THE ENCYCLOPAEDIA OF TYPE FACES

THE
ENCYCLOPAEDIA
OF TYPE FACES

W. PINCUS JASPERT

W. TURNER BERRY   A. F. JOHNSON

BLANDFORD PRESS
POOLE · DORSET

FIRST PUBLISHED IN THE UK IN 1953
BY BLANDFORD PRESS, LINK HOUSE, WEST STREET,
POOLE, DORSET BH15 1LL
SECOND EDITION (REVISED & ENLARGED) 1958
THIRD EDITION (FURTHER RESTYLED & ENLARGED) 1962
FOURTH EDITION (ENTIRELY RESTYLED & GREATLY ENLARGED) 1970
REPRINTED 1983

DISTRIBUTED IN THE UNITED STATES BY STERLING PUBLISHING CO., INC,
2 PARK AVENUE, NEW YORK, N.Y. 10016 35

ISBN 0 7137 1347 X

Printed and bound in Great Britain by
Richard Clay (The Chaucer Press) Ltd, Bungay, Suffolk

CONTENTS

Erratum—The typefounder for Eusebius on page 85 is Ludlow 1924.

REPRINT OF THE FOURTH EDITION

MUCH DISCUSSION PRECEDED this reprint of the fourth edition, the Publisher and the editor being well aware of inconsistencies in the book. The list, unfortunately, is quite long. As James Mosley, the learned librarian of St Bride Printing Library in the City of London points out, with the conversion to offset printing that took place with the fourth edition, some type specimens became mixed up, for example Temple Script on page 401 has a wrong lower case f. Also, some battered types are shown, but it seemed preferable to indicate designs than leave them out altogether. Only a complete revision could really cater for all the errors but regrettably this is impractical at the present time. The vexed question remains of dating accurately. In addition, some references are confusing, and may not necessarily always give greater clarity to the researcher. Specific points to note are as follows.

Ceska Uncials on page 43 and Unciala on page 229 are the same.

Cooper Old Style on page 57 is Cooper Black (see page 56).

On the same page, Cooper Old Style should be listed as Cooper Hilite.

Dante on page 63 was cut in 1947–52; Monotype cut their version in 1957.

Della Robbia on page 65 was modelled on Florentine not Roman capitals.

The first specimen showing of De Vinne is inappropriate on page 67.

On page 100, the *typi academiae* follow Jannon and not Garamond.

On pages 103 and 163, Genzsch and Nordische Antiqua should be listed as the same overall and basic design.

New Hammer Uncial is shown in page 111.

The first cutting of Joanna (page 124) by Monotype was in 11 point for the J. M. Dent publishing house in 1937–39.

Monastic on page 158 is really Erasmus Initials of Amsterdam Typefoundry.

On page 159 Monsoon is not shown; instead it is Kontakt, which is thus duplicated on page 130.

Open Roman Capitals on page 168 was for use with Antigone Greek as two-line capitals and not with Antique Greek.

Pilgrim on page 179 was designed in 1934 for use by Hague & Gill; Gill called the type Bunyan and the italic was added by Linotype.

Plantin Old Style on page 181 in Monotype Plantin.

Rockwell Shaded on page 195 is ATF Antique Shaded which also appears wrongly captioned on page 212; it is not Stymie.

Contact on page 262 is Imre Reiner's design; there is also a type by this name by Helmut Matheis for Ludwig & Mayer.

On page 370 the texts for Civilite and Clipper have been transposed.

Despite these and other shortcomings, it remains gratifying to find that there is a continuing demand for this work at a time when technical observers keep reminding the world of print that type is dead. Indeed, only very recently there has arisen a new awareness of the need to have typefaces designed in the disciplines of style and precision to which creators of metal type adhered. This is bringing improved type designs to even the most undisciplined of the manufacturers of phototypesetting machines. Digitisation of type face designs and the attention to precision and detail of especially some British, German and Swiss type designers are bringing about a return of fine typography.

W.P.J.

May 1983

PREFACE TO FOURTH EDITION

THIS NEW EDITION has had a further 400 specimens of new or recently resurrected type faces added to it. There has also been a substantial number of additions of older faces still in use, including in particular a variety from American sources. It had been hoped to include black letter types, but the physical difficulties of obtaining good specimens from founders and matrix suppliers have delayed this plan which will have to await a better opportunity, or possibly even a separate publication.

As in previous editions, almost all the elaborate designs from the latter part of the nineteenth century which were cut and cast in innumerable technically unsatisfactory variations and copies have been omitted. Those wishing to use such type designs are advised to look at the various style books now issued by photolettering studios.

Phototypesetting faces as such have only been included where they relate to keyboard-operated machines, that is machines which are governed by the limitations and restrictions of mechanical composition, whether by hot metal or photography. The numerous photo display alphabets available nowadays cannot claim to be subject to the disciplines of the typefounder's craft.

The introduction of the British Standard 2961:1967 classification system, now applied (and partly reprinted by kind permission of the British Standards Institute in London), should help considerably in classifying types. There are, however, still some types that defy any classification. These are found principally amongst those romans which originated during the Victorian era, together with others of more recent vintage from this century, including some which have basically lineale style but also scripts and "manuscript" designs.

The new, greatly enlarged format of this handbook is intended to enable users to keep the volume as a desk book in which annotations can easily be made. By arranging types alphabetically under three main sections—Romans, Lineales & Scripts, it is hoped to make the location of type faces easier for quick reference.

Typefounders and their agents, composing machine and matrix manufacturers, have once again given very considerable assistance and practical help in preparing this edition. However, in this issue we have again had to reproduce several designs from printed specimens because of the impossibility of obtaining actual specimen alphabet settings from readily available sources. Where the setting of specimens appears out of style, this is because of the difficulty of reconciling material from many different sources, including reproductions from type, slugs, electros, line blocks and even metal and plastic stereos.

It would not have been possible to revise this new edition without the very active help and advice of a number of people, Alan Hutt and A. D. B. Jones, both of London, Matthew Carter, New York, and in particular Dr G. W. Ovink, of Amsterdam. They provided notes of substantial value and have especially helped in clarifying references to source material and historical links.

I am also grateful to James Mosley, Librarian of the St. Bride Printing Library, for Index to Designers and for his general cooperation.

Much valuable help was also given by readers in many countries who provided information and corrections, suggestions and type specimens for reference.

Physically, the production of this book would have been extremely difficult but for the friendly assistance of Jerry Kuehl in Paris, and Roy Knightley in London, to whom my personal thanks are due.

The majority of type faces shown in this book are copyright designs, and may not be copied without permission from the appropriate foundry or owner of the design.

W.P.J.

TECHNICAL TERMS USED
IN THE DESCRIPTIONS

ARM: The projecting horizontal strokes on such letters as **T, E.**

ASCENDER: The part of a lower-case letter which projects above the mean-line, as in **b, h, l,** etc.

BASE LINE: The imaginary line on which the base of capital letters rests.

KERN: That part of a type which overhangs the body.

LIGATURE: The connecting link between two letters that are joined together. Often misused in the sense of logotype, that is, two or more letters cast on one body, generally comprising such characters as *fi, ff, fl, ffi, ffl, ct, ft, ll, tt, sp.*

LOOP: The lower part of **g,** also called the tail.

BOWL: The rounded part of such letters as **P, B** and the upper part of **g** to distinguish it from the lower part known as the loop or tail.

CAP-LINE: The imaginary line which rules along the top of capital letters.

COUNTER: The enclosed parts of a letter, such as lower-case **p, q.**

CURSIVE: Literally, resembling hand-writing; flowing rather than formal.

DESCENDER: Those parts of such letters as **g, p, q** which descend below the base line.

EAR: The projecting stroke on the bowl of the **g.**

EYE: The enclosed part of the lower-case **e.**

MEAN-LINE: The imaginary line that runs along the top of lower-case **a, n, x,** etc.

POINT OF MAXIMUM STRESS: The thickest part of curved letters, like **O, e,** etc.

SHORT-RANGING FIGURES: Numerals which range on the base line.

SPUR: The small beak on the end of arcs, as in **G.**

SWASH LETTERS: Flourished italic letters as **A, C, D, E, I, P, S,** etc.

UNCIALS: Rounded capital letters from which are derived lower-case letters, such as **e, u** etc.

X-HEIGHT: The face of the lower-case letters without ascenders and descenders.

INTRODUCTION

THIS SELECTION OF TYPE FACES has been compiled to provide a reference book for all those who use type—typographers, printers, publishers, advertisement designers and the business man who takes some interest in the choice of type for his stationery and publicity. It may also be of value to the lettering artist, the signwriter, and the engraver, who in consequence of the limitations of their own books of alphabets, often turn—we trust with a little uneasiness of conscience—to printers' type for inspiration.

Some explanation of the terms used in the descriptions of type faces seems to be required. This is not the place to enter into technical details on the making of types or to attempt a description of the cast type itself. We are concerned with the superficial impression made by the type when pressed on to paper, though, of course, many of the terms applied to the impression are originally used of the metal type itself. As we shall describe some types which are several centuries old, it may be as well to refer briefly to the existence of such things as punches and matrices. A letter is in the first place cut in reverse on the end of a steel punch, which in turn is driven into a matrix. The matrix receives an impression of the letter the correct way round, and from this is cast, again in reverse, the metal type actually set by the compositor. When a text is said to be composed in original CASLON type, this is a convenient shorthand. The type is, of course, more or less newly cast, but is derived from the original punches. Punches are all but indestructible, and, in fact, a number have survived from the fifteenth century.

The body of the type is the whole of the superficial area, which is not, of course, completely filled by any letter. What are called full-bodied letters occupy the whole height of the body, e.g. Q. Small letters like a, m, o, occupy the middle part of the body only. Ascending letters, like b, d, l, occupy the upper and middle parts, and descending letters, like p, q, the middle and lower parts. These three parts vary much in their proportions. When we speak of a type of small face we mean that the middle part is short in relation to the ascenders and descenders. The length of the ascenders and descenders is one of the principal points to be noted in describing a type. We speak also of bold-faced and light-faced types, referring to the thickness or thinness of the strokes of the letter. The face of a type is the same thing, then, as the impression of the letter. Types may also vary in width, laterally. Proportionally narrow types are called condensed. If the letters fill the body laterally, or fill it as nearly as possible, then the letters when set in line will have very small spaces of white between each other. The "set" is said to be close. This is a second point in which there is much variation among types. CASLON, for example, is a type which has a wide set, and a comparatively small face. The inside white spaces of the letters are called the counters, a term borrowed from the processes of punch cutting. From the seventeenth century onwards the sunk part of the letter, that is, the part which would be left in white, was made by driving into the punch another bar on which this area was engraved. This bar was called the counter-punch.

ix

IMPORTANCE OF SERIFS

In the designing of formal letters, not cursive or script characters, unconnected strokes are finished off by the addition of short cross-lines called serifs. These seemingly insignificant little lines have a surprising effect on the appearance of the face of a type and are therefore of great importance in typographical classification and description. They may be horizontal on the top, or inclined; they may be thick or thin, and of varying size in proportion to the main stem. On the underside they may be connected to the main stem by a triangular piece or in a curve, and are then described as bracketed; on the other hand the under-part may be entirely cut away, leaving a flat, unbracketed serif. In the case of foot serifs the bracketing, if any, is, of course, on top. Inclined serifs are normally confined to the lower case, on the m, n, p, r, u's, etc. Even when these are inclined those on the tops of the ascenders may be horizontal. The form of the foot serifs should also be noted.

Types were originally copied from manuscript letters written with broad-nibbed pens, or quills. The earliest printed books were in fact made to resemble contemporary manuscripts as nearly as possible. When a broad-nibbed pen, held at right angles to the paper, is used, it is clear that a vertical stroke will be of the same thickness as the pen's edge, and that a horizontal stroke will be a thin line, while curved strokes will vary in thickness from the one extreme to the other. In an "o" the two thickest parts will be directly opposite each other—due east and west, so to speak. In such a letter we describe the distribution of the thicks and thins, or the distribution of weight as vertical; we speak of the vertical colouring, stress, or shading. Holding the pen at right angles to the paper is a strained attitude, and we find that an angle of 45 degrees or less was more usual. This gives a diagonal shading; for example, the thickest parts of the "o" are diagonally opposite—north-east and south-west, or in some cases even north-east-north by south-west-south. Such shading is characteristic of early romans and of most of the book types in use today. Again, there can be variations in the gradation between thick strokes and thin; the gradation may be gradual and slight, or it may be extreme and abrupt. All book types show some variation of thick and thin; in the fifteenth century it was slight, and gradually became more pronounced, until it reached the extreme in the nineteenth century when they became called hair lines.

VARIATIONS IN DESIGN

All these points of variation so far referred to, differences in the degree and position of the shading or stress, differences in the forms of the serifs, and in the proportions of the different parts of the body, apply to the fount of type in general. Variations in the design of individual letters are perhaps even more helpful in distinguishing one type from another. A summary of the more obvious points to be observed in particular letters may be useful. The apex of A is sometimes pointed, sometimes flat, or again, oblique; the position of the bar varies. In the C the extent to which the circle is completed and the absence or presence of serifs or beaks and their shape, in E, F and L the width of the horizontal strokes or arms, are points to be noted. G is often C with a horizontal lower serif; sometimes the stroke below this serif is vertical, and sometimes there is a small projection on the right, which we call a beard or spur. H varies much in width and in the position of the bar. J was a non-existent letter at the time of the invention of printing, and our form is really the swash I. With the modern face it became a short-ranging letter; variations in the terminal or lower curve are to be noted. In the M the outer strokes may be upright or splayed, the middle strokes may meet on the line or at various points short of the line, while the top serifs vary considerably. The bowl of the P is often not closed. The tail of the Q varies greatly. The final stroke or tail of the R has undergone many changes. It may end in a serif on the line; it may taper to a point, even descending below the line; with the modern face it became curved and more vertical. The relation of the upper and lower curve in the S, and in the T the width of the horizontal stroke and the form of its serifs have varied. V originally did duty for U, which is a form dating from about 1600. For one period in the seventeenth century U assumed the same design as the lower-case u, with a foot serif, and that form has been revived in many recently designed romans. The middle strokes of the W meet at various heights, and when they meet at the top are sometimes without a serif.

Variations in the shape and size of the bowl of the a, in the extent to which the top arc curves downwards and the manner in which this is finished, make this letter useful for our purpose. In the eighteenth century b acquired a foot serif on the left. The foot serif on the d has changed from an inclined position to the horizontal. This applies to the u also. An important letter is e. The "eye" was in early days enclosed by an oblique stroke; when this stroke became horizontal the eye was very small and gradually grew larger, until in the nineteenth century it was as deep as half of the face of the letter. The position of the thickest part of the curve should be observed. g is equally important for the changes in the sizes of the bowl and the curves of the tail or loop. This tail is sometimes not closed. On the bowl is a projection, which we call the ear; this was originally a short horizontal stroke projecting from the right-hand top corner. Later it became curved, and sometimes started from a higher point on the bowl. h has changed little since, with JENSON, it acquired the straight shank, originally a curve. The dot over the i was in some early types not vertically over the stem, but away to the right; in other cases a dash took the place of the dot. The q in some modern faces has a top serif on the right. The height of the t and finish at the top, the cross-stroke, whether bracketed or not, and lastly the tail of the y are noteworthy. For the s and w the points noted in the capitals apply.

Besides the ordinary letters, the fount of roman includes also other sorts, tied letters or ligatures and punctuation marks. The ligatures, or combinations of two and even three letters cast on one body, have survived in a few cases, like the f combinations, ff, fl, etc. In types based on early models the earlier ligatures, such as ct and st, are still found. Full stops have at times been diamond-shaped, and commas have been oblique dashes. The arabic figures, too, are part of the fount. In the early designs 1 and 2 were short letters, 3, 4, 5, 7 and 9, descending letters, and 6 and 8 ascending letters. In the modern face all the figures were cut to range on the line, although there are now non-ranging figures for such types as TIMES ROMAN which look somewhat neater. Several typefounders provide alternative figures for many of their faces, modern or old style, so that the typography of these can best be suited to individual requirements and style preferences of the designer or typographer using them.

THE ITALICS

The italic letters are now also a part of the complete roman fount. Such is the sad fate of this once beautiful letter, originally an independent rival to roman. In origin it is a cursive form of the Italian hand on which roman types were based, and should properly be called *Cursive*, as in fact it is called in Germany, or *Chancery*, a name applied to it bacause it was used in the Papal Chancery at Rome. The earliest italic, that of the Venetian printer, Aldus Manutius, dating from 1501, was a niggardly sort of type devised for pocket editions. Later, under the influence of Italian writing masters like Lodovico Vicentino at Rome and Tagliente at Venice, more formal and graceful designs were produced, which ensured the popularity of italic in the sixteenth century. Such types have been the model for several modern italics, which will be described below. It was long before italic became merely a secondary letter to roman, and even longer before it was cut to harmonise with the roman. Our italics are inclined—this inclination is not essential and some few of the early models were upright—and the difficulty of inclining roman capitals at a uniform angle is evident in many of our old-face italics. Since this cursive letter was less bound by traditional forms than the roman, greater variety of design has been possible, with the result that italics are more easy to distinguish than romans. Not infrequently it is easier to recognise a roman from its accompanying italic than from the roman letter itself. On the other hand, our printers tend to use italic less and less, and one may search a text in vain for a word in italic. In view of the unimportant position which it now occupies, less space will be given in the following descriptions to the secondary letter.

The angle of inclination of an italic is the first characteristic to be observed. In the best early Italian models this angle was slight, and became more pronounced with the old-face group. Recent designs again tend more towards the upright. The lack of consistency of the angle of inclination is another characteristic of the old-face group. In some cases one can hardly imagine that the designer ever intended his italic capitals to combine together. Many italics have second forms for some upper-case letters, script forms, which are known as swash letters. These naturally were not meant to be used in the middle of words, though in fact they frequently are. In the lower case the greatest variation occurs in the serif formation, or rather what corresponds to the serif formation in the roman. It is here that italic especially retained the cursive quality of the hand on which it was modelled. The initial strokes are not serifs, but pen strokes. When deliberate attempts were made in the eighteenth century to harmonise the two designs, the italics did for a time acquire roman serifs, though never in this country. With our founders the calligraphic initial strokes of the Caslon italic degenerated into the pot-hooks of the nineteenth-century design.

W.T.B.

A.F.J.

TYPEFACE NOMENCLATURE

From the earliest days of printing, trade terms have been used which were passed orally from craftsman to apprentice; they related to the physical objects used in typographical printing processes, e.g. metal "types". Since the beginning of this century such terms have been used by designers and others outside the industry but, as they usually have no occasion to use the physical objects, they use the terms in more abstract senses. For example, the term "type face" now commonly refers to the printed character left on the paper by the printing surface ("face") of the physical "type".

Another factor which adds to the confusion is that (as in many other industries) established technical words are made to do service for new concepts that arise from new developments. Such confusion certainly arose after the invention of the pantographic mechanical punch-cutter and the hot-metal composing machine which largely replaced the hand-cut punch and hand composition. Photographic setting might have added to the danger of confusion in terminology, although the issue of the first edition of this standard reduced this to some extent.

Often the context will prevent any misunderstanding of the sense in which a particular word is used, but this is not always the case, and confusion does arise in practice. It is now common practice for publishers, advertisers and other print buyers to give detailed specifications to the printers and it is, therefore, important to define terms in a manner that will avoid embarrassing and costly misunderstandings in commercial transactions.

CLASSIFICATION

The names of groups of type faces now in general use have grown haphazardly over the past 150 years. Some of the names are descriptive but others are historical and, except to those well versed in the history of printing and type design, have little meaning. Since the end of the last century, several attempts have been made to evolve a classification of type faces, but none has found really wide acceptance. It has become increasingly evident, especially during the last ten years, that there is a real need for classification which can be accepted nationally, and preferably internationally, and which will facilitate discussions between type face designers and printers, printers and print-buyers, and teachers of typography and their students.

In 1954, Maximilian Vox, in France, published some proposals which were simpler than any of the earlier attempts. While they were generally welcomed, they were also criticized and were amended later. In 1959, a draft German Standard was issued, giving a classification which related to the principles adopted by Vox, but which was considerably more complex. After considering the comments which they received on this draft, the Deutscher Normenausschuss published a revised classification (DIN 16518) in 1964, which was almost identical to the Vox classification. The Vox classification is widely used in many European countries.

The difficulty arises that if the categories are rigidly defined and limited to a practical number, many type faces elude classification. On the other hand if the categories are loosely defined, each may contain type faces which are fundamentally different although having certain, perhaps arbitrary, factors in common. This classification attempts to limit the possibilities of confusion.

The actual nomenclature must, of course, differ in different countries according to language. The classification in the British Standard is based on the concepts of English-speaking countries.

CLASSIFICATION OF TYPE FACES

I	Humanist	Type faces in which the cross stroke of the lower case e is oblique; the axis of the curves is inclined to the left; there is no great contrast between thin and thick strokes; the serifs are bracketed; the serifs of the ascenders in the lower case are oblique. *Note.* This was formerly known as "Venetian", having been derived from the fifteenth-century minuscule written with a varying stroke thickness by means of an obliquely-held broad pen.	Verona Centaur Kennerley
II	Garalde	Type faces in which the axis of the curves is inclined to the left; there is generally a greater contrast in the relative thickness of the strokes than in Humanist designs; the serifs are bracketed; the bar of the lower case e is horizontal; the serifs of the ascenders in the lower case are oblique. *Note.* These are types in the Aldine and Garamond tradition and were formerly called "Old Face" and "Old Style".	Bembo Garamond Caslon Vendôme
III	Transitional	Type faces in which the axis of the curves is vertical or inclined slightly to the left; the serifs are bracketed, and those of the ascenders in the lower case are oblique. *Note.* Influenced by the letter-forms of the copperplate engraver. It may be regarded as a transition from Garalde to Didone, and incorporates some characteristics of each.	Fournier Baskerville Bell Caledonia Columbia

IV	Didone	Type faces having an abrupt contrast between thin and thick strokes; the axis of the curves is vertical; the serifs of the ascenders of the lower case are horizontal; there are often no brackets to the serifs. *Note.* These are type faces as developed by Didot and Bodoni. Formerly called "Modern".	Bodoni Corvinus Modern Extended
V	Slab-serif	Type faces with heavy, square-ended serifs, with or without brackets.	Rockwell Clarendon Playbill
VI	Lineale	Type faces without serifs. *Note.* Formerly called "Sans-serif".	
	a Grotesque	Lineale type faces with nineteenth-century origins. There is some contrast in thickness of strokes. They have squareness of curve, and curling close-set jaws. The R usually has a curled leg and the G is spurred. The ends of the curved strokes are usually horizontal.	SB Grotesque No. 6 Condensed Sans No 7 Headline
	b Neo-grotesque	Lineale type faces derived from the grotesque. They have less stroke contrast and are more regular in design. The jaws are more open than in the true grotesque and the g is often open-tailed. The ends of the curved strokes are usually oblique.	Edel/Wotan Univers Helvetica
	c Geometric	Lineale type faces constructed on simple geometric shapes, circle or rectangle. Usually monoline, and often with single-storey a.	Futura Erbar Eurostyle
	d Humanist	Lineale type faces based on the proportions of inscriptional Roman capitals and Humanist or Garalde lower case, rather than on early grotesques. They have some stroke contrast, with two-storey a and g.	Optima Gill Sans Pascal
VII	Glyphic	Type faces which are chiselled rather than calligraphic in form.	Latin Albertus Augustea
VIII	Script	Type faces that imitate cursive writing.	Palace Script Legend Mistral
IX	Graphic	Type faces whose characters suggest that they have been drawn rather than written.	Libra Cartoon Old English

Note. The impossibility of placing every type face into one of the categories above is recognized. In cases of difficulty the use of a compound term, e.g. Humanist/Garalde, is suggested.

Extracts from British Standards 2961:1967, on which the classification of type faces in this edition of *The Encyclopaedia of Type Faces* is based.

SELECTED LITERATURE ON TYPE & TYPE FOUNDING

Bastien, Alfred. ENCYCLOPAEDIA TYPOGRAPHICA. West Drayton 1953.
Bennett, Paul A. ON RECOGNISING TYPE FACES. In *The Dolphin*, Vol. II, New York 1935.
Berry, W. Turner & Johnson, A. F. CATALOGUE OF SPECIMENS OF PRINTING TYPES BY ENGLISH & SCOTTISH FOUNDRIES, 1665–1830. With an introduction by Stanley Morison. Oxford University Press, London 1935. (Supplement in *Signature*, New Series 16. New edition in preparation by J. Mosley.)
Biggs, J. R. AN APPROACH TO TYPE. Blandford Press, London. 2nd edition 1961.
Bohadti, Gustav. DIE BUCHDRUCKLETTER. Ein Handbuch für das Schriftgiesserei & Buchdruckgewerbe. Ullstein, Berlin 1954.
Burt, Sir Cyril. A PSYCHOLOGICAL STUDY OF TYPOGRAPHY. With an introduction by Stanley Morison. Cambridge University Press 1959.
Carter, Harry. FOURNIER ON TYPEFOUNDING. Soncino Press, London 1930.
Dowding, Geoffrey. AN INTRODUCTION TO THE HISTORY OF PRINTING TYPES. Wace, London 1961.
Falk, V. NUTIDA TYPSNIT, Upkomst & Utveckling. Lagerströms, Stockholm 1956.
Graphic Arts Typographers Inc. GRAPHIC ARTS TYPE BOOK. Reinhold, New York 1965.
Gray, Nicolette. NINETEENTH-CENTURY ORNAMENTED TYPES & TITLE PAGES. Faber & Faber, London 1938.
Hellinga, Wytze & Lotte. THE FIFTEENTH CENTURY PRINTING TYPES OF THE LOW COUNTRIES. 2 vols. Hertzberger, Amsterdam 1966.
SIXTEENTH CENTURY TYPE DESIGNS OF THE LOW COUNTRIES. Hertzberger, Amsterdam 1966.
Hlasta, S. PRINTING TYPES & HOW TO USE THEM. Carnegie Press, Pittsburgh 1950.
Hlavsa, O. & Sedlacek, F. A BOOK OF TYPE & DESIGN. Artia, Prague & Nevill, London. 2nd edition 1961.
Hutchings, R. S. A MANUAL OF DECORATED TYPE FACES. Cory Adams & Mackay, London 1965.
A MANUAL OF SCRIPT TYPE FACES. Cory Adams & Mackay, London 1965.
THE WESTERN HERITAGE OF TYPE DESIGN. Cory Adams & Mackay, London 1963.
Johnson, A. F. TYPE DESIGNS, Their history and development. André Deutsch, London. 3rd edition 1966.
Karch, R. Randolph. HOW TO RECOGNIZE TYPE FACES. McKnight & McKnight, Bloomington, Ill. 2nd edition 1959.
Kelly, R. R. AMERICAN WOOD TYPE 1828–1900 Van Nostrand Reinhold, New York 1970.
Lindegren, Erik. ABC OF LETTERING & PRINTING TYPES. 3 vols. Erik Lindegren Grafisk Studio, Askim 1964–65.
McMurtrie, Douglas C. TYPE DESIGN. An essay on American type designs with specimens of the outstanding types. With an introduction by Frederic W. Goudy. Pelham, New York 1927.
Mores, E. Rowe. A DISSERTATION UPON ENGLISH TYPOGRAPHICAL FOUNDERS & FOUNDRIES (1778). Edited with an introduction by Harry Carter & Christopher Ricks. Oxford University Press, London 1961.
Morison, Stanley. A TALLY OF TYPES. Cambridge University Press 1953.
ON TYPE DESIGNS OF THE PAST & PRESENT. Ernest Benn, London. Revised edition 1962.
Mosley, James. ENGLISH VERNACULA, A study in traditional letter forms. In *Motif*, 11.
Novarese, Aldo. ALFABETA. Progreso Grafico, Turin 1964.
Reed, Talbot R. HISTORY OF THE OLD ENGLISH LETTER FOUNDRIES. Edited by A. F. Johnson. Faber & Faber, London 1952.
Rosen, Ben. TYPE AND TYPOGRAPHY. Reinhold, New York 1963.
Scarfe, L. ALPHABETS. Written and printed letter forms. Batsford, London 1954.
Seemann, A. HANDBUCH DER SCHRIFTARTEN. Seemann, Leipzig 1926 and supplements to 1937.
Spencer, Herbert. THE VISIBLE WORD. Royal College of Art, London 1968, and Lund Humphries, London 1969.
Sutton, James & Bartram, Alan. AN ATLAS OF TYPE FORMS. Lund Humphries, London 1968.
Szántó, Tibor. A BETÜ. 2 vols. Akademia, Budapest 1965.
Thomas, D. TYPE FOR PRINT. Whitaker, London 1939.
Tschichold, Jan. MEISTERBUCH DER SCHRIFT. Otto Maier, Ravensburg 1953.
Updike, D. B. PRINTING TYPES. 2 vols. Harvard University Press, Cambridge, Massachusetts.

SOME TYPE FACE CLASSIFICATIONS

Association Typographique Internationale. CLASSIFICATION INTERNATIONALE DES CARACTERERES D'IMPRIMERIE. Verona 22 May 1962.
Bastien, Alfred. ENCYCLOPAEDIA TYPOGRAPHICA. West Drayton 1953.
British Standard. SPECIFICATION FOR TYPE FACE NOMENCLATURE & CLASSIFICATION BS 2961: 1967. British Standards Institution, London 1967.
Deutscher Normenausschuss DIN 16518. KLASSIFIZIERUNG DER SATZSCHRIFTEN. Beuth Vertrieb, Berlin 1962.
Hostettler, Rudolf. ZUR KLASSIFIZIERUNG DER SCHRIFTSCHNITTE. In *Typographische Monatsblaetter 5–1963.*—A commentary on the various schemes proposed in Europe, with notes pointing out the problems inherent in the schemes suggested.
Mosley, James. NEW APPROACH TO THE CLASSIFICATION OF TYPE FACES. In *British Printer* 3/1960.—A summary of the various schemes then proposed, prepared for the information of a British Standards Institute sub-committee (see above).
Munsch, René H. PHYSIONOMIE DE LA LETTRE CLASSIFICATION DES CRÉATIONS TYPOGRAPHIQUES ET CONSTRUCTION EN VUE D'OEUVRES PUBLICITAIRES. Editions Eyrolles, Paris 1958.
Novarese, Aldo. IL CARATTERRE, Sintesi storica, classificazione, accostamento eststico. Turin 1957.—An application of Vox, with modifications.
Pellitteri, Giuseppe. CLASSIFICAZIONE MORFOLOGICA DECIMALE DEI CARATTERI STAMPA. In *Annunciatore Poligrafico*, May 1962.—Decimal classification based on form or shape.
THE IDENTIFICATION OF TYPE FACES IN BIBLIOGRAPHICAL DESCRIPTIONS. *Journal of Typographic Research* 1/1967.
Schauer, Georg K. KLASSIFIKATION DER DRUCKSCHRIFTEN. In *Linotype Post*, Neue Folge, February 1958.—A German classification governed primarily by form or shape.
Thibaudeau, François. A LETTRE D'IMPRIMERIE. Paris, 2 vols. 1921.
LA CLASSIFICATION DES LETTRES D'IMPRIMERIE. In *Papyrus Typographie*, 1922.
Tschichold, Jan. MEISTERBUCH DER SCHRIFT. Otto Maier, Ravensburg 1952.
Vox, Maximilian. POUR UNE NOUVELLE CLASSIFICATION DES CARACTÈRES (with English translation). Paris 1954.
—The basis of BS 2961:1967 and DIN 16518.
Warde, Beatrice. TYPE FACES OLD AND NEW. In *The Library*, September 1935.
Zapf, Hermann. STILGRUPPEN DER ANTIQUA & IHRE CHARACTERISTISCHEN ELEMENTE. In *Gutenberg Jahrbuch*, 1954.

ROMAN TYPES

THERE ARE THREE PRINCIPAL FEATURES of the roman face which were gradually modified in the three centuries from JENSON to BODONI. In the earliest romans, copied as we have pointed out, from contemporary humanistic manuscripts, the serifs were inclined and bracketed, that is to say, the underpart of the serif was connected to the stem in a curve or by a triangular piece. On the upper case the serifs were often thick slabs extending to both sides of the uprights. In the typical modern face serifs are thin, flat and unbracketed. In between the two extremes various gradations are found. In all early romans the incidence of colour or stress is diagonal, while in the modern face it is vertical. If an O is drawn with a broad-nibbed pen held at an angle to the paper, the two thickest parts of the letter will be diagonally opposite. This was the manner in which the calligraphers of the fifteenth century drew an O; but by the year 1700 the writing masters, whose work was being reproduced on copper-engraved plates, had adopted the method of holding the pen at right angles to the paper, thus producing a vertical stress. The engravers of type who developed the modern face were adapting to typography a style already prevalent among the engravers. The third point in which the design was modified was in the amount of variation between the thick and thin strokes, and in the degree of abruptness of the variation. In the fifteenth century the stress was slight and gradual, in the nineteenth it was extreme and abrupt.

An inline with upper and lower case in which the left strokes are accentuated. In **A, M, N** and **U** the upstrokes are fine and not inline. All letters are condensed and somewhat angular. The serifs are flat.

ACROPOLIS
L. Wagner 1940

Das neue Modeheft REISE NACH ATHEN

iv

ACROPOLIS

Designed by H. Thannhaeuser. An inline sloped roman with minute serifs. The line passes right through the vertical strokes. There is also a set of swash capitals.

ADASTRA
Stempel 1928

Streamers DHER

ix

ADASTRA

ABCDEFGHIJKLM
NOPQRSTUVWXYZ

ix

ADASTRA SWASH CAPITALS

AETERNA or JOST MEDIAEVAL

Ludwig & Mayer 1927;

Intertype (Berlin)

Designed by Heinrich Jost. Mediaeval in German is used with much the same meaning as our Venetian. The type is of rich colour, has small serifs and short descenders. The capitals vary in width, **E**, **F** and **L** being narrow, corresponding with some well-known Roman inscriptions, *e.g.*, those of the Trajan column. There are two **M**'s and **N**'s, one having no top serifs. **U** has the lower-case design and **W** no middle serif. e has the Venetian form, the **g** an odd rectangular ear. The dot on the **i** is diamond-shaped. The italic has capitals consistent with the roman; the inclination is very slight and in the lower case some letters are upright. It is rather like a GOUDY italic. There is also an italic and a bold. AETERNA, as the type is now called, is a slightly revised version.

i

ABCDEFGHIJKLMNOPQRSTUVW
XYZ
abcdefghijklmnopqrstuvwxyz
1234567890

AETERNA ROMAN

i

ABCDEFGHIJKLMNOPQRSTUVW
XYZ
abcdefghijklmnopqrstuvwxyz
1234567890

AETERNA ITALIC

i

ABCDEFGHIJKLMNOPQRSTU
VWXYZ
abcdefghijklmnopqrstuvwxyz
1234567890

AETERNA BOLD

ALBERTINA

Monotype 1965

Designed by Chris Brand. This face is available only as Monophoto matrices, and it was first used for a catalogue of the work of Stanley Morison which was exhibited at the Albertina Library, Brussels, in 1966.

ii

ABCDEFGHIJKLMNOPQRSTUVWXYZ
abcdefghijklmnopqrstuvwxyz
1234567890

ii

ABCDEFGHIJKLMNOPQRSTUVWXYZ
abcdefghijklmnopqrstuvwxyz
1234567890

ALBERTINA

2

ALBERTUS
Monotype 1932–40

Designed by Berthold Wolpe. A display roman which has thickened terminals rather than serifs. In the **M** the middle strokes descend only half-way. There is also a second **M** and two **W**s. **U** has the lower-case design. In the lower case ascenders and descenders are short. The **e** has a large eye and the **g** a large bowl. There is no italic. The figures are short-ranging. There is also Albertus Light, a normal weight, and a Bold Titling.

ABCDEFGHIJKLMNOPQRSTUVWXY
abcdefghijklmnopqrstuvwxyz
1234567890

ALBERTUS LIGHT

ABCDEFGHIJKLMNOPQRSTUVWXY
abcdefghijklmnopqrstuvwxyz
1234567890

ALBERTUS

ABCDEFGHIJKLMNOPQRSTUVWXYZ
1234567890

ALBERTUS BOLD

ABCDEFGHIJKLMNOPQRSTU
VWXYZ 1234567890

ALBERTUS TITLING

ALBION
Monotype 1910

Letters have a strong vertical stress and are available in five different versions, including an extended one.

ABCDEFGHIJKLMNOPQRSTUVWXYZ
abcdefghijklmnopqrstuvwxyz
1234567890

ALBION

ABCDEFGHIJKLMNOPQRSTUVWXYZ
abcdefghijklmnopqrstuvwxyz
1234567890

ALBION BOLD

ALDUS
Stempel 1954;
Linotype (Frankfurt)

Designed by Hermann Zapf. A roman of old-face design. Serifs are small and only slightly inclined. The **Q** has an external tail. In the lower-case the **g** is particularly good. In the italic the upper case (except **U**) is the roman slightly inclined, but not the lower case.

ii

ABCDEFGHIJKLMNOPQRSTUVWXYZ
abcdefghijklmnopqrstuvwxyz
1234567890

ABCDEFGHIJKLMNOPQRSTUVWXYZ
abcdefghijklmnopqrstuvwxyz

ALDUS

ii

ABCDEFGHIJKLMNOPQRSTUVWXYZ
abcdefghijklmnopqrstuvwxyz
1234567890
ABCDEFGHIJKLMNOPQRSTUVWXYZ
abcdefghijklmnopqrstuvwxyz
1234567890

ALDUS BOOK

ALFRODITA
Nacional

A set of shaded capitals with very small serifs. The shading is formed by four parallel lines.

ix

ABCDEFGHIJKLMNOPQRSTUVWXYZ

ALFRODITA

ALLEGRO
Ludwig & Mayer 1936

Designed by Hans Bohn. A fat face italic of very slight inclination. The bulbous terminals of arcs, as in **a** and **r,** are much in evidence. Most of the bowls are not quite closed.

ix

ABCDEFGHIJKLMNOPQRSTUVWXYZ

abcdefghijklmnopqrstuvwxyz

1234567890

ALLEGRO

Designed by K.F. Bauer and Walter Baum. An italic of heavy weight and almost monotone. The serifs are stubby. There are two lower cases, hence the two names. The first is an inclined roman and the second a script of the brush variety. Ascenders and descenders are generous, more especially in the script.

ABCDEFGHIJKLMNOPQRSTUVWXYZ

ALPHA CAPS

abcdefghijklmnopqrstuvwxyz

ALPHA LOWER CASE

abcdefghijklmnopqrstuvwxyz

1234567890

BETA

A modern face with some modifications. The **A** has an oblique top, **G** a small spur and the **R** is more like OLD FACE. In the bracketing of the serifs and the size of the eye of the **e** it resembles SCOTCH ROMAN.

Games and Sports

Buntpapierindustrie und Export
Die Buntpapierfabrikation, eines von den vielerlei
Spezialgebieten in der Papierveredelung, kann auf

ALT LATEIN

Designed by Georg Trump. A very narrow type with short ascenders and descenders, and fine serifs. Rounded letters are slightly angular. The upper curve of the **c** ends in a dot, and the top of the **t** is finely tapered. The dot on the **i** is somewhat elongated. The serifs on the cross beam of the **T** are wedge shaped, and the **A** has a horizontal serif on the top.

ABCDEFGHIJKLMNOPQRSTUVWXYZ
abcdefghijklmnopqrstuvwxyz
1234567890

HOWARD YOUNG GALLERIES

AMATI

Designed by Richard Isbell. Serifs are short and the type is exceptional for its large x-height. Vertical strokes taper to the base and serifs are short.

ix

ABCDEFGHIJKL MNOPQRSTUV WXYZ abcdefghijklmn opqrstuvwxyz $£1234567890

AMERICANA

ix

ABCDEFGHIJK LMNOPQRSTU VWXYZ

abcde fghijklmnopqrstuvwxyz

1234567890 $$¢£%,,.:-----.*()[]P ?!""""&

AMERICANA ITALIC

A roman with small serifs, inclined in the lower case. The round capitals—**C, G, O** and **Q**—are wide. In the **M** the middle strokes stop short of the line.

ABCDEFGHIJKLMNOPQRSTUVWXYZ
abcdefghijklmnopqrstuvwxyz   1234567890
ABCDEFGHIJKLMNOPQRSTUVWXYZ
abcdefghijklmnopqrstuvwxyz   1234567890

ANCIEN

Designed by John Peters as a 4½ pt type face for Bible composition.

When jobs have type sizes fixed quickly margins of error widen unless determining calculations are based on factual rather than hypothetical figures. No variation in the amount of copy can affect the degree of error once that error has been made. If instead of ten point the estimator specifies nine point for the type size whether *When jobs have type sizes fixed quickly margins of error widen unless determining calculations are based on factual rather than hypothetical figures. No variation in the amount of copy can affect the degree of error once that error has been made. If instead of ten point the estimator specifies nine point for the type*

ANGELUS

Designed by Arno Drescher. This roman, which is very similar to CANDIDA, has little variation of stress. The lower case is wide with short ascenders and descenders. EGYPTIAN 505 is similar.

iv/v

ABCDEFGHIKLMNOPQRSTUVWXY
ZÄÖÜÇÆŒ abcdefghijklmnopqrsſtuv
wxyz äöüchckßʒàéîòúçæœ 1234567890

ABCDEFGHIJKLMNOPQRS
TUVWXYZ
abcdefghijklmnopqrstuvwxyz
1234567890

ANTIQUA 505

ABCDEFGHIJKLMNOPQRST
UVWXYZ
abcdefghijklmnopqrstuvwxyz
1234567890

iv/v

ANTIQUA 505 BOLD

ABCDEFGHIJKLMNOPQRS
TUVWXYZ
abcdefghijklmnopqrstuvwxyz
1234567890

iv/v

ANTIQUA 505 BOLD CONDENSED

ABCDEFGHIJKLMNOPQ
RSTUVWXYZ
abcdefghijklmnopqrst
uvwxyz
1234567890

ANTIQUA 505 EXTRA BOLD

Antique was one of the early names for an Egyptian. NO. 3 is a Clarendon and a revival of an early design; and No. 5 is a lighter face of the same basic design. No. 6 is a fat Egyptian, also in the English style and, like ANTIQUE No. 3, was taken over from the foundry of V. & J. Figgins.

v

ABCDEFGHIJKLMNOPQRSTUVWXYZ
abcdefghijklmnopqrstuvwxyz
1234567890

ANTIQUE No. 3

v

ABCDEFGHIJKLMNOPQRSTUVWXYZ
abcdefghijklmnopqrstuvwxyz

ANTIQUE No. 5

v

ABCDEFGHIJKLMNOPQRS
TUVWXYZÆŒ
abcdefghijklmnopqrstuvwxyz
fflffifflfioeæ£
1234567890

ANTIQUE No. 6

i

ABCDEFGHIJKLMNOPQRSTUVWXYZ
abcdefghijklmnopqrstuvwxyz
1234567890

ABCDEFGHIJKLMNOPQRSTUVWXYZ
abcdefghijklmnopqrstuvwxyz
1234567890

ANTIQUE OLD STYLE

Designed by Adrian Frutiger. This is the first new type face to be designed specifically for Monophoto filmsetters. One set of matrices covers the entire composition range from 6 to 24 pt. The weight is sufficiently heavy to produce a good impression when printed by photolithography on smooth papers, while at the same time light enough to contrast with the semi-bold version.

APOLLO

Monotype 1964

iv

ABCDEFGHIJKLMNOPQRSTUVWXYZ

abcdefghijklmnopqrstuvwxyz

1234567890

ABCDEFGHIJKLMNOPQRSTUVWXYZ

abcdefghijklmnopqrstuvwxyz

1234567890

APOLLO

ABCDEFGHIJKLMNOPQRSTUVWXYZ

abcdefghijklmnopqrstuvwxyz

1234567890

APOLLO BOLD

iv

Designed by G.G. Lange. A condensed roman of medium weight with short ascenders and descenders. The serifs are small, oblique and pointed. Numerals range on the line. There are two weights and an italic.

ARENA

Berthold 1951–59

ii

ABCDEFGHIJKLMNOPQRSTUVWXYZ

abcdefghijklmnopqrstuvwxyz

1234567890

ABCDEFGHIJKLMNOPQRSTUVWXYZ

abcdefghijklmnopqrstuvwxyz

1234567890

ARENA

ABCDEFGHIJKLMNOPQRSTUVWXYZÆŒ
abcdefghijklmnopqrstuvwxyz

ARMSTRONG

ARMSTRONG

Simoncini 1970

iv

ABCDEFGHIJKLMNOPQRSTUVWXYZÆŒ
abcdefghijklmnopqrstuvwxyz

ARMSTRONG BOLD

ARPKE ANTIQUA
Schriftguss 1928

Designed by Otto Arpke. A modified fat face, with thin horizontal serifs. It is more nearly monotone than some designs in this group. The vertical strokes are wedge-shaped, being thinner at the feet. There are no serifs at the top of the M, nor on the middle strokes of W. In the lower case unconnected strokes are terminated by a thin serif, *e.g.*, the arc of the **a** and the terminals of **e**, **g** and **t**. There is also a light face and a shaded version.

ix

Edita Horák Praha ZEICHNUNG

ARPKE ANTIQUA

ARRIGHI ITALIC
Monotype 1929

This italic cut for hand composition in 1925 by Plumet in Paris, was designed by Frederic Warde to accompany the Monotype Corporation's CENTAUR, resembles BLADO, but the capitals are narrower and in the lower case the serifs on the ascenders are flat. Warde had already designed as a private face an italic based on an earlier Chancery type of Arrighi, in which the ascenders have calligraphic terminals and with a number of swash varieties.

viii

ABCDEFGHIJKLMNOPQRSTUVWXYZ&
abcdefghijklmnopqrstuvwxyz   1234567890

ARRIGHI ITALIC OR CENTAUR ITALIC

ARTCRAFT
Ludlow 1930

Designed originally for Barnhart Bros. & Spindler by Robert Wiebking. A display roman with heavy, blunt serifs. The lower case is conspicuous for some freakish forms. The arc of the **a** extends beyond the bowl and the **g** has an ear rising out of the top of the bowl and curling backwards. The tail is wider than the bowl. There is an italic and a bold.

ix

Dainty or Lace-like
The Charming Face

ARTCRAFT

ix

Non-Distribution

ARTCRAFT BOLD

ASHLEY CRAWFORD
Monotype 1930

Designed by Ashley Havinden. A series of heavy monotone capitals, with very small serifs. The feet of the A, M and Y, and the tail of the R are cut off obliquely. The M is pointed at the top and splayed. The S is tilted over to the right. There is also a series of ranging figures.

ix

ABCDEFGHIJKLMNOPQRSTU
VWXYZ& 1234567890

ASHLEY CRAWFORD

ix

ABCDEFGHIJKLMNOPQRST
UVWXYZ& 1234567890

ASHLEY CRAWFORD PLAIN

Designed by Francesco Simoncini. A text type designed for book and newspaper work, with clear variation of stress, and a finely cut character.

ASTER
Simoncini 1958;
Ludwig & Mayer

ABCDEFGHIJKLMNOPQRSTUVWXYZ

abcdefghijklmnopqrstuvwxyz

1234567890

ABCDEFGHIJKLMNOPQRSTUVWXYZ

abcdefghijklmnopqrstuvwxyz

1234567890

ABCDEFGHIJKLMNOPQRSTUVWXYZ

ASTER

ii

ABCDEFGHIJKLMNOPQRSTUVWXYZ

abcdefghijklmnopqrstuvwxyz

1234567890

ASTER BOLD

ii

Designed by Robert Girard. A re-cutting of a baroque face. The bowl of the **P** is not closed, the **G** has no spur, and the tail of the **R** descends below the line. The spur of the lower-case **r** is slightly higher than other lower-case letters. There is an italic, and also special initials. Known as MAZARIN by Stephenson & Blake.

ASTREE
or MAZARIN
Deberny & Peignot 1921;
Stephenson Blake

ABCDEFGHI *ABCD EFGH*

peuples qui firent *Peuples, quelle ne*

ASTREE OR MAZARIN

ii

Designed by A. Butti, with initials by A. Novarese. A roman with small flat serifs and little variation of stress. **K** and **R** have curved tails. The **M** is splayed. The **C**, **G** and **Q** are almost script forms. The top of the ascenders are thickened. The distinguishing letter is a freak **g** which ends on the line. The figures are short ranging. The italic has serifs slightly inclined. There is also a bold face.

ATHENAEUM
Nebiolo 1945

ABCDEFGHIJKLMNOPQRSTUVWXYZ

Œabcdeghijklmnopqrstuvwxyz

1234567890

ABCDEFGHIJKLMNOPQRSTUVWXYZ

Œabcdefghijklmnopqrstuvwxyz

1234567890

ATHENAEUM

ix

ABCDEFGHIJKLMNOPQRSTUVWXYZ

abcdefghijklmnopqrstuvwxyz

1234567890

ATHENAEUM BOLD

ix

ATLANTIC 35
Lanston Monotype 1909–35

A type face first used by the *Atlantic Monthly* in 1909, and based on SCOTCH ROMAN, though the lower case is taller.

iv

ABCDEFGHIJKLMNOPQRSTUVWXYZ&ÆŒ
abcdefghijklmnopqrstuvwxyzæœ   fiflffffiffl $1234567890
ABCDEFGHIJKLMNOPQRSTUVWXYZ&ÆŒ
ABCDEFGHIJKLMNOPQRSTUVWXYZ&ÆŒ
abcdefghijklmnopqrstuvwxyzæœ   fiflffffiffl $1234567890

ATLANTIC 35

ATRAX
Bauer 1926

Designed by Heinrich Jost. Shaded bold roman capitals. The shading passes through the vertical strokes. There are also ranging figures.

ix

NEW YORK RANGERS

ATRAX

AUGUSTEA
Berthold 1905–25

A modern face roman with short ascenders and descenders. The italic has the serifs of the roman. There are two heavier weights. It has no resemblance to the Nebiolo foundry's capitals bearing this name, shown elsewhere. *Cf.* CENTURY.

iv

ABCDEFGHIJKLMNOPQRSTUVWXYZ
abcdefghijklmnopqrstuvwxyz   1234567890

ABCDEFGHIJKLMNOPQRSTUVWXYZ
abcdefghijklmnopqrstuvwxyz

AUGUSTEA LIGHT

iv

ABCDEFGHIJKLMNOPQRSTUVWXYZ
abcdefghijklmnopqrstuvwxyz

AUGUSTEA MEDIUM

iv

ABCDEFGHIJKLMNOPQRSTUVWX
abcdefghijklmnopqrstuvwxyz

AUGUSTEA BOLD

AUGUSTEA
Nebiolo 1951

Designed by A. Butti and A. Novarese. A set of inscriptional capitals and short-ranging figures. The **M**, which is splayed, has no top serifs. **W** has no middle serif.

vii

ABCDEFGHIJKLMNOPQRST
UVXYZWÇÆŒ   1234567890

AUGUSTEA

12

ABCDEFGHIJKLMNOPQR STUVXYZW 1234567890

AUGUSTEA OPEN

ABCDEFGHIJKLMNOPQRSTUV XYZW
abcdefghijklmnopqrstuvxyzw 1234567890

NOVA AUGUSTEA

Designed by Matthew Carter for phototypesetting and easy enlargement and reduction.

ABCDEFGHIJKLMNOPQRSTUVWXYZ
abcdefghijklmnopqrstuvwxyz   1234567890
ABCDEFGHIJKLMNOPQRSTUVWXYZ
abcdefghijklmnopqrstuvwxyz   1234567890

AURIGA

Designed by Georges Auriol. A calligraphic type with short ascenders and descenders. The pen-drawn qualities are very evident in the upper case. There are white gaps in some strokes. The **M** is curiously designed.

les feuilles éparpillées 1234567890
ABCDEFGHIJKLMNOPQR

AURIOL

Designed by Jackson Burke. This newspaper face was introduced primarily to meet the improved specifications adopted by Canadian news agencies for teletypesetter composition. AURORA of the Weber foundry is quite different and the same as NORMAL GROTESQUE.

ABCDEFGHIJKLMNOPQRSTUVWXYZ
abcdefghijklmnopqrstuvwxyz
1234567890

When it is considered that it was the intention to make the book one of practical instruction, and that it was written with the hope that it might be placed in the hands of each printer's boy on entering the business, I trust this sin of inelegance may [from Savage's Dictionary

AURORA

AUSTIN'S PICA No. 1

Austin c. 1819

iv

Designed and cut by Richard Austin for his own foundry and one of the earliest "modern" faces in Britain.

ABCDEFGHIJKLMNOPQRSTUVWXYZ
ABCDEFGHIJKLMNOPQRSTUVWXYZ
ABCDEFGHIJKLMNOPQRSTUVWXYZ
1234567890
ABCDEFGHIJKLMNOPQRSTUV WXYZÆŒ
ABCDEFGHIJKLMNOPQRST UVWXYZÆŒ

AUSTIN'S PICA NO. 1

BALLÉ INITIALS

Bauer

ix

Designed by Maria Ballé. A series of light, decorated initials, in which the main down strokes are inline.

BALLÉ INITIALS

P. T. BARNUM

American Typefounders

ix

A reversed Egyptian, that is with serifs thicker than the main strokes. In fact the heavy strokes are all in the wrong places. Such types were originally called Italian or French Antique. Barnhart Brothers & Spindler originally issued this type in the nineteenth century and called it FRENCH CLARENDON.

LOR Zero is the figure

P. T. BARNUM

BARBOU

Monotype 1925

iii

Based on one of the first transitional types of the eighteenth-century Paris founder, P.S. Fournier, to provide a bookish type which was narrow without being condensed. A 14-pt size was cut by The Monotype Corporation at the same time as the cutting of the better known FOURNIER, and this was used in several volumes of *The Flenron*, but it was not until 1959 that a 12 pt size was made available for the printing of *The Papers of Benjamin Franklin* by the Lakeside Press, Chicago. Additional smaller sizes have been added to the range.

ABCDEFGHIJKLMNOPQRSTUVWXYZ

abcdefghijklmnopqrstuvwxyz

1234567890

ABCDEFGHIJKLMNOPQRSTUVWXYZ

abcdefghijklmnopqrstuvwxyz

1234567890

BARBOU

14

Presumably a revival of a nineteenth century design. Capitals only, equal in width. The serifs, which are triangular, resemble those in the design known as LATIN FACE. The inclined version is called BARONESS.

SWAINE AND ADENEY
BARON

REGISTERED INSURANCE COM

BARONESS

The original punches of the types cut by John Baskerville of Birmingham are still in existence. They were sold by Baskerville's widow to Beaumarchais and have descended through various French foundries to Deberny & Peignot. Some of this material survives and is now at the Cambridge University Press. The story has been told by John Dreyfus. Baskerville is a round letter and appears to us to differ little from the old faces, but if compared in detail with CASLON it will be seen why we call it the first of the transitional romans in this country. There is more differentiation of thick and thin strokes, the serifs on lower-case letters are more nearly horizontal and the stress nearer the vertical. The **R** in some sizes has the eighteenth-century curled tail. The **W**, lower-case also, has no middle serif. In the **g** the tail is not closed, and the ear is curled. The

Amongst the feveral mechanic Arts that have engaged my attention, there is no one which I have purfued with fo much fteadinefs and pleafure, as that of Letter-Founding. Having been an early admirer of the beauty of Letters, I became infenfibly defirous of contributing to the perfection of them. I formed to my felf Ideas of greater accuracy than had yet appeared, and have endeavoured to produce a Sett of Types according to what I conceived to be their true proportion.

ABCDEFGHIJKLMNOPQRSTUVWXYZ Æ &
abcdefghijklmnopqrstuvwxyz .,;:!?-—()[] æ fi ff fl ffi ffl
£1234567890 * § ft & f fl « » Qu

ABCDEFGHIJKLMNOPQRSTUVWXYZ
abcdefghijklmnopqrstuvwxyz & 1234567890

ABCDEFGHIJKLMNOPQRSTUVWXYZ
abcdefghijklmnopqrstuvwxyz & 1234567890

DEBERNY & PEIGNOT BASKERVILLE

ABCDEFGHIJKLMNOPQRSTUVWXYZ
abcdefghijklmnopqrstuvwxyz
1234567890

ABCDEFGHIJKLMNOPQRSTUVWXYZ
abcdefghijklmnopqrstuvwxyz
1234567890

MONOTYPE BASKERVILLE

ABCDEFGHIJKLMNOPQRSTU
abcdefghijklmnopqrstuvwxyz 12

MONOTYPE BASKERVILLE BOLD

ABCDEFGHIJKLMNOPQRSTU
VWXYZ
abcdefghijklmnopqrstuvwxyz
1234567890
**ABCDEFGHIJKLMNOPQRSTU
VWXYZ
abcdefghijklmnopqrstuvwxyz
1234567890**
*ABCDEFGHIJKLMNOPQRSTU
VWXYZ
abcdefghijklmnopqrstuvwxyz
1234567890*

ABCDEFGHIJKLMNOPQRSTUVWXYZ &&£

INTERTYPE BASKERVILLE

ABCDEFGHIJKLMNOPQRSTUVWXYZ

abcdefghijklmnopqrstuvwxyz

1234567890

BASKERVILLE SEMI BOLD

ABCDEFGHIJKLMNOPQRSTUVWXYZ
abcdefghijklmnopqrstuvwxyz
1234567890
*ABCDEFGHIJKLMNOPQRSTUVWXYZ
abcdefghijklmnopqrstuvwxyz
1234567890*
ABCDEFGHIJKLMNOPQRSTUVWXYZ
1234567890
*ABCDEFGHIJKLMNOPQRSTUVWXYZ
1234567890*

ABCDEFGHIJKLMNOPQRSTUVWXYZ
Recut Italic: abcdefghijklmnopqrstuvwxyz

LINOTYPE BASKERVILLE

**ABCDEFGHIJKLMNOPQRSTUVWXYZ
abcdefghijklmnopqrstuvwxyz
1234567890**
***ABCDEFGHIJKLMNOPQRSTUVWXYZ
abcdefghijklmnopqrstuvwxyz
1234567890***

LINOTYPE BASKERVILLE BOLD

ABCDEFGHIJKLMNOPQRSTUVWXYZ
abcdefghijklmnopqrstuvwxyz
1234567890

ABCDEFGHIJKLMNOPQRSTUVWXYZ
abcdefghijklmnopqrstuvwxyz
1234567890

ATF TYPESETTER BASKERVILLE

ABCDEFGHIJKLMNOPQRSTUVWXYZ
abcdefghijklmnopqrstuvwxyz
1234567890

ATF TYPESETTER BASKERVILLE BOLD

ABCDEFGHIJKLMNOPQRS
abcdefghijklmnopqrstuvwxyz
1234567890

STEMPEL BASKERVILLE MEDIUM

ABCDEFGHIJKLMNOPQRSTU
abcdefghijklmnopqrstuvwxyz
1234567890

ABCDEFGHIJKLMNOPQRSTU
abcdefghijklmnopqrstuvwxyz
1234567890

STEMPEL BASKERVILLE

A design based on the sort of roman used at Basle and in Germany in the first half of the sixteenth century. It was cut by William Howard, a minor founder in Great Queen St. and first used in 1854. It belongs by its weight and distribution of colour to the Venetians rather than the Old Faces. There is a Venetian e and the long s is used. William Morris selected the type for the printing of two of his books in 1889, just before he started his own press. Morris however dropped the long s and had a new e cut. The matrices have now been deposited on permanent loan to the St. Bride Printing Library.

This Small Pica BASLE ROMAN was specially cut for Charles Whittingham in the early nineteenth century by William Howard, who had a Typefoundry in Great Queen Street, London. The Chiswick Press still possess the original punches and matrices, from which this Specimen has been cast.

A B C D E F G H I J K L M N O P Q R S T U V W X Y Z Æ Œ
a b c d e e f g h i j k l m n o p q r s t u v w x y z æ œ ſſ[(?!':;,-.

BASLE ROMAN

BAYER TYPE
Berthold 1935

iv

Designed by Herbert Bayer. A condensed type with short descenders.

HERBERT STEGEMANN GELSENKIRCHEN
Musik-Instrumente jeder Art kauft man am
besten und billigsten nur beim Fachmann

BAYER LIGHT

iv

PRESSEFOTO SCHERL BERLIN LEIPZIG
Wiesbaden pflegt Mode und Gesellschaft
HELSINGBORGS DAGBLAD
Studentkurser i Engelska och Latin
167890

BAYER MEDIUM

iv

STEINGUT IN NEUEN MUSTERN
Kristalle zu ermäßigten Preisen

BAYER BOLD

BEHRENS ROMAN
Klingspor c. 1900

ix

Designed by Peter Behrens. A pen-drawn roman.

ABCDEFGHIJKLMNOPQ
RSTUVWXYZ
abcdefghijklmnopqrſßst
uvwxyz
1234567890

ABCDEFGHIJKLMNOPQRSTUVWXYZ
abcdefghijklmnopqrſßstuvwxyz
1234567890

BEHRENS

BELINDA
Nacional

ix

The design is based on fifteenth-century Spanish calligraphic writings. Descenders are very short and ascenders high. The terminals of ascenders have fine, curved serifs; and the main strokes are heavy. There are also special decorative initials.

Por el ideal se identifica la desigualdad. Así lo dem

BELINDA

Stanley Morison has called this the first of our modern faces. It was cut by Richard Austin for Bell's British Foundry, and was influenced by Firmin Didot's new roman. We place it here with the eighteenth century types because of its date and because in one way it stands apart from the usual modern face. It has the flat serifs and vertical stress, but the stress is much less abrupt. The serifs are bracketed and sharply cut. There are two **J**'s, one short-ranging, two **K**'s, two **R**'s, one with a curved tail, and two **Q**'s, one with the tail starting inside the counter. The **e** has a large eye, and there are two **t**'s, one modern. The italic is commended for its harmony with the roman, with its wider letters. There are swash varieties of **A, J, N, Q, T** and **V**, and a swash **Y**. See S. Morison's *John Bell* for the interesting history of the type and specimen books. The Monotype Corporation's version dates from 1932.

ABCDEFGHIJKLMNOPQRSTUVWXYZ

abcdefghijklmnopqrstuvwxyz

ABCDEFGHIJKLMNOPQRSTUVWXYZ

abcdefghijklmnopqrstuvwyz

MONOTYPE BELL OR JOHN BELL

Designed by Georg Belwe. The type has old-face qualities, but short ascenders and very short descenders. Serifs are small, bracketed and oblique on the lower case. **A** has a slab serif, the **H, M, N** and **T** are narrow. In **M** the middle strokes stop half-way. **P** and **R** have deep bowls and **U** the lower case design. In the lower case **a** has a large bowl, the **g** a large bowl with the ear pointing north-east and the tail diminutive; **p** and **q** have no foot serifs, **t** is narrow and the bar unbracketed, and **v** is closed at the top. The italic is slightly inclined. On the lower case the serifs are as the roman except **h** and **k**, which have curved terminals. The figures are short-ranging. There are also Medium Bold, Bold and an Inline.

ABCDEFGHIJKLMNOPQRSTUVWXY
abcdefghijklmnopqrſstuvwxyz
1234567890

ABCDEFGHIJKLMNOPQRSTUVWXY
abcdefghijklmnopqrſstuvwxyz
BELWE ROMAN

ABCDEFGHIJKLMNOPQRSTUVWXY
abcdefghijklmnopqrſstuvwxyz
BELWE MEDIUM BOLD

ABCDEFGHIJKLMNOPQRSTUVWXY
abcdefghijklmnopqrſstuvwxyz
1234567890

ABCDEFGHIJKLMNOPQRSTUVWXY
abcdefghijklmnopqrſstuvwxyz
1234567890
BELWE BOLD

ABCDEFGHIJKLMNOPQRSTUVWXY
1234567890
BELWE INLINE

BEMBO
Monotype 1929

The first of the Old Faces is a copy of a roman cut by Francesco Griffo for the Venetian printer Aldus Manutius. It was first used in Cardinal Bembo's *De Aetna*, 1495, hence the name of the contemporary version. Although a type cut in the fifteenth century for a Venetian printer we group it with the Old Faces. Stanley Morison has shown that it was the model followed by Garamond and thus the forerunner of the standard European type of the next two centuries. The capitals are shorter than the ascending letters of the lower case, the serifs are slighter than in earlier romans and there are no slab serifs. The serifs on the **T** are divergent. In the lower case the **e** has a horizontal straight to the eye. The **h** has not the curved shank. There is also a TITLING and BEMBO CONDENSED ITALIC (designed by Alfred Fairbank). The bold italic was added in 1959.

ii

ABCDEFGHIJKLMNOPQRSTUVWXYZ
abcdefghijklmnopqrstuvwxyz
1234567890
ABCDEFGHIJKLMNOPQRSTUVWXYZ
abcdefghijklmnopqrstuvwxyz
1234567890

BEMBO

ii

ABCDEFGHIJKLMNOPQRSTUVWXYZ&
abcdefghijklmnopqrstuvwxyz   1234567890

BEMBO CONDENSED ITALIC

ii

ABCDEFGHIJKLMNOPQRSTU
VWXYZ

BEMBO TITLING

ii

ABCDEFGHIJKLMNOPQRSTUVWXYZ
abcdefghijklmnopqrstuvwxyz
1234567890
ABCDEFGHIJKLMNOPQRSTUVWXYZ
abcdefghijklmnopqrstuvwxyz   1234567890

BEMBO BOLD

BERLIN
Intertype (Berlin) 1962

A newspaper type with accentuated centres and serifs, available in two weights.

iv

ABCDEFGHIJKLMNOPQRSTUVWXYZ
abcdefghijklmnopqrstuvwxyz
1234567890
ABCDEFGHIJKLMNOPQRSTUVWXYZ
abcdefghijklmnopqrstuvwxyz
1234567890

BERLIN

iv

ABCDEFGHIJKLMNOPQRSTUVWXYZ
abcdefghijklmnopqrstuvwxyz
1234567890

BERLIN BOLD

Designed by K. E. Forsberg. A roman with the characteristics of an old face. The serifs are inclined and blunt. The **g** has a straight ear. There is also a bold version.

ABCDEFGHIJKLMNOPQRSTUVW XYZÄÖ

ii

abcdefghijklmnopqrstuvwxyzåäö

ABCDEFGHIJKLMNOPQRSTUV WXYZÅÄÖ

abcdefghijklmnopqrstuvwxyzåäö

BERLING

ABCDEFGHIJKLMNOPQRSTUV WXYZÅÄÖ

ii

abcdefghijklmnopqrstuvwxyzåäö

ii

BERLING BOLD

ABCDEFGHIJKLMNOPQRSTUVWXYZ

abcdefghijklmnopqrstuvwxyz

ii

1234567890

ABCDEFGHIJKLMNOPQRSTUVWXYZ

abcdefghijklmnopqrstuvwxyz

1234567890

BERLING MONOTYPE

ABCDEFGHIJKLMNOPQRSTUVWXYZ

abcdefghijklmņopqrstuvwxyz

ii

1234567890

BERLING MONOTYPE SEMI-BOLD

Designed by Albert Augspurg and originally a German type. A set of open capitals, slightly inclined and with hair lines for the thin strokes.

ABCDEFGHIJKLMNOPQRSTU VWXYZÅÄÖ

BERLING KORTVERSALER

BERNARD CONDENSED
Monotype 1926

ix

Berthold and Bauer and Berthold have BERNHARD types on which this face appears to be modelled.

ABCDEFGHIJKLMNOPQRSTUVWXYZ
abcdefghijklmnopqrstuvwxyz
1234567890

BERNARD CONDENSED

BERNHARD ROMAN
Bauer 1937

ix

Designed by Lucian Bernhard as a text and display type. Among distinguishing marks are the cross-over **W**, the open bowl of the **R** and a tilted **O**.

PHILHARMONISCHES KONZERT
Gold- und Silberscheideanstalt

BERNHARD ANTIQUA

ix

HAMBURGER ILLUSTRIERTE
Typographische Vereinigung

BERNHARD ANTIQUA ITALIC

ix

Gewerbe-Museum in Hamburg

BERNHARD ANTIQUA BOLD CONDENSED

ix

WORMSER ZEITUNG
Handel und Verkehr

BERNHARD ANTIQUA EXTRA BOLD

ix

Hotel zu den Drei Raben

BERNHARD ITALIC EXTRA BOLD

ix

Offenbacher Lederwaren
Letzte Pariser Neuheiten

BERNHARD ITALIC BOLD

BESSEMER
Stevens Shanks 1936

iv

Designed by Dennis Morgan. An elongated and condensed fat face based on mid-nineteenth century designs. The Alexander Wilson firm showed a type like this in 1843. Named after the elder Bessemer who had a foundry at Hitchin and later in London. *Cf.* SLIMBLACK.

ABCDEFGIJKLMNOPQRSTUVWXYZ
1234567890£ÆŒ&

BESSEMER

Designed by Heinrich Jost. **A** has a flat top, projecting to the left, **G** has a spur, and the **W** (lower-case also) no middle serif. The **a** has the two-storeyed design, with a serif terminating the arc, **g** has an open tail, **t** is vertical and has an oblique top, and **y** has a foot serif extending to the right.

There is a light face (which seems to contradict the essence of the design), a medium bold, bold and extra bold; also an open, really a three-dimensional letter.

ABCDEFGHIJKKLMNOPQRRSTUV
WXYZ
abcdefghijklmnopqrstuvwxyz
1234567890

BETON LIGHT

ABCDEFGHIJKKLMNOPQRRSTUV
WXYZ
abcdefghijklmnopqrstuvwxyz
1234567890

BETON MEDIUM

ABCDEFGHIJKKLMNOPQRRSTUV
WXYZ
abcdefghijklmnopqrstuvwx

BETON BOLD

ABCDEFGHIJKKLMNOPQRRS
TUVWXYZ
abcdefghijklmnopqrstuvwxyz
1234567890

BETON EXTRA BOLD

ABCDEFGHIJKKLMNOPQRRSTUVWXYZ
abcdefghijklmnopqrstuvwxyz
1234567890

BETON MEDIUM CONDENSED

23

ABCDEFGHIJKKLMNOPQRRSTUVW XYZ
abcdefghijklmnopqrstuvwxyz
1234567890

BETON BOLD CONDENSED

ABCDEFGHIJKKLMNOP QRRSTUVWXYZ
12345678

BETON OPEN

The type is similar to RONALDSON OLD STYLE, and was first cut in Scotland about 1863.

A B C D E F G H I J K L M N O P Q R S T U V W X Y Z & Æ Œ
a b c d e f g h i j k l m n o p q r s t u v w x y z
$1234567890£ $1234567890
æ œ fi fl ff ffi ffl   . , - ' : ; ! ?

ABCDEFGHIJKLMNOPQRSTUVWXYZ&ÆŒ
abcdefghijklmnopqrstuvwxyzææ   fiflffffiffl
$1234567890   :;!? $1234567890

BINNY OLD STYLE

The italic cut to accompany POLIPHILUS is based on a formal italic of the Roman calligrapher and printer Lodovico degli Arrighi, called Vicentino. It is named after the Roman printer Antonio Blado, who printed many books in this fount, using it as an individual type and not as a subsidiary to roman. In The Monotype Corporation's version the upper case closely resembles the roman and the inclination is slight. In the lower case the beginning strokes are angular and on the tops of ascenders become inclined serifs. The curves of the v and w are to be noted.

ABCDEFGHIJKLMNOPQRSTUVWXYZ
abcdefghijklmnopqrstuvwxyz
1234567890 &

BLADO ITALIC

Giambattista Bodoni of Parma was one of the most prolific type designers. In his earlier years he copied Fournier but in his later years carried the modern face to its logical conclusion. His serifs are both flat and unbracketed, the stress is mathematically vertical and the thins are hair lines. Bodoni believed in plenty of white space and therefore descenders are long. The **M** is narrow, in the **Q** the tail at first descends vertically and the **R** has a curled tail. In the lower case the **g** has a small bowl (in The Monotype Corporation's version it is not so small as in the original) and the **w**, in this version, no middle serif. The italic, like all continental modern faces, has roman serifs. The eighteenth century medial **v** and **w** may be noted.

There are two basic models in the modern re-cuttings,

I. American Typefounders by M.F. Benton, from 1907 onwards, possibly antedated by Nebiolo's version; copied by The Monotype Corporation (slightly squarer and heavier); and separately (following more closely, but on body) by Haas 1924–1939 (adopted by the Amsterdam Typefoundry, Stempel, Berthold), who also added an extra-bold with italic, and narrow extra-bold. The Linotype (1914–16), Intertype and Ludlow versions are likewise based on this. J. Wagner made a re-cutting in 1961.

II. Bauer. More delicate than the above re-cutting and not adopted by any other foundry or composing machine manufacturer.

ABCDEFGHIJKLMNOPQRSTUVWXYZ

abcdefghijklmnopqrstuvwxyz

1234567890

ABCDEFGHIJKLMNOPQRSTUVWXYZ

abcdefghijklmnopqrstuvwxyz

1234567890

ABCDEFGHIJKLMNOPQRSTUVWXYZ

abcdefghijklmnopqrstuvwxyz

1234567890

ABCDEFGHIJKLMNOPQRSTUVWXYZ

abcdefghijklmnopqrstuvwxyz

1234567890

MONOTYPE BODONI

ABCDEFGHIJKLMNOPQRSTUVWXYZ

abcdefghijklmnopqrstuvwxyz

1234567890

ABCDEFGHIJKLMNOPQRSTUVWXZ

abcdefghijklmnopqrstuvwxyz

MONOTYPE BODONI HEAVY

ABCDEFGHIJKLMNOPQRSTUVWXYZ

abcdefghijklmnopqrstuvwxyz

1234567980

MONOTYPE BODONI BOLD

iv

iv

ABCDEFGHIJKLMNOPQRSTUVWXYZ
abcdefghijklmnopqrstuvwxyz
1234567890
ABCDEFGHIJKLMNOPQRSTUVWXYZ
abcdefghijklmnopqrstuvwxyz
1234567890

MONOTYPE BODONI BOLD CONDENSED

iv

ABCDEFGHIJKLMNOPQRSTUVWXYZ&
abcdefghijklmnopqrstuvwxyz
1234567890

MERGENTHALER LINOTYPE BODONI BOLD CONDENSED

iv

ABCDEFGHIJKLMNOPQRSTUVWXYZ
abcdefghijklmnopqrstuvwxyz
ABCDEFGHIJKLMNOPQRSTUVWXYZ
abcdefghijklmnopqrstuvwxyz

HAAS BODONI LIGHT

iv

ABCDEFGHIJKLMNOPQRSTUVWXYZ
abcdefghijklmnopqrstuvwxyz
ABCDEFGHIJKLMNOPQRSTUVWXYZ
abcdefghijklmnopqrstuvwxyz

HAAS BODONI

iv

ABCDEFGHIJKLMNOPQRSTUVWXYZ
abcdefghijklmnopqrstuvwxyz
ABCDEFGHIJKLMNOPQRSTUVWXYZ
abcdefghijklmnopqrstuvwxyz

HAAS BODONI SEMI BOLD

iv

ABCDEFGHIJKLMNOPQRSTUVWXYZ
abcdefghijklmnopqrstuvwxyz
ABCDEFGHIJKLMNOPQRSTUVWXY
abcdefghijklmnopqrstuvwxyz

HAAS BODONI BOLD

ABCDEFGHIJKLMNOPQRSTUVWXYZ

abcdefghijklmnopqrstuvwxyz

HAAS BODONI BOLD CONDENSED

ABCDEFGHIJKLMNOPQRSTUVWXYZ

abcdefghijklmnopqrstuvwxyz

1234567890

ABCDEFGHIJKLMNOPQRSTUVWXYZ

abcdefghijklmnopqrstuvwxyz

1234567890

ABCDEFGHIJKLMNOPQRSTUVWXYZ

Recut Italic: abcdefghijklmnopqrstuvwxyz

ABCDEFGHIJKLMNOPQRSTUVWXYZ

ABCDEFGHIJKLMNOPQRSTUVWXYZ

MERGENTHALER LINOTYPE BODONI BOOK

iv

ABCDEFGHIJKLMNOPQRSTUVWXYZ

abcdefghijklmnopqrstuvwxyz

1234567890

ABCDEFGHIJKLMNOPQRSTUVWXYZ

abcdefghijklmnopqrstuvwxyz

1234567890

ABCDEFGHIJKLMNOPQRSTUVWXYZ

Recut Italic: abcdefghijklmnopqrstuvwxyz

ABCDEFGHIJKLMNOPQRSTUVWXYZ

ABCDEFGHIJKLMNOPQRSTUVWXYZ

MERGENTHALER LINOTYPE BODONI

iv

ABCDEFGHIJKLMNOPQRSTUVWXYZ

abcdefghijklmnopqrstuvwxyz

1234567890

ABCDEFGHIJKLMNOPQRSTUVWXYZ

abcdefghijklmnopqrstuvwxyz

1234567890

ABCDEFGHIJKLMNOPQRSTUVWXYZ

Recut Italic: abcdefghijklmnopqrstuvwxyz

ABCDEFGHIJKLMNOPQRSTUVWXYZ

ABCDEFGHIJKLMNOPQRSTUVWXYZ

MERGENTHALER LINOTYPE BODONI BOLD

iv

ABCDEFGHIJKLMNOPQRSTUVW
XYZ
abcdefghijklmnopqrstuvwxyz
1234567890
ABCDEFGHIJKLMNOPQRSTUVW
XYZ
abcdefghijklmnopqrstuvvwwxyz
1234567890

BAUER BODONI

iv

ABCDEFGHIJKLMNOPQRSTUVW
XYZ
abcdefghijklmnopqrstuvwxyz
1234567890
ABCDEFGHIJKLMNOPQRSTUV
WXYZ
abcdefghijklmnopqrstuvvww xyz
1234567890

BAUER BODONI BOLD

iv

ABCDEFGHIJKLMNOPQRSTUV
WXYZ
abcdefghijklmnopqrstuvwxyz
1234567890
ABCDEFGHIJKLMNOPQRSTU
VWXYZ
abcdefghijklmnopqrst uvvvw
xyz 1234567890

BAUER BODONI EXTRA BOLD

ABCDEFGHIJKLMNOPQRSTUV WXYZ&! abcdefghijklmnopqrstuvwxyz $1234567890

BODONI OPEN

ARCHIVIO

BAUER BODONI OPEN

ABCDEFGHIJKLMNOPQRSTUVWXYZ abcdefghijklmnopqrstuvwxyz

LANSTON MONOTYPE BODONI BOLD SHADED

New Face in the Bodoni Family 74
Tall Typeface in Narrow Measure

LUDLOW BODONI CAMPANILE

A B C D E F G H I J K L M N O P Q R S T U V
W X Y Z
& $ 1 2 3 4 5 6 7 8 9 0

AMERICAN TYPEFOUNDERS ENGRAVERS' BODONI

ABCDEFGHIJKLMNOPQRSTUVWXYZ
abcdefghijklmnopqrstuvwxyz
1234567890

ABCDEFGHJKLMNOPQRSTUVWXYZ
abcdefghijklmnopqrstuvwxyz
1234567890

MONOTYPE BODONI ULTRA BOLD

Very like CASLON BOLD FACE OPEN. It may be distinguished by the rounder arc of the lower-case **a**.

ABCDEFGHIJKLMNOPQRSTUVWXY
345   abcdefghijklmnopqrstuvwxyz   6

OUTLINE

BOLOGNA

Stephenson Blake 1946;
American Typefounders

A type based on the humanistic scripts of the fifteenth century and therefore resembling TREYFORD and SINIBALDI. Pen-qualities are evident in the serifs and in the gradation of colour in the round letters. The **M** is much splayed. Ascenders and descenders are ample. **v** and **w** have cursive forms.

i

ABCDEFGHIJKLMNOPQRSTUVWXYZQUQu

abcdefghijklmnopqrst uvwxyz   £&flfffifhffl's

1234567890.,-';:?!

BOLOGNA

BOOKMAN or ANTIQUE OLD STYLE

Ludlow 1925;
Mergenthaler Linotype c. 1936;
Monotype

ii

Originally cut as a bold face for Miller & Richard's OLD STYLE. The type has short ascenders and descenders. The upper case has heavy serifs and slight difference of stress. Lower-case serifs are thick and inclined more steeply than in OLD STYLE. The italic is the sloped roman.

ABCDEFGHIJKLMNOPQRSTUVWXYZ

abcdefghijklmnopqrstuvwxyz

1234567890

ABCDEFGHIJKLMNOPQRSTUVWXYZ

abcdefghijklmnopqrstuvwxyz

1234567890

ABCDEFGHIJKLMNOPQRSTUVWXYZ

ABCDEFGHIJKLMNOPQRSTUVWXY

BCDEFGHIJKLMNOPQRSTUVWXYZ

LINOTYPE BOOKMAN

BOUTIQUE

Haas c. 1900

ix

A Victorian design of narrow letters in which many of the capitals descend below the line. Letters are open with many of the strokes not joining.

ABCDEFGHIJKLMNOPQRSTUVWXYZ

abcdefghijklmnopqrstuvwxyz

1234567890

BOUTIQUE

BRAVOUR

Stempel 1912

ix

Designed by M. Jacoby-Boy. A monotone letter with flat serifs except those on the arms of **E**, **F** and **L**, and those terminating the arc of **C**, **G**, etc. These are oblique and long. **B**, **P** and **R** have large bowls. In the **M** the middle strokes descend half-way. Ascenders and descenders are short; the **g** has an open tail. The italic has some cursive capitals, *e.g.* the **H**, **L**, **V** and **W** and the serifs of the roman. There is also a bold, which is a heavy display type.

Kunst und Handwerk

BRAVOUR

Designed by Willy Wiegand and cut by Louis Hoell for the Flinsch Typefoundry in one size only (11 pt.), originally for the exclusive use of the Bremer Presse. It has a solid calligraphic quality and is distinguishable by the foot serifs pointing to the right only.

There are also 12 and 16 pt versions which are slightly different.

ABCDEFGHIJKLMNOPQRSTUVWXYZ
abcdefghijklmnopqrstuvwxyz
1234567890

BREMER PRESSE ROMAN

A modified fat face in which the main stroke only is fat, the thins taking over the rest of the letter. The thicks and thins meet at an angle and not in a curve. Several types of the American Typefounders have a similar design. CARLTON is an inline version of this design.

BRUXELLES NICE

BRISTOL

ENSURING

CARLTON

Designed by Jan Rambousek. There are a roman and an italic, as well as a bold. Letters are open and have little variations in stress, but in the lower case are somewhat uneven in weight. The tail of the **R** is vertical.

ABCDEFGHIJKLMNOPQRSTUVWXYZ
abcdefghikjlmnopqrstuvwxyz
1234567890

ABCDEFGHIJKLMNOPQRSTUVWXYZ
abcdefghijklmnopqrstuvwxyz
1234567890
BRNO Z

ABCDEFGHIJKLMNOPQRSTUVWXYZ
abcdefghikjlmnopqrstuvwxyz
1234567890

BRNO Z BOLD

Designed by Lucien Pissarro for his private press and named after his house in Hammersmith. The capitals are mostly broad and there are slab serifs on the **A** and **M**. The **g** has a large bowl and a squashed tail; the bowl of the **p** is circular and the **t** is narrow.

The type, now in the possession of the Cambridge University Press, was cut in pica only.

Next as to type. By instinct rather than by conscious thinking it over, I began by getting myself a fount of Roman type. And here what I wanted was letter pure in form; severe, without needless excrescenses; solid without the thickening and thinning of the line, which is the essential fault of the ordinary modern type, and which makes it difficult to read; and not compressed laterally, as all later type has grown to be owing to com-

ABCDEFGHIJKLMNOPRSTUVWXYZ QU Qu Æ Œ
abcdefghijklmnopqrstuvwxyz .,;:!?´'—...() æœ
£1234567890 «» àèéâêîôûëïü ç Ç &

BROOK TYPE

BRUCE OLD STYLE No. 31

Lanston Monotype 1909
iv

Designed by Sol Hess from the Bruce Foundry's BRUCE OLD STYLE NO. 20 which was first shown in 1869. The type is based on SCOTCH and similar faces.

ABCDEFGHIJKLMNOPQRSTUVWXYZ&ÆŒ
abcdefghijklmnopqrstuvwxyzæœ fiflffffiffl
$1234567890 .,-'':;!? $1234567890
ABCDEFGHIJKLMNOPQRSTUVWXYZ&ÆŒ
ABCDEFGHIJKLMNOPQRSTUVWXYZ&ÆŒ
abcdefghijklmnopqrstuvwxyzæœ fiflffffiffl
$1234567890 :;!? $1234567890

BRUCE OLD STYLE NO. 31

BRUDI MEDIAEVAL

Berthold 1953–54
Typograph
ii

Designed by Walter Brudi. Serifs are thin and unbracketed. The **M** is splayed and has no top serifs; the italic is only slightly inclined. Figures are ranging.

ABCDEFGHIJKLMNOPQRSTUVWXYZ
abcdefghijklmnopqrstuvwxyz
1234567890
ABCDEFGHIJKLMNOPQRSTUVWXYZ
abcdefghijklmnopqrstuvwxyz
1234567890

BRUDI MEDIAEVAL

BULMER

American Typefounders 1928;
Intertype;
Lanston Monotype;
Monotype

Designed by Morris F. Benton as a replica of a famous type in the history of English printing cut by William Martin about 1790 for William Bulmer of the Shakspeare Press.

The **R** has a curled tail. The **g** has a small bowl with a curved ear and gives the appearance of leaning backwards. **J**, **K**, **N**, **T** and **Y** in the italic are reminiscent of Baskerville, whose pupil Martin was. Figures are ranging.

iii

ABCDEFGHIJKLMNOPQRSTUVWXYZ
abcdefghijklmnopqrstuvwxyz
1234567890
ABCDEFGHIJKLMNOPQRSTUVWXYZ
ABCDEFGHIJKLMNOPQRSTUVWXYZ
abcdefghijklmnopqrstuvwxyz
1234567890

INTERTYPE BULMER

iii

ABCDEFGHIJKLMNOPQRSTUVWXYZ
abcdefghijklmnopqrstuvwxyz
1234567890
ABCDEFGHIJKLMNOPQRSTUVWXYZ
abcdefghijklmnopqrstuvwxyz
1234567890

MONOTYPE BULMER

ABCDEFGHIJKLMNOPQRSTUVWXYZ

abcdefghijklmnopqrstuvwxyz

1234567890

ABCDEFGHIJKLMNOPQRSTUVWXYZ

abcdefghijklmnopqrstuvwxyz

1234567890

AMERICAN TYPEFOUNDERS BULMER

This type face has some resemblance to MEMPHIS. **A** has the slab bar at the top, **G** has a spur, in the **M** the middle strokes stop short of the line, **R** has a curled tail. The lower case has slab serifs at the top and foot, and the **g** has a slab serif at the top and open tail.

ABCDEFGHIJKLMNOPQRSTUVWXYZ

abcdefghijklmnopqrstuvwxyz

1234567890 &£

v

CAIRO

ABCDEFGHIJKLMNOPQRSTUVWXYZ

abcdefghijklmnopqrstuvwxyz

1234567890 &£

v

CAIRO BOLD

ABCDEFGHIJKLMNOPQRSTUVWXYZ

abcdefghijklmnopqrstuvwxyz

1234567890

v

CAIRO HEAVY

ABCDEFGHIJKLMNOPQRSTUVWXYZ

abcdefghijklmnopqrstuvwxyz

1234567890

v

CAIRO EXTRA BOLD CONDENSED

ABCDEFGHIJKLMNOPQRSTUVWXYZ

abcdefghijklmnopqrstuvwxyz

1234567890

v

CAIRO BOLD CONDENSED

Mergenthaler Linotype 1938;
Stempel 1938;
Linotype (Frankfurt) 1939;
Linotype (London)

iv

Designed by W.A. Dwiggins. A modified SCOTCH, which accounts for the name. The stress is vertical and serifs are horizontal but not thin. The **G** is wide open and the **R** has a curled tail. The **g** has a wide tail and the ear is not curled. The **t** is unbracketed. In the italic **p** and **q** have no foot serifs. In Germany the type is called CORNELIA.

ABCDEFGHIJKLMNOPQRSTUVWXYZ
abcdefghijklmnopqrstuvwxyz
1234567890
ABCDEFGHIJKLMNOPQRSTUVWXYZ
abcdefghijklmnopqrstuvwxyz
1234567890

ABCDEFGHIJKLMNOPQRSTUVWXYZ
abcdefghijklmnopqrstuvwxyz
1234567890
1234567890

ABCDEFGHIJKLMNOPQRSTUVWXYZ
abcdefghijklmnopqrstuvwxyz
1234567890
1234567890

ABCDEFGHIJKLMNOPQRSTUVWXYZ

CALEDONIA

iv

ABCDEFGHIJKLMNOPQRSTUVWXYZ
abcdefghijklmnopqrstuvwxyz
1234567890
ABCDEFGHIJKLMNOPQRSTUVWXYZ
abcdefghijklmnopqrstuvwxyz
1234567890

ABCDEFGHIJKLMNOPQRSTUVWXYZ
abcdefghijklmnopqrstuvwxyz
1234567890
1234567890

ABCDEFGHIJKLMNOPQRSTUVWXYZ
abcdefghijklmnopqrstuvwxyz
1234567890
1234567890

ABCDEFGHIJKLMNOPQRSTUVWXYZ

CALEDONIA BOLD

34

Designed by Frederic W. Goudy in 1938 for the University of California Press. The type has flat serifs and an italic of slight inclination.

ABCDEFGHIJKLMNOPQRSTUVWXYZ
abcdefghijklmnopqrstuvwxyz
1234567890
ABCDEFGHIJKLMNOPQRSTUVWXYZ
abcdefghijklmnopqrstuvwxyz
1234567890

CALIFORNIAN

Designed by Jan van Krimpen, this italic, based on humanistic penscripts, has, when combined into words, a true hand lettering appeal. There are variations for most upper- and lower-case letters, and ascenders and descenders are ample. Swash letters are very much in evidence. The type complements the same founder's ROMULUS series.

ABCDEFGHIJKLMNOPQRSTUVWXYZÆŒ
abcdefghijklmnopqrstuvwxyzæœç
1234567890&

CANCELLERESCA BASTARDA

Designed by R. Hunter Middleton. A shaded roman and italic with thin serifs, which are inclined in the lower case. The italic has the serifs of the roman. The upper case is similar to NARCISSUS.

ABCDEFGHIJKLMNOPQRSTU
VWXYZ&   1234567890
abcdefghijklmnopqrstuvwxyz

CAMEO

Designed by J. Erbar. A roman with serifs like an "Egyptian" but thinner. Capitals are wide and the **W** and **w** without a middle serif. Lower-case serifs are horizontal and the **a** has a large bowl. ANTIQUA 505 is very similar.

iv

ABCDEFGHIJKLMNOPQRSTUV
WXYZ
abcdefghijklmnopqrstuvwxyz
1234567890

*ABCDEFGHIJKLMNOPQRSTUV
WXYZ
abcdefghijklmnopqrstuvwxyz
1234567890*

CANDIDA

iv

ABCDEFGHIJKLMNOPQRSTUV
WXYZ
abcdefghijklmnopqrstuvwxyz
1234567890

CANDIDA SEMI-BOLD

iv

ABCDEFGHIJKLMNOPQRSTUV
WXYZ
abcdefghijklmnopqrstuvwxyz
1234567890
*ABCDEFGHIJKLMNOPQRSTU
VWXYZ
abcdefghijklmnopqrstuvwxyz
1234567890*

CANDIDA BOLD

ABCDEFGHIJKLMNOPQRSTUVWXYZ
abcdefghijklmnopqrstuvwxyz
123467890

CANDIDA MEDIUM CONDENSED

ABCDEFGHIJKLMNOPQRSTUVWXYZ
abcdefghijklmnopqrstuvwxyz
1234567890

iv

CANDIDA BOLD CONDENSED

Designed by Karl Erik Forsberg. A set of pen-drawn capitals and ranging numerals with slight serifs. The **O** is nearly square.

ABCDEFGHIJKLMNOPQRST UVWXYZ

ix

CAROLUS

Designed by Carl Dair. First used by the Canadian printing house of Cape & Co, and designed specially for phototypesetting. There are no italic capitals.

ABCDEFGHIJKLMNOPQRSTUVW XYZ
abcdefghijklmnopqrstuvwxyz
1234567890
abcdefghijklmnopqrstuvwxyz
1234567890

ii

CARTIER

CASLON ANTIQUE
American Typefounders

Originally cast by Barnhart Brothers & Spindler as FIFTEENTH CENTURY about 1897, although an earlier specimen book with tipped-in pages would suggest 1894–95. An unusual design and oddly named. Some of the lower case letters are condensed, e.g., **a**, **n**, and **u**. The serifs are very blunt.

ii

ABCDEFGHIJKLMNOPQRSTUVWXYZ

&abcdefghijklmnopqrstuvwxyz?

1234567890

ABCDEFGHIJKLMNOPQRSTUVWX

YZ&

abcdefghijklmnopqrstuvwxyz?

1234567890

CASLON ANTIQUE

CASLON OLD FACE
Caslon and other founders

William Caslon started his foundry about the year 1720, but his first roman is not met with before 1725. He modelled his designs on Dutch types of the late seventeenth century, so that his type is classed among the Old Faces rather than with the eighteenth century types. In the upper case the **A** has a hollow in the apex, the **C** has two full serifs or beaks, and the **M** is wide and square. In the lower case the ear of the **g** is thickened at the end; the **s**, upper-case also, is a light letter. In the italic, as in many old-face italics, the capitals are irregular in their inclination; the **A**, **V** and **W** appear to be falling over. Some of the original swash capitals, **Q**, **T**, and **Y** seem to have been abandoned, but the **J** remains.

Matrices based on the original are still in existence at Enschedé, but since its revival the type has been so popular that many foundries have their own versions.

There are also much later-dated adaptations such as Caslon Old Face Heavy, and Old Face Open and an Old Face Open Heavy. The Caslon italic of American Typefounders has additional swash letters. Other series for this typefoundry were redesigned by Frank Bartuska.

Haas base their type on original matrices for roman and italic in small sizes, while the larger sizes were re-cut in 1944. Intertype (F) CASLON BOLD was re-designed and hand-cut in 1960 to match the lighter weight.

ii

ABCDEFGHIJKLMNOPQRSTUVWXYZ

abcdefghijklmnopqrstuvwxy

ABCDEFGHIJKLMNOPQRSTUVWXYZ

abcdedefghiiklmnopqrtuvwxyz

CASLON OLD FACE

ABCDEFGHIJKLMNOPQRSTUVWXYZ

abcdefghijklmnopqrstuvwxyz

1234567890

ABCDEFGHIJKLMNOPQRSTUV

abcdefghijklmnopqrstuvwxyz

HAAS CASLON

ABCDEGJKMNPQRTUY

HAAS CASLON SWASH CAPITALS

ABCDEFGHIJKLMNOPQRSTUVWXYZ
abcdefghijklmnopqrstuvwxyz
1234567   1234567890   ii
ABCDEFGHIJKLMNOPQRSTUVWXYZ
abcdefghijklmnopqrstuvwxyz
4567890   1234567890   ii
ABCDEFGHIJKLMNOPQRSTUVWXYZ
ABCDEFGHIJKLMNOPQRSTUVW
DEFGHIJKLMNOPQRSTUVWXYZ

MERGENTHALER LINOTYPE CASLON OLD FACE (1921)

ABCDEFGHIJKLMNOPQRSTUVWXYZ
abcdefghijklmnopqrstuvwxyz
12345678   1234567890
ABCDEFGHIJKLMNOPQRSTUVWXYZ
abcdefghijklmnopqrstuvwxyz   ii
34567890   1234567890
Recut Italic: abcdefghijklmnopqrstuvwxyz
ABCDEFGHIJKLMNOPQRSTUVWXYZ
ABCDEFGHIJKLMNOPQRSTUVWX
CDEFGHIJKLMNOPQRSTUVWXYZ

MERGENTHALER LINOTYPE CASLON NO. 3 (1913)

STRIKING NEW SERIES
suitable for every description
of modern commercial work
CASLON OLD FACE OPEN

DESIGNERS
number increased   ii
CASLON OLD FACE OPEN HEAVY

ABCDEFGHIJKLMNOPQRSTUVWXYZ
abcdefghijklmnopqrstuvwxyz
1234567890 &£
ABCDEFGHIJKLMNOPQRSTUVWXYZ   ii
abcdefghijklmnopqrstuvwxyz
1234567890 &£

CASLON OLD FACE HEAVY

ABCDEFGHIJKLMNOPQRSTUVWXYZ
abcdefghijklmnopqrstuvwxyz   ii
1234567890

CASLON 641

CASTELLAR
Monotype 1957

vii

Designed by John Peters. A set of shaded capitals and figures. The serifs are long and thin.

ABCDEFGHIJKL
MNOPQRSTUVX

CASTELLAR

CENTAUR
Monotype 1929

i

Designed by Bruce Rogers in 1914 as a titling fount only for the Metropolitan Museum of New York, and modelled on Jenson's roman. It is lighter in colour and more modelled than CLOISTER OLD FACE. The italic cut to accompany The Monotype Corporation's version is the ARRIGHI ITALIC shown separately.

ABCDEFGHIJKLMNOPQRSTUVWXYZ
abcdeghijklmnopqrstuvwxyz
1234567890

CENTAUR

CENTURY
American Typefounders;
Linotype;
Intertype;
Monotype;
Ludlow

iv

Cut in 1894 by Linn Boyd Benton in collaboration with T.L. De Vinne for the *Century Magazine* to supply a blacker and more readable face than the thin type used previously, and slightly condensed to fit the double-column setting of the magazine. It was first used in 1895.

Morris Fuller Benton designed several versions of this type; and in about 1900 American Typefounders brought out Century Expanded to meet the Typographical Union Standard of the day.

CENTURY NOVA, designed by Charles E. Hughes for American Typefounders in 1966, is a new condensed version of the expanded type.

ABCDEFGHIJKLMNOPQRSTUVW
XYZ
abcdefghijklmnopqrstuvwxyz
1234567890

CENTURY OLD STYLE

iv

ABCDEFGHIJKLMNOPQRSTUVW
XYZ
abcdefghijklmnopqrstuvwxyz
1234567890

CENTURY OLD STYLE ITALIC

ABCDEFGHIJKLMNOPQRSTU VWXYZ
abcdefghijklmnopqrstuvwxyz
1234567890

CENTURY OLD STYLE BOLD

ABCDEFGHIJKLMNOPQRSTUVW XYZ
abcdefghijklmnopqrstuvwxyz
1234567890

CENTURY EXPANDED

ABCDEFGHIJKLMNOPQRSTUV WXYZ
abcdefghijklmnopqrstuvwxyz
1234567890

CENTURY EXPANDED ITALIC

ABCDEFGHIJKLMNOPQRSTUVW XYZ
abcdefghijklmnopqrstuvwxyz
1234567890

ABCDEFGHIJKLMNOPQRSTUV WXYZ
abcdefghijklmnopqrstuvwxyz
1234567890

CENTURY SCHOOLBOOK

ABCDEFGHIJKLMNOPQRSTUVWXYZ
abcdefghijklmnopqrstuvwxyz
1234567890

ABCDEFGHIJKLMNOPQRSTUVWXYZ
abcdefghijklmnopqrstuvwxyz
1234567890

MONOTYPE CENTURY SCHOOLBOOK

iv

ABCDEFGHIJKLMNOPQRSTUVWXYZ
abcdefghijklmnopqrstuvwxyz
1234567890
ABCDEFGHIJKLMNOPQRSTUVWXYZ
ABCDEFGHIJKLMNOPQRSTUVWXYZ
abcdefghijklmnopqrstuvwxyz
1234567890

INTERTYPE CENTURY SCHOOLBOOK

iv

ABCDEFGHIJKLMNOPQRSTUVWXYZ
abcdefghijklmnopqrstuvwxyz
1234567890

INTERTYPE CENTURY SCHOOLBOOK BOLD

iv

ABCDEFGHIJKLMNOPQRSTUVWXYZ
abcdefghijklmnopqrstuvwxyz
1234567890

MONOTYPE CENTURY SCHOOLBOOK BOLD

iv

**ABCDEFGHIJKLMNOPQRST
UVWXYZ
abcdefghijklmnopqrstuvwxyz
1234567890**

CENTURY SCHOOLBOOK BOLD

iv

ABCDEFGHIJKLMNOPQRSTUVWXYZ
abcdefghijklmnopqrstuvwxyz
1234567890
ABCDEFGHIJKLMNOPQRSTUVWXYZ
abcdefghijklmnopqrstuvwxyz
1234567890

CENTURY CATALOGUE

iv

ABCDEFGHIJKLMNOPQRSTUVWXYZ
abcdefghijklmnopqrstuvw
12345
ABCDEFGHIJKLMNOPQRSTUVWXYZ
defghijklmnopqrstuvwxyz
67890
ABCDEFGHIJKLMNOPQRSTUVWXYZ

LINOTYPE CENTURY

42

ABCDEFGHIJKLMNOPQRSTUVW XYZ
abcdefghijklmnopqrstuvwxyz
1234567890

ABCDEFGHIJKLMNOPQRSTU VWXYZ
abcdefghijklmnopqrstuvwxyz
1234567890

CENTURY BOLD

ABCDEFGHIJKLMNOPQRSTUVWXYZ
abcdefghijklmnopqrstuvwxyz
1234567890

CENTURY BOLD CONDENSED

Designed by Charles Hughes as a variation on CENTURY EXPANDED, with a special emphasis on making the type suitable for printing by different printing processes. The lower case has a larger than normal x-height.

ABCDEFGHIJKLMNOPQRSTUVWXYZ
abcdefghijklmnopqrstuvwxyz
1234567890
ABCDEFGHIJKLMNOPQRSTUVWXYZ
abcdefghijklmnopqrstuvwxyz
1234567890

CENTURY NOVA

Designed by Oldrich Menhart. An angular "uncial" type face of calligraphic quality.

ABCDEFGHIJKLMNOPQRS TUVWXYZ
1234567890

CESKA UNCIALA

CHARLESTON
Ludwig & Mayer 1967

ix

Re-designed by Hace Frey as a revival of a Victorian bold angular roman.

ABCDEFGHIJKLMNOPQRSTUVWXYZ
abcdefghijklmnopqrstuvwxyz
1234567890

CHARLESTON

CHATSWORTH
Stephenson Blake 1904

A bold modern face with thick flat serifs almost Egyptian in appearance. Ascenders and descenders are short. The **t** has an oblique top. American Typefounders' KEYSTONE is similar.

iv

FRENCH INVENTION
Newer methods recognized
Papiers Autographiques

CHATSWORTH

CHELTENHAM
Many founders

Originally designed by Bertram G. Goodhue in 1896 for D.B. Updike on the suggestion of a Mr Kimball of the Cheltenham Press of New York. The type was made commercially available by American Typefounders, who produced 18 variations designed by M.F. Benton from 1904–11. The serifs are flat and stubby and although the stress is vertical, it is not abrupt. Descenders are short. The right stem of the **A** projects beyond the left. The **G** has a spur. The **e** is rather small and in the **g** the curve of the tail ends in a thickening and the tail is not closed, in the **r** the thickened ear projects above the top of the letter, the **s** ends in thickenings and the **w** has no middle serif. The italic has the serifs of the roman. The bowls of **e** and **p** are not closed, and **p** and **q** have no foot serifs.

   This type became popular and begot a large family, condensed, wide, elongated, bold open, etc. and had several imitators. Among these are WINCHESTER (Stephenson Blake), which may be distinguished by the curl of the ear on the **g** and the serifs of the **s**. The Monotype Corporation's GLOUCESTER has an italic **p** with the normal closed bowl. Intertype CHELTONIAN is another version. Berthold originally called their version SORBONNE (1905).

ii

ABCDEFGHIJKLMNOPQRSTUVWXYZ
abcdefghijklmnopqrstuvwxyz
1234567890

ii

ABCDEFGHIJKLMNOPQRSUVWYZ
abcdefghijklnopqrstuvwxyz
1234567890

CHELTENHAM

ii

ABCDEFGHIJKLMNOPQRSTUVWXYZ
abcdefghijklmnopqrstuvwxyz
1234567890

CHELTENHAM BOLD ITALIC

44

ABCDEFGHIJKLMNOPQRSTUVWXYZ
abcdefghijklmnopqrstuvwxyz

ii

BERTHOLD CHELTENHAM LIGHT

ABCDEFGHIJKLMNOPQRSTUVWXYZ
abcdefghijklmnopqrstuvwxyz
1234567890

ii

BERTHOLD CHELTENHAM MEDIUM

ABCDEFGHIJKLMNOPQRSTUVWXY
abcdefghijklmnopqrstuvwxyz

ii

BERTHOLD CHELTENHAM BOLD

ABCDEFGHIJKLMNOPQRSTUVWXYZ
abcdefghijklmnopqrstuvwxyz

ii

BERTHOLD CHELTENHAM BOLD CONDENSED

ABCDEFGHIKLMNOPQRST
UVWXY
abcdefghijklmnopqrstuvwxyz
14567890

ii

CHELTENHAM BOLD OUTLINE

ABCDEFGHIJKLMNOPQRSTUVWXYZ
abcdefghijklmnopqrstuvwxyz
1234567890
ABCDEFGHIJKLMNOPQRSTUVWXYZ
abcdefghijklmnopqrstuvwxyz
1234567890

ii

GLOUCESTER OLD STYLE

ABCDEFGHIJKLMNOPQRSTUVWXYZ
abcdefghijklmnopqrstuvwxyz
1234567890
ABCDEFGHIJKLMNOPQRSTUVWXYZ
abcdefghijklmnopqrstuvwxyz
1234567890

ii

GLOUCESTER BOLD

CHELTENHAM

iv

ABCDEFGHIJKLMNOPQRSTUVWXYZ

abcdefghijklmnopqrstuvwxyz

1234567890

GLOUCESTER BOLD CONDENSED

iv

ABCDEFGHIJKLMNOPQRSTUVWXYZ

abcdefghijklmnopqrstuvwxyz

1234567890

GLOUCESTER BOLD EXTRA CONDENSED

iv

ABCDEGHIJKLMNOPQRSTUVWXYZ

abcdefghijklmnopqrstuvwxyz

1234567890

GLOUCESTER BOLD EXTENDED

CHEVALIER
Haas

iv

A set of shaded capitals and figures, modern face or fat face in design. *Cf.* EXCELLENT.

ABCDEFGHIJKLMNOPQRSTUVWXYZ

1234567890

CHEVALIER

CHIC
American Typefounders 1928

ix

Designed by M.F. Benton. Doubly shaded capitals and figures. Each thick stroke is accompanied by two parallel hair lines. The flat serifs are hair lines and they are prolonged on the **C**, **G** and **S**.

ENCOURAGE

CHIC

CHISEL
Stephenson Blake 1939–56

ix

An inline version of LATIN BOLD CONDENSED, and designed on the suggestion of Robert Harling. There is a double white line, which was originally engraved in Latin type. Earlier experiments with such a method were made at the Cambridge University Press. Enschedé call this type BAVO.

ABCDEFGHIJKLM
NOPQRSTUVWXYZ
abcdefghijklmnopq
rstuvwxyz
1234567890

CHISEL

A roman of even colour, with ranging figures.

ABCDEFGHIJKLMNOPQRSTUVWXYZ
abcdefghijklmnopqrstuvwxyz
1234567890

ABCDEFGHIJKLMNOPQRSTUVWXYZ
abcdefghijklmnopqrstuvwxyz
1234567890

CHISWELL OLD FACE

Designed by Georg Trump. A rectangular letter. TOWER is similar.

ABCDEFGHIJKLMNOPQRSTUVWXYZ
abcdefghijklmnopqrstuvwxyz
1234567890

CITY LIGHT

ABCDEFGHIJKLMNOPQRSTUVWXYZ
abcdefghijklmnopqrstuvwxyz
1234567890

CITY MEDIUM

ABCDEFGHIJKLMNOPQRSTUVWXYZ
abcdefghijklmnopqrstuvwxyz
12345780

CITY BOLD

Designed by R.H. Stevens.

ABCDEFGHIJKLMNOPQRSTUVWXYZ ŒÆ
abcdefghijklmnopqrstuvwxyz
1234567890

CLARENCE CONDENSED

47

CLARENDON
Many founders

Originally put out in 1845 by R. Besley & Co. (the Fann St. Foundry) as a heavy face to accompany an ordinary roman in dictionaries and the like. It became very popular, was soon copied by the other founders and has become a word for a heavy type in the English vocabulary. It is a slab serif type with more differentiation of colour and lighter serifs than in the original model. Some letters follow the roman model, such as the **a**, **e**, **g** and **t**, and the **R** with its curls. This was also the characteristic of the first English "Egyptians". The revived version of the Haas'sche Schriftgiesserei (also cast by Stempel) was designed by Hermann Eidenbenz in 1951–53. Stempel have a revised type of this name designed under the direction of Erich Schulz-Anker. Ludlow introduced a new series in 1966.

v

ABCDEFGHIJKLMNOPQRSTUVWXYZ

abcdefghijklmnopqrstuvwxyz

1234567890

MONOTYPE CLARENDON

v

ABCDEFGHIJKLMNOPQRS
abcdefghijklmnopqrstuvwxy
1234567890

HAAS CLARENDON

v

ABCDEFGHIJKLMNOPQR
abcdefghijklmnopqrstuvwx

HAAS CLARENDON BOLD

v

ABCDEFGHIJKLMNOP
QRSTUVWXYZ
abcdefghijklmnopqrst
uvwxyz
1234567890

CLARENDON BOLD EXTENDED

v

ABCDEFGHIJKLMNOPQRSTUVWXYZ&
abcdefghijklmnopqrstuvwxyz
1234567890

MERGENTHALER LINOTYPE CLARENDON ROMAN

v

ABCDEFGHIJKLMNOPQRSTUVWXYZ&
abcdefghijklmnopqrstuvwxyz
1234567890

MERGENTHALER LINOTYPE CLARENDON BOLD ROMAN

48

ABCDEFGHIJKLMNOPQRS
abcdefghijklmnopqrstuvwxy
1234567890

HAAS LINOTYPE CLARENDON STEMPEL

v

ABCDEFGHIJKLMNOPQR
abcdefghijklmnopqrstuvwxy
1234567890

CLARENDON SEMI-BOLD

v

ABCDEFGHIJKLMNOPQRSTUVWXYZ
abcdefghijklmnopqrstuvwxyz
1234567890

CLARENDON CONDENSED

v

ABCDEFGHIJKL
abcdefghijklmnop
1234567890

CLARENDON EXTRA BOLD EXTENDED

v

This type was also known as BAUER BASKERVILLE although it has little relation to the real BASKERVILLE. Descenders are very short and the italic has the serifs of the roman.

ABCDEFGHIJKLMNOPQQuRS
TUVWXYZ
abcdefghijklmnopqrstuvwxyz
1234567890

iv

ABCDEFGHIJKLMNOPQQuR
STUVWXYZ
abcdefghijklmnopqr stuvwxyz
1234567890

CLASSIC

CLARITAS

Monotype;
Linotype (London) 1951

This is the name given to a small (4¾ point) version of the TIMES NEW ROMAN. It is claimed to be the clearest of all small types (hence the name), and is intended for use in newspaper "small" announcements.

iv

COMPANY actively engaged in the manufacture of mining equipment requires additional capital to finance current Government and like contracts. Enquiries from interested companies or individuals.—Box 324.
DIRECTOR of established financially sound firm, dealing retail stationers and stores only, apprehensive about rising cost travelling, seeks confidential discussion

ADELPHI. (Tem. 7611.) To-day, 2.30 & 7.30. ORIGINAL BALLET RUSSE. AURORA'S WEDDING. PRESAGES. PRINCE IGOR.
SADLER'S WELLS. (Ter. 1672.) Evgs., 7. To-night, THE BARBER OF SEVILLE. Wed., IL TROVATORE. Thurs., MARRIAGE OF FIGARO. Fri., SCHOOL FOR FATHERS. Sat., MADAME BUTTERFLY.

ABCDEFGHIJKLMNOPQRSTUVWXYZÆŒ abcdefghijklmnopqrstuvwxyzæœ fiflffffifl 1234567890 ABCDEFGHI
ABCDEFGHIJKLMNOPQRSTUVWXYZÆŒ abcdefghijklmnopqrstuvwxyzæœ fiflffffifl JKLMNOPQRSTU
ABCDEFGHIJKLMNOPQRSTUVWXYZÆŒ abcdefghijklmnopqrstuvwxyzæœ fiflffffifl 1234567890 VWXYZÆŒ

LINOTYPE CLARITAS WITH ITALIC, BOLD AND DROP INITIALS

CLEARFACE

American Typefounders;
Stephenson Blake;
Ludlow 1923;
Mergenthaler Linotype;
Linotype (London);
Monotype;
Lanston Monotype;
Intertype

iii

Designed by M.F. Benton. First produced in 1907 by the American Typefounders and now a stock type of many founders. The letters are rather condensed. Ascenders and descenders are short as in all bold faces. **A** has a flat top, in **M** the middle strokes stop short of the line, **V** and **W** have apparent serifs owing to the shortening of the thin strokes. In the lower case the thickened terminals sometimes found in modern faces in **a** and **c** are here found also in the **k, s, v, w** and **y**. The italic is regular. **f** ends on the line; **p** and **q** are without foot serifs.

ABCDEFGHIJKLMNOPQRSTUVWXYZ
abcdefghijklmnopqrstuvwxyz
1234567890

CLEARFACE

iii

ABCDEFGHIJKLMNOPQRSTUVWXYZ
abcdefghijklmnopqrstuvwxyz
123456

CLEARFACE BOLD

CLOISTER OLD STYLE

American
Typefounders c. 1897;
Monotype

This was among the first of the revived Venetians, apart from the types of the private presses, *e.g.*, William Morris's GOLDEN TYPE. It was designed in the United States by Morris Benton on the model of Jenson's roman. In the upper case note the thickened terminal of the **J**, the slab serifs on the **M**, the two **R**'s, and the parallel serifs on the **T**. In the lower case the **e** has an oblique bar to the eye and the **w** (a letter not in Jenson's fount) has no middle serif. Jenson of course had no italic and the Cloister italic is based on the Old Faces. In the upper case the **A** leans over to the right; on the **M** the slab serifs of the roman are copied. In the lower case the **h** has the curved shank, but curved less than in some early designs. Note the narrow **v** and **w**. There are also a number of swash capitals.

Intertype CLOISTER OLD STYLE has an **e** with a straight bar. American Typefounders had a JENSON after Morris by 1900. There is also a Linotype (London) CLOISTER BOLD.

i

ABCDEFGHIJKLMNOPQRRSTUVWXYZ
abcdefghijklmnopqrstuvwxyz
ABCDEFGHIJKLMNOPQRSTUVWXYZ
ABCDEFGMNPRTU
abcdefghijklmnqrstuvwxyz

CLOISTER OLD STYLE

i

ABCDEFGHIJKLMNOPQRRSTUVWXYZ & Qu
abcdefghijklmnopqrstuvwxyz
$1234567890
A ABBCDDEEFGGHIJJKLMMNNOPPQRRST TUVVWXYYZ& Qu
abcdefghijklmnopqrstuvvwwxyz
$1234567890

CLOISTER BOLD

This type was also known as SONDERDRUCK. The Deberny & Peignot version of which this type appears to be a copy, is called MOREAU-LE-JEUNE, and was also cut around 1912 as GRAVURE by Amsterdam, and these types also have an open version.

The Lanston Monotype COCHIN was first shown 1915, and adapted two years later by Sol Hess, with the bold following in the 1920s. NICOLAS COCHIN, of the same foundry, followed in 1929.

ABCDEFGHIJKLMNOPQRSTU
VWXYZ
abcdefghijklmnopqrstuvwxyz
1234567890

*ABCDEFGHIJKLMNOPQRTW
abcdefghijklmnopqrstuvwxyz
1234567*

COCHIN LUDWIG & MAYER

ABCDEFGHIJLI
abcdefghijklmnopqx
*ABCDEFGHIJKL
abcdefghijklmnopqrstu*

GRAVURE

ABCDEFGHIJKLMNOPQRSTUVWXYZ ÆOE
abcdefghijklmnopqrstuvwxyz
1234567890

NICOLAS COCHIN

ABCDEFGHIJKL
MNOPQURSTUVWXYZ
abcdefghijklmnopqrstuvwxyzœæ
1234567890

MOREAU-LE-JEUNE OPEN

iii

iii

ix

ix

COCHIN A B C D E F G H I J K L M N O P Q R S T U V W X Y
Z & Æ Œ
a b c d e f g h i j k l m n o p q r s t u v w x y z
1 2 3 4 5 6 7 8 9 0

ix

A B C D E F G H I J K L M N O P Q R S T U V
W X Y Z & Æ Œ
a b c d e f g h i j k l m n o p q r s t u v w x y z
1 2 3 4 5 6 7 8 9 0

COCHIN

CODEX
Weber 1954–1956

Designed by Georg Trump. A display roman which may be classified as calligraphic. The capitals are freely drawn and most of them very wide. The **M** is splayed. In the lower case the ascenders and descenders are short and the serifs seem to be made with a quill pen. The **g** has an open tail.

ix

ABCDEFGHIJKLMNOPQRS
TUVWXYZ
abcdefghijklmnopqrstuvwxyz
1234567890
EDINBURGH FESTIVAL

CODEX

COLONNA
Monotype 1927

An inline roman, the line passing through all strokes, including the round. The result is that in the round letters parts appear to be cut-off.

ix

ABCDEFGHIJKLMNOPQRSTUVWXYZ
abcdefghijklmnopqrstuvwxyz
1234567890

COLONNA

Designed by Walter H. McKay. A roman which is modern in serif treatment and stress. The **Q** has its tail entirely outside the bowl, the lower case **g** is almost an old face letter. The type is cast in two weights with italics. COLUMBIA BOLD CONDENSED was designed by Jeanette Kosmann-Markus after the sketches of Walter H. McKay. This design is not the earlier (1906) COLUMBIA by Morland.

ABCDEFGHIJKLMNOPQRSTUVW
XYZ
abcdefghijklmnopqrstuvwxyz
1234

ABCDEFGHIJKLMNOPQRSTUVW
XYZ
abcdefghijklmnopqrstuvwxyz
5678

COLUMBIA

iv

ABCDEFGHIJKLMNOPQRSTUVW
YXZ
abcdefghijklmnopqrstuvwxyz
90

ABCDEFGHIJKLMNOPQRSTUVW
XYZ
abcdefghijklmnopqrstuvwxyz
123

COLUMBIA BOLD

iv

ABCDEFGHIJKLMNOPQRSTUVXYZÆŒ
abcdefghijklmnopqrstuvwxyz
1234567890£&æœ

COLUMBIA BOLD CONDENSED

iv

ABCDEFGHIJKLMNOPQRSTUVWXYZ
abcdefghijklmnopqrstuvwxyz
1234567890
ABCDEFGHIJKLMNOPQRSTUVWXYZ
abcdefghijklmnopqrstuvwxyz
1234567890

INTERTYPE COLUMBIA

iv

ABCDEFGHIJKLMNOPQRSTUVWXYZ
abcdefghijklmnopqrstuvwxyz
1234567890

INTERTYPE COLUMBIA BOLD

53

COLUMNA
Bauer 1955

Designed by Max Caflisch. Originally a private type of the Benteli publishing house in Switzerland. Open capitals and ranging figures with very small, thin serifs. There are two **M**'s, one splayed, and two **R**'s, one with an extended tail.

vii

ABCDEFGHIJKLMMNNO
PQRRSTUVWXYZ1234567

COLUMNA

COMPACTES ITALIQUES
Deberny & Peignot

An inclined Egyptian, almost monotone in colour. The main strokes are slightly thicker than the secondary strokes.

v

ABCDEFGHIJKLMNOPQRSTUVWXYZ
abcdefghijklmnopqrstuvwxyz
1234567890

COMPACTES ITALIQUES

CONCORDE
Berthold 1968; Intertype (Berlin)

Designed by G.G. Lange. A text type of contemporary design following eighteenth-century style.

ii

ABCDEFGHIJKLMNOPQRSTU
abcdefghijklmnopqrstuvwxyzabcd
1234567890

ABCDEFGHIJKLMNOPQRSTU
abcdefghijklmnopqrstuvwxyzabcd
1234567890

CONCORDE

ii

ABCDEFGHIJKLMNOPQRSTU
abcdefghijklmnopqrstuvwxyzabc
1234567890

CONCORDE MEDIUM

A revival of the early English slab serif types, but with greater variation in the weight of the strokes. The original CLARENDON of 1845 is issued as CONSORT BOLD CONDENSED. The italic and the bold are new designs.

ABCDEFGHIJKLMNOPQRSTU
VWXYZÆŒ
abcdefghijklmnopqrstuvwxyz
1234567890

CONSORT LIGHT

ABCDEFGHIJKLMNOPQRSTUV
WXYZÆŒ
abcdefghijklmnopqrstuvwxyz
1234567890
ABCDEFGHIJKLMNOPQRSTUV
WXYZÆŒ
abcdefghijklmnopqrstuvwxyzœœ
1234567890

CONSORT

ABCDEFGHIJKLMNOPQRST
UVWXYZ
abcdefghijklmnopqrstuvwxyz
1234567890

CONSORT BOLD

ABCDEFGHIJKLMNOPQRSTUVWXYZÆŒ
abcdefghijklmnopqrstuvwxyzæœ
1234567890

CONSORT LIGHT CONDENSED

ABCDEFGHIJKLMNOPQRSTUVWXYZ
abcdefghijklmnopqrstuvwxyz
1234567890

CONSORT CONDENSED

ABCDEFGHIJKLMNOPQRSTUVWXYZÆ
abcdefghijklmnopqrstuvwxyz&£
123456789

CONSORT BOLD CONDENSED

CONTACT
American Typefounders 1944

Designed by F. H. Riley. A condensed type with short ascenders and descenders. The italic has the serifs of the roman. IDEAL ROMAN is similar.

v

ABCDEFGHIJKLMNOPQRSTUVWXYZ
abcdefghijklmnopqrstuvwxyz
ABCDEFGHIJKLMNOPQRSTUVWXYZ
abcdefghijklmnopqrstuvwxyz

CONTACT BOLD

CONTURA
Amsterdam 1966

Designed by Dick Dooijes. An outline type with ranging numerals.

ii

ABCDEFGHIJKLMNOPQRSTUVW
XYZ
abcdefghijklmnopqrstuvwxyz
1234567890

CONTURA

COOPER BLACK
American Typefounders;

Designed by Oswald B. Cooper for Barnhart Brothers & Spindler in 1921. An extra bold face based on COOPER OLD STYLE. The serifs are blurred and counters are naturally very small, in the **O** and **Q** they are tilted back. The dot on the **i** and **j** becomes elliptical. The italic is not far from the vertical and has the serifs of the roman. LUDLOW BLACK is very similar. There is also a condensed face and a shaded type called COOPER HILITE.

ix

ABCDEFGHIJKLMNOPQRSTUVWXY
abcdefghijklmnopqrstuvwxyz
£1234567890$

COOPER BLACK

COOPER OLD STYLE
Barnhart Bros. & Spindler 1919–24

Designed by Oswald B. Cooper for Barnhart Brothers & Spindler (1919–24). The design is old face with some calligraphic qualities reminding one of GOUDY. The serifs are unusual with foot serifs being convex. The apex of the **A** bends over to the left. The **Q** has a tail rather like GOUDY and the **R** a turned-up tail. The **f** is unkerned and the **j** has a buttonhook terminal. Descenders are short. The italic has only slight inclination and the final curves of **h**, **k**, **m** and **n** drop below the line. COOPER TOOLED ITALIC has the shading on the left.

iii

ABCDEFGHIJKLMNOPQRSTUV
WXYZ&$
abcdefghijklmnopqrstuvwxyz
1234567890
ABCDEFGHIJKLMNOPQRSTUV
WXYZ&$
abcdefghijklmnopqrstuvwxyz
1234567890

COOPER OLD STYLE

ABCDEFGHIJKLMNOPQRSTU
VWXYZ&
abcdefghijklmnopqrst
uvwxyz
$1234567890£

COOPER TOOLED ITALIC

ABCDEFGHIJKLMNO
PQRSTUVWXYZ
abcdefghijklmnopqrst
uvwxyz
1234567890

COOPER 570

ABCDEFGHIJKLMNOPQR
BDEFGMNPRT
abcdefghijklmnopqrsßtu
vwxyz
1234567890 &£$¢

COOPER 571

ABCDEFGHIJKLMNOPQR
STUVWXYZ
abcdefghijklmnopqrstu
vwxyz
1234567890 &£$¢

COOPER 579

The original type (American Typefounders) was designed by Frederic W. Goudy in 1901.
Capitals and figures in this titling and card type at first glance have the appearance of a sanserif
but there are in fact minute serifs. Capitals are wide and the centre arm of the **E** is short.
  SPARTAN (Monotype and Stephenson Blake), LINING PLATE GOTHIC (Ludlow), PLATE
GOTHIC, MIMOSA (Weber and Typoart) and ATALANTE (Nebiolo) are almost identical.

vii

ABCDEFGHIJKLMNOPQRST UVWXYZ&?!

AMERICAN TYPEFOUNDERS COPPERPLATE GOTHIC LIGHT

vii

ABCDEFGHIJKLMNOPQRST UVWXYZ&?!

AMERICAN TYPEFOUNDERS COPPERPLATE GOTHIC HEAVY

vii

ABCDEFGHIJKLMNOPQRS TUVWXYZ&?!

AMERICAN TYPEFOUNDERS COPPERPLATE GOTHIC ITALIC

vii

ABCDEFGHIJKLMNOPQRS TUVWXYZ&?!

AMERICAN TYPEFOUNDERS COPPERPLATE GOTHIC BOLD

vii

ABCDEFGHIJKLMNOPQRSTUVWXY

AMERICAN TYPEFOUNDERS COPPERPLATE GOTHIC LIGHT CONDENSED

vii

ABCDEFGHIJKLMNOPQRSTUVWXY

AMERICAN TYPEFOUNDERS COPPERPLATE GOTHIC HEAVY CONDENSED

vii

ABCDEFGHIJKLMNOP QRSTUVWXYZ&?!

AMERICAN TYPEFOUNDERS COPPERPLATE GOTHIC LIGHT EXTENDED

vii

ABCDEFGHIJKLMNOP QRSTUVWXYZ&?!

AMERICAN TYPEFOUNDERS COPPERPLATE GOTHIC HEAVY EXTENDED

vii

ABCDEFGHIJKLMNOPQRSTU VWXYZ

STEPHENSON BLAKE SPARTAN SHADED

vii

ABCDEFGHIJKLMNOPQRSTUVWXYZ

STEPHENSON BLAKE SPARTAN BOLD CONDENSED

58

ABCDEFGHIJKLMNOPQR STUVWXYZ

STEPHENSON BLAKE SPARTAN BOLD EXPANDED

ABCDEFGHIJKLMNOPQRST UVWXYZ

STEPHENSON BLAKE SPARTAN

ABCDEFGHIJKLMNOPQRSTUV WXYZ
ABCDEFGHIJKLMNOPQRST UVWXYZ

STEPHENSON BLAKE SPARTAN BOLD

ABCDEFGHIJKLMNOPQRSTUV WXYZ

STEPHENSON BLAKE SPARTAN EXTRA BOLD

Designed by George F. Trenholm. A roman with little variation of stress. The **Q** has a tail outside the bowl and the **R** has a curled tail. The italic has short descenders and the serifs of the roman.

CORNELL
Intertype (New York)

ABCDEFGHIJKLMNOPQRSTUVWXYZ
abcdefghijklmnopqrstuvwxyz
1234567890
ABCDEFGHIJKLMNOPQRSTUVWXYZ
ABCDEFGHIJKLMNOPQRSTUVWXYZ
abcdefghijklmnopqrstuvwxyz
1234567890

CORNELL

ABCDEFGHIJKLMNOPQRSTUVWXYZ
abcdefghijklmnopqrstuvwxyz
1234567890

CORNELL BOLD

Designed by C.H. Griffith. A newspaper type, which underwent some adaptation in 1952 to simplify teletypesetting use. Fairly narrow letters with large x-height. The thin strokes and serifs are firm, the counters are open as in **C**, **G**, **S**, **e**, **s**. ROYAL is very similar.

CORONA
Mergenthaler Linotype 1941; Linotype (London) 1961

ABCDEFGHIJKLMNOPQRSTUVWXYZ
abcdefghijklmnopqrstuvwxyz
1234567890
ABCDEFGHIJKLMNOPQRSTUVWXYZ
ABCDEFGHIJKLMNOPQRSTUVWXYZ
abcdefghijklmnopqrstuvwxyz
1234567890

CORONA

ABCDEFGHIJKLMNOPQRSTUVWXYZ
abcdefghijklmnopqrstuvwxyz
12345 67890

CORONA BOLD

CORONATION

Stephenson Blake c. 1937

A bold and somewhat condensed display roman face, with short descenders. The distinguishing features are the thickened terminals on the **C, E, F, G, T** and **S**, and the similar thickened ends of the arcs of the lower-case **a, e, r** and **s**.

iv

ABCDEFGHIJKLMNOPQRSTUVWXYZ

abcdefghijklmnopqrstuvwxyz

1234567890

CORONATION

CORVINUS

Bauer 1929–34

Designed by Imre Reiner. Ascenders and descenders are short. The condensation of the letters is achieved by flattening the sides of the round letters. Serifs are very thin. **A** and **M** have slab serifs, the **e** has a large eye and the **g** has the ear with link and tail squared up. In the italic the **g** has an unusual vertical shape, and **v** and **w** are cursive forms.

A condensed version of the type is called SKYLINE. EDEN is similar but has heavier square serifs on **E** and **T**. CORONATION is also similar. Lanston Monotype call this type GLAMOUR.

iv

ABCDEFGHIJKLMNOPQRSTUVWXYZ

abcdefghijklmnopqrstuvwxyz

1234567890

AABCDEEFGGHIJKKLMMNNOPQRSTUVW
XYZ

abcdefghijklmnopqrstuvvwwxyz

12345678

CORVINUS LIGHT

ABCDEFGHIJKLMNOPQRSTUVWXYZ

abcdefghijklmnopqrstuvwxyz

1234567

AABCDEEFGGHIJKKLMMNNOPQRSTU
VWXYZ

abcdefghijklmnopqrstuvvwwxyz

CORVINUS MEDIUM

ABCDEFGHIJKLMNOPQRSTUVWX
abcdefghijklmnopqrstuvwxyz
1234567890

CORVINUS BOLD

ABCDEFGHIJKLMNOPQRSTUVWXYZ
abcdefghijklmnopqrstuvwxyz
1234567890

CORVINUS SKYLINE

First cut in 1902 and used by the *Cosmopolitan* magazine. An extra condensed compact roman with a tall lower case.

ABCDEFGHIJKLMNOPQRSTUVWXYZ&ÆŒ
abcdefghijklmnopqrstuvwxyzæœ   fiflffffiffl
1234567890
ABCDEFGHIJKLMNOPQRSTUVWXYZ&ÆŒ
ABCDEFGHIJKLMNOPQRSTUVWXYZ&ÆŒ
abcdefghijklmnopqrstuvwxyzœæ   fiflffffiffl
1234567890

COSMOPOLITAN

Designed by Freeman Craw. The type follows closely the design of the first expanded CLARENDONS, and is one of many revivals and redesigned versions. Note the **G** in both upper and lower case.

ABCDEFGHIJKLMNOPQRSTUVWXYZ&
abcdefghijklmnopqrstuvwxyz
1234567890

CRAW CLARENDON BOOK

ABCDEFGHIJKLMNOPQRST
UVWXYZ&
abcdefghijklmnopqrstuvwxyz
1234567890£

CRAW CLARENDON

ABCDEFGHIJKLMNOPQRSTUVWXYZ
abcdefghijklmnopqrstuvwxyz?
1234567890

CRAW CLARENDON CONDENSED

Designed by Freeman Craw. Letters have considerable breadth and short ascenders and descenders.

ABCDEFGHIJKLMNOP QRSTUVWXYZ abcdefghijklmnopqrstu vwxyz 1234567890

ABCDEFGHIJKLMNOPQRSTUVWXYZ
abcdefghijklmnopqrstuvwxyz ffffifflfifl
1234567890

CRAW MODERN

ABCDEFGHIJKLMNO PQRSTUVWXYZ abcdefghijklmnopqrs tuvwxyz 1234567890

iv

CRAW MODERN BOLD

Designed by Rémy Peignot. A set of inline capitals with thin, pointed serifs. The double inline strokes are 'bulging.'

ABCDEFGHIJKLMNOPQRS TUVWXYZ 2468

CRISTAL

Named after a group of slightly related types probably commissioned by J. Stearns Cushing, a book printer of Norwood, Massachusetts. The type is monotone in appearance and has small-inclined serifs. Capitals are wide, ascenders and descenders are short. Figures are ranging. CUSHING OLD STYLE bears little relation to this type.

ABCDEFGHIJKLMNOPQRSTUVWXYZ abcdefghijklmnopqrstuvwxyz 12345

ABCDEFGHIJKLMNOPQRSTUVWXYZ
abcdefghijklmnopqrstuvwxyz

CUSHING

ABCDEFGHIJKLMNOPQRSTUVWXYZ&ŒÆ
abcdefghijklmnopqrstuvwxyzæœ fiflfffiffl
1234567890

ABCDEFGHIJKLMNOPQRSTUVWXYZ&ÆŒ

CUSHING MONOTONE

ii

The type was probably commissioned by J. Stearns Cushing (*cf.* CUSHING) from American Typefounders in 1898, with a redesign by F.W. Goudy in 1904. Cushing Antique follows the English Antiques in style. The Ludlow version is more condensed than the original.

ABCDEFGHIJKLMNOPQRSTUVWX
abcdefghijklmnopqrstuvwxyz

CUSHING ANTIQUE

A somewhat condensed type having large bracketed serifs and of fairly uniform weight.

A B C D E F G H I J K L M N O P Q R S T U V W X Y Z & Æ Œ

a b c d e f g h i j k l m n o p q r s t u v w x y z   æ œ fi fl ff ffi ffl

1234567890   1234567890

A B C D E F G H I J K L M N O P Q R S T U V W X Y Z & Æ Œ

a b c d e f g h i j k l m n o p q r s t u v w x y z   æ œ fi fl ff ffi ffl

1 2 3 4 5 6 7 8 9 0

CUSHING OLD STYLE

An inline series of roman capitals. The line passes through the vertical strokes. Serifs are minute. The **M** is slightly splayed. There are also figures. Resembles DELPHIAN.

PÓSITO MARÍT
DALIA

Designed by Giovanni Mardersteig and cut for hand composition by Charles Malin 1947–54. Originally a private press type for the Officina Bodoni at Verona. The capitals are wide and the italic has slight inclination. There is also a titling face.

ABCDEFGHIJKLMNOPQRSTUVWXYZ

ABCDEFGHIJKLMNOPQRSTUVWXYZ

abcdefghijklmnopqrstuvwxyz

ABCDEFGHIJKLMNOPQRSTUVWXYZ

abcdefghijklmnopqrstuvwxyz

1234567890

DANTE

ABCDEFGHIJKLMNOPQRSTUVWXYZ

ABCDEFGHIJKLMNOPQRSTUVWXYZ

abcdefghijklmnopqrstuvwxyz

ABCDEFGHIJKLMNOPQRSTUVWXYZ

abcdefghijklmnopqrstuvwxyz

MONOTYPE DANTE

ii

ii

ABCDEFGHIJKLMNOPQRSTUVWXYZ
1234567890

DANTE TITLING

ii

DAPHNIS
Klingspor 1931

Designed by Walter Tiemann. An outline roman with very small serifs. **E** and **F** are narrow. **M** is splayed. **U** has the lower-case design.

vii

NEUES PAPIER
Leipziger Messe

DAPHNIS

DEAUVILLE
Française 1927

Designed by M. Loewe. A fat face with modifications. The outer curves of the round letters, **D, O, R** and the round lower-case letters are unusual. The **M** has short middle strokes. The arc of the **a** has a thickened terminal, not a blob.

iv

Deauville MODER

DEAUVILLE

DEEPDENE
Lanston Monotype 1929–34

Designed by F.W. Goudy. The italics are narrow in appearance and include several swash characters and have calligraphic quality.

ii

ABCDEFGHIJKLMNOPQRSTUVWXYZ&

abcdefghijklmnopqrstuvwxyz

$1234567890

DEEPDENE 315

ii

ABCDEFGHIJKLMNOPQRSTUVWXYZ&

abcdefghijklmnopqrstuvwxyz

$1234567890

DEEPDENE ITALIC 315

ii

ABCDEFGHIJKLMNOPQRSTUVWXYZ&

abcdefghijklmnopqrstuvwxyz

$1234567890

DEEPDENE BOLD 317

ii

ABCDEFGHIJKLMNOPQRSTUVWXYZ&

DEEPDENE SMALL CAPS 315

64

Designed by Thomas Maitland Cleland. Based on rubbings of stone-cut capitals seen by the designer in Rome and almost a 'lineale with serifs'.

DELLA ROBBIA
Lanston Monotype 1902

A B C D E F G H I J K L M N O P Q R S T U V W
X Y Z &

vii

a b c d e f g h i j k l m n o p q r s t u v w x y z

vii

fi fl ff ffi ffl
$ 1 2 3 4 5 6 7 8 9 0

vii

DELLA ROBBIA

Designed by Georg Trump. This calligraphic type has capitals in which the tails of **K** and **R** descend below the line. In the slightly inclined lower case the ascenders of **h, l, b** are taller than the capitals. The lower-case **g** has an open tail and the **s** follows the style of German handwriting. DELPHIN II, is a heavier face of much the same design. There are two **z**'s and two **s**'s.

DELPHIN
Weber 1951–55

ABCDEFGHIJKLMNOPQRSTUVWXYZ

ix

abcddefgghijklmnopqrstuvwxyz

ix

1234567890

ix

DELPHIN I

ABCDEFGHIJKLMNOPQRSTUVWXYZ

ix

abcddefgghijklmnopqrstuvwxyz

1234567890

DELPHIN II

Designed by R. Hunter Middleton. Slender inline capitals, the line running through the vertical strokes. Serifs are very small and the variation in the width of the letters follows the model of the Trajan column.

DELPHIAN
OPEN TITLING
Ludlow 1928

ABCDEFGHIJKLMNOPQRSTU
VWXYZ&   1234567890

vii

DELPHIAN TITLING

Designed by P.A. Demeter, and originally a Schriftguss type. Shaded capitals with serifs like lead forms.

DEMETER
Typoart

ABCDEFGHIJKLMNOPQRSTUVWXYZ

ix

DEMETER

65

DE ROOS

Amsterdam 1947;
Intertype (New York);
American Typefoundry

The roman designed by S.H. De Roos. It is a light face with little variation in colour and somewhat condensed. The serifs are small and oblique on the lower case. The capitals are shorter than the ascenders and narrow, especially **H** and **T**. **U** has the lower-case design. **g** has a large bowl and the **w** no middle serif. The italic has a slight inclination. In the lower case the serifs are as the roman; the **g** has a script form. Numerals are short ranging. There are also in-line capitals.

ii

ABCDEFGHIJKLMNOPQRSTUVWXYZ

abcdefghijklmnopqrstuvwxyz

1234567890

ABCDEFGHIJKLMNOPQRSTUVWXYZ

abcdefghijklmnopqrstuvwxyz

DE ROOS

ii

ABCDEFGHIJKLMNOPQRSTUVWXYZ

abcdefghijklmnopqrstuvwxyz

DE ROOS SEMI-BOLD

ii

ABCDEFGHIJKLMNOPQRSTUVWXYZ

abcdefghijklmnopqrstuvwxyz

1234567890

ABCDEFGHIJ KLMNOPQRSTUVWXYZ

ABCDEFGHIJKLMNOPQRSTUVWXYZ

abcdefghijklmnopqrstuvwxyz

1234567890

INTERTYPE DE ROOS WITH ITALIC AND SMALL CAPS

DEUTSCH RÖMISCH

Weber 1926; Monotype

Designed by F.H.E. Schneidler. Serifs are small. The **A** has a flat apex, and the **M** slab serifs but thin. The **Q** has the tail outside the bowl. In the lower case round letters are condensed. The **f** is narrow, **g** has an oval-like bowl and wide tail. In the italic serifs on ascenders are flat.

ii

ABCDEFGHIJKLMNOPQRSTU
VWXYZ

abcdefghijklmnopqrs

ABCDEFGHIJKLMNOPQRSTU
VWXYZ

abcdefghijklmnopqrs

DEUTSCH RÖMISCH

ii

ABCDEFGHIJKL

DEUTSCH RÖMISCH BOLD

This type named after T.L. De Vinne, was cut for the Central Typefoundry (now American Typefounders) in 1894 by Gustav Schroeder; De Vinne Roman was cut by F.W. Goudy in 1898. Intertype LORIMER was based on a type called ROMAANS by Amsterdam Typefoundry with matrices supplied by Riegerl Weissenborn as an imitation of Schelter & Giesecke's ROMANISCH. Probably the principles of this series were applied in the USA to produce the De Vinne family; in turn this series was soon used as a related bold to all ROMANISCH, ROMISCH and ROMAANS series produced in Europe.

FRENCH OLD STYLE was derived from Gustave Mayeur's ROMAN XVIIe SIECLE of the Elzevier foundry (now Fonderie Typographique Française) and was the basis for the first Schelter & Giesecke re-cutting in 1889.

ABCDEFGHIJKLMNOPQRSTUVWXYZ&
ABCDEFGHIJKLMNOPQRSTUVWXYZ&
abcdefghijklmnopqrstuvwxyz
1234567890

ABCDEFGHIJKLMNOPQRSTUVWXYZ&
abcdefghijklmnopqrstuvwxyz
1234567890

MERGENTHALER LINOTYPE DE VINNE

ABCDEFGHIJKLMN
OPQRSTUVWXYZ&ÆŒ
abcdefghijklmnopqrstuvwxyz
1234567890

ABCDEFGHIJKLMNOPQ
RSTUVWXYZ&
abcdefghijklmnopqrstu
vwxyz 1234567890

DE VINNE NO. 11

ABCDEFGHIJKLMNOPQRSTUVWXYZ
abcdefghijklmnopqrstuvwxyz
12345 67890

DE VINNE CONDENSED

ABCDEFGHIJKLMNO
PQRSTUVWXYZ&ÆŒ
abcdefghijklmnopqrstuvwxyz
1234567890

ABCDEFGHIJKLMNO
PQRSTUVWXYZ&
abcdefghijklmnopqr
stuvwxyz
1234567890

DE VINNE OUTLINE

ii

67

ABCDEFGHIJKLMN
OPQRSTUVWXYZ
abcdefghijklmnopq
rstuvwxyz
£$1234567890

ABCDEFGHIJKLMNOP
QRSTUVWXYZ
abcdefghijklmnopqrstu
vwxyz.
£$1234567890

DE VINNE ORNAMENTAL

DIAMANT
Schriftguss 1937

Designed by J. Lehmann so shadowed as to produce a three-dimensional lineale.

vi

UNIVERSUM
DIAMANT

DIAPHANE
Warnery

Inline capitals to accompany MOZART NOIR.

iv

KILOMÈTRES
235768

DIAPHANE

Firmin Didot cut the first modern face about 1784. He and other members of the Didot family fixed the standard for book types in France in the nineteenth century. Among the capitals the **H** and **M** are narrower and the **R** has a vertical tail. In the Pierre Didot design the **g** has a contorted shape; The Monotype Corporation's **g** is more normal, but the upper part of the tail is flat. The italic is distinguished from English modern-face italics by the flat serifs on **m**, **n**, **p**, etc. **v** and **w** have eighteenth-century curves. The Monotype Corporation have another version, very similar, called NEO DIDOT. Pierre Didot, elder brother of Firmin, at a later date had his own foundry with types cut by one Vibert. FIRMIN DIDOT of Deberny & Peignot, who hold the original punches, is true to the original, and the Ludwig & Mayer version follows it closely. The FRENCH ROMAN of Typograph also follows this style.

DIDOT

*Deberny & Peignot;
Monotype;
Ludwig & Mayer;
Typograph*

ABCDEFGHIJKLMNOPQRSTUVWXYZ
abcdefghijklmnopqrstuvwxyz
1234567890
ABCDEFGHIJKLMNOPQRSTUVWXYZ
abcdefghijklmnopqrstuvwxyz
1234567890

FIRMIN DIDOT

iv

A B C D E F G H I J K L M N O P Q R S T U V
W X Y Z &
a b c d e f g h i j k l m n o p q r s t u v w x y z
1 2 3 4 5 6 7 8 9 0

LUDWIG & MAYER FIRMIN DIDOT BOLD

iv

ABCDEFGHIJKLMNOPQRSTUVWXYZ&
abcdefghijklmnopqrstuvwxyz
1234567890
ABCDEFGHIJKLMNOPQRSTUVWXYZ&
abcdefghijklmnopqrstuvwxyz

DIDOT

iv

ABCDEFGHIJKLMNOPQRSTUVWXYZ&
abcdefghijklmnopqrstuvwxyz
1234567890
ABCDEFGHIJKLMNOPQRSTUVWXYZ&
abcdefghijklmnopqrstuvwxyz

NEO DIDOT

iv

ABCDEFGHIJKLMNOPQRSTUVWXYZ&
abcdefghijklmnopqrstuvwxyz
1234567890
ABCDEFGHIJKLMNOPQRSTUVWXYZ&
abcdefghijklmnopqrstuvwxyz

NEO DIDOT (VARIATION)

iv

ABCDEFGHIJKLMNOPQRSTUVWXYZ&
abcdefghijklmnopqrstuvwxyz
1234567890
ABCDEFGHIJKLMNOPQRSTUVWXYZ&
abcdefghijklmnopqrstuvwxyz

PIERRE DIDOT

iv

**DIDOT
FLORIATED
CAPITALS**
Enschedé

Decorated capitals cut by Pierre Didot l'aîné c. 1820. The main strokes are decorated with a floral pattern, the thins are hair lines and the design modern face. The Didot material was acquired by Enschedé in 1850.

iv

ABCDEHFGIJKLM
NOQPRSTUVW
XYZ

DIDOT FLORIATED CAPITALS

**DIETHELM
ROMAN**
*Haas 1948–50;
Linotype (Frankfurt) 1957*

A new roman designed by Walter Diethelm. Ascenders and descenders are short, serifs are flat. The eye of the **e** is large. The italic is regular and slightly inclined. There are some swash capitals. The serifs on the tops of ascenders are large and inclined.

ii

ABCDEFGHIJKLMNOPQRSTUV
abcdefghijklmnopqrstuvwxyz
1234567890 1234567890
ABCDEFGHIJKLMNOPQRST
abcdefghijklmnopqrstuvwxyz
ABCDEGJKMNPRTU

DIETHELM WITH SWASH CAPITALS

ii

ABCDEFGHIJLMNOPQRSTUV
abcdefghijklmnopqrstuvwxyz

DIETHELM BOLD

DIOTIMA
Stempel 1954

Designed by Gudrun Zapf-v.Hesse. A light roman with thin, flat serifs and wide letters in the lower case. The broad, splayed **M** has no top serifs. The tail of the **g** is not closed; **m, n, w** and the round letters are all very wide. The figures are old face. The italic is of slight inclination and the letters much narrower than in the roman.

ii

ABCDEFGHIJKLMNOPQRSTUVW
abcdefghijklmnopqrstuvwxyz
1234567890
ABCDEFGHIJKLMNOPQRSTUVW
abcdefghijklmnopqrstuvwxyz

DIOTIMA

Designed by Lucien Pissarro and cut by E.P. Prince as a private-press-type for the printers in Holland. A calligraphic roman in which several letters have flourished tails and some capitals vertical strokes descending beneath the line. The t has miniscule form, and so has the E.

❡ Als eerste boek der KUNERA PERS zal eer-
lang verschijnen: ❧ OOSTERSCH. Verzen
naar PERZISCHE en ARABISCHE DICH-
TERS door J. H. LEOPOLD, het vierde boek
voor de Vereeniging der Vijftig.

DISTEL

A face designed to match IBM electric typewriter composition.

ABCDEFGHIJKLMNOPQRSTUVWXYZ
abcdefghijklmnopqrstuvwxyz
1234567890
ABCDEFGHIJKLMNOPQRSTUVWXYZ
abcdefghijklmnopqrstuvwxyz
1234567890

DOCUMENT

Designed by Johannes Schweitzer. A monotone type with some squaring up of letters which leads to a condensed appearance. The e has an unusual vertical terminal and the g a minute ear.

ABCDEFGHIJKLMNOPQRSTUVWXYZ
abcdefghijklmnopqrstuvwxyz
1234567890
ABCDEFGHIJKLMNOPQRSTUVWXYZ
abcdefghijklmnopqrstuvwxyz
1234567890

ABCDEFGHIJKLMNOPQRSTUVWXYZ
abcdefghijklmnopqrstuvwxyz
1234567890

DOMINANTE

ABCDEFGHIJKLMNOPQRSTUVWXYZ
abcdefghijklmnopqrstuvwxyz
1234567890
ABCDEFGHIJKLMNOPQRSTUVWXYZ
abcdefghijklmnopqrstuvwxyz
1234567890

DOMINANTE BOLD

DOMINO
Ludwig & Mayer

iv

Designed by Alfred Riedel a fat face roman with short ascenders and descenders. The uprights are concave.

THE PRIMARY FUNCTION
of type is that it shall be read

DOMINO

DOMINUS
Stephenson Blake 1925

ix

A shaded roman with a resemblance to NARCISSUS, but the capitals are narrower. In the **M** the middle strokes stop short of the line. The arcs of **a**, **c** and **r** are terminated in thickenings. The eye of the **e** has an oblique stroke. In all these points the type differs from NARCISSUS. The type is also known as CLEARFACE OPEN or HANDTOOLED.

FORCEFULNESS
news announcem

DOMINUS

DOVES ROMAN
Doves Press 1900

i

The Doves Press was started in 1896 by T.J. Cobden Sanderson and Sir Emery Walker. It was named after an inn in Hammersmith, and possessed only one roman type in one size. This roman, first used in a book in 1900, was based on the favourite model of the early private presses, the type of Nicolas Jenson. It is nearer the original than Morris's GOLDEN TYPE, and is not so black. When the press was closed down the type was thrown into the Thames.

OFFICINA COLUMBARUM excuderunt T. J. Cobden-Sanderson et Emery Walker textum recensu it J. W. Mackail typos composuit J. H. Mason prelum exercuit H. Gage-Cole XIV Kal. Nov. MDCCCC

DOVES ROMAN

DRYNKOV
Grafotechna

ix

Designed by K. Drynkov. A calligraphic roman light in weight.

ABCDEFGHIJK
LMNOPQRSTU
VWXYZ
abcdefghijklmno
pqrstuvwxyz
1234567890

DRYNKOV

Designed by A. Finsterer. Three-dimensional capitals and figures; in design like an Egyptian. DUO SOLID has the face of the letters in black, and DUO OUTLINE in white.

ABCDEFGHIJKLM
NOPQRSTUWXZ
1234567890

DUO OUTLINE

ABCDEFGHIJKLM
NOPQRSTUWXZ

DUO SOLID

Designed by Otto Eckmann. A heavy type characterised by flowery characters. There is also a light and a heavy. In concept the type was meant to lean on black letter.

ABCDEFGHIJKLMNOPQRSTUV
WXYZ
abcdefghijklmnopqrsituvwxyz
1234567890

ECKMANN

A shaded roman, in which the shading takes the form of horizontal lines. Such shading always imparts a feeling of movement. Ascenders and descenders are short. The arcs of **a**, **c** and **r** are terminated by blobs.

ABCDEFGHIJKL
MNOPQRSTUV
WXY&Z
Æ Œ
1234567890

ÉCLAIR

EDEN

Ludlow 1934

Designed by R.H. Middleton. An angular type with horizontal serifs and thin upstrokes. There are two weights. Descenders are shorter than ascenders. The lower bowl of the **B** is slightly wider than the upper bowl, and the **R** is also wider at the bottom. The **G** has no spur. It resembles CORVINUS.

iv

ABCDEFGHIJKLMNOPQRSTUVWXYZ&
abcdefghijklmnopqrstuvwxyz 1234567890

EDEN

iv

ABCDEFGHIJKLMNOPQRSTUVWXYZ&
abcdefghijklmnopqrstuvwxyz
1234567890$

EDEN BOLD

EDITOR

Française 1937

Designed by Henri Chaix. A display roman with short ascenders and descenders. The serifs are thin and flat, and the thins are hair lines. In the **M** the middle strokes stop half-way The **g** has an open tail.

ix

Les artistes graphiques
Les artistes graphiques italiens de l'époque présentent leurs

EDITOR

ix

Les artistes graphiques

EDITOR BOLD

EGIPCIA PROGRESO

Gans c. 1923

A monotone type with heavy and oblique serifs in the lower case. Ascenders and descenders are short. *Cf.* PROGRESO.

i

Perfumería Regional BENAMOR 249 586

EGIPCIA PROGRESO

EGIZIANO

Nebiolo 1905

A heavy slab serif type.

v

ABCDEFGHIJKLMNOPQRSTUVWXYZ
abcdefghijklmnopqrstuvxyzw
1234567890

EGIZIANO

74

Designed by Aldo Novarese. Capitals are wide, ascenders and descenders are short. Serifs are flat though there is little variation of stress. The italic has the serifs of the roman.

EGIZIO
Nebiolo 1955–58

ABCDEFGHIJKLMNOPQRST
UVWXYZÇÆŒ&
abcdefghijklmnopqrstuvwxyz
1234567890

ABCDEFGHIJKLMNOPQRST
UVXYZWÇÆŒ&
abcdefghijklmnopqrstuvxyzw
1234567890

EGIZIO

iv/v

A B C D E F G H I J K L M N O P Q R S T U
V W X Y Z
a b c d e f g h i j k l m n o p q r s t u v w x y z
1 2 3 4 5 6 7 8 9 0

EGIZIO CONDENSED

iv/v

ABCDEFGHIJKLMNOPQRS
TUVXYZWÇÆŒ&
abcdefghijklmnopqrstuvwxyz
1234567890

ABCDEFGHIJKLMNOPQRS
TUVWXYZÇÆŒ&
abcdefghijklmnopqrstuvwxyz
1234567890

EGIZIO BOLD

iv/v

EGMONT
Amsterdam 1933;
Intertype 1937

A light-faced roman designed by S.H. De Roos. The type has vertical stress, rather thin flat serifs, extending both ways on the top of ascenders. Ascenders are tall and descenders short. The capitals are wide; in **M** the middle strokes stop short of the line. The round **a** has a final top serif, **g** has a large bowl and **t** is tall. Numerals are short ranging. The italic has slight inclination and the serifs of the roman.

iv

ABCDEFGHIJKLMNOPQRSTUVW
XYZ

abcdefghijklmnopqrstuvwxyz   12345

*ABCDEFGHIJKLMNOPQRSTUVW
XYZ*

abcdefghijklmnopqrstuvwxyz   67890

EGMONT LIGHT

iv

ABCDEFGHIJKLMNOPQRSTUVW
XYZ

abcdefghijklmnopqrstuvwxyz   123

*ABCDEFGHIJKLMNOPQRSTUVW
XYZ*

abcdefghijklmnopqrstuvwxyz   456

EGMONT

iv

**ABCDEFGHIJKLMNOPQRSTUV
WXYZ**

abcdefghijklmnopqrstuvwxyz   7

EGMONT BOLD

iv

ABCDEFGHIJKLMNOPQRS
TUVWXYZ
1234567890

EGMONT INLINE CAPITALS

EGYPTIAN
Monotype

v

ABCDEFGHIJKLMNOPQRSTUVWXYZ
abcdefghijklmnopqrstuvwxyz
1234567890

EGYPTIAN

76

The condensed type is a revival of a nineteenth-century design. Descenders are very short.

ABCDEFGHIJKLMNOPQRSTUVWXYZ
abcdefghijklmnopqrstuvwxyz
1234567890

EGYPTIAN BOLD CONDENSED

ABCDEFGHIJKLMN
OPQRSTUVWXYZ

EGYPTIAN BOLD EXTENDED

v

abcdefghijklmnopqrs
tuvwxyz
1234567890

EGYPTIAN BOLD EXTENDED

v

Originally a nineteenth-century Miller & Richard's design. The type is an extra extended bold design with very pronounced serifs. The open version is a later three-dimension addition to the type range.

ABCDEFGHIJKLMNO
PQRSTUVWXYZ
abcdefghijklmnopqrst
uvwxyz
1234567890

EGYPTIAN EXPANDED

v

ABCDEFGHI
JKLMNOPQ
RSTUVWXY
ZÆŒ
abcdefghijkl
mnopqrstuvw
xyz
1234567890

EGYPTIAN EXPANDED OPEN

EGYPTIENNES
Française

Distinguishing letters are the upper- and lower-case J which end in a round dot.

v

ABCDEFGHIJKLMNOPQRSTUVWXYZÆŒ
abcdefghijklmnopqrstuvwxyzæœ 1234567890

EGYPTIENNES NARROW

v

ABCDEFGHIJKLMNOPQRST
UVWXYZÆŒ
abcdefghijklmnopqrstuvwx
yzæœ   1234567890

EGYPTIENNES BOLD

v

*ABCDEFGHIJKLMNO
PQRSTUVWXYZ
abcdefghijklmnopqrstu
vwxyz   1234567890*

EGYPTIENNE ITALIC

EHMCKE
Bauer

Designed by F. H. Ehmcke in 1908 for the Flinsch Foundry.

ix

ABCDEFGHIJKLMNOPPQ
RSſßTTUVWXYZ
abcdefghijklmnopqrſßstu
vwxyz
1234567890
ABCDEFGHIJKLMNOPPQRSſßTTUVW
XYZ
abcdefghijklmnopqrſßstuvwxyz
1234567890

EHMCKE

The original types were in the Ehrhardt foundry at Leipzig in the early eighteenth century. The type is another version of JANSON. The upper case M is splayed and the g has a curved ear. There is also a semi-bold and italic. Special matrices of the Monotype series are available for the composition of the PITMAN INITIAL TEACHING ALPHABET.

EHRHARDT
Monotype 1938;
Lanston Monotype

ABCDEFGHIJKLMNOPQRSTUVWX

abcdefghijklmnopqrstuvwxyz

12345

ABCDEFGHIJKLMNOPQRSTUVWXYZ

abcdefghijklmnopqrstuvwxyz

1234567890

EHRHARDT

ii

ABCDEFGHIJKLMNOPQRSTUVWXYZ

abcdefghijklmnopqrstuvwxyz

1234567890

EHRHARDT SEMI-BOLD

ii

ABCDEFGHIJKLMNOPQRSTUVWXYZ

abcdefghijklmnopqrstuvwxyz

1234567890

EHRHARDT SEMI-BOLD ITALIC

ii

Designed by W.A. Dwiggins. A book type which is old face in its serif formation and stress. The italic has several swash capitals. There are two sets of figures, non-ranging and ranging.

ELDORADO
Mergenthaler Linotype 1951

ABCDEFGHIJKLMNOPQRSTUVWXYZ

abcdefghijklmnopqrstuvwxyz

1234567890   1234567890

ABCDEFGHIJKLMNOPQRSTUVWXYZ

ABCDEFGHIJKLMNOPQRSTUVWXYZ

abcdefghijklmnopqrstuvwxyz

1234567890   1234567890

ii

ELDORADO

ELECTRA
Nacional

Designed by W.A. Dwiggins. The serifs are flat, but otherwise old face traditions are observed. The letters are so unobtrusive that it is not easy to pick anything out—a compliment to a type. The **Q** has a distinctive tail, the **g** is slightly idiosyncratic. In common with other Linotype faces the **f** is unkerned, and the **t** is unbracketed. The italic is the roman slightly inclined, without any exception. ELECTRA CURSIVE is an alternative italic of orthodox design.

ii

ABCDEFGHIJKLMNOPQRSTUVWXYZ
abcdefghijklmnopqrstuvwxyz
1234567890   1234567890
ABCDEFGHIJKLMNOPQRSTUVWXYZ
ABCDEFGHIJKLMNOPQRSTUVWXYZ
abcdefghijklmnopqrstuvwxyz   abcdefghijklmnopqrstuvwxyz
1234567890   1234567890

ELECTRA

ii

ABCDEFGHIJKLMNOPQRSTUVWXYZ
abcdefghijklmnopqrstuvwxyz
1234567890   1234567890
ABCDEFGHIJKLMNOPQRSTUVWXYZ
ABCDEFGHIJKLMNOPQRSTUVWXYZ
abcdefghijklmnopqrstuvwxyz   abcdefghijklmnopqrstuvwxyz
1234567890   1234567890

ELECTRA BOLD

ELIZABETH ROMAN
Bauer 1937

Designed by Miss E. Friedländer, a pupil of Weiss. A roman almost monotone in colour, with small serifs and short descenders. The **E** and **F** are narrow, **J** ranges on the line, **M** has no top serifs as in many contemporary German romans, **U** has the lower-case design and **W**, lower-case also, no middle serif. The **g** has an open tail. Note the serif on the bar of the **t**. Figures are short-ranging. The inclination of the italic is slight; beginning strokes are angular. There is a second series of swash capitals.

ii

ABCDEFGHIJKLMNOPQRSTUVWXYZ
abcdefghijklmnopqrstuvwxyz
1234567890
ABCDEFGHIJKLMNOPQRSTUVWXYZ
abcdefghijkklmnopqrstuvwxyzz
1234567890

CAABDEFGHIJKLMNPRTWZ

ELIZABETH ROMAN

A text roman for phototypesetting and named after the street address of the type founders.

ABCDEFGHIJKLMNOPQRSTUVWXYZ
abcdefghijklmnopqrstuvwxyz
1 2 3 4 5 6 7 8 9 0

ELMORA

ABCDEFGHIJKLMNOPQRSTUVWXYZ
abcdefghijklmnopqrstuvwxyz
1 2 3 4 5 6 7 8 9 0

ELMORA BOLD

A revival of the Victorian condensed and elongated fat faces, a fashion started by SLIMBLACK.

ABCDEFGHIJKLMNOPQRSTUVWXYZ

1234567890

ELONGATED ROMAN

ABCDEFGHIJKLMNOPQRSTUVWXYZ

1234567

ELONGATED ROMAN SHADED

Originally a French type (one version is known as FRENCH OLD STYLE), designed by Théophile Beaudoire in 1858. The upper case is derived from Louis Perrin's LYONS CAPITALS. Note the splayed **M** and the tail of the **R**. The type is somewhat condensed and has short ascenders and descenders. In the **c** and **e** the thickest parts of the curves are very low; the **g** has a steeply inclined tail and there is a tall **t**. The italic has a slight inclination. Linotype (London) OLD STYLE NO. 33 is similar and so is DE VINNE.

ABCDEFGHIJKLMNOPQRSTUVWXYZ&

abcdefghijklmnopqrstuvwxyz

1234567890

ABCDEFGHIJKLMNOPQRSTUVWXYZ&

abcdefghijklmnopqrstuvwxyz

ELZEVIR

ELZEVIR INITIALS

Chiswick Press c. 1900

ix

Sets of quaintly decorated Victorian initials for the Elzevir Press.

ABCDEFG
HIJKLMNO
PQRSTUV

ix

ABCDEFGH
IJKLMNOPQ
RSTUVWYZ

ELZEVIR INITIALS

EMERGO

Enschedé 1948–53

Designed and cut by S.L. Hartz. A light face with little variation in colour, small capitals and serifs, horizontal on the lower case. The **G** has a spur; **H** is wide and has the bar rather high. There are two **R**'s, one with an extended tail. The **g** has a rather wide tail. In the slightly inclined italic capitals are even smaller. In its angularity the type is of the BLADO school. Numerals are non-ranging.

ABCDEFGHIJKLMNOPQRR STUVWXYZÆŒ&1234567890

ii

ABCDEFGHIJKLMNOPQRSTUVWXYZÆŒ&1234567890

abcdefghijklmnopqrstuvwxyzijæœ1234567890

ABCDEFGHIJKLMNOPQRR STTUVWXYZÆŒQU

ii

abcdefghijklmnopqrstuvwxyzijæœ&1234567890

&fb ff ffi ffl fh fi fj fk fl Qu

EMERGO

EMERSON

Monotype 1936–39

Designed by Joseph Blumenthal and based on his SPIRAL type, which was cut by Louis Hoell. A type with little differentiation of colour and with blunt, horizontal serifs. The italic has a slight inclination and conforms to the roman, even in the serifs of the lower case. The numerals are non-ranging.

ii

ABCDEFGHIJKLMNOPQRSTUVWXYZ

abcdefghijklmnopqrstuvwxyz

1234567890

EMERSON

ABCDEFGHIJKLMNOPQRSTUVWXYZ EMERSON
abcdefghijklmnopqrstuvwxyz
1234567890

EMERSON ITALIC

A roman following BODONI.

ABCDEFGHIJKLMNOPQRS
TUVWXYZ
abcdefghijklmnopqrstuvwxyz
1234567890

EMPIRIANA
Grafotechna 1920

ABCDEFGHIJKLMNOPQRS
TUVWXYZ
abcdefghijklmnopqrstuvwxyz
1234567890

EMPIRIANA

ABCDEFGHIJKLMNOPQRS
TUVWXYZ
abcdefghijklmnopqrstuvwxyz
1234567890

EMPIRIANA BOLD

ABCDEFGHIJKLMNOPQRS
TUVWXYZ   1234567890

EMPIRIANA SHADED

ENDEAVOUR TYPE
Essex House Press 1901

A black face with heavy serifs, designed by C.R. Ashbee, the punches cut by E.P. Prince. This is perhaps the most exotic of the private press types. Few of the letters have a normal design. The bowls of the **B** are divided diagonally. **H** has a very high bar. The **M** has slab serifs and very short middle strokes. **W** has foot serifs and brief middle strokes. In the lower case **e** is a cursive form, **g** has no link and a contorted tail, in the **h**, **m** and **n** the last stroke is curved and descends below the line, **w** has the foot serifs of the capitals. Ascenders and descenders are short. The ampersand is curious. The name is derived from the title of the first book in which the type was used, *An Endeavour towards the Teachings of Ruskin and Morris*. The PRAYER BOOK TYPE of 1903, is the same design in Great Primer.

ix

And his mother said unto him, Upon 13
me be thy curse, my son: only obey my
voice, and go fetch me them. And he 14

ENDEAVOUR TYPE

ENGRAVERS' TITLING BOLD
Monotype 1924

A titling type originally cast by American Typefounder's as ENGRAVER'S BOLD, available on Ludlow since 1926, and cast Inland Typefounders as LITHO. Ludlow call their version of 1940 LINING LITHO. In 1914 GNOM, designed by W. Augspurg, was cast by Schelter & Giesecke whose inline version is known as PERKEO or DIAPHANE by Warnery who call the type MOZART. Bauer's NOBLESSE of 1870 is based on the American designs.

iv

ABCDEFGHIJKLMNOPQRSTUVWXYZ
1234567890

ENGRAVERS' TITLING BOLD

ERASMUS
Amsterdam 1923

Designed by S.H. de Roos. Light serifs and short descenders, with many of the serifs shaped as though drawn with a pen. **E** and **F** have centre arms high; the **H** has a high bar and the **U** follows the lower-case design. The **g** has a short tail drawn from right to left; **p** and **q** have oblique foot serifs. The italic has slight inclination and the serifs of the roman.

ix

BORN AT ROTTERDAM
Pension at the Duke of Cleves

ERASMUS

ix

ABCDEFGHIJKLMNOPQRSTUWXZ

abcdefghijklmnopqrstuvwxyzabcdefgir

ERASMUS GRATIUS

ERLER TITLING
Typoart 1953

Designed by Herbert Thannhaeuser. A set of inline capitals with thin serifs and of light weight.

A B C D E F G H I J K L M N O P Q R S T U V W X Y Z

ERLER TITLING

ix

Designed by Aldo Novarese. Many letters have script quality.

ABCDEFGHIJKLMNOPQRS TUVWXYZ abcdefghijklmnopqrstuvwxyz 1234567890

ESTRO

Another Garamond design due to G.W. Jones, named after the famous family of Paris printers. This roman differs from GRANJON in the greater height of the ascenders and length of the descenders. It is also lighter in colour. Other distinguishing marks are, the **R** which tapers off and descends below the line, and the **g** with a larger bowl.

The italic has less inclination than the Granjon. The **Q** has a tail after the Goudy model. In the lower case the serifs on the tops of ascenders are inclined; the curve of the bowl of the **p** continues beyond the main stroke. The Haas ESTIENNE is an entirely different design.

ABCDEFGHIJKLMNOPQRSTUVWXYZ

abcdefghijklmnopqrstuvwxyz

1234567890

ABCDEFGHIJKLMNOPQRSTUVWXYZ

ABCDEFGHIJKLMNOPQRSTUVWXYZ

abcdefghijklmnopqrstuvwxyz

1234567890

ESTIENNE

ii

Probably a Wagner & Schmidt face of 1902. An elongated and condensed roman with small, pointed serifs. Not to be confused with the Linotype ESTIENNE.

ABCDEFGHIJKLMNOPQRSTUVWXYZ

abcdefghijklmnopqrstuvwxyz

1234567890

ETIENNE

The roman was designed by E. F. Detterer, and the other weights by R. H. Middleton. A faithful copy of the original after Nicolas Jenson, retaining the slab serifs on the **M**. The **Q** has a tail like CLOISTER, while the **W** is like CENTAUR. The lower-case **g** has the appearance of leaning backwards. The italic resembles ARRIGHI, but the capitals are wider. The type's old name is NICOLAS JENSON.

ABCDEFGHIJKLMNOPQRSTUVWXY

i

EUSEBIUS

ABCDEFGHIJKLMNOPQRSTUVWXYZ

i

EUSEBIUS BOLD

ABCDEFGHIJKLMNOPQRSTUVW

i

EUSEBIUS OPEN

EXECUTIVE

Monotype;
Wagner and others 1960

ii

Designed by The Monotype Corporation to provide a printing type compatible with an IBM typewriter face. The alphabet has been divided into four set widths.

ABCDEFGHIJKLMNOPQRSTUVWXYZ

abcdefghijklmnopqrstuvwxyz

1234567890

EXECUTIVE

EXCELSIOR

Mergenthaler Linotype 1931;
Linotype (London);
Linotype (Frankfurt)

iv

Designed by C.H. Griffith. A newspaper type of even colour, and No. 2 of the "Linotype Legibility Group". The roman has horizontal serifs and generally follows the Didone style. The numerals are ranging.

ABCDEFGHIJKLMNOPQRSTUVWXYZ

abcdefghijklmnopqrstuvwxyz

123456789

ABCDEFGHIJKLMNOPQRSTUVWXYZ

ABCDEFGHIJKLMNOPQRSTUVWXYZ

abcdefghijklmnopqrstuvwxyz

234567890

EXCELSIOR

EXPANDED ANTIQUE

Stevens Shanks c. 1880

v

An expanded titling taken over from the foundry of V. & J. Figgins.

ABCDEFGHIJ
KLMNOPQRS
TUVWXYZ
1234567890£&

EXPANDED ANTIQUE

EXTRA ORNAMENTED 2

Stevens Shanks

ix

A set of inline and ornamented capitals and figures. In plan the letters are English modern face.

ABCDEFGHIJKLMNOPQRST
UVWXYZ 1234567890

EXTRA ORNAMENTED No. 2

EXTENDED 3

Stevens Shanks

iv

An expanded type with short ascenders and descenders. Serifs are thin and there are many hair lines. American Typefounders call the type CARD MERCANTILE.

ABCDEFGHIJKLMNOP
QRSTUVWXYZ

abcdefghijklmnopqrstuvwxyz

1234567890

EXTENDED No. 3

Designed by Rudolph Ruzicka. There are ranging and non-ranging numerals. The **R** has a curled tail and the **U** follows the lower-case design. The **g** has a large bowl with a minute ear. In the italic **b**, **h**, **m** and **n** the upstrokes take off from the very feet of the downstrokes.

ABCDEFGHIJKLMNOPQRSTUVWXYZ

abcdefghijklmnopqrstuvwxyz

iv

1234567890 1234567890

ABCDEFGHIJKLMNOPQRSTUVWXYZ

ABCDEFGHIJKLMNOPQRSTUVWXYZ

abcdefghijklmnopqrstuvwxyz

1234567890 *1234567890*

FAIRFIELD

ABCDEFGHIJKLMNOPQRSTUVWXYZ

abcdefghijklmnopqrstuvwxyz

iv

1234567890 1234567890

ABCDEFGHIJKLMNOPQRSTUVWXYZ

ABCDEFGHIJKLMNOPQRSTUVWXYZ

abcdefghijklmnopqrstuvwxyz

1234567890 *1234567890*

FAIRFIELD MEDIUM

Designed by W.A. Dwiggins. A book face with narrow characters and of calligraphic simple design. The **Q** has an unusual angular hooked tail. The italic **y** is almost closed, as are the **v** and **w**.

ABCDEFGHIJKLMNOPQRSTUVWXYZ

abcdefghijklmnopqrstuvwxyz

ii

1234567890 1234567890

ABCDEFGHIJKLMNOPQRSTUVWXYZ

ABCDEFGHIJKLMNOPQRSTUVWXYZ

abcdefghijklmnopqrstuvwxyz

1234567890 *1234567890*

FALCON

A fat face following the traditional English design.

ABCDEFGHIJKLMNOPQRSTUVWXYZ

iv

abcdefghijklmnopqrstuvwxyz

iv

1234567890

iv

ABCDEFGHIJKLMNOPQRSTUVWXYZ

iv

abcdefghijklmnopqrstuvwxyz

iv

1234567890

iv

FALSTAFF

FARMER'S OLD STYLE

Lanston Monotype 1909

ii

One of the first types made available for Monotype machine composition, this face was first cut in 1899 adapted from OLD STYLE NO. 5 of the former A.D. Farmer & Son Foundry, of New York City. The type has not been cut larger than 12 pt.

ABCDEFGHIJKLMNOPQRSTUVWXYZ&ÆŒ

abcdefghijklmnopqrstuvwxyzæœ

1234567890   1234567890

ABCDEFGHIJKLMNOPQRSTUVWXYZ&ÆŒ

ABCDEFGHIJKLMNOPQRSTUVWXYZ&ÆŒ

abcdefghijklmnopqrstuvwxyzæœ

1234567890   1234567890

FARMER'S OLD STYLE

FAUST

Typoart 1959

ix

Designed by Albert Kapr. A roman with many unusual letters. The most conspicuous are the **n**, **m**, and **r**, with inclined top strokes. There is some squaring-up of the round letters. The capitals are wide and lower than the ascenders. There is an italic, slightly inclined.

ABCDEFGHIJKLMNOPQRSTU
VWXYZ&
abcdefghijklmnopqrstuvwxyz?
1234567890

*ABCDEFGHIJKLMNOPQRSTU
VWXYZ&
abcdefghijklmnopqrstuvwxyz?
1234567890*

FAUST

FELIX

Monotype 1934

vii

A titling based on the inscriptional letters designed by Felice Feliciano of Verona in 1463. The manuscript is in the Vatican Library and was reproduced in the Italian periodical *La Bibliofilia* in 1935 and in an edition by Dr Giovanni Mardersteig entitled ALPHABETUM ROMANUM published in 1960 at Verona.

MONOTYPE

FELIX

Many of the old types of the Oxford University Press were bought by John Fell, Bishop of Oxford, about the year 1672, through his agents in Holland. But some of these types, like the one here shown, are probably of French origin. It has recently been established that the larger sizes, formerly thought to be Dutch, were cut at Oxford by Peter Walpergen.

The Oxford Printing House holds the oldest punches and matrices surviving in England, material not only treasured but used; types cast therefrom being employed for the composition of books and other printed matter.

ABCDEFGHIJKLMNOPQRSTUVWXYZÆ
ABCDEFGHIJKLMNOPQRSTUVWXYZÆ
abcdefghijklmnopqrstuvwxyzæœ
1234567890
ct ff fi fl ffi ffl ſ ſh ſi ſl ſſ ſt ſſi

FELL ROMAN

A monoline type with short descenders and some terminal flourishes.

Forstwirtschaft
Land- und

FEMINA

A condensed reversed slab serif type resembling PLAYBILL but having greater colour contrast. HIDALGO is very similar.

ABCDEFGHIJKLMNOPQRSTUVWXYZ
abcdefghijklmnopqrstuvwxyz
1234567890

FIGARO

A condensed fat face following the usual English design of the time and taken over from the foundry of V. & J. Figgins.

ABCDEFGHIJKLMNOPQRSTU
VWXYZÆŒ
abcdefghijklmnopqrstuvwxyz
1224567890

FIGGINS CONDENSED NO. 2

FIGGINS SHADED

Stevens Shanks

Three-dimensional capitals and figures with white faces. In this type there are two distinct designs, 10 and 30 point, first shown by Vincent Figgins in 1815. The 14 and 18 point derive from the foundry of Bessemer and Catherwood and were first shown in their specimen of 1825.

iv

ABCDEFGHIJKLMNOPQRSTUVW
XYZÆŒ&£1234567800

18 POINT FIGGINS SHADED

iv

ABCDEFG

30 POINT FIGGINS SHADED

FIGURA

Klingspor 1955

Designed by Alfred Finsterer. A condensed and elongated fat face, like SLIMBLACK. Ascenders and descenders are very short. The design is Victorian, except perhaps the **t**.

iv

ABCDEFGHIJKLMNOPQRSTUVWXYZ

abcdefghijklmnopqrstuvwxyz

1234567890

FIGURA

FIGURAL

Grafotechna

Designed by Oldrich Menhart. A type leaning somewhat on JENSON but having strong pen characteristics, which become particularly obvious in the italic, where lower-case letters are angular and of varying inclination. In the italic the **R** and **K** have a tail descending below the line, the **U** follows the lower-case design. The swash capitals were added in 1959.

ii

ABCDEFGHIJKLMNOPQRSTUVWXYZ
abcdefghijklmnopqrstuvwxyz
1234567890
ABCDEFGHIJKLMNOPQRSTUVWXYZ
abcdefghijklmnopqrstuvwxyz
1234567890

FIGURAL

viii

ABCDEFGHIJKLMN
OPQRSTUVWXYZ

FIGURAL SWASH CAPS

Designed by John Peters, and presumably intended for newspaper display headings.

632-18 pt

ABCDEFGHIJKLMNOPQRSTUVWXYZ 1234567890

FLEET TITLING

J.M. Fleischman was born in Germany in 1701, but for most of his life he was cutting types for Dutch founders, including the Enschedé firm in their earliest days. All his surviving punches and matrices are now in the possession of the Enschedés. His roman types are rather condensed and of a large x-height. His design is approaching the modern; the stress in some letters is vertical and the serifs are nearer the horizontal. The long arms of the **E** and the squareness of the **M** are to be noted. The **g** is conspicuous with its bulbous ear and rounded link. The italic is moderately inclined, but is somewhat irregular. The modern re-cutting was designed by Georg Belwe for L. Wagner, who spell the name of the type as FLEISCHMANN, following original German style.

ABCDEFGHIJKLMNOPQRSTUVWXYZÆŒ&

ABCDEFGHIJKLMNOPQRSTUVWXYZÆŒ

abcdefghijklmnopqrsſtuvwxyzijæœ1234567890

ct fb ff ffi ffl fh fi fk fl fb fh fi fl ſſ ß fh fll ft

ABCDEFGHIJKLMNOPQRSTUVWXYZIJÆŒ&

AB C D F M N P Q R

abcdefghijklmnopqrsſtuvvwxyzijæœ

ENSCHEDE FLEISCHMAN

ABCDEFGHIJKLMNOPQRSTU VWXYZ&

abcdefghijklmnopqrstuvwxyz?

1234567890

ABCDEFGHIJJKLMNOPQQuRSTU

VWXYTZ&&

abcdefghhijklmnopqrstuvwxyz?

1234567890

FLEISCHMANN

ABCDEFGHIJKLMNOPQRSTU VWXYZ&

abcdefghijklmnopqrstuvwxyz?

1234567890

FLEISCHMANN BOLD

FLORENCE PRESS TYPE

Chatto & Windus 1908

ix

A roman designed by H.P. Horne, resembling his other romans, MONTALLEGRO and RICCARDI. Serifs are small and inclined on the lower case. The capitals are broader than in Montallegro. **e** has a large bowl with a straight bar. The ampersand has the tall form found in some italics.

'Lear,' although we can hardly imagine they would ever marry, kept single out of a cynical humour or for a broken heart, and not, as we do nowadays, from a spirit of incredulity and preference for the single state. For that matter, if you turn to George Sand's French version of 'As You Like

FLORENCE PRESS TYPE

FLORENZ

L. Wagner 1960

i

Designed by Paul Zimmermann. The type resembles ALDUS. Serifs are very small, the **W** is wide and has no middle serif.

ANTIQUA   FLORENZ

Als der fünfzehnjährige Erhard Ratdolt mit Augsburger Kauffahrern zum erstenmal nach Venedig kam, faßte er eine tiefe Liebe zu dieser Stadt. Im Jahre 1476 zog er als junger Buchdrucker wieder über die Alpen, um sich ganz in Venedig niederzulassen. Dort richtete er mit zwei Deutschen eine Offizin ein, die bald seinen Ruhm über alle Lande tragen sollte.

FLORENZ

FLORIATED CAPITALS

Monotype 1935

ix

Designed by Eric Gill. A set of open capitals with decorative leaf forms.

FLORIATED CAPITALS

FOLKWANG

Klingspor 1954–55

ix

Designed by Hermann Schardt. A somewhat exotic roman in which the lower case is like an upright italic. The serifs at the ends of the arms of **E** and **F** are on the under side only. The **J** has an unusual design. The italic has some characteristics of a script, e.g. in the pen drawn serifs. Numerals are short ranging. The bold differs in many ways from the roman.

ABCDEFGHIJKLMNOPQRSTUV
abcdefghijklmnopqrstuvwxyz
1234567890
ABCDEFGHIJKLMNOPQRST
abcdefghijklmnopqrstuvwxyz

FOLKWANG

92

ABCDEFGHIJKLMNOPQRST
abcdefghijklmnopqrstuvwxyz

FOLKWANG BOLD

Designed by Giovanni Mardersteig for Collins, the Glasgow publishers and printers in 1936, and based on a type cut by Alexander Wilson of the Glasgow Letter Foundry about 1770. It is a round letter with some affinity to BASKERVILLE. The ascenders are rather short and the capitals modest in height and weight.

FONTANA
Monotype 1961

ABCDEFGHIJKLMNOPQRSTUVWXYZ
abcdefghijklmnopqrstuvwxyz
1234567890
ABCDEFGHIJKLMNOPQRSTUVWXYZ
abcdefghijklmnopqrstuvwxyz
1234567890

FONTANA

Designed by A. Novarese. A set of decorated capitals and figures. All serifs are rounded forms and there are roundels in the centre of the main strokes.

FONTANESI
Nebiolo

ABCDRFGHIJKLMN
OPQRSUVWXYZ
ÇÆŒ&
1234567890

FONTANESI

Designed by Friedrich Bauer. An inline series of roman capitals. The line passes right through vertical strokes. Serifs are very small. In the **M** the middle strokes stop short of the line. *Cf.* DALIA.

FORTUNA
Trennert 1930

GEISENHEIM

FORTUNA

FORTUNE
or **VOLTA**
Bauer 1955

Designed by K.F. Bauer and Walter Baum. A display roman whose stubby flat serifs give it the appearance of a Clarendon. It is an expanded face and the lower case has very short ascenders and descenders. There are three weights.

iv

ABCDEFGHIJKLMNOPQ
RSTUVWXYZ
abcdefghijklmnopqrstuvw
xyz
1234567

FORTUNE LIGHT

iv

ABCDEFGHIJKLMNOP
QRSTUVWXYZ
abcdefghijklmnopqrstu
vwxyz
1234567890

ABCDEFGHIJKLMNOPQX
abcdefghijklmnopqrstuvwx
1234567890

FORTUNE BOLD

v

ABCDEFGHIJKLMN
OPQRSTUVWXYZ
abcdefghijklmnop
qrstuvwxyz
1234567890

FORTUNE EXTRA BOLD

94

Designed by Georg Trump. A slab serif type with light (FORUM I) and heavy (FORUM II) **FORUM**
The type is quite different from FORUM CAPITALS.

Weber

ABCDEFGHIJKLMNOPQRSTUVW
XYZ
1234567890

FORUM I

ABCDEFGHIJKLMNOP
QRSTUVWXYZ
1243567890

FORUM II

Designed by F.W. Goudy and first shown 1912. The serifs have pen-stroke qualities like other **FORUM**
Goudy designs. The U has the lower-case design and the upper limbs of the Y are curved. **CAPITALS**

Lanston Monotype 1924; Caslon

ABCDEFGHIJKLMNOPQRS
TUVWXYZ

FORUM CAPITALS

The new roman of the famous Paris founder P.S. Fournier is, apart from the privately owned **FOURNIER**
ROMAINS DU ROI, the first of the "transitional" types. The type is somewhat condensed, though
much less so than others designed by Fournier, such as his POETIQUE. The capitals are tall. *Monotype 1925*
BARBOU is related. There is a short-ranging **J** and an **R** with a curved tail. In the lower
case the **b** has a foot serif which is flat. The italic is notable for its inclined roman serifs on the
m, n, p, z, no doubt designed for the sake of harmony with the roman; nevertheless the Fournier
italic can stand on its own. The curves of the **v, w** and **y** are influenced by contemporary
calligraphy.

ABCDEFGHIJKLMNOPQRSTUVWXYZ

abcdefghijklmnopqrstuvwxyz

1234567890

ABCDEFGHIJKLMNOPQRSTUVWXYZ

abcdefghijklmnopqrstuvwxyz

1234567890

FOURNIER

95

FOURNIER

Typoart

ix

Designed by P. A. Demeter in 1922.

ABCDEFGHIJKLMNOPQRSTUVWX
DIE SCHRIFT WURDE DIE TRÄGE

FOURNIER

FOURNIER
LE JEUNE

Deberny & Peignot 1913;
Amsterdam

ix

Shaded italic capitals, in which the thick strokes are broken in the middle by the insertion of diamond-shaped ornaments. Based on the decorated letters designed by P.S. Fournier *c.* 1746 and reproduced by Peignot.

FOURNIER LE JEUNE (American Typefounders) is a similar type. It can be distinguished by the thin serifs which curve downwards and end in thickenings.

LETTTERS BULLETIN

DEBERNY & PEIGNOT FOURNIER LE JEUNE

ix

ABCDEFGHI
JKLMNNO
PQRSTUVWY

AMSTERDAM FOURNIER LE JEUNE

FRENCH FACE
EXTENDED

Monotype

iv

A modern face with short ascenders and descenders. In spite of its name the design follows English models.

ABCDEFGHIJKLMNOPQRSTUVWXYZ

abcdefghijklmnopqrstuvwxyz

12345

ABCDEFGHIJKLMNOPQRSTUVWXYZ

abcdefghijklmnopqrstuvwxyz

FRENCH FACE EXTENDED

FRENCH
OLD STYLE

Monotype 1908

ii

A type similar to DE VINNE.

ABCDEFGHIJKLMNOPQRSTUVWXYZ

abcdefghijklmnopqrstuvwxyz

1234567890

ABCDEFGHIJKLMNOPQRSTUVWXYZ

abcdefghijklmnopqrstuvwxyz

FRENCH OLD STYLE

ii

ABCDEFGHIJKLMNOPQRSTUVWXYZ

abcdefghijklmnopqrstuvwxyz

1234567890

FRENCH OLD STYLE BOLD

A type similar to ELZEVIR, DE VINNE and OLD STYLE NO. 33.

ABCDEFGHIJKLMNOPQRSTUVWXYZ
abcdefghijklmnopqrstuvwxyz
1234567890
ABCDEFGHIJKLMNOPQRSTUVWXYZ
abcdefghijklmnopqrstuvwxyz

FRENCH ROUND FACE

Designed by Frederick W. Goudy. Almost an italic with swash capitals.

ABCDEFGHIJKLMNOPQRTSUV
WXYZ

abcdefghijklmnopqrstuvwxyz

FRENCHWOOD RONDE

Designed by Lin Yu-Bingnan. A calligraphic type. Bowls of **B**, **P** and **R** do not close in the centre, and in the **g** the tail does not close. In the italic the tail of the **Q** is freely suspended.

ABCDEFGHIJKLMNOPQR
STUVWXYZ
abcdefghijklmnopqrstuvw
xyz

1234567890

ABCDEFGHIJKLMNOPQRST
UVWXYZ
abcdefghijklmnopqrstuvwxyz
1234567890

FREUNDSCHAFT

FRY'S BASKERVILLE
Stephenson Blake

Stephenson Blake give the date as 1768, and the type was perhaps cut by Isaac Moore under the influence of Baskerville. In the **Q** the tail is like BASKERVILLE and the **R** had a straight tail. There are two **w**'s, one with and one without a middle serif.

iii

DETER printed

FRY'S BASKERVILLE

FRY'S CANON
Kynoch Press

This type, originally from Fry's foundry was cast by Stephenson Blake for Kynoch Press and Curwen Press.
One of the earliest of the Fat Faces, dating from 1808. The design is that of the modern face, with an exaggeration of the contrast between thick and thin strokes. The exaggeration is however less than in the contemporary type THOROWGOOD.

iv

ABCDEFGH
abcdefghijkl
123456789
ABCDEFG
abcdefghijkl
mnopqrstuvw

FRY'S CANON

FRY'S ORNAMENTED
Stephenson Blake

Cut by Richard Austin in 1796. A series of inline capitals in which the centre of the main strokes is further decorated with an oval.

ii

ABCDEFGHIJKLMNOP
QRSTUVWXYZ

FRY'S ORNAMENTED

A quaintly decorated tooled display face.

ABCDEFGHIJ KLMNOPQRS ſ'STUVWXYZ 1234567890

GALLIA

A set of inscriptional capitals and ranging figures. The serifs are fairly large and shaped. E and F are narrow; the variation of stress in O and Q is oblique. P has the bowl unclosed. U has the lower-case design.

CURIOUS EPITAPH

GANTON

Designed by A. Novarese. A type closely following the style of GARAMOND, but in the bold the slight irregularity of the original type is no longer apparent.

ABCDEFGHIJKLMNOPQRSTUVXYZWQu

abcdefghijklmnopqrsſtuvxyzwfiffflffifl

1234567890 1234567890

ABCDEFGHIJKLMNOPQRSTUVXYZÆŒW

abcdefghijklmnopqrstuvxyzæœwfifffflffiffl

1234567890 1234567890

GARALDUS

ABCDEFGHIJKLMNOPQRSTU VWXYZ 1234567890
abcdefghijklmnopqrstuvwxyz

ABCDEFGHIJKLMNOPQRSTU
VWXYZ 1234567890
abcdefghijklmnopqrstuvwxyz

GARALDUS BOLD

GARAMOND or GARAMONT

Many founders

Claude Garamond (1480–1561) based his ROMAIN DE L'UNIVERSITÉ on designs by Aldus Manutius, and first specimens are found in books printed in Paris around 1532. Many of the present-day versions of this type are based on the TYPI ACADEMIAE of Jean Jannon cut in Sedan around 1615. The Imprimerie Nationale in Paris towards the end of the nineteenth century revived the JANNON type of 1641 cut for the then Imprimerie Royale. Ambroise Vollard in 1897 was given permission to use the type for Verlaine's *Paralellement*.

There are the following basic models:

Deberny & Peignot, 1912-28. This design, supervised by Georges and later Charles Peignot —not copied by any other foundry or matrix manufacturer—is based on the original types in the Imprimerie Nationale.

American Typefounders, 1917, designed by M.F. Benton and T.M. Cleland after the original Jannon types. From this source the versions of the Amsterdam Typefoundry, Linotype Garamond No. 3 (1936) and Intertype have been derived.

Lanston Monotype, 1921, designed by F.W. Goudy after Jannon. This version was also adopted by The Monotype Corporation and has not been copied by others. The Monotype Corporation's version follows Jannon in the roman and Granjon in the italic.

Stempel, 1924. This design is based on the Egenolff-Berner sheet, but the characters have been regularised. The design is available on Linotypes.

Mergenthaler Linotype, 1925, issued an adaptation by Joseph Hill. This was also based on the Egenolff-Berner sheet, but considerably bolder and less closely setting than the other Linotype version. This design is no longer available.

Nebiolo's GARALDUS, 1956, designed by Aldo Novarese, is another re-cutting and is shown separately.

Simoncini in Italy—later in co-operation with Ludwig & Mayer, have also issued a Garamond in 1958–61, designed by F. Simoncini and W. Bilz.

Grafotechna introduced a Garamond in 1959 designed by Stanislav Marso.

There are also a number of other adaptations of the American Typefounders' design (based on Jannon). The Ludlow version designed by R. Hunter Middleton in 1930, the Berling version designed by Henri Alm partly based on Granjon designs; and the Typoart version.

ii

ABCDEFGHIJKLMNOPQRSTUVWXYZ
abcdefghijklmnopqrstuvwxyz
1 2 3 4 5 QU & Qu 6 7 8 9 0

ABCDEFGHIJKLMNOPQRSTUVWXYZ
abcdefghijklmnopqrstuvwxyz
1 2 3 4 5 QU & Qu 6 7 8 9 0

DEBERNY & PEIGNOT GARAMONT

ii

ABCDEFGHIJKLMNOPQRSTUVWXYZ
abcdefghijklmnopqrstuvwxyz
123456789 1234567890
ABCDEFGHIJKLMNOPQRSTUVWXYZ
ABCDEFGHIJKLMNOPQRSTUVWXY

ABCDEFGHIJKLMNOPQRSTUVWXYZ
abcdefghijklmnopqrstuvwxyz
1234567890 234567890
BCDEFGHIJKLMNOPQRSTUVWXYZ
Recut Italic: abcdefghijklmnopqrstuvwxyz

LINOTYPE GARAMOND NO. 3

ABCDEFGHIJKLMNOPQRSTUVWXYZ
abcdefghijklmnopqrstuvwxyz
12345678   1234567890

ABCDEFGHIJKLMNOPQRSTUVWXYZ
ABCDEFGHIJKLMNOPQRSTUVWXYZ

ABCDEFGHIJKLMNOPQRSTUVWXYZ
abcdefghijklmnopqrstuvwxyz
34567890   1234567890

ABCDEFGHIJKLMNOPQRSTUVWXYZ
Recut Italic: abcdefghijklmnopqrstuvwxyz

LINOTYPE GARAMOND BOLD NO. 3

ii

ABCDEFGHIJKLMNOPQRSTUVWXYZ
abcdefghijklmnopqrstuvwxyz
1234567890

ABCDEFGHIJKLMNOPQRSTUVWXYZ &&£

ABCDEFGHIJKLMNOPQRSTUVWXYZ
abcdefghijklmnopqrstuvwxyz
1234567890

INTERTYPE GARAMOND

ii

ABCDEFGHIJKLMNOPQRSTUVWXYZ
abcdefghijklmnopqrstuvwxyz 1234567890
ABCDEFGHIJKLMNOPQRSTUVWXYZ
abcdefghijklmnopqrstuvwxyz 1234567890
1234567890 1234567890

INTERTYPE GARAMOND BOLD

ii

ABCDEFGHIJKLMNOPQRSTUVWXYZ
abcdefghijklmnopqrstuvwxyz
1234567890

ABCDEFGHIJKLMNOPQRSTUVWXYZ
abcdefghijklmnopqrstuvwxyz
1234567890

MONOTYPE GARAMOND

ABCDEFGHIJKLMNOPQRSTUVWXYZ
abcdefghijklmnopqrstuvwxyz
1234567890
ABCDEFGHIJKLMNOPQRSTUVWXYZ
abcdefghijklmnopqrstuvwxyz
1234567890

MONOTYPE GARAMOND BOLD

ii

ABCDEFGHIJKLMNOPQRS
TUVWXYZ
abcdefghijklmnopqrstuvwxyz
1234567890

ii

ABCDEFGHIJKLMNOPQRS
TUVWXYZ
abcdefghijklmnopqrstuvwxyz
1234567890

GRAFOTECHNA GARAMOND

ii

ABCDEFGHIJKLMNOPQRS
TUVWXYZ
ABCDEFGHIJKLMNOPQRSTUVW
XYZ
1234567890

ABCDEFGHIJKLMNOPQRST
UVWXYZ
1234567890

SIMONCINI GARAMOND

ABCDEFGHIJKLMNOPQRSTUVWXYZ&

abcdefghijklmnopqrstuvwxyz 1234567890$

LUDLOW GARAMOND ITALIC

ABCDEFGHIJKLMNOPQRSTUV
WXYZ&

abcdefghijklmnopqrstuvwxyz 1234567890$

LUDLOW GARAMOND BOLD ITALIC

A text type derived from a design of the former Genzsch & Heyse Foundry. Tall ascenders characterise this type, which is basically old face, but has ranging figures.

ABCDEFGHIJKLMNOPQRSTU VWXYZ

abcdefghijklmnopqrstuvwxyz   1234567890

ABCDEFGHIJKLMNOPQRSTUVWXYZ

abcdefghijklmnopqrstuvwxyz   1234567890

GENZSCH ANTIQUA

ABCDEFGHIJKLMNOPQRSTU VWXYZ

abcdefghijklmnopqrstuvwxyz   1234567890

GENZSCH ANTIQUA BOLD

A roman dating from *c.* 1790, perhaps from the Fry Foundry, but its early history is obscure. The serif formation and differentiation of colour are approaching the modern face. The capitals, in larger sizes, are rather heavy. Descenders are short. The **g** has a curled ear. The italic seems to be an earlier design, a Fry copy of CASLON ITALIC. *Cf.* the slope of the **A**, the swash **J** and **T**.

Linotype GEORGIAN designed by G.W. Jones (and VICTORIAN) are similar to the Stephenson Blake design, but there are a number of small differences, *e.g.* the serif on the lower arc of the **C** and the straight serifs on the arms of the **E**.

ABCDEFGHIJKLMNOPQRSTUVWXYZ

abcdefghijklmnopqrstuvwxyz   123456789

ABCDEFGHIJKLMNOPQRSTUVWXYZ

ABCDEFGHIJKLMNOPQRSTUVWXYZ

abcdefghijklmnopqrstuvwxyz   234567890

LINOTYPE GEORGIAN

GLOBUS CURSIVE

Stempel 1932

iv

Designed by Friedrich Wobst. A fat face italic or script. In the lower case there are not the usual flat serifs, but hooks. The **g** has an open tail. This appears to be a separate face.

Continental Regenmäntel

GLOBUS CURSIVE

GOLDEN COCKEREL TYPE

Golden Cockerel Press 1929

ii

Designed by Eric Gill, a rounder form of his PERPETUA. It has the modest capitals, horizontal serifs and slight differentiation of colour of Gill's other romans. The **M** is somewhat splayed. The **g** has a rather large bowl. The **t** is very short. The italic, cut only for the 14 pt. size, is a sloped roman except for the **a** and with it are used the roman capitals, as in the case of JOANNA.

ABCDEFGHIJKLMNOPQuRSTUVWXYZ

abcdefghijklmnopqrstuvwxyz

abcdefghijklmnopqrstuvwxyz

1234567890

GOLDEN COCKEREL TYPE

GOLDEN TYPE

Kelmscott Press 1890

Designed by William Morris and of importance in the history of modern typography since it began the revolution which has taken place in the design of our type faces. The punches were cut by E.P. Prince and the first book in which it was used was the *Golden Legend*, 1892.

Morris tells us that there was only one source in which to find the model for his first roman, namely, the printers of fifteenth-century Venice and especially Nicolas Jenson. The designer reinforced the type, made it a blacker face than the model and in particular weighted the serifs on the lower case. The **g** is a narrower letter and has an incorrect ear.

American Typefounders made a copy of this type before 1900 and called it NICOLAS JENSON.

All Morris's punches and matrices and some of the types are now in the possession of the Cambridge University Press.

i

Next as to type. By instinct rather than by conscious thinking it over, I began by getting myself a fount of Roman type. And here what I wanted was letter pure in form; severe, without needless excrescenses; solid without the thickening and thinning of the line, which is the essential fault of the ordinary modern type, and which makes it difficult to read; and not compressed laterally, as all later type has grown to be

ABCDEFGHIJKLMNOPQRSTUVWXYZ

abcdefghijklmnopqrstuvwxyz

1234567890

GOLDEN TYPE

GOLDRUSH

Bruce c. 1885

v

A three-dimensional rather square slab serif type of Victorian style. NUBIAN (not the American Typefounders' version) is very similar.

ABCDEFGHIJKLMNO PQRSTUVWXYZ 1234567890

GOLDRUSH

Designed by H.R. Möller. Inline fat face capitals and figures. The white line occupies only a small portion of the main strokes. The letters are wide, especially **M** and **W**.

REGATTA is a similar face with horizontal inline. There are two parallel white lines.

MUSEOS   **ODAIR**

GOLF   REGATTA

Begun, says F.W. Goudy, in 1919. It is a Venetian in some respects, but it was intended as a Bold Face, and has the abbreviated descenders of such faces. The **H** has a high bar and there is the usual Goudy **Q**. In the lower case note the narrow **f** and the position of the dot over the **i** and **j**.

GOUDY ANTIQUE is the name, first applied to Caslon's RATDOLT ROMAN, but it was later applied to design No. 39, cut in 1930 by Goudy himself.

ABCDEFGHIJKLMNOPQRS TUVWXYZ
abcdefghijklmnopqrstuvwxyz

GOUDY ANTIQUE or RATDOLT ROMAN

Designed by Bruce Rogers in collaboration with Sol Hess and based on GOUDY NEWSTYLE of Lanston Monotype, 1920, as a type for the second Lectern Bible.

ABCDEFGHIJKLMNOPQRRSTUVWXYZ
abcdefghijklmnopqrstuvwxyz
1234567890

GOUDY BIBLE

Designed by Morris F. Benton as an adaptation of a basic Goudy design. GOUDY HANDTOOLED is a shaded letter based on this type.

ABCDEFGHIJKLMNOPQRSTUVW XYZ
abcdefghijklmnopqrstuvwxyz
1234567890

GOUDY CATALOGUE

Herds Judges

GOUDY HANDTOOLED

A type bolder than GOUDY BOLD and approaching COOPER BLACK. The serifs are less blurred. The M is wider than in Cooper. **Q** has the Goudy tail. The **e** has an oblique stroke to the eye; in the **b** the upright tapers to a point below the line. There is no italic.

LUDLOW BLACK, 1924, is a similar design and weight. The **e** is as in COOPER BLACK, but the **w** has no middle serif. Intertype RUGGED BLACK, 1929, is again similar, but more condensed.

ABCDEFGHIJKLMNOPQRSTUVWXYZ
abcdefghijklmnopqrstuvwxyz
1234567890
Italic for a Poster Job

LUDLOW BLACK

GOUDY
MODERN

*Lanston Monotype 1918;
Monotype 1928;
Caslon 1929*

ii/iv

The serifs are flat but strong and bracketed; the stress is neither vertical nor abrupt. The capitals are shorter than the ascenders. The shadow version is GOUDY OPEN.

ABCDEFGHIJKLMNOPQRSTUVWXYZ
abcdefghijklmnopqrstuvwxyz

ABCDEFGHIJKLMNOPQRSTUVWX
abcdefghijklmopqrstuvwxyz

GOUDY MODERN

The capitals were modelled on Renaissance lettering, as F.W. Goudy himself relates. The serifs are small. The lower case is marred, as the designer himself says, by its short descenders. The ear of the **g** projects upwards. The italic is nearly upright, in fact **m** and **n** are upright. Goudy's designs were cut by Robert Wiebking, as indeed most of his work after 1911 until 1926, whereafter Goudy also cut his own types. Several bold versions were designed by Morris F. Benton.

ABCDEFGHIJKLMNOPQRSTUVWXYZ
abcdefghijklmnopqrstuvwxyz
1234567890

ABCDEFGHIJKLMNOPQRSTUVWXYZ
abcdefghijklmnopqrstuvwxyz
ABCDEFGHIJKLMNOPQRSTUVWXYZ
abcdefghijklmnopqrstuvwxyz

GOUDY OLD STYLE

DINERS Engulfed

GOUDY BOLD ITALIC (1919)

Regal Interesting Place

GOUDY EXTRA BOLD (1925)

Designed by F.W. Goudy. A pen-drawn calligraphic roman. Note the slab serifs on the **A**, the open **G** and the pen-drawn **M**. The **a** is one-storeyed, the **g** has an open tail, and the **y** a calligraphic terminal.

GOUDY
THIRTY

ix

Before he died in 1947, Frederic W. Goudy, America's greatest and most prolific type designer, prepared the drawings for a new

GOUDY THIRTY

Designed by Frederic W. Goudy. Serifs on the capitals are unusual. There are a number of swash. Numerals range on the line.

GOUDYTYPE

*American
Typefounders 1916
Lanston Monotype*

i

New Story

GOUDYTYPE

Designed by F.W. Goudy and a revision of the first book face by this designer cut around 1905. FRANCISCAN is similar.

GOUDY
VILLAGE

Lanston Monotype 1936

iv

A B C D E F G H I J K L M N O P Q R S T U V W X Y Z

a b c d e f g h i j k l m n o p q r s t u v w x y z

1 2 3 4 5 6 7 8 9 0
1 2 3 4 5 6 7 8 9 0

A B C D E F G H I J K L M N O P Q R S T U V W X Y Z

a b c d e f g h i j k l m n o p q r s t u v w x y z

1 2 3 4 5 6 7 8 9 0

GOUDY VILLAGE

GRANJON

Mergenthaler Linotype;
Linotype (London)
1928–1931

Designed for Linotype under the supervision of George W. Jones. Although named after another French type designer, Robert Granjon, this roman is the best reproduction of the Garamond type we have. It was based on a sixteenth century Paris book printed in a roman which appears under the name GARAMOND on a specimen sheet of the Egenolff-Berner foundry at Frankfurt, 1592. The capitals are tall in comparison with BEMBO, but sufficiently narrow and light to prevent their being too conspicuous. The middle strokes of the **M** are slightly over-hanging, the bowl of the **P** is not closed, the **R** ends in a foot serif on the line. The lower-case Garamond **g** with a small bowl is well reproduced. The italic is less distinguished than the true old-face italics. The **A** is rather like CASLON. There is a straight shanked **h** and a number of swash capitals. The large bowl of the **g** differentiates this design from the "Garamond," so-called, italics. The Linotype & Machinery bold is also called BERNARD.

ii

ABCDEFGHIJKLMNOPQRSTUVWXYZ

abcdefghijklmnopqrstuvwxyz

1234567890   1234567890

ABCDEFGHIJKLMNOPQRSTUVWXYZ

abcdefghijklmnopqrstuvwxyz

1234567890   1234567890

ABCDEFGHIJKLMNOPQRSTUVWXYZ

GRANJON

ii

ABCDEFGHIJKLMNOPQRSTUVWXYZ

abcdefghijklmnopqrstuvwxyz

1234567890   1234567890

GRANJON BOLD

GRASSET

Deberny & Peignot 1898

Designed by Eugène Grasset. A roman rich in colour, partly derived from script. The blunt serifs are generally on the outside only, *e.g.*, in the F, H, M and P. The M is splayed. In the lower case similar serifs are found at the feet of letters. Note also the feet of **v** and **w** in both cases. The italic also has some unusual terminals on the capitals and on the ascender of the lower-case **t**.

ix

ABCDEFGHIJKLMN
OPQRSTUVWXYZ
abcdefghijklmnopqrstuvw
xyz   1234567890
ABCDEFGHIJKLMNOP
QRSTUVWXYZ
abcdefghijklmnopqrstuvw
xyz   1234567890

GRASSET

Designed by Herbert Thannhaeuser. A double inline roman. The main strokes have two white spaces. The stress is vertical and there is sharp variation of weight. The serifs are hair lines, and the thin strokes in general hair lines.

GRAVIRA

Schelter & Giesecke 1935

ix

A B C D E F G H I J K L M N O P Q R S T U V W X Y Z

GRAVIRA

A shaded bold roman. The serifs are thin and inclined on the lower case. In the lower case the **a** is one-storeyed, **b** has a foot serif and the eye of the **e** has an oblique stroke. The **g**, **v**, **w** and **y** are cursive forms like italic.

GRAVURE

American Typefounders
c. 1929

ix

Hosiery

GRAVURE

A type with some calligraphic qualities. The serifs are rather large, especially at the ends of the arms of **E**, **F** and **L** and on **S** and **T**. The right-hand stroke of the **A** and the middle strokes of **M** and **N** are pen-drawn and overlap. The serifs on the lower case are concave and descenders are short. The **g** has a nearly vertical ear and wide tail. The italic is the roman inclined, except for the terminals at the tops of some ascenders, which are pen strokes.

There are also Semi-Bold (Negra), Bold, Ornamented (Adornado) and initials. The ornamented titling fount resembles VESTA, but the serrated edges are on the left of the black strokes. Stevens Shanks call the ornamented version ROSART.

GRECO or
BRISTOL

Gans 1925; Stevens Shanks

ix

Que la suprema elegancia se consigue a base de sencillez y de sobriedad es un hecho innegable. En todas las

Que la suprema elegancia se consigue a base de sencillez y de sobriedad es un hecho innegable. En todas las artes

GRECO

Agrupación Deportiva Gans
FUNDACIÓN EGUILAR

Librería y Papelería Oriental
ESTACIÓN DE MADRID

GRECO BOLD

REGLAMENTO DE IMPRESORE

GRECO ADORNADO ROSART*

ix

ix

ix

Designed by William E. Fink. A very condensed elongated type in which the lower case has short ascenders and descenders. Rounded letters are slightly angular, and upstrokes very thin. Serifs are fine. The dots on **r** and **a** are elongated. The bar of the **A** is rather near the foot line.

GREENWICH

Ludlow 1940

iv

ABCDEFGHIJKLMNOPQRSTUVWXYZ&

abcdefghijklmnopqrstuvwxyz

1234567890

GREENWICH

Originally from the Vincent Figgins foundry, *c.* 1796, and with lower case and figures, as well as 42 pt. capitals added in 1925. A shaded roman with thin, flat serifs. The design is that of a modern face, with short ascenders and descenders.

GRESHAM

Stevens Shanks 1925

iv

ABCDEGHMRS13467

GRESHAM

GRIFFO
Officina Bodini 1928–30

ii

Designed by Giovanni Mardersteig for use in his private press. The design bears resemblance to DANTE and ZENO. Numerals are non-ranging.

ABCDEFGHIJKLMNOPQURRSTUVWXYZ

abcdefghijklmnopqrstuvwxyz

1234567890

ABCDEFGHIJKLMNOPQRRSTUVWXYZ

abcdefghijklmnopqrstuvwxyz

GRIFFO

GWENDOLIN
Monotype
for Gregynog Press 1935

i

Designed by Graily Hewitt and cut by The Monotype Corporation. In general this roman is humanist but reminiscent of the calligrapher in many of the serifs for example on the **E, L** and the feet of **m, n** and **u**. The capitals are mostly wide, especially the splayed **M. U** has the lower-case design. The lower-case **g** has a very broad tail and the **w** a cursive form.

ABCDEFGHIJKLMNOPRSTUVWXYZ

abcdefghijklmnopqrstuvwxyz

1234567890

GWENDOLIN

HAARLEMMER
Monotype c. 1938

ii

Designed by Jan van Krimpen, and commissioned in 1938 by the Vereeniging voor Druk- en Boekkunst. This originally private type was intended for an edition of the *Staten Bijbel* to be printed in small folio format. The type has the qualities of an old face. The serifs on the capitals are thin; on the lower case they are stronger and not quite horizontal. The capitals are wide, especially the **M**. The **g** has a large bowl. The italic is slightly inclined and has angular beginning strokes; the **g** has a calligraphic tail; **v** and **w** have cursive forms. Two styles of figures are provided.

ABCDEFGHIJKLMNOPQRSTUVWXYZÆŒ&

abcdefghijklmnopqrstuvwxyz

ABCDEFGHIJKLMNOPQRSTUVWXYZÆŒ&

abcdefghijklmnopqrstuvwxyz

HAARLEMMER

HADRIANO
Goudy 1918
Lanston Monotype 1929

vii

Designed by F.W. Goudy in 1918 for the Continental Typefounders Association after a Roman inscription seen in the Louvre. The **A** has an extended apex, the **M** is unusually wide and the **Q** has swash form. The serifs, here large, have the usual Goudy pen qualities.

This titling is heavier than FORUM. In 1930 Goudy cut a lower case for Hadriano (which is No. 71 in his *A Half Century of Type Design*).

ABCDEFGHIJKLMNOPQRS
TUVWXYZ&

HADRIANO

ABCDEFGHIJKLMNOP
QRSTUVWXYZ&
1234567890

HADRIANO STONECUT

110

Designed by Victor Hammer in 1923 for Klingspor together with a set of initials. In 1953 a NEW HAMMER UNCIAL, also known as AMERICAN UNCIAL, was issued, which stems from the new version cut by Nussbaumer in 1945. The characters go back to letter forms practised before black letter or roman were evolved.

ABCDEFGHIJKLMNOPQRSTUVWXYZ
abcdefghijklmnopqrstuvwxyz ch ck ff ß tt
1234567890 1234567890 &Et

HAMMER UNCIAL

Serifs are long and thin, and flat. The **g** has an ear like CASLON. Serifs in the italic are those of the roman.

Graphischer Zirkel   *Meißner Porzellan*

HÄRTEL

Chemical Industries

HÄRTEL BOLD

Designed by F.W. Kleukens. A roman with moderate variation of stress and very small serifs, flat and bracketed. The round letters, notably the capitals **G**, **O** and **Q**, have a pen-drawn quality. **A** and **H** have high bars. **M** and **U** (with the lower-case design) are narrow letters. The descenders are short. The round lower-case letters are wide.

Das Lob des Buches kann nie ausgesungen werde

Alle Jahrhunderte, alle großen Geister vereinige

HELGA ANTIQUA

A linear slab serif type.

ABCDEFGHIJKLMN
OPQRSTUVWXYZ
abcdefghijklmnopqrs
tuvwxyz
1234567890

HELLENIC WIDE

A tooling of NEW CASLON and a shaded letter resembling NARCISSUS. It may be distinguished by the more usual **a** and the **g**, on which the ear rises out of the top of the bowl.

Typographic World STEA

HERMES

HEROLD

Berthold 1901

ix

A bold condensed display type with foot serifs pointing right, following end nineteenth-century style.

ABCDEFGHIJKLMNOPQRSTUVWXYZ
abcdefghijklmnopqrstuvwxyz
1234567890

HEROLD

HESS BOLD

Lanston Monotype 1910

ii

Designed by Sol Hess, and not strictly a bold face, though the serifs are drawn to suit a bold type. The design is based on GOUDY LIGHT.

ABCDEFGHIJKLMNOPQRSTUVWX
YZ&ÆŒ
abcdefghijklmnopqrstuvwxyzæœ
fi fl ff ffi ffl 1234567890

ABCDEFGHIJKLMNOPQRSTUVWX
YZ&
abcdefghijklmnopqrstuvwxyz
fi fl ff ffi ffl 1234567890

HESS BOLD

**HESS
NEOBOLD**

Lanston Monotype 1933

ix

Designed by Sol Hess, cast in only one size, and intended as a thin-serifed companion face to light lineales of the period.

ABCDEFGHIJKL
MNOPQRSTUVWX
YZ&
1234567890

HESS NEOBOLD

112

Designed by Sol Hess to follow JENSON.

A B C D E F G H I J K L M N O P Q R S T U V
W X Y Z & Æ Œ

a b c d e f g h i j k l m n o p q r s t u v w x y z æ

fi fl ff ffi ffl

1 2 3 4 5 6 7 8 9 0

ABCDEFGHIJKLMNOPQRSTUVWXYZ&ÆŒ

abcdefghijklmnopqrstuvwxyzæœ

fiflffffiffl

1234567890

HESS OLD STYLE

Designed by Friedrich Bauer. The serifs are sharp and rather long on the arms of the **E, L, S, Z** and on the **T**. They are similar in the lower case but oblique. The **W** has no middle serif. The **g** has the ear pointing north-east and a wide tail. The italic has the serifs of the roman. The **S** has curled terminals. The **a** is one-storeyed. There is also a Semi-Bold.

Wir fahren nach *Süden* allmählich von der arkadischen

Wir tun noch einen Blick auf die unbedeutenden Reste
HEYSE

Ausstellung von Reiseliteratur
HEYSE SEMI-BOLD

Designed by Stefan Schlesinger. A condensed reversed slab serif type similar to FIGARO and PLAYBILL.

ABCDEFGHIJKLMNOPQRSTUVWXYZ

1234567890

HIDALGO

Designed by Hiero Rhode, with the italic designed by Karl Hans Walter. The type is characterised by concave strokes and the variation in the stress is particularly apparent in the bold. Serifs are only slightly inclined. **E** and **F** have arms which extend over the vertical stroke.

ix

ABCDEFGHIJKLMNOPQRSTUVW
abcdefghijklmnopqrstuvwxyz
1234567890
*ABCDEFGHIJKLMNOPQRSTU
VWXYZ*
ABCDEFGHIJKLMNOPQRSTU
VWXYZ
*abcdefghijklmnopqrstuvwxyz
1234567890*

HIERO RHODE ROMAN

ix

**ABCDEFGHIJKLMNOPQRSTUV
abcdefghijklmnopqrstuvwxyz**

HIERO RHODE ROMAN BOLD

Ascenders are tall and there are two titlings. Upper- and lower-case **V** has a foot serif, and the bowl of the **P** is open.

ix

Nuevas ideas LUISA DE TAPIAS
Palma de Mallorca es

HISPALIS

ix

Ultimas Creaciones DE UNA MA

HISPALIS BOLD

ix

GRACIA Y UN

HISPALIS TITLING

ix

PRIMAVERA

HISPALIS BOLD TITLING

Designed by P.A. Demeter. Shaded roman capitals with thin, flat serifs. There is also a bold and an extended face.

HOLLÄNDISCH
Weber 1922–26

iii

ABCDEFGHIJKLMNOPQRS
TUVWXYZ 1234567890

HOLLÄNDISCH

BOZEN   SIEG   iii

HOLLÄNDISCH BOLD   HOLLÄNDISCH EXTENDED

Designed by S.H. De Roos. A Venetian with short descenders. There are slab serifs on the **A** and **M**. The **U** has the lower-case design. The **g** has a brief open tail. The italic is the roman inclined except for the cursive **v** and **w**. The figures are short-ranging.

There are also a bold, a condensed bold, and special initials.

Intertype called their now obsolete version MEDIAEVAL.

HOLLANDSE
MEDIAEVAL
Amsterdam 1912; Intertype

i

ABCDEFGHIJKLMNOPQRSTUV
abcdefghijklmnopqrstuvwxyz
1234567890

ABCDEFGHIJKLMNOPQRTSUVWXYZ
abcdefghijklmnoprstuvwxyz   1234567890

HOLLANDSE MEDIAEVAL

ABCDEFGHIJKLMNOPQRSTU
abcdefghijklmnopqrstuvwxyz

HOLLANDSE MEDIAEVAL SEMI-BOLD

i

ABCDEFGHIJKLMNOPQRSTUVWXYZ
abcdefghijklmnopqrstuvwxyz

HOLLANDSE MEDIAEVAL SEMI-BOLD CONDENSED

i

ABCDEFGHIJKLMNOPQRSTUVWXYZ
abcdefghijklmnopqrstuvwxyz 1234567890

ABCDEFGHIJKLMNOPQRSTUVWXYZ
abcdefghijklmnopqrstuvwxyz

INTERTYPE MEDIAEVAL

A B C D E F G H   ix

HOLLANDSE MEDIAEVAL INITIALS

115

Designed by K.F. Bauer and Walter Baum. A narrow roman combining several older alphabets in its design. The letters, with not very pronounced serifs, combine to give an even grey when formed into words. **L**, **P**, **E**, **B** and **S** are very narrow, the ascenders of some lower-case letters are higher than the caps, and the descenders of lower-case letters are short.

iv

ABCDEFGHIJKLMNOPQRSTUVWXYZ
abcdefghijklmnopqrstuvwxyz
123456789

ABCDEFGHIJKLMNOPQRSTUVWX
abcdefghijklmnopqrstuvwxyz
12345678

HORIZON

iv

ABCDEFGHIJKLMNOPQRSTUVWX
YZ
abcdefghijklmnopqrstuvwxyz
123456

HORIZON MEDIUM

iv

ABCDEFGHIJKLMNOPQRSTUV
WXYZ
abcdefghijklmnopqrstuvwxyz
1234567890

HORIZON BOLD

iv

ABCDEFGHIJKLMNOPQRSTUVWXYZ
abcdefghijklmnopqrstuvwxyz
1234567890

HORIZON BOLD CONDENSED

iv

ABCDEFGHIJKLMNOPQRSTUVWXYZ
abcdefghijklmnopqrstuvwxyz
1234567890

ABCDEFGHIJKLMNOPQRSTUVWXYZ
abcdefghijklmnopqrstuvwxyz
1234567890

INTERTYPE HORIZON

iv

ABCDEFGHIJKLMNOPQRSTUVWXYZ
abcdefghijklmnopqrstuvwxyz
1234567890

INTERTYPE HORIZON BOLD

The type has little differentiation of colour. The capitals are wide. **H** has a high bar. In the lower case serifs are inclined, **e** has an oblique stroke to the eye, **g** has the tail unclosed and the **t** is tall. There is also a heavy face and no italic.

ABCDEFGHIJKLMNOPQRSTUVWXYZ

abcdefghijklmnopqrstuvwxyz

1234567890

HORLEY OLD STYLE

ABCDEFGHIJKLMNOPQRSTUVWXYZ

abcdefghijklmnopqrstuvwxyz

1234567890

HORLEY OLD STYLE BOLD

Designed by Hermann Zapf as a private press type for the Hunt Botanical Library, of Pittsburg, Pennsylvania. A fine calligraphic roman of great clarity. Numerals are non-ranging.

ABCDÉFGHIJKLMÑOPQRSTÜVWXYZÆŒ

abcdefghijklmnopqrstuvwxyz

1234567890

HUNT ROMAN

Designed by Berthold Wolpe. An angular pen-lettered design, with several unusual letters. The right hand serifs of upper- and lower-case **V** and **W** run inwards, the **Y** descends below the line and has a pronounced serif running to the right.

ABCDEFGHIJKLMNOPQRSTUVW

XYZ abcdefghijklmnopqrstuvwxyz 123456

HYPERION

A narrow roman with short descenders and comparatively tall ascenders.

El Congreso de la Federación Gráfica

UNIVERSIDAD DE VALENCIA

Gremio Patronal de Tipógrafos, Cádiz

ECONÓMICO Y FINANCIERO

IBARRA

IBERICA
Nacional 1942

Designed by Carlos Winkow. An open and shaded, that is three-dimensional inclined lineale. Ascenders are tall. The middle and top bar of the A extend to the left.

ix

ABCDEFGHIJKLM
NOPQRSTUV
WXY&Z
abcdefghijklmnopqrst
uvwxyz
1234567890

IBERICA

IDEAL
Intertype; Amsterdam

This type closely follows IONIC and was first used in the Intertype version for *The New York Times*. Haas IDEAL is a condensed fat face and quite different. IDEAL NEWS is called PRESSA on the Continent.

iv

ABCDEFGHIJKLMNOPQRSTUVWXYZ
abcdefghijklmnopqrstuvwxyz
1234567890

ABCDEFGHIJKLMNOPQRSTUVWXYZ

abcdefghijklmnopqrstuvwxyz

AMSTERDAM IDEAL NEWS

ABCDEFGHIJKLMNOPQRSTUVWXYZ

abcdefghijklmnopqrstuvwxyz

AMSTERDAM IDEAL BOLD

iv

ABCDEFGHIJKLMNOPQRSTUVWXYZ
ABCDEFGHIJKLMNOPQRSTUVWXYZ
abcdefghijklmnopqrstuvwxyz
1234567890

ABCDEFGHIJKLMNOPQRSTUVWXYZ
abcdefghijklmnopqrstuvwxyz
1234567890

INTERTYPE IDEAL

ABCDEFGHIJKLMNOPQRSTUVWXYZ
abcdefghijklmnopqrstuvwxyz
1234567890

INTERTYPE IDEAL BOLD

ABCDEFGHIJKLMNOPQRSTUVWXYZ
abcdefghijklmnopqrstuvwxyz
1234567890
ABCDEFGHIJKLMNOPQRSTUVWXYZ
abcdefghijklmnopqrstuvwxyz
1234567890

IDEAL NEWS SPECIAL

ABCDEFGHIJKLMNOPQRSTUVWXYZ
abcdefghijklmnopqrstuvwxyz
1234567890

IDEAL NEWS SPECIAL BOLD

This Haas revival is a condensed semi-bold nineteenth-century design, which is almost a Fat Face. There is the usual long spur to the **G,** curled tail to the **R,** and long serifs in the **E, F** and **T.** Ascenders and descenders in the lower case are very short. *Cf.* CONTACT. The present design is cast from 1941 matrices, and the identical type is cast by Stempel, who call it JEANNETTE. The type is quite different from Amsterdam and Intertype IDEAL.

ABCDEFGHIJKLMNOPQRSTUVWXYZ
abcdefghijklmnopqrstuvwxyz
1234567890

IDEAL ROMAN

Designed by Edwin W. Shaar. A newspaper type with very short ascenders and descenders The serifs are slightly inclined and the stress is vertical. The italic has the serifs of the roman, and there is also a bold roman.

ABCDEFGHIJKLMNOPQRSTUVWXYZ
abcdefghijklmnopqrstuvwxyz
1234567890
ABCDEFGHIJKLMNOPQRSTUVWXYZ

ABCDEFGHIJKLMNOPQRSTUVWXYZ
abcdefghijklmnopqrstuvwxyz
1234567890

IMPERIAL

ABCDEFGHIJKLMNOPQRSTUVWXYZ
abcdefghijklmnopqrstuvwxyz
1234567890

IMPERIAL BOLD

IMPRESSUM

Amsterdam;
Bauer 1962; Adler Traldi

ii

Designed by Konrad F. Bauer and Walter Baum as a text type, with affinity to IMPRIMATUR.

ABCDEFGHIJKLMNOPQRSTUV
WXYZ
abcdefghijklmnopqrstuvwxyz
1234567890
ABCDEFGHIJKLMNOPQRSTUV
WXYZ
abcdefghijklmnopqrstuvwxyz
1234567890

IMPRESSUM

ii

ABCDEFGHIJKLMNOPQRSTUV
WXYZ
abcdefghijklmnopqrstuvwxyz
1234567890

IMPRESSUM BOLD

IMPRINT

Monotype 1913

A type cut for the periodical of the same name, instigated by Gerald Meynell, J.H. Mason, Ernest Jackson and Edward Johnston. It is modelled on CASLON but has a large x-height. The italic differs much more; the inclination has been regularised and the letters widened. It has lost the character of an independent letter but harmonises better with the roman, which is what printers now desire. There is also Imprint Shadow.

ii

ABCDEFGHIJKLMNOPQRSTUV
WXYZ
abcdefghijklmnopqrstuvwxyz
1234567890
ABCDEFGHIKLMNOPQRSTVYZ
abcdefghijklmnoqrstuvwxyz
1234567890

IMPRINT

ii

ABCDEFGHIJKLMNOPQRSTUVWXYZ
abcdefghijklmnopqrstuvwxyz 1234567890

IMPRINT BOLD (310)

ABCDEFGHIJKLMNOPQRSTUVWXYZ
abcdefghijklmnopqrstuvwxyz 12345
ABCDEFGHIJKLMNOPQRSTUVWXYZ
abcdefghijklmnopqrstuvwxyz 12345

IMPRINT BOLD (410)

ii

ABCDEFGHIJKLMNOPQRSTUV
abcdefghijklmnopqrstuvwxyz

IMPRINT SHADOW

120

A bold roman with short ascenders and descenders.

ABCDEFGHIJKLMNOPQRSTUVWXYZ

abcdefghijklmnopqrstuvwxyz

1234567890

INDUSTRIE ANTIQUA

INDUSTRIE
ANTIQUA
*Wagner;
Linotype* (*Frankfurt*)

iv

The **A** is very narrow, and so are the **M** and **N**. The top serifs of the **T** are pointed out-wards. The **G** has a spur and the **R** a curved tail. In the lower case serifs are finer. Ascenders and descenders are comparatively short. Lower-case letters in the italic have very round hair lines.

INGLÉS
Nacional

iv

construída en la terminación de la calle de Alcalá por
SOCIEDAD ESPAÑOLA DE PAVIMENTACIONES
CAPACIDAD CREADORA DE DIVERSOS IDEALES POLÍTICOS
*El entendimiento corto y el alma algo pequeña de ciertos
críticos pueden asustar a ingenios por demás eminentes*
VIAJE ALREDEDOR DEL MUNDO EN BALANDRO

INGLÉS

Designed by Raffaello Bertieri and based on the roman of Erhard Ratdolt. There are slab serifs on **A**, **M** and **N**. In the **G** the thickest part of the curve is unusually low. The **h** has a curved shank, a form which disappeared with Nicolas Jenson. The italic has swash capitals and a large bowl in the **g**. There are also shaded capitals and a titling.

INKUNABULA
Nebiolo 1911

Raffaello dipinse quarantadue Madonne e fra

Prescindendo dalle funzioni strategiche, navali

INKUNABULA

i

The first IONIC was a bold face cut by Caslon and shown 1842. The original design is similar to Beasley's EXTENDED CLARENDON. It has been revived as a suitable newspaper type. With its strong serifs it has been found to be legible in small sizes (No. 1 in the "Linotype Legibility Group"). It has short ascenders and descenders and considerable differentiation of colour. The eye of the **e** is large.

Linotype IONIC was introduced in 1926 in the *Newark Evening News*, and Intertype later cut their version of IDEAL for the *New York Times*. There is also The Monotype Corporation's version of IONIC.

IONIC
*Mergenthaler Linotype 1925;
Linotype* (*London*); *Monotype
Simoncini*

ABCDEFGHIJKLMNOPQRSTUVWXYZ
abcdefghijklmnopqrstuvwxyz 1234567890
ABCDEFGHIJKLMNOPQRSTUVWXYZ
abcdefghijklmnopqrstuvwxyz 1234567890
ABCDEFGHIJKLMNOPQRSTUVWXYZ

LINOTYPE IONIC

iv

ABCDEFGHIJKLMNOPQRSTUVWXYZ
abcdefghijklmnopqrstuvwxyz 1234567890

LINOTYPE IONIC BOLD

iv

ITALIANA CURSIVA
Gans

A condensed reversed slab serif type with the serifs heavier than the main strokes, and similar to MAGNET.

v

Sindicato Provincial del Metal

ITALIENNE
Française

A revival of an early reversed Egyptian. The founders give the date as 1820. The English founders called the design French Antique and the earliest English fount, according to Mrs. N. Gray's *Nineteenth Century Ornamental Types*, was considerably later than 1820.

v

furieuse tempête dans les mers du sud
IMPRESO COMERCIAL, PUBLICITARIO

ITALIENNE

JANSON
Mergenthaler Linotype 1937;
Stempel;
Linotype (London);
Linotype (Frankfurt);
Lanston Monotype

Another type which has been misnamed. The original dates from about 1690 and was cut by Nicholas Kis, a Hungarian in Amsterdam. The original matrices have survived in Germany and have since 1919 been held by the Stempel foundry. The type was not cut by Anton Janson, a Dutchman who worked at Leipzig. In the upper case the **M** is an easily remembered letter and in the lower case the **g**, which has a curved ear. In general the thin strokes are thinner than in earlier types. In the italic the **m** and **n** are more squared up. Note also the curves of the **v** and **w**. The Linotype version follows the original and was designed under the direction of C.H. Griffith. The Monotype Corporation's EHRHARDT (because the original types were in the Ehrhardt Foundry at Leipzig in the early eighteenth century) is a version of this type. Herman Zapf has redesigned some of the weights and sizes for Stempel, basing his revisions on the original type.

ii

ABCDEFGHIJKLMNOPQRSTUVW
abcdefghijklmnopqrstuvwxyz
1234567890
ABCDEFGHIJKLMNOPQRSTUVWXY
abcdefghijklmnopqrstuvwxyz

STEMPEL JANSON

ii

ABCDEFGHIJKLMNOPQRSTUVWXYZ
abcdefghijklmnopqrstuvwxyz
1234567890   1234567890
ABCDEFGHIJKLMNOPQRSTUVWXYZ
ABCDEFGHIJKLMNOPQRSTUVWXYZ
ABCDEFGHIJKLMNOPQRSTUVWXYZ
abcdefghijklmnopqrstuvwxyz
1234567890   1234567890
ABCDEFGHIJKLMNOPQRSTUVWXYZ
Recut Italic: abcdefghijklmnopqrstuvwxyz

LINOTYPE JANSON

ABCDEFGHIJKLMNOPQRSTUVWXYZ

abcdefghijklmnopqrstuvwxyz

1234567890

ABCDEFGHIJKLMNOPQRSTUVWXYZ

abcdefghijklmnopqrstuvwxyz

1234567890

MERGENTHALER LINOTYPE JANSON

Designed by Jos W. Phinney for American Typefounders (also called NICOLAS JENSON) and a copy of Morris's GOLDEN TYPE.

The Monotype Corporation's ITALIAN OLD STYLE with which the display sizes of the quite different VERONESE are combined, has a companion bold face. The ITALIAN OLD STYLE of F.W. Goudy is another re-cutting, made for the Lanston Monotype. It has an unusual italic with some swash capitals.

JENSON or
ITALIAN
OLD STYLE

Stephenson Blake;
Monotype;
Lanston Monotype;
American Typefounders

i

ABCDEFGHIJKLMNOPQRSTUVWX

abcdefghijklmnopqrstuvwxyz

1234567890

ABCDEFGHIJKLMNOPQRSTUVWXYZ

abcdefghijklmnopqrstuvwxyz

1234567890

ITALIAN OLD STYLE

ABCDEFGHIJKLMNOPQRSTUVWXYZ

abcdefghijklmnopqrstuvwxy

MERGENTHALER JENSON

ABCDEFGHIJKLMNOPQRSTUVWXYZ

abcdefghijklmnopqrstuvwxyz

1234567890

ITALIAN OLD STYLE BOLD

A B C D E F G H I J K L M N O P Q R S

T U V W X Y Z

a b c d e f g h i j k l m n o p q r s t u v w x y z

1 2 3 4 5 6 7 8 9 0

JENSON CONDENSED

JESSEN
Stempel

ix

Designed by Rudolf Koch in 1930 for Klingspor, and cut by the artist as a type for the setting of the Bible. The A has a wide bar at the top, and the S vertical serifs. Lower-case characters lean on black letter forms.

ĀBCDEFGHIJKLMNOPQRSTUV WXYZ
abcdefghijklmnopqrſstuvwxyz
1234567890 &

JESSEN

JOANNA
Monotype 1958

Designed by Eric Gill for Hague & Gill in 1930. A light roman with small horizontal serifs and little differentiation of colour. The type is remarkable for the smallness of the capitals, which do not reach the height of the ascenders, themselves not tall. The bowl of the **g** is rather large. The italic is the roman inclined except for **a** and **g**. The inclination is very slight. There are no specially cut capitals, but the modest roman capitals are used. This was the practice of Aldus, the first printer to use italic. Eric Gill's *Essay on Typography*, 1931 is printed in Joanna.

ii/iv

as a man who does not know his road can only be on it by accident), so a good clear training in the making of normal letters will enable a man to indulge more efficiently in fancy and impudence.

(Figure 17 : 1, normal sans-serif; 2–5, unseemly abnormalities & exaggerations; 6, normal with serifs; 7, normal bold; 8, overbold and fatuous; 9–13, 15 and 16, seemly 'fancy' varieties of the normal; 14 & 17, R's with normal

HAGUE & GILL JOANNA

ii/iv

ABCDEFGHIJKLMNOPQRSTUVWXYZ
abcdefghijklmnopqrstuvwxyz
1234567890
ABCDEFGHIJKLMNOPQRSTUVWXYZ
abcdefghijklmnopqrstuvwxyz
1234567890

MONOTYPE JOANNA

JOHN HANCOCK
Lanston Monotype 1909

iv

A bold roman originally cut by the Keystone Type Foundry in 1905. A condensed version was added in 1917.

ABCDEFGHIJKLMNOPQRSTUVWXYZ&ÆŒ
abcdefghijklmnopqrstuvwxyzæœ   fiflfffiffl
1234567890

JOHN HANCOCK

iv

ABCDEFGHIJKLMNOPQRSTUVWXYZ
abcdefghijklmnopqrstuvwxyz
1234567890

JOHN HANCOCK CONDENSED

Designed under the direction of Walter Tracy, it was first used by the *Glasgow Herald*. It is not to be confused with Stephenson Blake's JUBILEE, which was designed by Eric Gill. A roman with moderate stress and slightly inclined serifs. Ascenders and descenders are short. There is no middle serif on the **W**. The numerals are ranging. The bold has much greater variation of stress.

JUBILEE

Linotype (London) 1954

ii

ABCDEFGHIJKLMNOPQRSTUVWXYZ

abcdefghijklmnopqrstuvwxyz

1234567890

ABCDEFGHIJKLMNOPQRSTUVWXYZ

ABCDEFGHIJKLMNOPQRSTUVWXYZ

abcdefghijklmnopqrstuvwxyz

1234567890

JUBILEE

ABCDEFGHIJKLMNOPQRSTUVWXYZ

abcdefghijklmnopqrstuvwxyz

12345 67890

ii

JUBILEE BOLD

Designed by S.L. Hartz as a book type. The characters are fairly narrow. The **C** has two serifs, the **U** has arms of equal weight, the **W** is crossed. The **b** has a foot serif, **i** and **j** have diamond dots. The italic is calligraphic in style but fairly upright.

JULIANA

Linotype (London) 1958

ii

ABCDEFGHIJKLMNOPQRSTUVWXYZ

abcdefghijklmnopqrstuvwxyz

1234567890

ABCDEFGHIJKLMNOPQRSTUVWXYZ

ABCDEFGHIJKLMNOPQRSTUVWXYZ

abcdefghijklmnopqrstuvwxyz

1234567890

JULIANA

Shaded italic capitals and figures, very like Peignot's FOURNIER LE JEUNE. The serifs themselves are ornamented, by which the type may be distinguished. JUNE is rather more ornamented in the serifs than Fournier.

JUNE

Stephenson Blake 1927

ix

ABCDEFGHIJKLMN
OPQRSTUVWXYZ&

1234567890

ix

JUNE

Inline capitals. The letters are rather wide and have thin bracketed serifs.

JUNO

Amsterdam

iv

ABCDEFGHIJKLMNOPQRSTU
VWXYZ
1234567890

JUNO

KAATSKILL
Lanston Monotype 1929

Designed by F.W. Goudy, originally for an edition of Washington Irving's *Rip van Winkle*. The bowls of the **C**, **D**, **G** and **O** have high arches and similar arches are in the **m** and **n**. The **Q** has the characteristic Goudy tail.

ii

ABCDEFGHIJKLMNOPQRSTUVWXYZ

abcdefghijklmnopqrstuvwxyz

1234567890

KAATSKILL

KALAB
Grafotechna

Designed by Method Kalab. A roman with fine straight serifs and thin hairlines. Figures are ranging.

ii

A B C D E F G H I J K L M N O P Q R
S T U V W X Y Z
a b c d e f g h i j k l m n o p q r s t u v w
x y z
1 2 3 4 5 6 7 8 9 0

KALAB

KARNAK
Ludlow 1931–42

Designed by R.H. Middleton. **A** has a slab serif, **G** no spur and in **M** the middle strokes stop short of the line. **a** has the lower-case design but no top serif, **g** an open tail and **t** a foot serif on the right only. There is an italic. There are some additional round capitals. There are four weights, and condensed faces, one being called OBELISK.

v

ABCDEFGHIJKLMNOPQRSTUVWX
YZ&
abcdefghijklmnopqrstuvwxyz
1234567890

KARNAK LIGHT

v

ABCDEFGHIJKLMNOPQRSTUVW
XYZ&
abcdefghijklmnopqrstuvwxyz
1234567890

*ABCDEFGHIJKLMNOPQRSTUVW
XYZ&
abcdefghijklmnopqrstuvwxyz
1234567890*

KARNAK INTERMEDIATE

ABCDEFGHIJKLMNOPQRSTUV
WXYZ&
abcdefghijklmnopqrstuvwxyz
1234567890

KARNAK

KARNAK MEDIUM

ABCDEFGHIJKLMNOPQRSTUV
WXYZ&
abcdefghijklmnopqrstuvwxyz
1234567890

KARNAK BLACK

ABCDEFGHIJKLMNOPQRSTUVWXYZ&
abcdefghijklmnopqrstuvwxyz
1234567890

KARNAK BLACK CONDENSED

ABCDEFGHIJKLMNOPQRSTUVWXYZ&
abcdefghijklmnopqrstuvwxyz
1234567890

KARNAK OBELISK

Designed by F.W. Goudy for the New York publisher Mitchell Kennerley in 1911 and cut by Robert Wiebking. Short ascenders and descenders. Note the spur on the **G**, the high bar on the **H**, the tail of the **Q** and **R**. The italic is almost upright and has a pen quality common to most of the Goudy italics.

Intertype KENNTONIAN was another version of this type.

KENNERLEY
Lanston Monotype;
Caslon 1930

BCDEFGHIJKLMNOPQRSTUVW
abcdefghijklmnopqrstuvwxyz
BCDEFGHIJKLMNOPQRSTUVW
abcdefghijklmnopqrstuvwxyz

KENNERLEY

ABCDEFGHIJKLMNOPQRSTU VW
abcdefghijklmnopqrstuvwxyz
123456 7890&£

INTERTYPE KENNTONIAN

127

KEYBOARD
Stephenson Blake 1951

A condensed and elongated slab serif type with thin serifs.

iv

ABCDEFGHIJKLMNOPQRSTUVWXYZ

abcdefghijklmnopqrstuvwxyz

1234567890£

KEYBOARD

iv

ABCDEFGHIJKLMNOPQRSTUVWXYZ

abcdefghijklmnopqrstuvwxyz

1234567890£

KEYBOARD LIGHT

KING'S FOUNT
Vale Press 1903

Another black face with heavy serifs and a number of uncial letters, designed by Charles Ricketts. It was first used in an edition of the King's (James I of Scotland) Quair. In the upper case E has the uncial form and in the lower case **a**, **e**, and **g**. **f**, **r** and **t** have the designs of capitals. An exotic, surpassed only by the ENDEAVOUR and PRAYER BOOK types.

ix

Erectus his sermonibus, consulere pruden-
tiores cœpi ætates tabularum, et quædam
argumenta mihi obscura, simulque causam de-
sidiæ præsentis excutere, quum pulcherrimæ
artes periissent, inter quas pictura ne mini-

KING'S FOUNT

KINGSTON
Stephenson Blake

A bold roman with rather thick serifs. Thick and thin strokes meet at an angle. The eye of the **e** is almost square. Descenders are short.

iv

ABCDEFGHIJKLMNOPQRSTUV

abcdefghijklmnopqrstuvwxyzæœ

KINGSTON BOLD*

KLANG
*Monotype 1955;
Stephenson Blake*

Designed by Will Carter. A slightly inclined and slightly shaped sans serif with short ascenders and descenders; Stephenson Blake also have a bold. LYDIAN has some letters that are similar in design.

ix

ABCDEFGHIJKLMNOPQRSTUVWXYZ

abcdefghijklmnopqrstuvwxyz

12345

KLANG

ix

ABCDEFGHIJKLMNOPQRSTUVWXYZ

abcdefghijklmnopqrstuvwxyz

1234567890

STEPHENSON BLAKE KLANG BOLD

Designed by F. W. Kleukens. An angular narrow roman of large x-height.

KLEUKENS
ANTIQUA
Bauer c. 1900

ix

ABCDEFGHIJKLMN OPQRSTUVWXYZ

abcdefghijklmnopq
rſsßtuvwxyz
1234567890

KLEUKENS ANTIQUA

Designed by S. Duda, K. Misek and J. Tyfa. A text face in two weights with one italic. There is little variation in stress. The **b** has a pointed spur. The italic has roman serifs and the figures are ranging.

KOLEKTIV
Grafotechna 1952

iii

ABCDEFGHIJKLMNOPQRS
TUVWXYZ
abcdefghijklmnopqrstuvwxyz
1234567890
ABCDEFGHIJKLMNOPQRS
TUVWXYZ
abcdefghijklmnopqrstuvwxyz
1234567890

KOLEKTIV

iii

ABCDEFGHIJKLMNOPQRS TUVWXYZ abcdefghijklmnopqrstuvwxyz 1234567890

KOLEKTIV BOLD

KOLONIAL
Woellmer

A heavy display type similar to POST OLD ROMAN. It is somewhat condensed and has short ascenders and descenders. Serifs are thick, blunt and horizontal (except on the **d**). The **K** has a very high waist, the middle strokes of the **M** descend only half-way, the **R** has a tapering tail. The ear of the **g** points north-east. The arches of the **h**, **m** and **n** are splayed. The italic has the serifs of the roman and some swash capitals. There are also a Shaded and an Extended face.

Before World War II the type was also sold as COLUMBIA by the Amsterdam Typefoundry, and is the BUFFALO of the H.C. Hansen Foundry of Boston. It belongs with MORLAND (BLANCHARD of the Inland Type Foundry) to the group of heavy display types of which many American foundries had their own version.

ix

ABCDEFGHIJKLMNO
PQRSTUVWXYZ
abcdefghijklmnopq
rſßstuvwxyz
1234567890

KOLONIAL

ix

ABCDEFGHIJKLMNOPQ
RSTUVWXYZ
abcdefghijklmnopqrſßstu
vwxyz
1234567890

KOLONIAL CONDENSED

KOMPAKT
Stempel 1954

Designed by Hermann Zapf. A fat, slightly inclined roman of large x-height and with short descenders and ascenders. The dots on **i** and **j** are diamond-shaped.

ix

ABCDEFGHIJKLM
NOPQRSTUVWXYZ

KOMPAKT

130

abcdefghijklmnopq rst uvwxyz 1234567890

KOMPAKT

Designed by F. H. Schneidler as a bold titling type.

DAS ROSTFREIE UND TAFEL IDEAL=METALL SÄUREFESTE FÜR KÜCHE

KONTRAST

Designed by Albert Augspurg. A monotone display roman. Some of the capitals in design resemble the capitals of SCHWABACHER. The lower case is without serifs and vertical strokes are cut off at an angle. The **e** has an oblique stroke to the eye and the **g** a short open tail. There is also a Bold.

ABCDEF abcdefghch

KRIMHILDE

A narrow roman text and display type designed by Akke Kumlien. There are slab serifs on the ascenders, and also on some lower-case letters like **i, u, n, m,** and **r.** Foot serifs of **d, a,** and **u** point upwards. The tail of the **R** is straight. The italic has calligraphic qualities and is also supplied with swash caps. There are two weights.

ABCDEFGHIJKLMNOPQRST abcdefghijklmnopqrstuvwxyz 1234567890 *ABCDEFGHIJKLMNOPQRSTUVW abcdefghijklmnopqrstuvwxyz 1234567890*

KUMLIEN

ABCDEFGHIJKLMNOPQRS
abcdefghijklmnopqrstuvwxyz
1234567890

KUMLIEN BOLD

LAFAYETTE
Ludlow 1932

Designed by R. Hunter Middleton. An extra condensed bold roman with fine serifs. The dots on **i** and **j** are square.

ABCDEFGHIJKLMNOPQRSTUVWXYZ&
abcdefghijklmnopqrstuvwxyz
1234567890

LAFAYETTE

LANDI
Nebiolo 1939–43

This type is shown under its original name WELT.

LANDI ECHO, designed by A. Butti, is a slab serif type with inclined inline. LANDI LINEAR, designed by A. Novarese, is an outline type with black horizontal feet and tops of letters.

v

ABCDEFGHIJK LMNOPQRST UVXYZW 1234567890

LANDI LINEAR

v

ABCDEFGHIJK LMNOPQRST UVXYZW 1234567890

LANDI ECHO

LARGO
Ludwig & Mayer

A set of roman capitals with very small serifs. Many letters, notably the **A**, **H** and **M** (which is splayed) are very wide.

vii

ABCDEFGHIJKLMNOP QRSTUVWXYZ 1234567890

LARGO

ABCDEFGHIJKLMNO PQRSTUVWXYZ 1234567890

LARGO BOLD

ABCDEFGHIJKLMNOP QRSTUVWXYZ& 1234567890

LARGO OPEN

The type is characterised by horizontal serifs, cut to a point and connected to the main strokes by a stout triangular piece. Ascenders and descenders are short.

ABCDEFGHIJKLMNOPQRSTUVWXYZ&

abcdefghijklmnopqrstuvwxyz

1234567890

MONOTYPE LATIN ANTIQUE

ABCDEFGHIJKLMNOPQRSTUVWXYZ&

abcdefghijklmnopqrstuvwxyz

1234567890

MONOTYPE LATIN ANTIQUE No. 2

ABCDEFGHIJKLMNOPQRSTUVWXYZ&

abcdefghijklmnopqrstuvwxyz

1234567890

MONOTYPE LATIN ANTIQUE No. 3

ABCDEFGHIJKLMNOPQRSTUVWXYZ&

abcdefghijklmnopqrstuvwxyz

1234567890

MONOTYPE LATIN ANTIQUE No. 4

ABCDEFGHIJKLMNOPQRSTUVWXYZ abcdefghijklmnopqrstuvwxyz 1234567890

MONOTYPE LATIN CONDENSED

**LATIN
ANTIQUE**

ix

ABCDEFGHIJKL MNOPQRSTUVW XYZ

abcdefghijklmnop qrstuvwxyz

STEPHENSON BLAKE WIDE LATIN

LAUDIAN

Monotype

ii

ABCDEFGHIJKLMNOPQRSTUVWXYZ&ÆŒ

abcdefghijklmnopqrstuvwxyzfiflffffifflæœ

1234567890

ABCDEFGHIJKLMNOPQRSTUVWXYZÆŒ

ABCDEFGHIJKLMNOPQRSTUVWXYZ&ÆŒ

abcdefghijklmnopqrstuvwxyzfiflffffifiæœ

1234567890

LAUDIAN OLD STYLE

LAUREATE

Ludlow 1926

A bold display roman.

ABCDEFGHIJKLMNOPQRSTUV WXYZ&

abcdefghijklmnopqrstuvwxyz
1234567890

LAUREATE

LAUREL

Intertype (F) 1960

iv

A roman with the characteristics of a modern face, except for the **g** which resembles the CASLON **g**. The serifs are bracketed.

ABCDEFGHIJKLMNOPQRSTUVWXYZ&

abcdefghijklmnopqrstuvwxyz

1234567890   fi fl ff ffi ffl   1234567890

ABCDEFGHIJKLMNOPQRSTUVWXYZ&

ABCDEFGHIJKLMNOPQRSTUVWXYZ&

abcdefghijklmnopqrstuvwxyz

1234567890   fi fl ff ffi ffl   1234567890

LAUREL

ABCDEFGHIJKLMNOPQRSTUVWXYZ&

abcdefghijklmnopqrstuvwxyz

12345   fi fl ff ffi ffl   67890

ABCDEFGHIJKLMNOPQRSTUVWXYZ&

ABCDEFGHIJKLMNOPQRSTUVWXYZ&

abcdefghijklmnopqrstuvwxyz

12345   fi fl ff ffi ffl   67890

LAUREL BOLD

Adapted from EMERSON for 18-pt settings of Bibles, prayer-books, etc.

ABCDEFGHIJKLMNOPQRSTUVWXYZ

abcdefghijklmnopqrstuvwxyz

1234567890

LECTERN MISSAL

Designed by Dick Dooijes. A book type designed for improved legibility.

ABCDEFGHIJKLMNOPQRSTUVWXYZ

abcdefghijklmnopqrstuvwxyz

1234567890

ABCDEFGHIJKLMNOPQRSTUVWXYZ

abcdefghijklmnopqrstuvwxyz

1234567890

LECTURA

ABCDEFGHIJKLMNOPQRSTUVWXYZ

abcdefghijklmnopqrstuvwxyz

LECTURA BOLD

ABCDEFGHIJKLMNOPQRSTUVWXYZ

abcdefghijklmnopqrstuvwxyz

LECTURA BOLD CONDENSED

ABCDEFGHIJKLMNOPQRSTUV WXYZ

abcdefghijklmnopqr stuvwxyz   1234567890

ABCDEFGHIJKL MNOPQRSTUVWXYZ

abcdefghijklmnopqr stuvwxyz   1234567890

INTERTYPE LECTURA

ABCDEFGHIJKL MNOPQRSTUV WXYZ

abcdefghijklmnopqr stuvwxyz   1234567890

INTERTYPE LECTURA BOLD

LEIPZIG
Typoart 1963

ix

Designed by Albert Kapr and cut by Otto Erler. A text type of large x-height with angular characters.

ABCDEFGHIJKL MNOPQR
STUVWX YZ ÄÖÜ
abcdefghijklmnopqrsßtuvwx
yzäöüchckfift
1234567890
ABCDEFGHIJKLM NOPQRS
TUVWXY Z ÄÖÜ
abcdefghijk lmnopqrstuvwxy
zß&
1234567890

LEIPZIG

LETTRES ORNÉES
Deberny & Peignot

v

Richly decorated, three-dimensional capitals. The founders say from the "fonds de Gillé" and give the date as 1820. The English founder Edmund Fry showed somewhat similar letters in 1824.

LETTRES ORNÉES

LIBERTA
Typoart 1960

ii

Designed by Herbert Thannhaeuser. The **M** is splayed. The **g** has an open tail. The italic is slightly inclined and has roman serifs. The numerals are ranging. The italic has the serifs of the roman. There is a semi-bold.

ABCDEFGHIJKLMNOPQRSTUV
WXYZ&
abcdefghijklmnopqrstuvwxyz?
1234567890
ABCDEFGHIJKLMNOPQRSTUVW
XYZ&
abcdefghijklmnopqrstuvwxyz?
1234567890

LIBERTA

ABCDEFGHIJKLMNOPQRST UVWXYZ&
abcdefghijklmnopqrstuvwxyz?
1234567890

LIBERTA BOLD

ABCDEFGHIJKLMNOPQRSTUVWXYZ&
abcdefghijklmnopqrstuvwxyz?
1234567890

LIBERTA BOLD CONDENSED

This type face, designed by S.H. De Roos, closely follows the pattern of uncial scripts combining the liveliness of a lower case with the emphasis of a capital line. There are two weights.

aBcDefGhijklmnopqrstuvwxyz

LIBRA LIGHT

aBcDefGhijklmnopqrstuvwxyz
1234567890

LIBRA

A newspaper and text type designed for legibility. Angular points are exaggerated to compensate for loss of detail in reproduction.

ABCDEFGHIJKLMNOPQRSTUVWXYZ
abcdefghijklmnopqrstuvwxyz
1234567890
ABCDEFGHIJKLMNOPQRSTUVWXYZ
abcdefghijklmnopqrstuvwxyz
1234567890
ABCDEFGHIJKLMNOPQRSTUVWXYZ

LIFE

ABCDEFGHIJKLMNOPQRSTUVWXYZ
abcdefghijklmnopqrstuvwxyz
1234567890

LIFE BOLD

A condensed fat face of nineteenth-century design. The serifs are very small, but note the beak-like terminations in the **C, E, F, S** and **T**. *Cf.* SLIMBLACK.

ABCDEFGHIJKLMNOPQRSTUVWXYZÆŒ
abcdefghijklmnopqrstuvwxyzæœ
1234567890

LILIOM

LILITH
Bauer 1930

ix

Designed by Lucian Bernhard. A shaded fat face italic of a slight inclination. The capitals are further decorated with nodules. The ascending **b**, **h** and **k** are looped; the **l** and **t** have cleft tops.

Famous Pleasure Garden

LILITH

LINOTYPE MODERN
Linotype (London) 1969

iv

Designed by Walter Tracy as a newspaper type and first used by *The Daily Telegraph*. The type was designed to offer compensation for the effects of multiple moulding and high-speed printing on newsprint. Angles of strokes are almost unconnected. Crotches in v-angles of **M** and **W** have been enlarged.

ABCDEFGHIJKLMNOPQRSTUVWXYZ
abcdefghijklmnopqrstuvwxyz
1234567890
ABCDEFGHIJKLMNOPQRSTUVWXYZ
abcdefghijklmnopqrstuvwxyz
1234567890
ABCDEFGHIJKLMNOPQRSTUVWXYZ
LINOTYPE MODERN

iv

ABCDEFGHIJKLMNOPQRSTUVWXYZ
abcdefghijklmnopqrstuvwxyz
1234567890
LINOTYPE MODERN BOLD

LITURGICA
Flinsch

ix

Designed by Willy Wiegand for the *Missale Romanum* of Editio Lacensis, which was set by the Bremer Presse. The punches were cut by Louis Hoell.

In méntibus nostris, quæsumus, Domine, veræ fidei sacramenta Virgine Deum verum et hominem confirma: ut, qui conceptum de

LITURGICA

LOCARNO or KOCH ANTIQUA
Klingspor 1922

An unusual but popular roman designed by Rudolf Koch. The name is no doubt connected with political events of the year. The vertical strokes taper. Serifs are very small; on the tops of the ascenders they extend both ways. **A** is wide and has a high bar. **C**, **G**, **O** and **Q** are wide and round, while **B**, **E**, **F**, **P**, **R**, **S** and **T** are narrow. **U** has the lower-case design. The **M** is splayed. The lower case has extravagantly tall ascenders. The **a** has a pinched bowl, **e** an oblique bar. In the **g** the link between bowl and tail is omitted and the tail is open. **w** has no middle serif. The figures are short-ranging.
The italic called KOCH CURSIVE, has a shaded upper case. The lower case is the roman inclined except that **p** and **g** are without foot serifs. In spite of all its oddities the type has proved a success, but is no book type. RIVOLI is of very similar design.

ix

ABCDEFGHIJKLMNOPQRSTU
abcdefghijklmnopqrstuvwxyz
1234567890
LOCARNO

ix

ABCDEFGHIJKLMNOPQRSTU
abcdefghijklmnopqrstuvwxyz

LOCARNO BOLD

ABCDEFGHIJJKLMNOPQRSTUVWXYZ

abcdefghijklmnopqrstuvwxyzchckfffiflft

1234567890

ABDEGHKLMRS

A display face designed by M.F. Benton, based on a Bodoni model, but with the peculiarity found in a number of modernistic types of making the thicks and thins meet at an angle. This is especially noticeable in the **O** and **S**. The **g** and **y** have cursive tails. The italic is the roman inclined, except for **a**, which has a flat-foot serif, **v** and **w**. There are three weights, the light having the colour of a normal book type.

Mysterious Flight

Beautiful Drawing

iv

LOUVAINE LIGHT

Simple Design

iv

LOUVAINE MEDIUM

Quaint Styles

iv

LOUVAINE BOLD

A light design by Lucian Bernhard with unusually tall ascenders. The serifs are small and horizontal. All the capitals are wide. In the **M** the middle strokes stop short of the line, **Q** has an extravagant tail and the **W** is unusual. In the **g**, bowl and tail are equal and the ear rises out of the top of the bowl. In **p** and **q** the uprights are extended. The **s** has thickened terminals. The italic is the roman inclined including the **a**, but the **R** tapers.
There are bold, extra-bold and open faces. The extra-bold has an irregular outline. The roman is also known as BERNHARD ROMAN.

ABCDEFGHIJKLMNOPQRSTUVWXYZ

abcdefghijklmnopqrstuvwxyz

1234567890   1234567890

iv

ABCDEFGHIJKLMNOPQRSTUVWXYZ

abcdefghijklmnopqrstuvwxyz

1234567890   1234567890

LUCIAN LIGHT

ABCDEFGHIJKLMNOPQRSTUVWXYZ

abcdefghijklmnopqrstuvwxyz

1234567890

iv

ABCDEFGHIJKLMNOPQRSTUVWXYZ

abcdefghijklmnopqrstuvwxyz

1234567890

LUCIAN

ABCDEFGHIJKLMNOPQRSTUVWXYZ
abcdefghijklmnopqrstuvwxyz
1234567890
LUCIAN BOLD

ABCDEFGHIJKLMNOPQRSTUVWXYZ
abcdefghijklmnopqrstuvwxyz
1234567890
LUCIAN OPEN

LUDLOW
BLACK
Ludlow 1924

iv

Designed by R. Hunter Middleton. The type is similar to COOPER BLACK but the **w** has no middle serif.

ABCDEFGHIJKLMNOPQRSTU VWXYZ abcdefghijklmnopqrstuvwxyz 1234567

LUDLOW BLACK

LUNDA
Berling 1941

iv

Designed by K. E. Forsberg. An inclined roman or italic with short ascenders and descenders. The thins are hairlines and the letters have somewhat rigid appearance because of the straight hairlines.

ABCDEFGHIJKLMNOPQRSTUVW
abcdefghijklmnopqrstuvwxyzäöå

LUNDA

LUTETIA
Enschedé 1925;

Monotype 1928

ii

Designed by Jan van Krimpen. The type shares some of the qualities which we have found in a number of contemporary types, small serifs and unobtrusive capitals. The capitals are wide, note especially **E** and **F**. **U** has the lower-case design. In the lower case the **e** has an oblique stroke to the eye, the **g** a large bowl, and the **t** is very short. The figures are old style. In the italic there is a swash series of capitals with prolonged strokes in **A**, **K**, **M**, **N** and **R**. The lower case, very slightly inclined, resembles BLADO in the angularity of the begininng strokes, but the serifs on ascenders are flat. The **g** has a calligraphic form. It is an italic which, again like Blado, will stand on its own. The roman alphabet shown here is the first LUTETIA of 1925 designed 1923–24. With the co-operation of Jan van Krimpen an American printer, Porter Garnett, had it revised in 1928. The present Enschedé Lutetia is of the first form with the exception of the horizontal bar to the **e**, and was adapted by the designer for use on Monotype machines. Lutetia Open was cut about 1930 on the model of hand-tooled capitals which the designer had been using occasionally.

ABCDEFGHIJKLMNOPQ RSTUVWXYZÆŒQU&

abcdefghijklmnopqrsſtuvwxyz

1234567890   1234567890
LUTETIA

ABCDEFGHIJKLMNOPQRSTUVWXYZÆŒQU&

abcdefghijklmnopqrsʃtuvwxyz

1234567890   *1234567890*

A B C D E F G H I K M N P Q R T U V Y

ENSCHEDE LUTETIA ITALIC WITH CAPS AND SWASH CAPS

Designed by Warren Chappell. A pen-drawn type without serifs with the bars of the **A** and **H**, the arms of **E** and **F** and other strokes being thinner than the main strokes. Ascenders and descenders are short. Numerals are short ranging.

ABCDEFGHIJKLMNOPQRSTUVWXYZ

abcdefghijklmnopqrstuvwxyz

1234567890

ABCDEFGHIJKLMNOPQRSTUVWXYZ

abcdefghijklmnopqrstuvwxyz

1234567890

INTERTYPE LYDIAN

ABCDEFGHIJKLMNOPQRSTUVWXYZ

abcdefghijklmnopqrstuvwxyz

1234567890

ABCDEFGHIJKLMNOPQRSTUVWXYZ

abcdefghijklmnopqrstuvwxyz

1234567890

INTERTYPE LYDIAN BOLD

Designed by Louis Perrin about 1846. Serifs are small and bracketed. Letters vary in width, the round letters **C**, **D** and **O** being the wider. The **J** is short ranging, and the tail of the **R** tapers to a point. Perrin's original CARACTÈRES AUGUSTAUX included the lower case and numerals, but the capitals only seem to have been preserved.

TWENTY FOUR POINT LYONS TITLING FOUNDRY CAST IN

LYONS TITLING

Designed by Douglas C. McMurtrie. Shaded capitals with thin, flat serifs. It resembles NARCISSUS and is based on ROSART.

ABCDEFGHIJKLM

McMURTRIE TITLE

This type face, originally called AMTS-ANTIQUA, was redesigned in 1965 and is characterised by large x-height and strong serifs.

ABCDEFGHIJKLMNOPQRSTUVWXYZ
abcdefghijklmnopqrstuvwxyz
1234567890

ABCDEFGHIJKLMNOPQRSTUVWX
abcdefghijklmnopqrstuvwxyz
1234567890

MADISON

iv

ABCDEFGHIJKLMNOPQRSTU
abcdefghijklmnopqrstuvwxyz
1234567890

MADISON BOLD

iv

ABCDEFGHIJKLMNOPQRSTUVWXYZ
abcdefghijklmnopqrstuvwxyz
1234567890

MADISON CONDENSED

iv

ABCDEFGHIJKLMNOPQRSTUVWXYZ
abcdefghijklmnopqrstuvwxyz
1234567890

MADISON BOLD CONDENSED

Designed by Aldo Novarese as a text type of large x-height.

ABCDEFGHIJKLMNOPQRSTUVX
YZW
abcdefghijklmnopqrstuvxyzw
1234567890

ABCDEFGHIJKLMNOPQRSTUVX
YZW
abcdefghijklmnopqrstuvxyzw
1234567890

MAGISTER

ABCDEFGHIJKLMNOPQRSTUVX YZW
abcdefghijklmnopqrstuvxyzw
1234567890

MAGISTER BOLD

ABCDEFGHIJKLMNOPQ RSTUVWXYZ &
abcdefghijklmnopqrstuv wxyzß
1234567890

MAGISTER WIDE

A text type having narrow letters.

ABCDEFGHIJKLMNOPQRSTUVWXYZ
abcdefghijklmnopqrstuvwxyz ff fi fl ft &
1234567890

ABCDEFGHIJKLMNOPQRSTUVWXYZ
abcdefghijklmnopqrstuvwxyz ff fi fl ft &
1234567890

MAGNA

ABCDEFGHIJKLMNOPQRSTUVWXYZ
abcdefghijklmnopqrstuvwxyz ff fi fl ft &
1234567890

MAGNA BOLD

Designed by Arthur Murawski and based on the nineteenth-century ITALIENNE. A condensed type of heavy colour. The **g** has an open tail and ascenders and descenders are short.

ABCDEFGHIJKLMNOPQRSTUVWXYZ
abcdefghijklmnopqrstuvwxyz
1234567890

MAGNET

MAJESTIC
Bauer 1926

ix

Designed by R. Gipkens. A fat face with some flourishes and diamond-shaped dots on the **i**.

Eine Schrift von Wirkung

MAJESTIC

MAJESTIC
Mergenthaler Linotype 1953–56

iv

Designed by Jackson Burke. Another of the important newspaper types introduced in the 1950s and 60s, designed for teletypesetter operation.

ABCDEFGHIJKLMNOPQRSTUVWXYZ
abcdefghijklmnopqrstuvwxyz
12345 67890

ABCDEFGHIJKLMNOPQRSTUVWXYZ
abcdefghijklmnopqrstuvwxyz
12345 67890

MAJESTIC

iv

ABCDEFGHIJKLMNOPQRSTUVWXYZ
abcdefghijklmnopqrstuvwxyz
12345 67890

MAJESTIC BOLD

MANILA
Lanston Monotype 1909

iv

A bold text type with heavy serifs.

ABCDEFGHIJKLMNOPQRSTUVWXYZ&ÆŒ
abcdefghijklmnopqrstuvwxyzæœ fiflffffiffl
1234567890

MANILA

MANUSCRIPT
Grafotechna 1944–50

ix

Designed by Oldrich Menhart. A pen-drawn type closely following the designer's hand-writing. The lower-case italic is similar to that of FIGURAL. The **k** and the **x** in the roman have no right-foot serif, all letters have irregular outlines.

ABCDEFGHIJKLMNOPQRSTUVWXYZ
abcdefghijklmnopqrstuvwxyz
1234567890
ABCDEFGHIJKLMNOPQRSTUVWXYZ
abcdefghijklmnopqrstuvwxyz
1234567890

MANUSCRIPT

Named after the Venetian printer and publisher Aldus Manutius, but by no means a Venetian type! Instead, the design resembles IONIC or even SCHADOW. Unusual is the r in the italics which has a rounded foot pointing to the right, and the open design of some swash capital, like L, N, P, etc. Ascenders and descenders are short; and there are three weights.

MANUTIUS

L. Wagner

iv/v

ABCDEFGHIJKLMNOPQRSTUV
abcdefghijklmnopqrstuvwxyz
ABCDEFGHIJKLMNOPRSTUV
abcdefghijklmnopqrstuvwxy
ABCDEFGHIJKLMNOPRS

MANUTIUS WITH SWASH CAPITALS

ABCDEFGHIJKLMNOPQRSTUV
abcdefghijklmnopqrstuvwxyz

iv/v

MANUTIUS BOLD

ABCDEFGHIJKLMNOPQRSTUVWXYZ
abcdefghijklmnopqrstuvwxyz

iv/v

MANUTIUS EXTRA BOLD CONDENSED

Designed by Rudolf Koch. A roman with short ascenders and descenders. The serifs are small, but longer at the ends of the arms of E, F and L, M is rather splayed and is without top serifs, like the M in other types designed by Koch. The lower-case g has no link and an open tail, again like the g in other Koch types. U has the lower-case design. In the W the middle strokes cross; the lower case w has no middle serif. The figures are short-ranging.

MARATHON

Klingspor 1931

ii

ABCDEFGHIJKLMNOPQRSTUV
abcdefghijklmnopqrstuvwxyz
1234567890

MARATHON

A card titling with hair-line serifs. *Cf.* ORLANDO or ENGRAVERS' BODONI.

MARKO

Weber

iv

ABCDEFGHIJKLMNOPQRSTUVWXYZ
1234567890

MARKO

MASTERMAN
Lanston Monotype 1910

iv

A rather legible version of a bold variation of DORIC.

A B C D E F G H I J K L M N O P Q R S T U V
W X Y Z & Æ Œ

a b c d e f g h i j k l m n o p q r s t u v w x y z
æ œ fi fl ff ffi ffl

1 2 3 4 5 6 7 8 9 0

MASTERMAN

MATHEIS MOBIL
Ludwig & Mayer 1960

ix

Designed by Helmut Matheis. A design of medium weight which is almost without serifs and very nearly monotone. The letters are wide. The **T** has an unusual terminal, found also in the lower-case **r**. There are script qualities in many letters.

ABCDEFGHIJKLMNOPQRSTUVWXYZ
abcdefghijklmnopqrstuvwxyz
1234567890

MATHEIS MOBIL

MATRO NEWS
Matrotype 1968

iv

A newspaper text type designed for legibility and similar to OPTICON.

ABCDEFGHIJKLMNOPQRSTUVWXYZÆŒ
abcdefghijklmnopqrstuvwxyzæœ
1234567890

ABCDEFGHIJKLMNOPQRSTUVWXYZÆŒ
abcdefghijklmnopqrstuvwxyzæœ
1234567890

MATRO NEWS

MATURA
Monotype 1938

ix

Designed by Imre Reiner. A modified bold calligraphic type of sans serif style. It is not quite monotone nor entirely without serifs. **A** has a slab serif and there are serifs on the **C, N, S, V, W** and **Y**, and also on the lower-case **m** and **n**. The **a** is one-storeyed and the **g** has an open tail. There is also a set of scriptorial caps.

ABCDEFGHIJKLMNOPQRSTUVWXYZ&
abcdefghijklmnopqrstuvwxyz
£1234567890   ÆŒæœ   fifffl

MATURA

ix

ABCDEFGHIJKLMN
OPQRSTUVWXYZ

MATURA SCRIPTORIAL CAPITALS

Designed by Georg Trump. A roman with large x-height.

ABCDEFGHIJKLMNOPQRSTU VWXYZ
abcdefghijklmnopqrstuvwxyz
1234567890

MAURITIUS

ABCDEFGHIJKLMNOPQRSTUV WXYZ

abcdefghijklmnopqrstuvwxyz
1234567890

MAURITIUS ITALIC

ii

ABCDEFGHIJKLMNOPQRSTU VWXYZ

abcdefghijklmnopqrstuvwxyz
1234567890

MAURITIUS BOLD

ii

Designed by Rudolf Koch. A shaded series of capitals with ranging figures. The serifs are thin. The rounded letters, **C**, **O** and **Q**, have the thickest part low down. **M** is splayed and the inner strokes stop short of the line.

MERCHANTS SOCIE

MAXIMILIAN ANTIQUA

A newspaper type for classified advertising.

COMPANY actively engaged in the manufacture of mining equipment requires additional capital to finance current Government and like contracts. Enquiries from interested companies or individuals.— DIRECTOR of established financially sound firm, dealing retail stationers and stores only, apprehensive about rising cost travelling, seeks confiden-

ADELPHI. (Tem. 7611.) To-day, 2.30 & 7.30. ORIGINAL BALLET RUSSE. Aurora's Wedding. Presages. Prince Igor. SADLER'S WELLS. (Ter. 1672.) Evgs., 7. To-night The Barber of Seville. Wed. Il Trovatore. Thurs., Marriage of Figaro. Fri., School for Fathers. Sat., Madame Butterfly.

ABCDEFGHIJKLMNOPQRSTUVWXYZÆŒ abcdefghijklmnopqrstuvwxyzæœ fiflffffifl 1234567890
ABCDEFGHIJKLMNOPQRSTUVWXYZÆŒ abcdefghijklmnopqrstuvwxyzæœ fiflffffifl 1234567890

MAXIMUS

MEIDOORN

Heuvelspers 1927

Designed by S.H. de Roos. **A** and **M** have slab serifs. The **g** has a rather conspicuous tail and **p** and **q** have oblique foot serifs.

Cut by the German punchcutters Wagner & Schmidt in 14 pt only, the type was cast by Amsterdam Typefoundry for the exclusive use of the Heuvelspers. It is now the property of J.F. Duwaer & Zonen of Amsterdam.

i

Aa Bb Cc Dd Ee Ff Gg Hh Ii Jj Kk
Ll Mm Nn Oo Pp Qq Rr Ss Tt
Uu Vv Ww Xx Yy Zz

MEIDOORN

MEISTER

Typoart c. 1951

Designed by Herbert Thannhaeuser. Serifs are not very pronounced, and most strokes are expanded towards the ends. The **g** has an open tail in both the roman and italic, the **J** descends below the line and the **G** has no spur.

ix

ABCDEFGHIJKLMNOPQRSTUVWX
YZ&
abcdefghijklmnopqrſstuvwxyz?
1234567890
ABCDEFGHIJKLMNOPQRSTUVWX
YZ&
abcdefghijklmnopqrſstuvwxyz?
1234567890

MEISTER

ix

ABCDEFGHIJKLMNOPQ
RSTUVWXYZ

MEISTER INITIALS

ix

ABCDEFGHIJKLMNOPQRSTUVW
XYZ&
abcdefghijklmnopqrsſtuvwxyz?
1234567890

MEISTER BOLD

Designed by Hermann Zapf. A rather heavy roman with short ascenders and descenders. The **c** and **g** are rather square. The italic is the roman inclined except for the one-storeyed **a**, the **f** and the **k**.

MELIOR

Stempel 1952;

Linotype (Frankfurt)

iv

ABCDEFGHIJKLMNOPQRSTUVW
abcdefghijklmnopqrstuvwxyz
1234567890

ABCDEFGHIJKLMNOPQRSTUV
abcdefghijklmnopqrstuvwxyz

MELIOR

iv

ABCDEFGHIJKLMNOPQRSTUV
abcdefghijklmnopqrstuvwxyz

MELIOR BOLD

iv

ABCDEFGHIJKLMNOPQRSTUVWX
abcdefghijklmnopqrstuvwxyz

MELIOR BOLD CONDENSED

Designed by Rudolf Weiss. This is the earliest modern revival of the EGYPTIAN. In this design and in those that followed it there is a more thorough adoption of the slab serif, especially in the lower case. **A** has a slab serif; there is also a second **A** with a rounded top. **G** has a spur. In the **M** the middle strokes stop short of the line. In the lower case **a** has the one-storeyed form, with top and foot serifs on the right. **g** has a top serif instead of an ear and an open tail. There are two **f**'s and two **t**'s; in one there is a foot serif extending both ways. The italic is as the roman. There are four weights; and also condensed versions, an open and a three-dimensional letter called LUNA; the two latter designs cast by Stempel only.

MEMPHIS

Stempel 1929;
Mergenthaler Linotype
1935–36;
Linotype (London);
Linotype (Frankfurt)

v

ABCDEFGHIJKLMNOPQRSTUVWXYZ
abcdefghijklmnopqrstuvwxyz
1234567890
AJQ aafgt

ABCDEFGHIJKLMNOPQRSTUVWXYZ

ABCDEFGHIJKLMNOPQRSTUVWXYZ
abcdefghijklmnopqrstuvwxyz
1234567890
AJQ aafgt

ABCDEFGHIJKLMNOPQRSTUVWXYZ

LINOTYPE MEMPHIS LIGHT

v

ABCDEFGHIJKLMNOPQRSTUVWXYZ
abcdefghijklmnopqrstuvwxyz   1234567890
ABCDEFGHIJKLMNOPQRSTUVWX   AJQ   aafgt
ABCDEFGHIJKLMNOPQRSTUVWXYZ
abcdefghijklmnopqrstuvwxyz   1234567890
CDEFGHIJKLMNOPQRSTUVWXYZ   AJQ   aafgt

LINOTYPE MEMPHIS MEDIUM

v

ABCDEFGHIJKLMNOPQRSTUVWXYZ
abcdefghijklmnopqrstuvwxyz   1234567890
ABCDEFGHIJKLMNOPQRSTUVWX   AJQ   aafgt
ABCDEFGHIJKLMNOPQRSTUVWXYZ
abcdefghijklmnopqrstuvwxyz   1234567890
CDEFGHIJKLMNOPQRSTUVWXYZ   AJQ   aafgt

LINOTYPE MEMPHIS BOLD

v

ABCDEFGHIJKLMNOPQRSTUVWXYZ
abcdefghijklmnopqrstuvw   1234567890
AJQ   aafgt
ABCDEFGHIJKLMNOPQRSTUVWXYZ
defghijklmnopqrstuvwxyz   1234567890
AJQ   aafgt

LINOTYPE MEMPHIS EXTRA BOLD

v

ABCDEFGHIJKLMNOPQRSTUVWXYZ
abcdefghijklmnopqrstuvwxyz

STEMPEL MEMPHIS UNIVERSAL MEDIUM

v

ABCDEFGHIJKLMNOPQRSTUVWXYZ
abcdefghijklmnopqrstuvwxyz

STEMPEL MEMPHIS UNIVERSAL HEAVY

v

ABCDEFGHIJKLMNOPQRSTUVWXYZ
abcdefghijklmnopqrstuvwxyz

STEMPEL MEMPHIS UNIVERSAL BOLD

v

ABCDEFGHIJKLMNOPQRST

STEMPEL MEMPHIS OPEN

v

ABCDEFGHIJKLMNOP

STEMPEL MEMPHIS LUNA

Designed by Oldrich Menhart. A roman with small serifs, which are horizontal in the lower case, except on the tops of the ascenders. The italic has the serifs of the roman. The round letters and arcs have a certain angularity, and it is this angularity which is the most striking feature of the italic. Originally this type was cut for use in Czechoslovakia.

MENHART

Monotype 1938;
Grafotechna

ii

ABCDEFGHIJKLMNOPQRSTUVWXYZ
abcdefghijklmnopqrstuvwxyz
1234567890
ABCDEFGHIJKLMNOPQRSTUVWXYZ
abcdefghijklmnopqrstuvwxyz
1234567890

MENHART

Designed by O. Menhart. A roman more or less old face in design with the small serifs which are characteristic of contemporary romans. In the upper case **B, E, F** and **P** are narrow letters, the **M** is slightly splayed and **Q** has its tail outside the bowl. In the **e** the straight to the eye is not quite horizontal. The **g** has a large bowl. The figures range on the line. The italic has a slight inclination. There is also a bold. Different from the Monotype Corporation's MENHART.

MENHART
ROMAN

Bauer 1939

ii

ABCDEFGHIJKLMNOPQRSTUVW
XYZ
abcdefghijklmnopqrstuvwxyz
1234567
ABCDEFGHIJKLMNOPQRSTUVW
XYZ
abcdefghijklmnopqrstuvwxyz
1234567890

MENHART ROMAN

ABCDEFGHIJKLMNOPQRSTUV
WXYZ
abcdefghijklmnopqrstuvwxyz
1234567890

MENHART BOLD

ii

**MERGEN-
THALER**

Linotype (Frankfurt) 1961

iv

Designed by Hermann Zapf. A newspaper type, modern-face in design like SCOTCH ROMAN. There is also a bold.

ABCDEFGHIJKLMNOPQRSTUVWXYZ

abcdefghijklmnopqrstuvwxyz

67890

ABCDEFGHIJKLMNOPQRSTUVWXYZ

ABCDEFGHIJKLMNOPQRSTUVWXYZ

abcdefghijklmnopqrstuvwxyz

12345

MERGENTHALER

iv

ABCDEFGHIJKLMNOPQRSTUVWXYZ

abcdefghijklmnopqrstuvwxyz

12345

MERGENTHALER BOLD

MERIDIEN

Deberny & Peignot 1957

vii

Designed by A. Frutiger. A classical roman with foot serifs on the **p** and **q**. The **M** is wide and splayed. PRESIDENT is similar.

ABCDEFGHIJKLMN
OPQRSTUVWXYZ
abcdefghijklmnopqrs
tuvwxyz
1234567890

MERIDIEN

**MERRY-
MOUNT**

Merrymount Press 1894

i

Designed by Bertram G. Goodhue and cut by Woerner of A.D. Farmer & Son. The design is probably influenced by the work of William Morris. The **G** has a small spur, **M** has slab serifs and the tail of the **R** tapers. The **g** has a squat tail and there is a serif on the bar of the **t**.

Et quibus bellum volentibus erat, probare exemplum ac recentis legati animum opperiri, cum Agricola, quamquam transvecta

MERRYMOUNT TYPE

A text and display type face with heavy serifs and designed for phototypesetting.

ABCDEFGHIJKLMNOPQRSTUVWXYZ
abcdefghijklmnopqrstuvwxyz
1 2 3 4 5 6 7 8 9 0

ABCDEFGHIJKLMNOPQRSTUVWXYZ
abcdefghijklmnopqrstuvwxyz
1 2 3 4 5 6 7 8 9 0

iv

METRION

ABCDEFGHIJKLMNOPQRSTUVWXYZ
abcdefghijklmnopqrstuvwxyz
1 2 3 4 5 6 7 8 9 0

iv

METRION BOLD

Designed by W. Schwerdtner. Vertical strokes are wedge-shaped and thicker at the top. The **g** has an open tail. The light version of the type looses much of the essential character of the design.

ABCDEFGHIJKLMNOPQ
abcdefghijklmnopqrstuvwx
1234567890

ix

METROPOLIS BOLD

ABCDEFGHIJKLMNOP
QRSTUVWXYZ&
£1234567890

ix

METROPOLIS SHADED

MINERVA

Linotype (London) 1954

Designed by Reynolds Stone. The **B**, **E**, **F**, **P** and **R** are narrow letters. The italic has the serifs of the roman. Numerals are both ranging and non-ranging.

ii

ABCDEFGHIJKLMNOPQRSTUVWXYZ
abcdefghijklmnopqrstuvwxyz
1234567890   1234567890

ABCDEFGHIJKLMNOPQRSTUVWXYZ
abcdefghijklmnopqrstuvwxyz
1234567890   1234567890

ii

MINERVA

ii

ABCDEFGHIJKLMNOPQRSTUVWXYZ
abcdefghijklmnopqrstuvwxyz
1234567890   1234567890

MINERVA BOLD

MINISTER

Schriftguss 1929

Designed by M. Fahrenwaldt. Capitals are wide. Serifs on the upper case are shaped and oblique and slightly concave on the lower case. The bowl of the **P** is not closed, the **V** has cursive form. Numerals are short ranging. Decorated initials are called SYMBOL and PROMINENT, and a white on black titling was called KREIS VERSALIEN.

i|ii

ABCDEFGHIJKLMNOPQRSTUVW
XYZ&

abcdefghijklmnopqrstuvwxyz?

1234567890

ABCDEFGHIJKLMNOPQRSTUVW
XYZ&

abcdefghijklmnopqrstuvwxyz?

1234567890

MINISTER

ABCDEFGHIJKLMNOPQRSTUV
WXYZ&
abcdefghijklmnopqrstuvwxyz?
1234567890

MINISTER BOLD

ABCDEFGHIJKLMNOPQRS
TUVWXYZ&
abcdefghijklmnopqrstuvwxyz?
1234567890

i/ii

MINISTER EXTRA BOLD

ABCDEFGHIJKLMNOPQRSTUVWXYZ
abcdefghijklmnopqrstuvwxyz?
1234567890

i/ii

MINISTER BOLD CONDENSED

MONTBLANC

i/ii

KREIS VERSALIEN

ABCDEFG
HIJKLMN
OPQRSTU
VWXY&Z
1234567890

ix

SYMBOL

155

A type with stubby serifs, oblique on the lower case. Capitals are wide, notably the N. Descenders are very short, as indicated by the name. The eye of the **e** has an oblique stroke.

MODERN to meet the needs

FOUNDRY in England

MINSTER LINING OLD STYLE

HIGHEST-CLASS work

MINSTER LINING OLD STYLE BOLD

MODERN

Monotype

A characteristic English face, of which The Monotype Corporation has several versions.

iv

ABCDEFGHIJKLMNOPQRSTUVWXYZ

abcdefghijklmnopqrstuvwxyz

1234567890

ABCDEFGHIJKLMNOPQRSTUVWXYZ

abcdefghijklmnopqrstuvwxyz

MODERN

iv

ABCDEFGHIJKLMNOPQRSTUVWXYZ

abcdefghijklmnopqrstuvwxyz

1234567890

ABCDEFGHIJKLMNOPQRSTUVWXYZ

abcdefghijklmnopqrstuvwxyz

1234567890

MODERN BOLD

iv

ABCDEFGHIJKLMNOPQRSTUVWXYZ

abcdefghijklmnopqrstuvwxyz

1234567890

ABCDEFGHIJKLMNOPQRSTUVWXYZ

abcdefghijklmnopqrstuvwxyz

1234567890

MODERN CONDENSED

iv

ABCDEFGHIJKLMNOPQRSTUVWXYZ

abcdefghijklmnopqrstuvwxyz

1234567890

ABCDEFGHIJKLMNOPQRSTUVWXYZ

abcdefghijklmnopqrstuvwxyz

MODERN WIDE

ABCDEFGHIJKLMNOPQRSTUVWX
YZ
1234567890

ABCDEFGHIJKLMNOPQRSTUVWXYZ

abcdefghijklmnopqrstuvwxyz

fifffliffifflqu& £$12345678

Designed by W.A. Parker. Similar to the same founders' GALLIA, but with an additional decoration of the main strokes.

ABCDEFGHIJKL
MNOPQRSTUV
WXYZ~
1234567890

MODERNISTIC

A type with similarity to STEELPLATE.

ABCDEFGHIJKLMNOPQRSTUVWXYZ
1234567890

ABCDEFGHIJKLMNOPQRSTUVWXYZ
1234567890

MODULARIO

Redrawn by S.L. Hartz from a design by the Paris founder Molé. Floral decoration on the open face of three dimensional letters.

ABCDEFGHIJKL
MNOPQRSTUV
WXYZ

MOLÉ FOLIATE

MONA LISA

Ludwig & Mayer 1930

Designed by Albert Auspurg. An inline roman of modern-face design not unlike the same founders' FIRMIN DIDOT. The central arm of the A and other capitals is extended to the left. Ascenders are tall, but descenders are short. The f and t are unusual in design.

ix

ABCDEFGHIJKLMNOPQRSTUVWXYZ

abcdefghijklmnopqrstuvwxyz

1234567890

MONA LISA

MONASTIC

Ludwig & Mayer

A calligraphic open titling type.

ix

A B C D E F G
H I J K L M N
O P Q R S T U
V W X Y Z

MONASTIC

MONDIAL

Stempel 1936

Designed by Hans Bohn. A type like CORVINUS, with straight edges to the round letters. The A and M do not have the slab serifs of CORVINUS. The italic is a sloped roman.

iv

ABCDEFGHIJKLMNOPQRSTUVWXYZ

abcdefghijklmnopqrstuvwxyz

ABCDEFGHIJKLMNOPQRSTUVWXYZ

abcdefghijklmnopqrstuvwxyz

MONDIAL

ABCDEFGHIJKLMNOPQRSTUVWXYZ
abcdefghijklmnopqrstuvwxyz
1234567890

MONDIAL SEMI-BOLD

ABCDEFGHIJKLMNOPQRSTU
abcdefghijklmnopqrstuvwxyz

MONDIAL BOLD

ABCDEFGHIJKLMNOPQRSTUVWXYZ
abcdefghijklmnopqrstuvwxyz

MONDIAL BOLD CONDENSED

Designed by Karlgeorg Hoefer as a fat face with almost slab serifs. The type is slightly inclined.

ABCDEFGHIJKLM
NOPQRSTUVWXY
Z
abcdefghijklmnop
qrstuvwxyz
1234567890

MONSOON

Designed by Herbert P. Horne and cut by E.P. Prince. The type has very small serifs, oblique on the lower case. Capitals are rather narrow and the **R** has an extended tail. The **a** has a wide bowl, the **e** a large eye and the **g** a large bowl. The **v** is a wide letter.

virtue and ancient descent, and also of their having inter-married with imperial blood; inasmuch as Beatrice, sister of the emperor, Henry II, was wife to Count Bonifazio da Canossa, then lord of Mantua, of whom was born the Countess Matilda, a lady of rare and singular prudence and

MONTALLEGRO TYPE

MONTICELLO
Mergenthaler Linotype 1946

Designed by C.H. Griffith and based on RONALDSON ROMAN NO. 1 or OXFORD. The serifs, slightly inclined, have a scooped-out appearance. The lower-case **g** both roman and italic, has an open tail ending in a blob.

iii

ABCDEFGHIJKLMNOPQRSTUVWXYZ

abcdefghijklmnopqrstuvwxyz

1234567890

ABCDEFGHIJKLMNOPQRSTUVWXYZ

ABCDEFGHIJKLMNOPQRSTUVWXYZ

abcdefghijklmnopqrstuvwxyz

1234567890

Recut Italic: abcdefghijklmnopqrstuvwxyz

MONTICELLO

MONUMENT
Grafotechna 1950–52

Designed by Oldrich Menhart. A pen-drawn and calligraphic type with irregular outlines. The bowl of the **P** is open and the **U** is lower case. The descending tail of the **J** is very short.

ix

ABCDEFGHIJKLMNOPQRS
TUVWXYZ
1234567890

MONUMENT

MORLAND
Caslon 1900

Based on BLANCHARD of the Inland Typefoundry. A bold face with uneven outlines, a characteristic visible only in the larger sizes. The serifs are inclined but blurred. The letters are wide. The **H** has a high bar. The **R** is conspicuous with a swollen and extended tail. In the lower case the **a** leans back, **p** and **q** have foot serifs on the outer side only. The italic has the serifs of the roman. In the **M** the middle strokes stop short of the line. The **h** has a curved main stroke; **v** and **w** have initial loops.

One of Goudy's early designs, PABST OLD STYLE, has similar characteristics, and M.F. Benton's ROYCROFT is also similar but narrower.

ix

Latest Estimates *Charming Scenes*

MORLAND

MÖWE
Genzsch & Heyse 1929

Designed by H. Beck. An outline roman in which the open part of each stroke is divided by a second stroke. As a result the counters of **e** and **o** have an unusual appearance.

iv

Moderne Druckarb

MÖWE

MOZART NOIR
Warnery

A set of modern-face capitals in which the thins are hair lines. The letters are of equal width and somewhat extended. An Inline version is called DIAPHANE.

iv

BIEN QUE LES PROCÉD

MOZART NOIR

Designed by W. Schwerdtner. Mainly a display type, if one may judge from its blackness and very short ascenders and descenders. The serifs are very slight and like chisel strokes. The capitals vary in width and in this case among the narrow letters are H and N. M, N and W have no top serifs. *Cf.* the capitals of JOST MEDIAEVAL. **a** has a large bowl and an unusual finish to the top arc. The **g** has no link and the tail is open. The **i** has a dash in place of the dot. The lower-case letters have crushed down serifs. There is also a light face.

MUNDUS
Stempel 1929;

Linotype (Frankfurt)

Ein Werk der Neuzeit

MUNDUS LIGHT

ix

Cerises d'Itxassou

MUNDUS BOLD

ix

Designed by Carlos Winkow. A calligraphic roman. The serifs are steeply inclined and slightly modelled. On some upper case letters there are hooks, and some lower case letters, especially the **e**, have pen-drawn qualities. The italic has the serifs of the roman, and there is also a bold.

NACIONAL
Nacional 1941

El dibujo de los tipos ofrece mucha dificultad
DISTINCIONES MERECIDAS
La bella historia de las amazonas en Viena
LOS AMANTES DE TERUEL

CLÁSICO NACIONAL I

ix

Penetrando profundamente en la cavidad
REFERENCIA LOCALIZADA

CLÁSICO NACIONAL NEGRO

ix

A type designed by Bernard Naudin with some resemblance in the roman to NICOLAS COCHIN. The serifs are thick, inclined in the lower case. In the capitals the vertical strokes are thickened in the middle. The arm of the **L** is very wide. The middle strokes of the **M** stop short of the line. The **S** ends in a big serif. The ascenders and descenders are ample. Serifs on the tops of ascenders extend both ways. **c** and **e** have extended curves; **g** is a squat letter with a wide tail; **s** is as in the upper case. There are two sets of figures, one short-ranging. The roman is accompanied by a script, not an italic, based on the designer's own hand. In the upper case many of the serifs have curved ends. **G** has an odd lower serif. In the **H** the bar extends to the left. The middle strokes of the **M** stop half-way. The lower case has pen strokes for serifs. The bowls of **a, d, g** and **o** are not closed; **g** has an open tail drawn from right to left; the curve of the **v** extends above the letter. A set of open capitals is called NAUDIN CHAMPLEVÉ. This type is not to be confused with Berthold's TRADITION.

NAUDIN or **TRADITION**
Deberny & Peignot 1911–24;
Stephenson Blake

se présente, comme des 2345

ABCDEFGHIJKLM

ii

Dans mille ans d'ici, il fera verser
des larmes; il sera l'admiration des

TRADITION

ABCDEFGHIJKLMNO
1234567890

CHAMPLEVÉ

ii

NEUTRA

Typoart 1968

v

A roman following CLARENDON.

ABCDEFGHIJKLMNOPQR
STUVWXYZ
abcdefghijklmnopqrstuvwxyz
1234567890

NEUTRA

NEW CLARENDON

Monotype 1960

v

A text face following English style for these types.

ABCDEFGHIJKLMNOPQRSTUVWXYZ
abcdefghijklmnopqrstuvwxyz
1234567890

NEW CLARENDON

ABCDEFGHIJKLMNOPQRSTUVWXYZ
abcdefghijklmnopqrstuvwxyz
1234567890

NEW CLARENDON BOLD

NEWPORT

*American Typefounders
c. 1890*

ix

A quaint elongated slab serif type which lends to two-colour printing, giving a three-dimensional effect.

ABCDEFGHIJKLMNOP
QRSTUVWXYZ

NEWPORT

ix

ABCDEFGHIJKLMNOP
QRSTUVWXYZ

NEWPORT OUTLINE

NOBLESSE

Bauer c. 1870

iv

A set of modern face capitals and ranging figures with hairline serifs. The thin strokes also are hairline. Ludwig & Mayer's COPPERPLATE and Nebiolo's ORLANDO are very similar and many founders cast such types.

ABCDEFGHIJKLMNOP
QRSTUVWXYZ 1234567

NOBLESSE

A text roman with tall ascenders.

A B C D E F G H I J K L M N O P Q R S T U
V W X Y Z

a b c d e f g h i j k l m n o p q r s t u v w x y z

1 2 3 4 5 6 7 8 9 0

NORDISCHE ANTIQUA

A fat face following the original designs of the early nineteenth century. Note the heavy spur on the **G** and the design of the lower-case **g**. See also the blob on the arc of the **c** and other similar letters.

A B C D E F G H I J K L M N O P Q R S T U
a b c d e f g h i j k l m n o p q r s t u v w x y z
1 2 3 4 5 6 7 8 9 0

HAAS NORMANDE SEMI-BOLD

A B C D E F G H I J K L M N O P
a b c d e f g h i j k l m n o p q r s t u

HAAS NORMANDE

A B C D E F G H I J K L M N O P Q R S T U
V W X Y Z
a b c d e f g h i j k l m n o p q r s t u v w x y z
1 2 3 4 5 6 7 8 9 0

A B C D E F G H I J K L M N O P Q R S
T U V W X Y Z
a b c d e f g h i j k l m n o p q r s t u v w x y z
1 2 3 4 5 6 7 8 9 0

NORMANDE

A B C D E F G H I J K L M N O P Q R S T U V W X Y Z
a b c d e f g h i j k l m n o p q r s t u v w x y z
1 2 3 4 5 6 7 8 9 0

NORMANDE CONDENSED

NORMANDIA

Nebiolo 1946–49

Designed by A. Butti and A. Novarese. A fat face after the Bodoni design. Differing from ULTRA BODONI, this face has thin strokes that curve into the thick strokes. The **b** in the italic has a spur. There is also an outline version.

iv

ABCDEFGHIJKLMNOPQRS
abcdefghijklmnopqrstuvwxyz
1234567890

ABDEFGHIJKLMNOPQ
RSWXYZÇÆŒ&
abcdefghijklmnopqrstuvw
xyzçæœfiflffffifffifl
1234567890

NORMANDIA

iv

ABCDEFGHIJKLMNOPQRSTUVWXYZÇÆŒ&

abcdefghijklmnopqrstuvwxyzçæœfiflffffiffl

1234567890

NORMANDIA ELONGATED

iv

ABCDEFGHIJKLMNOPQR
STUVWXYZÇÆŒ&
abcdefghijklmnopqrstuvwx
yzçæœfifl ff ffi ffl
1234567890

NORMANDIA OUTLINE

NUBIAN

American Typefounders 1928

Designed by W.T. Sniffin. A fat face of extra weight. The G has no spur. In the lower-case ascenders and descenders are extremely short. The tail of the **g** is unfinished. The dot over **i** and **j** is a solid segment. There are none of the globular endings of arcs found in early fat faces.

ix

Leaving Boston March 11th
on the S.S. San Petro. Will

NUBIAN *

The lower-case letters of this type are based on Spanish uncial forms. Ascenders are high, while the descenders are rather shorter. The capitals follow the style of roman letters and are condensed. The foot of the U is somewhat angular.

Elevando lo pensado
MIENTRAS BUSQUE

NUMANTINA

Designed by Will Carter and David Kindersley. This type face owes much of its character to classical inscriptional letters. Mr Carter writes: "While the ultimate authority is the ancient inscriptional pattern, the special characteristics of the present rendering are manifest in the economic propositions of the shapes and the modified relations of the strokes. Thus, the letters are narrower than the classical forms and their weight heavier."

ABCDEFGHIJKLMNOPQRSTUVWXYZ&ÆŒ

abcdefghijklmnopqrstuvwxyzfiflffffifflæœ

1234567890

ABCDEFGHIJKLMNOPQRSTUVWXYZÆŒ

ABCDEFGHIJKLMNOPQRSTUVWXYZ&ÆŒ

abcdefghijklmnopqrstuvwxyzfiflffffifflæœ

1234567890

OCTAVIAN

Designed by Walter Tiemann. A roman with short ascenders and descenders; in design not unlike CASLON, except for the R with a curled tail and the ear of the g. The numerals range on the line.

ABCDEFGHIJKLMNOPQRS
TUVWXYZ
abcdefghijklmnopqrstuvwxyz
1234567890

OFFIZIN

Designed by Richard McMurtrie. Open and decorated capitals. In the centre of each main stroke is a circle. The serifs are also decorated.

GIGANTIC

OLD DUTCH

An open roman which first appeared in Fry's specimen book of 1788. The design of the letters is like that of FRY'S BASKERVILLE. The Q has a curled tail starting inside the counter.

ABCDFGHIJKLMNOPQRSTUVW
XYZ
1234&

OLD FACE OPEN

OLD STYLE
Many founders

Originally cut by Miller & Richard's employee, Alexander Phemister, and first shown in a specimen of 1860. It was so successful that it was soon copied by all the other founders. Its purpose was to cut a type which would overcome what was regarded as archaic in CASLON. The serifs are slighter and more sharply cut. Stress is vertical, though not abruptly so. Note the curves of **c**, **e** and **p**. Ascenders and descenders are rather short. The eye of the **e** is larger than in Caslon, and the **t** taller. The down stroke of the **g** tail is thickened and steeply inclined. The italic is regularly but steeply inclined.

The adapted Intertype versions of this design was called BOOKFACE, and the Linotype (London) version is BOOKPRINT. The Mergenthaler Linotype versions are OLD STYLE No. 1 and No. 3. There is a Monotype version (Series 2) with a companion bold (Series 544). By a change of seven capitals and small capitals, OLD STYLE No. 1 may be converted to RONALDSON (the characters are **C, E, F, G, L, S, T**).

ii

ABCDEFGHIJKLMNOPQRSTUVWXYZ

abcdefghijklmnopqrstuvwxyz

1234567890

ABCDEFGHIJKLMNOPQRSTUVWXYZ

abcdefghijklmnopqrstuvwxyz

MONOTYPE OLD STYLE

ii

ABCDEFGHIJKLMNOPQRSTUVWXYZ

abcdefghijklmnopqrstuvwxyz

1234567890

MONOTYPE OLD STYLE BOLD

ii

ABCDEFGHIJKLMNOPQRSTUVWXYZ&
ABCDEFGHIJKLMNOPQRSTUVWXYZ&
abcdefghijklmnopqrstuvwxyz
1234567890
ABCDEFGHIJKLMNOPQRSTUVWXYZ&
abcdefghijklmnopqrstuvwxyz
1234567890

MERGENTHALER LINOTYPE OLD STYLE NO. 1

ii

ABCDEFGHIJKLMNOPQRSTUVWXYZ&
ABCDEFGHIJKLMNOPQRSTUVWXYZ&
abcdefghijklmnopqrstuvwxyz
1234567890
ABCDEFGHIJKLMNOPQRSTUVWXYZ&
abcdefghijklmnopqrstuvwxyz
1234567890

MERGENTHALER LINOTYPE OLD STYLE NO. 2

ii

ABCDEGHIJKLMNOPQRSTUVWXYZ

abcdefghijklmnopqrstuvwxyz

1234567890

ABCDEFGHIJKLMNOPQRSTUVWXYZ

abcdefghijklmnopqrstuvwxyz

1234567890

MONOTYPE OLD STYLE BOLD NO. 53

ii

ABCDEFGHIJKLMNOPQRSTUVWXYZ

abcdefghijklmnopqrstuvwxyz

1234567890

MONOTYPE OLD STYLE BOLD NO. 159

ABCDEFGHIJKLMNOPQRSTUVWXYZ OLD STYLE

abcdefghijklmnopqrstuvwxyz 1234567890 ii

AABCDDEℰFGHIJKLMMNℕOPP
QRRSSTTUVXYZ
abcdefghijklmnopqrstuvwxyz
1234567890

OLD STYLE NO. 5

Designed by Matthew Carter as a newspaper type with large x-height, and believed to have the distinction of being the first copyrighted type in the United States.

ABCDEFGHIJKLMNOPQRSTUVWXYZ&
abcdefghijklmnopqrstuvwxyz
$1234567890

OLYMPIAN

ABCDEFGHIJKLMNOPQRSTUVWXYZ&
abcdefghijklmnopqrstuvwxyz
$1234567890

OLYMPIAN BOLD

OLYMPIAN

Mergenthaler
Linotype 1970

ii

A revival of a mid-nineteenth century condensed and elongated fat face. Such a type was shown by the Wilson foundry as early as 1843. Capitals only. VERTICAL is similar but narrower.

ABCDEFGHIJKLMNO

SLIMBLACK

OLYMPIC or
SLIMBLACK

Deberny & Peignot 1937

iv

Designed by Gerry Powell. A condensed and elongated fat face in the style of SLIMBLACK. It follows the design of the early fat faces, except for the rather angular **a**.

ABCDEFGHIJKLMNOPQRSTUVWXYZ
abcdefghijklmnopqrstuvwxyz 1234567890

ARSIS

ABCDEFGHIJKLMNOPQRSTUVWXYZ
abcdefghijklmnopqrstuvwxyz 12345

MONOTYPE ONYX

ONYX or ARSIS

American Typefounders 1937;
Amsterdam Typefoundry;
Monotype 1955

iv

iv

A set of decorated capitals of fat face design. The decoration consists of horizontal lines on the vertical strokes.

ABCDEFGHIJKLMNOP
QRSTUVWXYZ 12345678

OPAL

OPAL

Weber

iv

167

OPEN ROMAN CAPITALS
Enschedé 1929

vii

Designed by Jan van Krimpen for use with ANTIQUE GREEK or two-line capitals.

ABCDEFGHIJKLMNOPQ RST UVWXYZ

OPEN ROMAN CAPITALS

OPERA
Sofratype 1960

ii

ii

Designed by Adrien Frutiger. Ascenders and descenders are short, the italic is the roman slightly sloped, except for **a** and an open-tailed **g**. Numerals are ranging.

ABCDEFGHIJKLMNOPQRSTUVWXYZ

abcdefghijklmnopqrstuvwxyz

1234567890

ABCDEFGHIJKLMNOPQRSTUVWXYZ

ABCDEFGHIJKLMNOPQRSTUVWXYZ

abcdefghijklmnopqrstuvwxyz

1234567890

OPERA

ABCDEFGHIJKLMNOPQRSTUVWXYZ

abcdefghijklmnopqrstuvwxyz

1234567890

OPERA BOLD

OPTICON
Mergenthaler Linotype 1935–36

iv

Designed by C.H. Griffith. A newspaper type ranging as No. 3 in the "Linotype Legibility Group", and specially designed to suit newspapers running heavy pictures and a lot of ink.

ABCDEFGHIJKLMNOPQRSTUVWXYZ

abcdefghijklmnopqrstuvwxyz

1234567890

ABCDEFGHIJKLMNOPQRSTUVWXYZ

abcdefghijklmnopqrstuvwxyz

1234567890

OPTICON

ORATOR
Amsterdam 1962

iv

Designed by Leonard H.D. Smit. A bold companion to PROMOTOR, with capitals resembling card types. The type has some similarities to CRAW MODERN, but is more rounded and has less variation in stress between thick and hair-line strokes.

ABCDEFGHIJKLMNOPQ RSTUVWXYZÆŒ

abcdefghijklmnopqrstu vwxyz

1234567890£&æœ

ORATOR

These lavishly ornamented letters are in white except for parts of the lower halves, which are in black. The type comes from the foundry of V. and J. Figgins. ROMANTIQUES NO. 1 is identical.

ORNAMENTED
OUTLINE
Stevens Shanks c. 1870

ABCDEFGHIJKLMNOPQRSTUVWXY
1234567890 & Æ Œ

ORNAMENTED OUTLINE

ix

Designed by O.H.W. Hadank. A bold copperplate roman in which the black has been replaced by a fine herring-bone inline design. The capitals also have a star in the centre of the down strokes.

ORNATA
Klingspor 1943

ABCDEFGHIJKLMNOPQ
abcdefghijklmnopqrstuvw
1234567890

ORNATA

iv

Designed by Walter Tiemann. A roman with small serifs, slightly oblique on the lower case and with short ascenders and descenders. The **M** is splayed and has no top serifs. In the **W** the middle strokes cross. The swash caps are also called EUPHORION.

ORPHEUS
Klingspor 1928

ABCDEFGHIJKLMNOPQRSTUV
abcdefghijklmnopqrstuvwxyz
1234567890
ABCDEFGHIJKLMNOPQRSTUV
abcdefghijklmnopqrstuvwxyz

ORPHEUS

ii

ABCDEFGHIJKLMNOPQRST
abcdefghijklmnopqrstuvwxyz

ORPHEUS BOLD

ii

ABCDEFGHIJKLMNOPQRS
TUVWXYZ

EUPHORION

ii

OTTOCENTO
Nebiolo 1930

ix

Shaded capitals in which the left edges of the black strokes are serrated. The letters are wide and the serifs bracketed.

ABCDEFGHIJKLMNOP
QRSTUVXYZW
1234567890

OTTOCENTO

OXFORD
American Typefounders

iv

Designed by James Ronaldson and first shown in a specimen book in 1812 by Binny & Ronaldson in Philadelphia, who called it ROMAN No. 1. The type is influenced by the work of Didot. It was used by Updike for the text of his *Printing Types*. Cf. MONTICELLO.

ABCDEFGHIJKLMNOPQRSTUVWXYZ&

abcdefghijklmnopqrstuvwxyz

ABCDEFGHIJKLMNOPQRSTUVWXYZ

1234567890

ABCDEFGHIJKLMNOPQRSTUVWXYZ

abcdefghijklmnopqrstuvwxyz

fifflffiflffl   *fifflffiflffl*

OXFORD

PABST OLD STYLE
Lanston Monotype

ix

Designed by Frederick W. Goudy, but quite unlike PABST ROMAN. Letters have an uneven outline and blurred serifs.

ABCDEFGHIJKLMNOPQRSTUWVX

abcdefghijklmnopqrstuvwxyz

1234567890

PABST OLD STYLE

PABST ROMAN
American Typefounders 1902

ix

Designed by Frederic W. Goudy. Wide letters and somewhat uneven outline characterise this bold type. AVIL was a copy of this type made by the former Inland Typefoundry. Krebs made a copy which was called LATINA.

ABCDEFGHIJKLMNOPQR

klmnopqrstuvwxyz

1234567890

ABCDEFGHIJKLMNOPQR

klmnopqrstuvwxyz

1234567890

PABST ROMAN

170

Designed by A. Butti under the direction of Raffaello Bertieri. Serifs are small. The **M** is splayed. The **e** has a small eye, the **g** a wide tail and the **y** a flowing tail. The italic has the serifs of the roman.

ABCDEFGHIJKLMNOPQQuRR
STUVXYWZÇÆŒ&
abcdefghijklmnopqrsſtuvxywzç
1234567890
ABCDEFGHIJKLMNOPQQu
RSTUVXYWZÇÆŒ&
abcdefghijklmnopqrstuvxywz
123457890

PAGANINI

iv

ABCDEFGHIJKLMNOPQQuRR
STUVXYWZÇÆŒ&
§ abcdefghijklmnopqrsſtuvxywz çæœ fiflff
1234567890
ABCDEFGHIJKLMNOPQQuR
STUVXYWZÇÆŒ&
abcdefghijklmnopqrstuvyxwz
1234567890

PAGANINI LIGHT

iv

ABCDEFGHIJKLMNOPQQu
RRSTUVXYWZÇÆŒ&
abcdefghijklmnopqrsſtuvxywzç
1234567890

PAGANINI BOLD

iv

171

ABCDEFGHIJKLMNO
QPRSTUVXYWZÇÆ
1234567890

PAGANINI OPEN

Designed by M. Jacoby-Boy to accompany BRAVOUR.

Denomination

PALADIN BOLD CONDENSED

Decorative

PALADIN SHADED

Designed by Hermann Zapf. A roman with broad letters and strong, inclined serifs. The capitals especially **M** and **W** are wide. The **e** has a large eye, the **g** is wide, and the foot serifs on the final strokes of the **h**, **m** and **n** are on the outside only. Descenders are short. MICHELANGELO and SISTINA are companion titlings.

ABCDEFGHIJKLMNOPQRSTUVW
abcdefghijklmnopqrstuvwxyz
1234567890

ABCDEFGHIJKLMNOPQRSTUVW
abcdefghijklmnopqrstuvwxyz

PALATINO

ABCDEFGHIJKLMNOPQRSTUV
abcdefghijklmnopqrstuvwxyz

PALATINO BOLD

ABCDEFGHIJKLMNOPQRSTUVW
1234567890

MICHELANGELO

ABCDEFGHIJKLMNOPQRSTUV
1234567890

SISTINA

172

Designed by K. E. Forsberg. A set of double-inline capitals with ranging figures. The thins are hairlines.

PARAD
Berling 1938

ix

ABCDEFGHIJKKLMNOPQRSTUVW XYZÅÄÖ
PARAD

Designed by C.H. Griffith. Very fine up-strokes. The lower case italic **g** has a large bowl and a curiously short tail. The type is a lighter version of EXCELSIOR.

PARAGON
Mergenthaler Linotype 1935;
Linotype (London)

iv

ABCDEFGHIJKLMNOPQRSTUVWXYZ
abcdefghijklmnopqrstuvwxyz
1234567890
ABCDEFGHIJKLMNOPQRSTUVWXYZ
abcdefghijklmnopqrstuvwxyz
1234567890
ABCDEFGHIJKLMNOPQRSTUVWXYZ
PARAGON

ABCDEFGHIJKLMNOPQRSTUVWXYZ
abcdefghijklmnopqrstuvwxyz
12345 67890
PARAGON BOLD

iv

Designed by Herbert Thannhaeuser. A heavy type with short descenders and small serifs. **A** has the bar high, the middle strokes of **M** stop short of the line, **R** has a curled tail and **T** is narrow. The **g** has a squashed tail and the **t** is narrow. The italic has slight inclination. The italic **a** has the roman form but serifs are not roman; the **g** has an open tail.

PARCIVAL
Schelter & Giesecke 1930

Eine Type von zeitloser Schönheit ist unsere Parcival-Antiqua. Ihre

ix

Die Parcival-Kursiv zeichnet sich aus durch die freie Bewegung
PARCIVAL

Ihre kraftvolle Schwere und künstlerische Form
PARCIVAL BOLD

ix

Designed by Oldrich Menhart for the printing of the new Czech Constitution. The type was then melted down. It is a calligraphic type of individual angular character.

PARLAMENT
Czech Government
Printing Office 1950

ix

KAPITOLA TŘETÍ
přítomna nadpoloviční většina poslanců. Zvolen je ten, pro koho
PARLAMENT

A type with great variation of stress and almost a heavy design. LINING MODERN No. 25 is the same type; but Stephenson Blake's MODERN No. 20 is not the same design and has cupped ends to the **h**, **k**, **n** and **r**.

PARMA
Stevens Shanks c. 1870

ABCDEFGHIJKLMNOPQRSTU?
abcdefghijklmnopqrstuvwxyzæœ
£1234567890&

iv

PARMA

PARSONS
American Typefounders 1918

Designed by Will Ransom. A monotone display face with a peculiarity in the serifs. At the tops of the letters the serifs extend to the left only, and at the feet to the right. Some of the capitals have the same design, in a larger size, as the lower-case letters, *e.g.*, the **M, N, P, U, V, W,** and **Y.** There is also a more normal variety of **M** and **N.** There are some additional sorts with extra long ascenders and descenders. The figures are short-ranging. There is no italic and there are two weights. Originally designed for Barnhart Bros. & Spindler.

ix

Printed Things
PARSONS

ix

RESPONSIBLE
Big Advertising

PARSONS BOLD

PASTONCHI
Monotype 1927

Designed by F. Pastonchi and E. Cotti. The serifs are small and bracketed.

i

ABCDEFGHIJKLMNOPQRSTUVWXYZ
abcdefghijklmnopqrstuvwxyz
1234567890

ABCDEFGHIJKLMNOPQRSTUVWXYZ
abcdefghijklmnopqrstuvwxyz
1234567890

PASTONCHI

PEARL FOURNIER
Schriftguss 1922

Decorated capitals designed by P.A. Demeter. Many of the strokes assume leaf forms. In Germany the type is called GEPERLTE FOURNIER.

ix

ABCDEFGHIJKLMNOPQRSTUVWXYZ

PEARL FOURNIER

PEGASUS
Monotype c. 1937

Designed by Berthold Wolpe. A somewhat condensed roman designed to complement ALBERTUS.

ii

ABCDEFGHIJKLMNOPQRSTUVWXYZÆŒ&
abcdefghijklmnopqrstuvwxyz
1234567890

PEGASUS

A heavy face with sharply cut serifs, oblique on the lower case, and with vertical stress.

PENTLAND
Miller & Richard 1920

AUSTRALIA TO HONOLU
The quiet cart road leading

PENTLAND

Designed by Alfons Schneider. A roman in five weights. Ascenders are of the same height as the capitals, and descenders are short. Serifs are flat. The capital **G**, like the **g** has a spur, and the lower-case letter an open tail. The **f** curves inward at the top to form a heavy dot.

PERGAMON
L. Wagner 1932; Typoart

ABCDEFGHIJKLMNOPQRSTUVW
XYZ&
abcdefghijklmnopqrstuvwxyz?
1234567890

ABCDEFGHIJKLMNOPQRSTUVW
XYZ&
abcdefghijklmnopqrstuvwxyz?
1234567890

PERGAMON

ABCDEFGHIJKLMNOPQRSTUVW
XYZ&
abcdefghijklmnopqrstuvwxyz?
1234567890

ABCDEFGHIJKLMNOPQRSTUVW
XYZ&
abcdefghijklmnopqrstuvwxyz?
1234567890

PERGAMON BOLD

ABCDEFGHIJKLMNOPQRSTU VWXYZ&
abcdefghijklmnopqrstuvwxyz?
1234567890

ABCDEFGHIJKLMNOPQRSTU VWXYZ&
abcdefghijklmnopqrstuvwxyz?
1234567890

PERGAMON EXTRA BOLD

ABCDEFGHIJKLMNOPQRSTUVWXYZ&
abcdefghijklmnopqrstuvwxyz?
1234567890

PERGAMON BOLD CONDENSED

ABCDEFGHIJKLMNOPQRSTUVWXYZ&
abcdefghijklmnopqrstuvwxyz?
1234567890

PERGAMON BOLD EXTRA CONDENSED

This type is a reproduction of IMPRINT but has a more regular inclination in the italic. Numerals are short ranging. Ascenders and descenders are short.

ABCDEFGHIJKLMNOPQRSTUVWXYZ

abcdefghijklmnopqrstuvwxyz

1234567890

ABCDEFGHIJKLMNOPQRSTUVWXYZ

abcdefghijklmnopqrstuvwxyz

1234567890

ABCDEFGHIJKLMNOPQRSTUVWXYZ &&£

PERIOD OLD STYLE

Designed by Eric Gill, and his most popular roman. First used in a privately printed translation made by Walter Shrewring of *The Passion of Perpetua and Felicity*. The roman was named PERPETUA and the italic, cut later, FELICITY. The serifs are small, sharply cut and horizontal. The stress and gradation of colour are akin to old face. The italic is slightly inclined and is much as the roman. The titling of the same design is widely used. The bold italic was added by The Monotype Corporation in 1959.
    Stephenson Blake's foundry type is somewhat different in design.

ABCDEFGHIJKLMNOPQRSTUVWXYZ&
abcdefghijklmnopqrstuvwxyz   1234567890

ABCDEFGHIJKLMNOPQRSTUVWXYZ&
abcdefghijklmnopqrstuvwxyz   1234567890

MONOTYPE PERPETUA

ii

ABCDEFGHIJKLMNOPQRSTUVWXYZ?!&ÆŒ£
abccdefghijklmnopqrstuvwxyzfifffflfflffiæœ   1234567890

STEPHENSON BLAKE PERPETUA

ii

ABCDEFGHIJKLMNOPQRSTUVWXYZ
abcdefghijklmnopqrstuvwxyz &
1234567890

ABCDEFGHIJKLMNOPQRSTUVWXYZ
abcdefghijklmnopqrstuvwxyz
1234567890

MONOTYPE PERPETUA BOLD

ii

ABCDEFGHIJKLMNOPQRSTU
VWXYZ&
1234567890

MONOTYPE PERPETUA TITLING

ii

ABCDEFGHIJKLMNOPQ
RSTUVWXYZ&

MONOTYPE PERPETUA BOLD TITLING

ii

ABCDEFGHIJKLMNOPQRSTUV
WXYZ&
1234567890

MONOTYPE PERPETUA LIGHT TITLING

ii

PHALANX

Genzsch & Heyse 1928

Designed by Hans Möhring. A monotone roman which has thickened terminals rather than serifs. The **e** has a large bowl. The **t** has a thickened terminal to the vertical stroke and a bracketed bar.

ix

Ullsteinbuch

PHALANX

PHARAON

Deberny & Peignot 1933

A type with small variation in the weight of the strokes. The **M** has a short middle stroke and the **g** an open tail. The inline version is called PHARAON WHITE.

v

ABCDEFGHIJKLMNOPQRSTUVW XYZ&

abcdefghijklmnopqrstuvwxyz

1234567890

PHARAON SEMI-BOLD

v

ABCDEFGHIJKLMNOPQRSTU VWXYZ

PHARAON WHITE

PHOEBUS

Deberny & Peignot 1953

Designed by A. Frutiger. Inclined, shaded capitals and figures. Serifs are pointed. The **A** has a rounded apex, and the **V** and **W**, as well as the alternative **M** and **N**, are lower-case in design.

ix

ABCDEFGHIJKLMMMNOPQRSTUVW XYZ & 1234567890

PHOEBUS

PIEHLER SCRIPT

Schriftguss

Designed by A. Piehler. Decorated capitals. Both thick and thin strokes are terminated by curled serifs. The bar of the **H**, arms of the **E**, etc., are hair lines and curved. There are also italic capitals.

HEINE BUR

PIEHLER SCRIPT

178

This type, originally designed by Eric Gill for a book published by the Limited Editions Club of New York, who called this face BUNYAN, is a re-cutting by Linotype. In its general appearance it resembles Gill's JOANNA type. The face is even in colour, and the shading of round characters is vertical. The thick and thin strokes of the letters are not strongly contrasted. Capitals are not as tall as the lower case ascenders. The serifs are bracketed. Distinguishing marks are the equal thickness of the arms of the **U** and the two serifs of the **C**, as well at the flat foot of the **a** and **b**.

PILGRIM

Linotype (London) 1953

iv

ABCDEFGHIJKLMNOPQRSTUVWXYZ

abcdefghijklmnopqrstuvwxyz

1234567890

ABCDEFGHIJKLMNOPQRSTUVWXYZ

ABCDEFGHIJKLMNOPQRSTUVWXYZ

abcdefghijklmnopqrstuvwxyz

1234567890

ABCDEFGHIJKLMNOPQRSTUVWXYZ

PILGRIM

Designed by W.T. Sniffin. A light display face with thin flat serifs and tall ascenders. **M** is slightly splayed. The **e** has an oblique stroke to the eye; **g** has an ear starting from near the top of the bowl; the serifs on **m** and **w** are oblique. The italic is almost a script.

PIRANESI

American Typefounders 1930

ix

PRINTING IN THE ROMAN LETTER

will follow from the conventions of alphabetical

PIRANESI

ix

ABCDEFGHIJKLMNOPQRSTUVWX
YZ

abcdefghijklmnopqrstuvwxyz ct st

1234567890

MODERN   Cottage Sold

PIRANESI BOLD

PLANTIN

Monotype; Linotype (London);

Stephenson Blake; Intertype

A roman named after the famous Antwerp printer, Christophe Plantin, and designed for The Monotype Corporation by F. H. Pierpont. However, the 16th century type on which it is modelled never seems to have been used by that printer, although it belongs to his generation, being found at Frankfurt and at Basle about 1570. It is a heavy face of large x-height, a pioneer type of the ever-recurring attempt to design founts which would consume less paper. Conspicuous letters are in the upper case the flat-topped **A** and the splayed **M**, and in lower case the **a** with a large bowl and a narrow **t**. The italic is of a regular slope and has very short descenders. There is also a semi-bold face.

ii ABCDEFGHIJKLMNOPQRSTUV
ii abcdefghijklmnopqrstuvwxyz
ii 1234567890
ii *ABCDEFGHIJKLMNOPQRSUVX*
ii *abcdefghijklmnopqrstuxwxyz*
ii *1234567890*

MONOTYPE PLANTIN

ii ABCDEFGHIJKLMNOPQRSTUVWXYZ
abcdefghijklmnopqrstuvwxyz
1234567890
ABCDEFGHIJKLMNOPQRSTUVWXYZ
abcdefghijklmnopqrstuvwxyz
1234567890

PLANTIN LIGHT

ii **ABCDEFGHIJKLMLOPQRSTU**
VWXYZ
ii **abcdefghijklmnopqrstuv**
ii ***ABCDEFGHIJKLMNOPQRSTU***
ii ***abcdefghijklmnopqrstu***

MONOTYPE PLANTIN BOLD

ii **ABCDEFGHIJKLMNOPQRSTUVWXYZ**
ii **abcdefghijklmnopqrstuvwxyz**
ii **1234567890**

MONOTYPE PLANTIN BOLD CONDENSED

ABCDEFGHIJKLMNOPQRSTUVWXYZ
abcdefghijklmnopqrstuvwxyz
1234567890.

ABCDEFGHIJKLMNOPQRSTUVWXYZ
abcdefghijklmnopqrstuvwxyz
1234597890

STEPHENSON BLAKE PLANTIN

ABCDEFGHIJKLMNOPQRSTUVWXYZ
abcdefghijklmnopqrstuvwxyz   1234567890
ABCDEFGHIJKLMNOPQRSTUVWXYZ
ABCDEFGHIJKLMNOPQRSTUVWXYZ
abcdefghijklmnopqrstuvwxyz   *1234567890*

LINOTYPE PLANTIN

ABCDEFGHIJKLMNOPQRSTUVWXYZ
abcdefghijklmnopqrstuvwxyz
ABCDEFGHIJKLMNOPQRSTUVWXYZ &&£
ABCDEFGHIJKLMNOPQRSTUVWXYZ
abcdefghijklmnopqrstuvwxyz

INTERTYPE PLANTIN

ABCDEFGHIJKLMNOPQRSTUVWXYZ
abcdefghijklmnopqrstuvwxyz
1234567890

INTERTYPE PLANTIN BOLD

In spite of its name, this type has little connection with PLANTIN, except that it is a heavy face of large x-height. Serifs are very thin on the capitals, and there is abruptness of stress. American Typefounders' NEW CASLON is identical.

ABCDEFGHIJKLMNOPQRSTUV
WXYZ
abcdefghijklmnopqrstuvwxyz
1234567890

ABCDEFGHIJKLMNOPQRSTUV
WXYZ
abcdefghijklmnopqrstuvwxyz
1234567890

PLANTIN OLD STYLE

PLAYBILL

Stephenson Blake 1938

Designed after sketches by Robert Harling. A condensed reversed type face in which the serifs are heavier than the main strokes. It is a revival of a Victorian type. The style was at first called FRENCH ANTIQUE, or sometimes ITALIAN. The Monotype Corporation's FIGARO is a type of this style.

v

ABCDEFGHIJKLMNOPQRSTUVWXYZ

abcdefghijklmnopqrstuvwxyz

1234567890

PLAYBILL

PLYMOUTH

Lanston Monotype 1905–6

A bold display type, also cast in text sizes, and similar to ROYCROFT. **E** and **F** have stumpy cross strokes, the **M** is wide and the italic has swash characters.

ix

ABCDEF GHIJKLMNOPQRSTUV WXYZ@ÆŒ

abcdefghijklmnopqrstuvwxyzæœ

$1234567890£

ABCDEFGHIJKLMNÑOPQRRRSTU VWXYZ&ÆŒ

abcdefghijklmnopqrstuvwxyzœœ

$1234567890£

PLYMOUTH

POLIPHILUS

Monotype 1923

Before BEMBO was cut The Monotype Corporation had already designed a roman based on another Aldine type, that of the *Hypnerotomachia Poliphili*, 1499, which was in fact Griffo's second version of his roman. The upper case is rather taller than that of Bembo. The curve of the **C** is less complete and the **G** has a spur not present in Bembo. The bowl of the **P** is not closed and there is a second variety of **Y** with curved upper limbs. In the lower case there are only slight differences. In the **w** the middle strokes meet at a lower level and the **y** is narrower. The italic is called BLADO.

ii

ABCDEFGHIJKLMNOPQRSTUVWXYZ

ABCDEFGHIJKLMNOPQRSTUVWXYZ

abcdefghijklmnopqrstuvwxyz

1234567890

POLIPHILUS

Designed by Herbert Post. A book and display type of almost calligraphic quality. Characteristic are the **U**, which is in the style of the lower-case **u**, the bowl of the **G**, which is narrow at the bottom, the top serifs of the **T** which point downward to the left, and the concave strokes of the **A.** The strokes of upper- and lower-case letters are of uneven width. There are two weights and an italic with swash caps.

POST
MEDIAEVAL
Berthold 1951;
Intertype (Frankfurt)

All Tourist Clubs of the United States are private organisations of

Orchestras and Musical Societies give classical concerts in Radioprogrammes

POST MEDIAEVAL

ABCDEFGHIJKLMNOPQRSTUVWXYZ

POST MEDIAEVAL SWASH CAPITALS

The woodcut has become one of the most attractive of the arts

POST MEDIAEVAL MEDIUM

Designed by Herbert Post. A display roman with slight variation of colour. The capitals are almost without serifs and most of them are wide. The lower case has small, strong, horizontal serifs and short descenders. The **e** has an oblique stroke to the eye; **g** has a normal tail but not closed. The figures are short-ranging. There are three weights. The italic is of slight inclination and has the serif formation of the roman.

POST ROMAN

Berthold 1937

ABCDEFGHIJKLMNOPQRSTUVWXYZ
abcdefghijklmnopqrstuvwxyz

POST ROMAN LIGHT

ABCDEFGHIJKLMNOPQRSTUVWX
abcdefghijklmnopqrstuvwxyz
1234567890

POST ROMAN MEDIUM

ABCDEFGHIJKLMNOPQRSTUVWX
abcdefghijklmnopqrstuvwxyz

POST ROMAN BOLD

ABCDEFGHIJKLMNOPQRSTUVWXYZ

POST TITLE LIGHT

ABCDEFGHIJKLMNOPQRSTUVWX

POST TITLE MEDIUM

ABCDEFGHIJKLMNOPQRSTUVWX

POST TITLE BOLD

Designed by C.H. Griffith. A fat face following the general style of fat face romans. *Cf.*
ULTRA BODONI.

ABCDEFGHIJKLMNOPQRSTUVWXYZ
abcdefghijklmnopqrstuvw 12345
ABCDEFGHIJKLMNOPQRSTUVWXYZ
defghijklmnopqrstuvwxyz 67890

POSTER BODONI

iv

ABCDEFGHIJKLMNOPQRSTUVWXYZ&
abcdefghijklmnopqrstuvwxyz
1234567890

MERGENTHALER LINOTYPE POSTER BODONI COMPRESSED

POWELL

Ludlow 1925

A heavy roman with rugged outlines and short descenders. The bowls of **B** and **P** are open.

ABCDEFGHIJKLMNOPQRSTUV
abcdefghijklmnopqrstuvwxyz 1234

POWELL

PRACHT

J. Wagner

Designed by Carl Pracht in 1941. A display roman in which the lower case is rather like an upright italic with pen-drawn qualities. The **G** has a long spur and **K** and **R** are unusual. In the italic the capitals have the qualities of a script, while the lower case is the roman inclined. There is a bold and bold condensed.

ix

ABCDEFGHIJKLMNOPQRSTUVW
abcdefghijklmnopqrstuvwxyz
1234567890

ABCDEFGHIJKLMNOPQRST
UVWXYZ
1234567890
abcdefghijklmnopqrstuvwxyz

PRACHT ROMAN

ix

ABCDEFGHIJKLMNOPQRS
TUVWXYZ

PRACHT CURSIVE INITIALS

ABCDEFGHIJKLMNOPQRSTUV
abcdefghijklmnopqrstuvwxyz

PRACHT

ix

PRACHT BOLD

ABCDEFGHIJKLMNOPQRSTUVWXYZ
abcdefghijklmnopqrstuvwxyz

ix

PRACHT BOLD CONDENSED

A calligraphic roman, light in weight.

PRAHA

Grafotechna 1968

ii

ABCDEFGHIJKLMNOPQRSTUV WXYZ
abcdefghijklmnopqrstuvwxyz
1234567890

ABCDEFGHIJKLMNOPQRS TUV WXYZ
abcdefghijklmnopqrstuvwxyz
1234567890

PRAHA

Designed by Vojtech Preissig from 1924–27 for the Government Printing Office in Prague. An angular type with slight inclination in the italic, in which the lower case is even more uneven in outlines than the roman. Numerals are non-ranging. In the roman the **f** does not descend below the line, and in the italic has a pointed descender.

PREISSIG

Grafotechna 1924–27

ix

ABCDEFGHIJKLMNOP
abcdefghijkm nopqrstuvwyz
1234567890

ABCDEFGHIJKLMNOPQ
abcdefghijklmnopqrstuvwyz
1234567890

PREISSIG

PRESIDENT
Deberny & Peignot 1954

vii

Designed by A. Frutiger. A set of capitals and ranging figures with very small serifs. Note the wide, splayed **M**.

A B C D E F G H I J K L M N O P Q R S T U V W X Y Z

1 2 3 4 5 & Œ Ç 6 7 8 9 0

PRESIDENT

PRIMER
Mergenthaler Linotype 1951

iv

Designed by Rudolph Ruzicka. A newspaper type with short ascenders and descenders. There are ranging and non-ranging numerals.

ABCDEFGHIJKLMNOPQRSTUVWXYZ
abcdefghijklmnopqrstuvwxyz
1234567890
ABCDEFGHIJKLMNOPQRSTUVWXYZ
abcdefghijklmnopqrstuvwxyz
1234567890
ABCDEFGHIJKLMNOPQRSTUVWXYZ
1234567890   *1234567890*

PRIMER

PRIMUS
Berthold 1964

iv

Designed by Friedrich Berthold. A fat face for book and display work.

A B C D E F G H I J K L M N O P Q R S T U V W X Y Z
a b c d e f g h i j k l m n o p q r s t u v w x y z ff fi fl ft &
1 2 3 4 5 6 7 8 9 0

A B C D E F G H I J K L M N O P Q R S T U V W X Y Z
a b c d e f g h i j k l m n o p q r s t u v w x y z ff fi fl ft &
1 2 3 4 5 6 7 8 9 0

PRIMUS

iv

A B C D E F G H I J K L M N O P Q R S T U V W X Y Z
a b c d e f g h i j k l m n o p q r s t u v w x y z ff fi fl ft &
1 2 3 4 5 6 7 8 9 0

PRIMUS BOLD

PRO ARTE
Haas 1954

v

Designed by Max Miedinger. Like FIGARO, etc., this is a revival of a nineteenth-century design. It follows the style of PLAYBILL very closely, but the letters are even more condensed. The tail of the **R** is cut off, and the **Q** is an O resting on a flourish.

ABCEEFGHIJKLMNOPQRSTUVWXYZ

1234567890

PRO ARTE

Designed by Eugen and Max Lenz. A set of three-dimensional capitals and figures, which are inclined. The heavy black letters are rimmed with a white line.

PROFIL

Haas 1946

v

ABCDEFGHIJKLM
NOPQRSTUVWXYZ
1234567890

PROFIL

A display roman with heavy serifs. They are especially heavy on the arms of the **E** and the terminals of the **S**. Ascenders and descenders are short. The tail of the **g** is not closed. There is also a bold, and a closely similar face called EGIPCIA PROGRESO.

PROGRESO

Gans c. 1923

ix

ix

Ropa Egeo

PROGRESO

Enrejados
MOREDA

PROGRESO BOLD

Designed by Leonard H.D. Smit. An expanded face of medium weight with short ascenders and descenders. The serifs are bracketed, as also is the apex of the **t**.

PROMOTOR

Amsterdam 1960

iv

ABCDEFGHIJKLMNOPQ
RSTUVWXYZÆŒ
abcdefghijklmnopqrstuvw
xyz
1234567890£&æœ

PROMOTOR

A lighter face than SUBIACO. It is based on the roman used at Ulm by Leonhard Holle in an edition of *Ptolemy*, 1482. The punches were cut mechanically. The **U** follows the lower-case design. The **g** has a large bowl and also a large tail, and the **h** has a curved shank. This type is now in the possession of the Cambridge University Press.

PTOLEMY
ROMAN

Ashendene Press 1927

i

QUESTO DANTE FU HONOREVOLE ANTICO

cittadino di Firenze di porta San Piero, & il suo esilio da

PTOLEMY ROMAN

Designed by Stanislav Marso. A heavy face with flat serifs and very short ascenders. Round letters are squared-up, e.g., in the **b**, **c**, **e**, **p** and **q**. The **f** has a button-hook terminal. There is also an italic on line composition matrices of the Tos matrix factory.

iv

ABCDEFGHIJKLMNOPQRST
UVWXYZ
abcdefghijklmnopqrstu
vwxyz
1234567890

PUBLIC

iv

ABCDEFGHIJKLMNOPQRSTU
VWXYZ
abcdefghijklmnopqrstuvwxyz
1234567890

PUBLIC CONDENSED

Designed by Joachim Romann. A set of outline and decorated capitals and ranging figures. The decoration consists of knotted work and is found on the serifs also.

ix

QUEEN

Designed by Alessandro Butti. A display type like CORVINUS. It has the same distinguishing feature of square sides to the normally round letters. But the **M** is square and in the lower case the tops of the ascenders are without serifs. The italic, except for a one-storeyed **a**, is the roman inclined. There are two weights.

iv

ABCDEFGHIJKLMNOPQRSTUVXYWZ
abcdefghijklmnopqrstuvxywz
1234567890

QUIRINUS

ABCDEFGHIJKLMNOPQRSTUVXYWZ

abcdefghijklmnopqrstuvxy

1234567890

QUIRINUS ITALIC

ABCDEFGHIJKLMNOPQRSTUVXYWZ

abcdefghijklmnopqrstuvxywz

1234567890

QUIRINUS BOLD

Designed by Adolf Behrmann. A fat face with very small serifs, in which the thins have a moderate weight. Some of the round letters, *e.g.*, **C** and **G**, and the insides of the counters have straight edges. Ascenders are fairly tall and descenders short. There are also capitals shaded horizontally.

RUNDFUNK is the same design with taller capitals and ascenders.

Sidenhuset Eckström 56789

RADIO

Handwerker HOTEL REICHS

RUNDFUNK   RADIO SHADED CAPITALS

A fat face of nineteenth century design and with hair line serifs and very short ascenders and descenders.

ABCDEFGHIJKLMNO PQRSTUVWXYZ abcdefghijklmnopqrstu 1234567890 VWXYZ

RAKETE

An extra bold titling fount in which the letters have also been expanded. The negative parts are outlined by fine hair lines and the three-dimensional shading is comparatively thin. Serifs are flat and square-edged. The lower part of **R** and **P** are shorter than the upper parts, while the horizontal strokes in **B, E** and **G** are central.

ERZGEBIRGE

RAMONA

A monotone roman with minute serifs, wide letters and very short ascenders and descenders. The round letters are quite circular.

Grand-Hotel Metro

RASSE

Designed by F.W. Kleukens. A type in the BODONI style. In the **a**, **c** and **e** the terminals are blobs, as in the ear of the **g**. The italic has roman serifs.

ABCDEFGHIJKLMNOPQRSTU
abcdefghijklmnopqrstuvwxyz
1234567890
ABCDEFGHIJKLMNOPQRST
abcdefghijklmnopqrstuvwxyz

RATIO

ABCDEFGHIJKLMNOPQRSTU
abcdefghijklmnopqrstuvwxyz

RATIO BOLD

ABCDEFGHIJKLMNOPQRST
abcdefghijklmnopqrstuvwxy

RATIO EXTRA BOLD

THE VOCAL MUSIC OF BRAHMS

OPEN RATIO TITLING

Designed under the direction of H.R. Freund. A newspaper face with short ascenders and descenders. The serifs are less solid than in types like IDEAL; capitals are wide. There is also a bold roman.

ABCDEFGHIJKLMNOPQRSTUVWXYZ
abcdefghijklmnopqrstuvwxyz   1234567890
ABCDEFGHIJKLMNOPQRSTUVWXYZ

ABCDEFGHIJKLMNOPQRSTUVWXYZ
abcdefghijklmnopqrstuvwxyz   1234567890

REGAL

ABCDEFGHIJKLMNOPQRSTUVWXYZ
abcdefghijklmnopqrstuvwxyz   1234567890

REGAL BOLD

A condensed three-dimension titling. The design is an engraved version of this founder's NORMANDE CONDENSED.

REGINA
Berthold 1955

iv

ABCDEFGHIJKLMNOPQRSTUVWXYZ
1234567890

REGINA

Designed by Wilhelm Scheffel. A roman of a pronounced pen-drawn quality. The serifs are oblique and on some letters shaped. The upper arm of the **E** and other strokes also are shaped. The **U** has the lower-case design. The **a** is one-storeyed and the eye of the **e** has an oblique stroke. There is also a semi-bold.

REMBRANDT
Bauer 1914

ix

REMBRANDT

REMBRANDT

A series of inline roman capitals. Serifs are sharp and bracketed. The bars of the **A, H,** and similar strokes are very thin.

REX
Genzsch & Heyse 1924

ix

BUCKINGHAM

REX

Originally a German roman cut in Leipzig and called UNIVERSITY ROMAN or DRUCKHAUS. It is a heavy face with short ascenders and descenders, modern-face in design, except for the lower case **g**. There are bold and extra bold faces and a condensed bold.

RHENANIA
Haas and other founders

iv

ABCDEFGHIJKLMNOPQRSTUVWX
abcdefghijklmnopqrstuvwxyz
1234567890

RHENANIA

iv

ABCDEFGHIJKLMNOPQRSTU
abcdefghijklmnopqrstuvwxyz

RHENANIA BOLD

iv

ABCDEFGHIJKLMNOPQRST
abcdefghijklmnopqrstuvwx

RHENANIA EXTRA BOLD

iv

ABCDEFGHIJKLMNOPQRSTUVWXYZ
abcdefghijklmnopqrstuvwxyz

RHENANIA BOLD CONDENSED

**RICCARDI
PRESS
FOUNT**

Medici Society 1909

ii

ii

ii

vii

Designed by Herbert P. Horne. Capitals are made of a uniform width, for instance, the **E** is as broad as the **M**. The **R** has a wide bowl and the tail tapers. The **a** and **e** are broad, and lower-case serifs are small and oblique. Numerals are non-ranging.

Fourteen Point Riccardi together with a selection of the Initial Letters

A private typeface owned by The Medici Society

1234567890 £

RICCARDI

ABCDEKOPRUW

RICCARDI OPEN

ACDEFGINPQSTWV

RICCARDI BOLD

RICCARDO

Haas 1941

ix

Designed by Richard Gerbig. An open three-dimensional titling in which many of the letters are lineale in design. The bars of **A** and **H** extend to the left of the main strokes.

ABCDEFGHIJKLMNOPQR
STUVWXYZ
1234567890

RICCARDO

**RIEDINGER
MEDIAEVAL**

Krebs 1929

ii

Designed by Franz Riedinger. Serifs are strong and bracketed, slightly concave on the lower case. Ascenders and descenders are short. The italic is lightly inclined and has pen strokes in the place of serifs.

Geschwister Bernstein

RIEDINGER MEDIAEVAL ITALIC

192

Designed by William T. Sniffin. A roman closely resembling Koch's LOCARNO, except that the capitals are shaded like the capitals of the KOCH CURSIV. The serifs at the tops of ascenders are smaller than in LOCARNO. The italic is very close to KOCH CURSIV.

RIVOLI
American Typefounders 1928

MUSIC

Delightful girl entertainer

OLD AUTOMOBILE

Manufacturer displayed relic

RIVOLI

ix

A heavy roman with blurred serifs and short ascenders and descenders. CLAIRE DE LUNE is the inline version. ROYAL LINING is another name for the shaded version of the type.

ROBUR PALE
or
ROYAL LINING
*Deberny & Peignot c. 1912;
Stevens Shanks 1924*

Inventions

ROBUR BLACK

Quotidien

ROBUR BLACK ITALIC

ix

Arts

ROBUR TIGRE

Pianos

CLAIRE DE LUNE

ix

LES CHAMPIONS

CLAIRE DE LUNE ELONGATED

ix

Côte d'Azur Polaires

ROBUR ELONGATED

ix

Récit LETTERS

with advertisers

ix

ROYAL LINING

ROCKWELL
Monotype 1934

The **A** has a slab serif, the **G** no spur, the **M** is wide, the **Q** has the tail entirely outside the bowl. The **a** is two-storeyed, the **g** has an open tail, and the **t** has a curved foot.
There are four weights, condensed faces, and a SHADOW, which is three-dimensional.

v

ABCDEFGHIJKLMNOPQRSTUVWXYZ
abcdefghijklmnopqrstuvwxyz
1234567890

ROCKWELL LIGHT

v

ABCDEFGHIJKLMNOPQRSTUVWXYZ
abcdefghijklmnopqrstuvwxyz
1234567890

CASTLES and cathedrals of France

ROCKWELL MEDIUM

v

ABCDEFGHIJKLMNOPQRSTUVWXYZ
abcdefghijklmnopqrstuvwxyz
1234567890

ROCKWELL HEAVY

v

ABCDEFGHIJKLMNOPQRSTUVWXYZ
abcdefghijklmnopqrstuvwxyz
1234567890

ROCKWELL BOLD CONDENSED

v

v

v

ABCDEFGHIJKLMNOPQRSTUVWXYZ
abcdefghijklmnopqrstuvwxyz
1234567890

ROCKWELL CONDENSED

v

ABCDEFGHIJKLMNOPQRSTUVWXYZ
abcdefghijklmnopqrstuvwxyz
1234567890

ROCKWELL EXTRA BOLD

GEOMETRY

ROCKWELL SHADOW

ABCDEFGHIJKLMNOPQRSTUVW
XYZ

abcdefghijklmnopqrstuvwxyz

1234567890

ROCKWELL SHADED

Designed by J. Roesner. A pen-drawn titling.

ABCDEFGHIJKLMNOPQRSTU
VWXYZ

1234567890 &

ROESNER

Designed by Johann Christian Bauer, the founder of the Bauer Typefoundry. Another fat face of the usual early nineteenth-century design. FALSTAFF and RAKETE are similar.

ABCDEFGHIJKLMNOPQRST
UVWXYZ

abcdefghijklmnopqrstuvwxyz

1234567890

ABCDEFGHIJKLMNOPQRS
TUVWXYZ

abcdefghijklmnopqrstuvwxyz

1234567890

ROMAN EXTRA BOLD

195

ROMANA
J. Wagner c. 1904

A display roman of some weight and short ascenders and descenders, and basically a German DE VINNE adaptation. The serif formation is old face. The central arms of **E**, **F** and **H** are above the centre. The final upright in the **G** is tall and the **M** is splayed. There is also a bold.

ii

ABCDEFGHIJKLMNOPQRST
UVWXYZ

abcdefghijklmnopqrstuvwxyz

1234567890

ROMANA

ii

ABCDEFGHIJKLMNOPQRS
TUVWXYZ
abcdefghijklmnopqrstuvwxyz

ROMANA BOLD

ROMANÉE
Enschedé 1928–1949

Designed by Jan van Krimpen to accompany the only surviving italic of the seventeenth-century Amsterdam founder Christoffel van Dijck. Romanée, named after a wine drunk by the designer at El Vino's in London's Fleet Street, has a considerable resemblance to BEMBO, both in colour and in the modest height of the capitals. The **A** has a sharper apex and the **J** a straight tail. There are no italic capitals. The slightly-inclined italic shown here was added twenty-one years after the roman and the designer himself comments that "the distance of twenty years between the coming into existence of the one and the other in a way tells".

ii

ABCDEFGHIJKLMNOPQ_RSTUVWXYZ

abcdefghijklmnopqrstuvwxyz

1234567890

abcdefghijklmnopqrstuvwxyz   *1234567890*

ROMANÉE

ii

ABCDEEFGHIJJKLMNPQRSTUVWXYZ&

ROMANÉE SWASH CAPS

196

Decorated capitals of Victorian design. In Nos. 1 and 3 the serifs are rounded, in No. 2 the top serifs run to points. In No. 1 the upper halves of letters are white and the lower halves black; in No. 2 the colours are reversed. No. 5 is shaded. ORNAMENTED OUTLINE, which is identical with No. 1 is shown elsewhere.

ROMANTIQUES

Fonderie Typographique Française

ix

ABCDEFGHIJKLMNOPQRST
UVWXYZÆŒ
1234567890

ROMANTIQUES No. 2

ix

ABCDEFGHIJKLMNOPQRSTUV
WXYZÆŒ

ROMANTIQUES No. 3

ix

ABCDEFGHIJKLMNOPQ
RSTUVWXYZÆŒ
1234567890

ROMANTIQUES No. 5

Designed by A. Anklam (capitals) and Heinz Koenig (lower case). The type is also known as BRADFORD, HADDONIAN or MCFARLAND.

RÖMISCHE ANTIQUA

Genzsch & Heyse 1988

ix

ABCDEFGHIJKLMN
OPQRSTUVWXYZ
abcdefghijklmnopqrst
uvwxyz
1234567890
ABCDEFGHIJKL·MNOP
QRSTUVWXYZ
abcdefghijklmnopqrst
uvwxyz
1234567890

RÖMISCHE ANTIQUA

ROMULUS

Enschedé 1931;
Monotype 1936

Designed by Jan van Krimpen. One of those contemporary romans which cut across the old divisions of type families. In gradation of colour it is akin to the old faces, but the serifs are almost horizontal and the stress nearly vertical. The capitals are unobtrusive and the serifs light. The bowl of the g is large. The italic is an interesting experiment in the sloped roman, carried out in every detail with the letters as wide as the roman. The figures are short-ranging. There is also a bold and open versions designed in 1955, and a calligraphic type called CANCELLARESCA BASTARDA shown separately. The type was intended to have a complete range of weights, a related sanserif and Greek. These were cut but do not seem to be generally used.

iii

ABCDEFGHIJKLMNOPQRSTUVWXY
abcdefghijklmnopqrstuvwxyz   Z&
1234567890

ABCDEFGHIJKLMNOPQRSTUVWXY
abcdefghijklmnopqrstuvwxyz   Z&
1234567890

ROMULUS

iii

ABCDEFGHIJKLMNOPQRSTUVWXYZ&
abcdefghijklmnopqrstuvwxyz
1234567890

ROMULUS BOLD

iii

ABCEFGHIJKLMNOPQRSTUVWXYZ
1234567890

ROMULUS OPEN CAPS

RONALDSON OLD STYLE

Monotype 1903;
Linotype (London)

Originally cut in 1884 by the American founders, MacKellar, Smiths & Jordan, and no doubt named after one of the original founders of their house, James Ronaldson, who with Archibald Binny established a typefoundry in Philadelphia in 1796. It is easily distinguished by the beak-like serifs on the capitals and lower case and by the squared-up shoulders of **m** and **n**. In the italic the serifs are more normal and the design becomes very like OLD STYLE. The Monotype Corporation's version has short ascenders and descenders and capitals not rising above the ascenders.

ii

ABCDEFGHIJKLMNOPQRSTUVWXYZ&
abcdefghijklmnopqrstuvwxyz
1234567890

ABCDEFGHIJKLMNOPQRSTUVWXYZ&
abcdefghijklmnopqrstuvwxyz

MONOTYPE RONALDSON OLD STYLE

The original by J.F. Rosart, (1714-77,) a typefounder at Haarlem and later at Brussels. The shaded capitals have since been in the possession of the Enschedé foundry. The type is a series of inline roman capitals almost three-dimensional in appearance. The **Q** has a long descending tail and the **J**, descending below the line, a curled tail. Characters vary in different sizes.

ROSART
Enschedé 1759

ii

ABCDEFGHIJ
KLMNOPQRS
TUVWXYZ

ROSART

Designed by Walter Schneider and H. Vollenweider and cut in one size only by the Haas foundry. The lower case is based on 15th century type known as ROTUNDA. The originals are now in the Kunstgewerbemuseum, Zürich.

ROTUNDA
Johannes Presse 1948

ix

A B C D E F G H I J K L M N O P Q R S T u v w x y z Ä Ö Ü Æ

abcdefghijklmnopqrsßſtuvwxyʒ fffiflftſiſtttäöüæ

1234567890

ROTUNDA

The type was initially designed for use by *The Scotsman*. A newspaper type for classified advertisements and editorials SCOTSMAN ROYAL is based on the standard version of ROYAL. Ascenders and descenders are short and serifs strong, as in other types designed for newspaper work. Very similar to CORONA. Like CLARITAS, MAXIMUS and ADSANS, this type is available in 4¾ point.

ROYAL
Intertype 1960

iv

This example of Intertype's new typeface ROYAL is set in the 9 point size. Royal owes much of its clarity to generous x-height and slightly elongated form. **The bold face** *and complementary italic* are equally successful.
Standard characters
CGKQRW agktw 57 **CGKQRW agktw 57**

ROYAL

ABCDEFGHIJKLMNOPQRSTUVWXYZÆŒ

abcdefghijklmnopqrstuvwxyzæœ

12345 67890

ABCDEFGHIJKLMNOPQRSTUVWXYZÆŒ

abcdefghijklmnopqrstuvwxyzæœ

12345 67890

SCOTSMAN ROYAL

A monoline extra condensed bold roman.

ABCDEFGHIJKLMNOPQRSTUVWXYZ

abcdefghijklmnopqrstuvwxyz

1234567890

RUNIC CONDENSED

A type based on manuscript hands of the Italian fifteenth century. The serifs are shaped, as though made with a pen; many of the round letters also follow the rule of the pen. The **G** has a deep spur and **U** the lower-case design. The **g** has an open tail; **v, w** and **y** are cursive forms. It is a black type. The figures are short-ranging. Originally an American type called MOTTO.

Exhibition of Printed Books

RUNNYMEDE

Designed by Paul Hayden-Duensing for his private press. This calligraphic titling lacks a cross-bar in the **A**, and has unparallel left-hand strokes in the **M**.

ABCDEFGHIJKLMNOPQRSTUVWXYZ

RUSTICA

Designed by Jan Tschichold and jointly developed by Linotype, Monotype and Stempel, in response to a common need of German master printers for a type face to be made in identical form for mechanical composition by linecasting and single-type methods, and also for hand composition in foundry type.

The sources for the design are to be found on a specimen sheet of the Frankfurt type-founder, Konrad Berner, who married the widow of another typefounder, Jacques Sabon—hence the name of the face. The roman is based on a fount engraved by Garamond and the italic on a fount by Granjon, but Tschichold has introduced many refinements to make these models suitable for the typographic needs of today and for the varying requirements of the three manufacturing companies.

ABCDEFGHIJKLMNOPQRSTUVWXYZ

abcdefghijklmnopqrstuvwxyz

1234567890

ABCDEFGHIJKLMNOPQRSTUVWXYZ

abcdefghijklmnopqrstuvwxyz

1234567890

SABON

ABCDEFGHIJKLMNOPQRSTUVWXYZ

abcdefghijklmnopqrstuvwxyz

1234567890

SABON BOLD

Designed by H. Maehler. A close-set linear extra bold face with moderate variation in colour.

ABCDEFGHIJKLMNOPQ
abcdefghijklmnopqrstuv
1234567890

SALUT

Designed by Hermann Zapf. Decorated capitals of fat face design. The decoration is based on leaf forms. There is also a set of ranging figures (FESTIVAL NUMERALS).

ABCDEFGHIJKLMNOPQR

SAPPHIRE

1234567890

FESTIVAL NUMERALS

Designed by Jan Tschichold. An italic with considerable variation of stress and short ascenders and descenders. It is without serifs but there are thickened terminals of the arcs of **c, s** and similar letters. The eye of the **e** and the bowls are not quite closed. ZEUSS is somewhat similar.

Eigenart voll Vornehmheit und Eleganz zutage, die sie weit erhebt über alles Hergebrachte und Alltägliche. Wer eindrucksvoll und doch voll Milde

SASKIA •

The **A** has no top serif, **J** has a round loop, **R** a slightly curved tail and the **W** no middle serif. The **a** is two-storeyed, **b** has no foot serif, **g** has the open tail of the continental versions and **t** a curved terminal. There is an italic, a light face and a bold.

ABCDEFGHIJKLMNOPQRSTUVXYZ
abcdefghijklmnopqrstuvwxyz
1234567890£

SCARAB LIGHT

ABCDEFGHIJKLMNOPQRSTUVWXYZ
abcdefghijklmnopqrstuvwxyz
1234567890
ABCDEFGHIJKLMNOPQRSTUVWXYZ
abcdefghijklmnopqrstuvwxyz
1234567890£

SCARAB

Designed by Georg Trump. An angular type with horizontal serifs. The **g** has flourished but open tail.

v

ABCDEFGHIJKLMNOPQRSTUVW
XYZ
abcdefghijklmnopqrstuvwxyz
1234567890

SCHADOW LIGHT

v

ABCDEFGHIJKLMNOPQRSTU
VWXYZ
abcdefghijklmnopqrstuvwxyz
1234567890
ABCDEFGHIJKLMNOPQRSTU
VXYZ
abcdefghijklmnopqrstuvwxyz
1234567890

SCHADOW WERK

v

ABCDEFGHIJKLMNOPQRS
TUVWXYZ
abcdefghijklmnopqrstuvwxy
1234567890

SCHADOW BOLD

v

ABCDEFGHIJKLMNOPQRST
UVWXYZ
abcdefghijklmnopqrstuvwxy
1234567890

SCHADOW EXTRA BOLD

v

ABCDEFGHIJKLMNOPQRSTUVWXYZ
abcdefghijklmnopqrstuvwxyz
1234567890

SCHADOW BOLD CONDENSED

Designed by F.H.E. Schneidler. Similar to MENHART but with less variation of stress. The **M** is splayed and without top serifs. The **Q** has a brief tail outside the bowl and does not descend below the line. Numerals range. SCHNEIDLER INITIALS have pointed and very small serifs. **B**, **E**, **F**, **P** and **R** are narrow letters. The **M** is wide and splayed, and the **U** of lower-case design. AMALTHEA (1957) is an italic companion design.

SCHNEIDLER OLD STYLE or BAUER TEXT

ABCDEFGHIJKLMNOPQRSTUVWXYZ

abcdefghijklmnopqrstuvwxyz

12345678

vii

SCHNEIDLER OLD STYLE

ABCDEFGHIJKLMNOPQR

vii

SCHNEIDLER INITIALS

Designed by Albert Auspurg. A heavy shaded italic. The shading is horizontal. The capitals are of the swash variety and the serifs thin.

SCHÖNBRUNN
Krebs 1928

Bremer Ratskeller

ix

SCHÖNBRUNN

An important type and a revival of some ninety years ago of a series of types which appear in the specimens of William Miller, of Edinburgh, for 1813. The type in its original may be the work of Richard Austin. It was for a time perhaps the most favoured of English faces in use for literary texts, because it avoids some of the extremes. The letters are sturdy and the serifs bracketed.

Monotype SCOTCH ROMAN (46) was cut in 1907, and (137) in 1920 for R. & R. Clark, the printers, as an accurate re-cutting of the Miller & Richard type (though the 14 pt size is not strictly derived from the original). There are variations in the design of different sizes.

SCOTCH ROMAN
Miller & Richard;

Linotype (London);

Mergenthaler Linotype;

Monotype; Intertype

ABCDEFGHIJKLMNOPQRSTUVWXYZ
abcdefghijklmnopqrstuvwxyz
1234567890

iv

ABCDEFGHIJKLMNOPQRSTUVWXYZ
abcdefghijklmnopqrstuvwxyz
1234567890

MONOTYPE SCOTCH ROMAN

ABCDEFGHIJKLMNOPQRSTUVWXYZ&
ABCDEFGHIJKLMNOPQRSTUVWXYZ&
abcdefghijklmnopqrstuvwxyz
1234567890

iv

ABCDEFGHIJKLMNOPQRSTUVWXYZ&
abcdefghijklmnopqrstuvwxyz
1234567890

MERGENTHALER LINOTYPE SCOTCH NO. 2 ROMAN

SCROLL SHADED

Stevens Shanks

ix

Three-dimensional, decorated capitals from the foundry of V. & J. Figgins. The style was originated around 1815 by Figgins as an ORNAMENTED ETRUSCAN.

ABCDEFGHIJKLMNOPQR
STUVWXYZÆŒ&

SCROLL SHADED

SELECT or ALBERT

Berling;
Amsterdam c. 1936

iv

Designed by Albert Augspurg. Shaded capitals, the shading being horizontal. The graduation of stress is abrupt and the serifs thin.

ABCDEFGHIJKLMNOPQRS
TUVWXYZ
1234567890

SELECT

SERIE 16

Deberny & Peignot;
Linotype (London);
Mergenthaler Linotype

iv

A modern face with rather short ascenders and descenders. The **Q** has the tail entirely outside the bowl. The italic, as frequently in French types, has the serifs of the roman. The Linotype version is called No. 61.

ABCDEFGHIJKLMNOPQRSTUVWXYZ
abcdefghijklmnopqrstuvwxyz
1234567890
ABCDEFGHIJKLMNOPQRSTUVWXYZ
abcdefghijklmnopqrstuvwxyz
1234567890

SERIE 16

SERIE 18

Deberny & Peignot

iv

A roman with considerable variation of stress. Serifs are small and slightly inclined. There are both ranging and non-ranging figures. The italic has some of the qualities of a script, as in the upper arms of the **E** and **F**, and in the **R**. Linotype called their version TRANSIT, which was also known as BASKERVILLE OLD STYLE, and is no longer available.

ABCDEFGHIJKLMNOPQRSTUVWXYZ
abcdefghijklmnopqrstuvwxyz
1234567890 & 1234567890
ABCDEFGHIJKLMNOPQRSTUVWXYZ
abcdefghijklmnopqrstuvwxyz
1234567890 & 1234567890

SERIE 18

Designed by Adrian Frutiger. A type based on the geometric linear forms of UNIVERS to which slab serifs have been added.

ABCDEFGHIJKLMNOPQRSTUV
WXYZ
abcdefghijklmnopqrstuvwxyz
1234567890

SERIFA LIGHT

ABCDEFGHIJKLMNOPQRSTUV
WXYZ
abcdefghijklmnopqrstuvwxyz
1234567890

SERIFA MEDIUM

Designed by Karl Michel. A shaded roman, the shading being horizontal.

History of Scot

SHADED ROMAN

Designed by Georg Belwe, a display face of rich colour, even in the lightest weight. The serifs are strong and stubby in the lower case. The **A** has a slab serif and the **R** a wide, shallow bowl. In the **M** the middle strokes stop short of the line. The descenders are very short. The italic has a moderate inclination. The middle strokes of the **M** are curved. The **y** is a script form. There is also a bold, an extra bold, and condensed faces.

MINERALOGIA E GEOLO

Carta della provincia di Per

Editore Ferdinando Dalmo Mi

SHAKESPEARE MEDIAEVAL

DAMPFSCHIFF-VERKE

Jahresausſtellung in Barcel

Conférence internationale 1

SHAKESPEARE MEDIAEVAL BOLD

Publication du Gouvern

SHAKESPEARE MEDIAEVAL EXTRA BOLD CONDENSED

Designed by Paul Hayden-Duensing for his private press after a set of very rough punches acquired by the designer in Italy from which after much work castable matrices were produced. Some letters were added by engraving new punches.

ABCDEFGHIJKLMNOPQuRSTUVVXYZ

abcdefghijklmnopqrstuvvvxyz

Ⓓæꝛⱦāđēꞓīñóꝓꝗꝙꝓꞇū✠

XVITH CENTURY ROMAN

SLENDER

Ludwig & Mayer 1939

Designed by Walter Höhnisch. A condensed roman with most of the characteristics of a modern face. Some of the serifs, *e.g.*, on the E and S, are heavier. The M is splayed. The ascenders and descenders are short. The thickened terminals of arcs are blobs and the **g** has an open tail. There is also a Bold face. In Germany the founders call the type SCHLANKE.

iv

ABCDEFGHIJKLMNOPQRSTUVWXYZ
abcdefghijklmnopqrstuvwxyz
1234567890

ABCDEFGHIJKLMNOPQRSTUVWXYZ
abcdefghijklmnopqrstuvwxyz
1234567890

SLENDER

iv

ABCDEFGHIJKLMNOPQRSTUVWXYZ
abcdefghijklmnopqrstuvwxyz
1234567890

SLENDER SEMIBOLD

iv

ABCDEFGHIJKLMNOPQRSTUVWXYZ
abcdefghijklmnopqrstuvwxyz
1234567890

SLENDER BOLD

Designed by G. Zapf-v. Hesse. A set of outline capitals with hair-line serifs.

SMARAGD
Stempel 1953

iv

ABCDEFGHIJKLMNOPQRSTUVWXYZ

SMARAGD

Designed by G.G. Lange. An uncial type. *Cf.* AMERICAN UNCIAL and LIBRA. There is one case only, some letters resembling those of the upper case and others those of the lower case.

SOLEMNIS
Berthold 1954

ix

ABCDEFGHIJKLMNOPQRSTUVWXYZ
1234567890

SOLEMNIS

Designed by Eric Gill. A roman with slight variation of stress and horizontal serifs. There are two **M**'s, one slightly splayed, and the other with the middle strokes descending half-way. The lower case **g** has a resemblance to that letter in Gill's PERPETUA. There is no italic and the numerals are short ranging.

SOLUS
Monotype 1929

ii/iv

MUCH DIFFERENT, AND THE CHANGES
worse than the garden of one hundred years

SOLUS

A condensed fat face with short ascenders and descenders. The **a** and **r**, but not the **s**, have the bulbous terminations frequent in fat faces. The **f** has a button-hook top and the **g** an open tail.

SPARTA
Genzsch & Heyse 1939

iv

HOCHSCHULEN

Königsberg

SPARTA

SPECTRUM

Enschedé 1952;
Monotype 1955
ii

Designed by Jan van Krimpen. A roman in the Aldine tradition. The **W** is composed of two **V**'s and comparatively narrow. The italic is based on the calligraphy of Arrighi.

ABCDEFGHIJKLMNOPQRSTUVWXYZ

abcdefghijklmnopqrstuvwxyz

1234567890 1234567890

As Frederic Warde aptly put it, 'as long as we work with the arbitrary signs of the alphabet, we shall be dependent on the past and—like

ABCDEFGHIJKLMNOPQRSTUVWXYZ

abcdefghijklmnopqrstuvwxyz

1234567890 1234567890

SPECTRUM

SPHINX

Deberny & Peignot 1925

A fat face in which the thin strokes are not hair lines. In the lower case the terminations of the arcs of **a**, **c** and **r** are not quite circular. The **g** has an open tail. In the italic lower case the serifs are blunted.

There is also a condensed face and a set of inline capitals. There are also special modernistic borders for this fount.

iv

ABCDEFGHJKLMNOPQRSTUVXYZ

SPHINX

iv

VIGNETTES

SPHINX INLINE CAPITALS

SPIRE

Lanston Monotype 1938

Designed by Sol Hess as an extra condensed fat face.

ix

AABCDEFGHIJKKLMMNOPQRRSTUUV

WWXYZ&

$1234567890ᶜ

SPIRE

Designed by Sol Hess and based on STYMIE EXTRABOLD.

SQUAREFACE

Lanston Monotype 1939

v

A A B C D E F G H I J K L M N O P Q R S T U V W X Y Z &

a a b c d e f g h i j k l m n o p q r s t u v w x y z

1234567890

SQUAREFACE

A heavy display italic, in which the serifs are merely thickenings of the ends of strokes. The capitals are of the swash variety. Ascenders and descenders are extremely short.

STABIL

Woellmer 1926

ix

Gewerbe und Hand

STABIL

Designed by E. Grundeis. **A** has a rounded top, and the bars of **A** and **H**, arms of **E** and similar strokes are extended beyond the main strokes. **M**, **U** and **W** follow lower-case design. Short serifs are cut off obliquely.

STADION

Schriftguss 1929

ix

Kunstausstellung München Heinrich Zille und sein Werk

STADION

A fat face with tall capitals and ascenders, in which the thins have a certain weight. The capitals are rather narrow, but the lower-case letters are wide. The **g** has a curled ear on top of the bowl. The **t** has its top cut off obliquely.

STAFETTE

Woellmer 1930

iv

Moderne Handarbeit

STAFETTE

STAR NEWS

Star Parts 1962

A newspaper type designed for printing on rough papers and for teletypesetter work. The 8 and 9 pt are cut to the same alphabet length.

ii

ABCDEFGHIJKLMNOPQRSTUVWXYZ

abcdefghijklmnopqrstuvwxyz fiflffffiffl

1234567890

STAR NEWS

ii

ABCDEFGHIJKLMNOPQRSTUVWXYZ

abcdefghijklmnopqrstuvwxyz

1234567890

STAR NEWS BOLD

STEEL

Klingspor 1939

Designed by Rudolf Koch (capitals derived from his OFFENBACH) and Hans Kuehne (lower case). A pen-drawn roman called STAHL in Germany. It is without serifs but not monotone. The capitals vary in width as in the other Koch romans. The **M** is splayed and the **U** has the lower-case design. In the lower case descenders are very short. The **g** has an open tail. The most striking characteristic is the pen-drawn quality of the letters.

ix

ABCDEFGHIJKLMNOPQRSTU

abcdefghijklmnopqrstuvwxyz

1234567890

ABCDEFGHIJKLMNOPQRSTU

abcdefghijklmnopqrstuvwxyz

STEEL

ix

ABCDEFGHIJKLMNOPQRST

abcdefghijklmnopqrstuvwxyz

STEEL BOLD

ix

Chinese porcelain and V

STEEL BOLD CONDENSED

STEELPLATE GOTHIC BOLD

American Typefounders

vii

Capitals with minute serifs. Wide letters of Victorian design. The face was designed to complement Frederic Goudy's COPPERPLATE GOTHIC. *Cf.* PLATE GOTHIC.

FINE QUALITY CON

STEELPLATE GOTHIC BOLD

210

Designed by R. Hunter Middleton. A set of bold capitals with stubby serifs and with white gaps between some strokes. The round letters have a break in the top and another at the foot. American Typefounders' STENCIL is similar.

STENCIL
Ludlow 1938

iv

MODERN 896

STENCIL

A condensed and elongated fat face. *Cf.* ONYX and SLIMBLACK. Another nineteenth century revival. In Germany the type is called STEPHANIE.

STEPHANA or STEPHANIE
Bauer c. 1870

iv

ABCDEFGHIJKLMNOPQRSTUVWXYZ

abcdefghijklmnopqrstuvwxyz

1234567890

STEPHANA

Designed by Morris F. Benton with later additions by Sol Hess for Lanston Monotype and Garry Powell for American Typefounders. **A** has a slab serif, **G** has a spur, the middle strokes of **M** stop short of the line. The **a** is two-storeyed—but the one-storeyed **a** is also supplied, **g** has an open tail and **t** a foot serif to the right only. The italic has the one-storeyed **a**. In other respects it conforms to the roman. There are four weights, and a compressed. STYMIE ANTIQUE SHADED does not really belong in this group.

STYMIE
American Typefounders 1931;

Lanston Monotype

v

ABCDEFGHIJKLMNOPQRSTUV
WXYZ&
abcdefghijklmnopqrstuvwxyz
1234567890
ABCDEFGHIJKLMNOPQRSTUV
WXYZ&
abcdeffghijklmnopqrrstuvwxyz
1234567890

STYMIE MEDIUM

v

AAABCDEFGHIJKLMNOPQRRSTU
VWXYZ&
aabcdeffghijklmnopqrs
ABCDEFGHIJKLMNOPQRSTUV
WXYZ&
abcdeffghijklmnopqrstuvwxyz
1234567890

STYMIE LIGHT

ABCDEFGHIJKLMNOPQRRSTU
VWXYZ&$$^$

abcdefghijklmnopqrstuvwxyz
1234567890

ABCDEFGHIJKLMNOPQRSTUV
WXYZ&$

abcdeffghijklmnopqrrstuvwxyz
1234567890

STYMIE BOLD

ABCDEFGHIJKLMNOPQRSTUV
WXYZ&$$

abcdefghijklmnopqrstuvwxyz
1234567890

STYMIE BLACK

ABCDEFGHIJKLMNOPQRSTU
VWXYZ&$

abcdefghijklmnopqrstuvwxyz
1234567890

STYMIE ANTIQUE SHADED

SUBIACO
Ashendene Press 1902

Designed for C.H.St.J. Hornby after the first roman used in Italy about 1464 by Sweynheym and Pannartz at Subiaco. The punches were cut by E.P. Prince. It is a black face with small serifs and capitals much less conspicuous than is usual with early romans. E and F are narrow. G has a large terminal. In H the right-hand vertical stroke is short. The middle stroke of N reaches neither top nor foot of the uprights. M is splayed and has no middle serifs. W also has no middle serif. In the lower case the g is a straighter letter than the original; h has the curved shank common in early romans; i has an accent for the dot. This face is now in the possession of the Cambridge University Press.

Conrad Sweynheym and Arnold Pannartz
introduced printing into Italy, setting up a
press at Subiaco in 1465. Their type, though

SUBIACO

A text type.

ABCDEFGHIJKLMNOPQRSTUVWXYZ&ÆŒ

abcdefghijklmnopqrstuvwxyzæœ   fiflffffiffl

1234567890

ABCDEFGHIJKLMNOPQRSTUVWXYZ&ÆŒ

ABCDEFGHIJKLMNOPQRSTUVWXYZ&ÆŒ

abcdefghijklmnopqrstuvwxyzæœ   fiflffffiffl

1234567890

SUBURBAN FRENCH

Designed by Franz Deixler. A heavy display italic with blunt serifs. Some of the capitals resemble those of the traditional German gothic types.

Stadion in Berlin
SUGGESTION

A condensed type face with short ascenders and descenders. The dots on **i** and the German *Umlaut*-vowels are square. Many letters are very similar to Ludwig & Mayer's TEMPO, but the **A** has no slab serif and the arcs of **a** and **r** are curved down. SUPERBA ILLUSTRA is a three-dimensional type. There is also a bold version. Berling's SMALFET EGYPTIENNE is another very similar type.

ABCDEFGHIJKLMNOPQRSTUVWXYZ
abcdefghijklmnopqrstuvwxyz
1234567890

SUPERBA CONDENSED

ABCDEFGHIJKLMNOPQRSTU
abcdefghijklmnopqrstuvwxyz

SUPERBA BOLD

ABCDEFGHIJKLMNOPQRSTU
1234567890

SUPERBA ILLUSTRA

TALLONE

Alberto Tallone 1952

ii

Designed by Alberto Tallone for his private press. A text face of even colour with fine serifs. The downward serifs of the **T** point outwards, the **b** has no lower serif. The tail of the **g** in the italic is open and flourished, the lower-case **k** has a bowl. Old style numerals.

A Womans face with natures owne hand painted,
Haste thou the Master Mistris of my passion,
A womans gentle hart but not acquainted
With shifting change as is false womens fashion,

Fra le molte e molte centinaia, ch' io ho visto
e catalogato nella mia Bibliografia manzoniana,
dovrei forse risalire alla prima del Ferrario, per
trovare il quasi perfetto accordo testo-stampa.

TALLONE

TALLONE
MAX FACTOR

Lanston Monotype 1959
ii

Designed by Alberto Tallone for the use of a cosmetics manufacturer. Descenders and ascenders are tall. Figures are cut ranging and non-ranging. The **T** has a bowl-shaped wide top. Serifs are fine.

ABCDEFGHIJKLMNOPQRSTUVWXYZ

abcdefghijklmnopqrstuvwxyz

1234567890   1234567890

ABCDEFGHIJKLMNOPQRSTUVWXYZ

abcdefghijklmnopqrstuvwxyz

1234567890   *1234567890*

TALLONE MAX FACTOR

TEA CHEST

Stephenson Blake 1939

ix

A set of bold, condensed capitals with stubby serifs and with white gaps in some strokes, that is to say a stencil letter. The round letters have a break in the top and another at the foot. The **T** has two breaks in the top. **W** has two breaks between thick and thin strokes. There are also figures. Ludlow STENCIL is similar but not condensed.

ABCDEFGHIJKLMN
OPQRSTUVWXYZ
1234567890

TEA CHEST

214

A slab serif type with some gradation of colour. The **A** has a top serif pointing to the left only, **G** has a spur and the **b** has no foot serif.

ABCDEFGHIJKLMNOPQRSTUV
WXYZ&
abcdefghijklmnopqrstuvwxyz?
1234567890

ABCDEFGHIJKLMNOPQRSTUV
WXYZ&
abcdefghijklmnopqrstuvwxyz?
1234567890

TECHNOTYP

ABCDEFGHIJKLMNOPQRSTU
VWXYZ&
abcdefghijklmnopqrstuvwxyz?
1234567890

TECHNOTYP MEDIUM

ABCDEFGHIJKLMNOPQRSTUVWXYZ&
abcdefghijklmnopqrstuvwxyz?
1234567890

TECHNOTYP MEDIUM CONDENSED

ABCDEFGHIJKLMNOPQRST
UVWXYZ&
abcdefghijklmnopqrstuvwxyz?
1234567890

TECHNOTYP BOLD

TECHNOTYP
v

ABCDEFGHIJKLMNOPQRSTUVWXYZ&
abcdefghijklmnopqrstuvwxyz?
1234567890

v

ABCDEFGHIJKLMNOPQRST
UVWXYZ&
abcdefghijklmnopqrstuvwxyz?
1234567890

TEIMER
Grafotechna

iv

Designed by S. Teimer. A roman with italic, ranging and non-ranging figures. Weight of characters is even, and serifs are straight.

ABCDEFGHIJKLMNOP
QRSTUVWXYZ
abcdefghijklmnopqrstu
vwxyz
1234567890 1234567890
ABCDEFGHIJKLMNOP
QRSTUVWXYZ
abcdefghijklmnopqrstu
vwxyz
1234567890 1234567890

TEMPO
Ludwig & Mayer

v

A condensed Egyptian. The A has a slab serif. The lower-case **a** is two-storeyed and the **g** has an open tail. The arc of the **r** is a circle, an unusual form in an Egyptian. This type should not be confused with Ludlow's TEMPO, a sans serif.

PRIMARY FUNCTION is that it shall be

A newspaper type like IDEAL and IONIC, with stubby serifs, little variation of stress and long ascenders.

TEXTYPE

Mergenthaler Linotype 1929

iv

ABCDEFGHIJKLMNOPQRSTUVWXYZ

abcdefghijklmnopqrstuvwxyz

1234567890

ABCDEFGHIJKLMNOPQRSTUVWXYZ

ABCDEFGHIJKLMNOPQRSTUVWXYZ

abcdefghijklmnopqrstuvwxyz

1234567890

TEXTYPE

Designed by Herbert Thannhaeuser. A type of linear appearance but with minute serifs which in some letters are simple thickenings of strokes. There is slight variation of stress. The **a** is one-storeyed and the **e** has a large eye.

THANN-HAEUSER

Schriftguss 1929

vii

ABCDEFGHIJKLMNOPQRSTUVWX YZ&

abcdefghijklmnopqrstuvwxyz?

1234567890

ABCDEFGHIJKLMNOPQRSTUVW X YZ&

abcdefghijklmnopqrstuvwxyz?

1234567890

THANNHAEUSER

vii

ACBCDEFGHIJKLMNOPQRSTUV WXYZ&

abcdefghijklmnopqrstuvwxyz?

1234567890

THANNHAEUSER BOLD

ix

ABCDEFGHIJKL MNOPQRSTUV WXYZ

THANNHAEUSER INITIALS

THOMAS TYPE

Typoart 1956

Designed by F. Thomas. Among the capitals are a round-topped **A** and a round **E**. In the lower case there are the rudiments of serifs and some modelled strokes.

ix

ABCDEFGHIJKLMNOPQRSTUVWXYZ

abcdefghijklmnopqrstuvwxyz

THOMAS TYPE

THORNE SHADED

Stephenson Blake 1938–48

One of the earliest three-dimensional letters, dating from about 1820. The greatly modified design is based on the contemporary fat face capitals, but with thicker serifs. The proportions of the larger sizes are different.

v

ABCDEFGHIJKLMNOPQ
RSTUVWXYZ
1234567890

THORNE SHADED

THOROWGOOD

Stephenson Blake

Cut by the English type-founder Robert Thorne, predecessor of William Thorowgood, and first shown in his specimen books in the early nineteenth century. The larger series probably derived from the Thorne Foundry, but the smaller 12 pt and the 18 pt (shown here) did not appear until 1836. The fat face has been revived in roman (1953) and italic. **S** and **C** appear to be smaller than other capitals. Most serifs are flat and thin horizontals. In the italic the main strokes of **h**, **k**, **m**, **n** and **r** are curved inwards at the foot.

iv

ABCDEFGHIJKLMNOPQRSTUV
WXYZ
abcdefghijklmnopqrstuvxwyz
1234567890£

ABCDEFGHIJKLMNOPQRSTU
VWXYZ
abcdefghijklmnopqrstuvwxyz
1234567890£

THOROWGOOD

218

A German modern face designed by Walter Tiemann, said to be after DIDOT. It is a heavy face with short descenders, perhaps intended for display. The serifs are brief hair lines. The arms of **E** and **F** also are hair lines. The **J** has a button-hook termination, the **M** is slightly splayed and the **W** (lower-case also) has no middle serif. The **b** has a rudimentary foot serif. In the italic the **Q** has a tail like GOUDY. **Y** is a swash letter. In the lower case the serifs are inclined like FOURNIER, and the curves of **v** and **w** also resemble FOURNIER.

ABCDEFGHIJKLMNOPQRS

abcdefghijklmnopqrstuvwxyz

1234567890

ABCDEFGHIJKLMNOPQRST

abcdefghijklmnopqrstuvwxyz

TIEMANN

Care is an enemy to life

iv

Hermann und Dorot

iv

NARCISS

Designed by Walter Tiemann. A calligraphic italic, cast as WREN by Pavyers & Bullens.

ABCDEFGGHIJKRLM

MNNOPQRS STUVWX

YZ

TIEMANN MEDIAEVAL

Monotype 1932;

Linotype (London) 1932;

Mergenthaler Linotype 1935;

Linotype (Frankfurt);

Intertype 1954;

Intertype (F) 1955;

Ludlow;

Stephenson Blake 1955

Commissioned by *The Times*, 1931, the design was supervised by Stanley Morison. A newspaper type with short ascenders and descenders. Serifs are small and sharply cut. It is a rather black type, in comparison for instance with the previous TIMES roman. The capitals, being no higher than the short ascenders, are small, and unobtrusive. On the lower case the serifs are oblique and the stress is neither abrupt nor vertical. The thickest parts of **c** and **e** are very low down. The **g** has a wide tail. The italic is regular, of a moderate inclination, and has the serifs of the roman. The figures are ranging, but non-ranging figures are also available.

A modified version, with longer descenders, for book work, is available. There are also Titlings in two weights and a Condensed Titling. The special small design to this type is called CLARITAS, and is shown separately. For German setting special light capitals are available. TIMES HEVER TITLING presumaby named after Lord Astor of Hever, is not really similar to the TIMES NEW ROMAN series.

ii

ABCDEFGHIJKLMNOPQRSTUVWXYZ

abcdefghijklmnopqrstuvwxyz

1234567890

ABCDEFGHIJKLMNOPQRSTUVWXYZ

abcdefghijklmnopqrstuvwxyz

1234567890

TIMES NEW ROMAN

ii

ABCDEFGHIJKLMNOPQRSTUVWXYZ

abcdefghijklmnopqrstuvwxyz

1234567890

ABCDEFGHIJKLMNOPQRSTUVWXYZ

abcdefghijklmnopqrstuvwxyz

1234567890

TIMES BOLD

ii

ABCDEFGHIJKLMNOPQRSTUVWXYZ

abcdefghijklmnopqrstuvwxyz

1234567890

TIMES SEMI-BOLD

ii

ABCDEFGHIJKLMNOPQRSTUVWXYZ

abcdefghijklmnopqrstuvwxyz

1234567890

ABCDEFGHIJKLMNOPQRSTUVWXYZ

abcdefghijklmnopqrstuvwxyz

1234567890

TIMES WIDE

ABCDEFGHIJKLMNOPQRSTUVWXYZ
1234567890

TIMES TITLING

ABCDEFGHIJKLMNOPQRSTUVWXYZ
1234567890

TIMES BOLD TITLING

ABCDEGHJKMNOPQRSTUVWXYZ
1234567890

TIMES EXTENDED TITLING

ABCDEFGHIJKLMNOPQRSTUVWXYZ
1234567890

TIMES HEVER TITLING

ABCDEFGHIJKLMNOPQRS TUVWXYZ&
abcdefghijklmnopqrstuvw xyz
1234567890

TIMES NEW ROMAN HEAVY

Shaded capitals based on COPPERPLATE ROMAN and originally a type of the Inland Typefoundry. The letters are wide and the shading horizontal. ENGRAVERS' SHADED (Stephenson Blake and American Typefounders), designed by Morris F. Benton, is very similar in treatment. The type is also known as AZURE. Bauer called their version EXCELLENT.

ABCDEFGHIJKLMNO PQRSTUVWXYZ
1234

EXCELLENT

TORINO

Nebiolo c. 1908

A somewhat condensed roman with abrupt variation of colour. Hair lines are frequent. The tail of the **g** is not closed. The type is also known as ROMANO MODERNO.

iv

ABCDEFGHIJKLMNOPQRST
UVWXYZ
abcdefghijklmnopqrstuvwxyz
1234567890

*ABCDEFGHIJKLMNOPQRS
TUVWXYZ
abcdefghijklmnopqrstuvwxyz
1234567890*

TORINO

TOTFALUSI

Magyar 1956

Designed by Antal Thalwieser and Wenzel Wendler.

ii

ABCDEFGHIJKLMNOPQRSTUVWXYZ
ÁÉÍÓÚÖÜŐŰÄ
abcdefghijklmnopqrstuvwxyzáéíóúöüőűäàßfffffiflft
1234567890

*ABCDEFGHIJKLMNOPQRSTUVWXYZ
ÁÉÍÓÚÖÜŐŰÄE
abcdefghijklmnopqrstuvwxyzáéíóúöüőűäëàèßfffffiflft
1234567890*

TOTFALUSI

ii

ABCDEFGHIJKLM
NOPQRSTUVWXYZ

TOTFALUSI

TOWER

American Typefounders 1934

Designed by Morris F. Benton. The type is completely monotone in colour. The top serif on the **A** points to the left only.

v

ALL KNIGHTS OF THE MID
After an apprenticeship

TOWER

A set of capitals and figures with hair-line serifs. Almost a fat face and following English models; *e.g.* note the spurred **G**. *Cf.* the same founder's NORMANDE. Not to be confused with the type also known as NAUDIN or TRADITION.

TRADITION

Berthold 1955

iv

ABCDEFGHIJKLMNOPQRSTU

TRADITION

The serifs are small and descenders short. The **J** ends on the line, in the **M** the middle stroke stops half-way, **Q** has an unusual tail and **R** tapers to a point. The **f** is narrow, the ear of the **g** projects north-east.

TRAJAN

Miller & Richard c. 1925

i

USE OF THE CAMERA

About five hundred years ago experiments for photo etching were made in Lille.

TRAJAN

Designed by Albert Auspurg. Shaded roman capitals. Presumably the name derives from the lettering on the Trajan column, but that model is not closely followed. The arms of **E** and **F** and the bar of the **H** are high. The **M** is splayed.

TRAJAN
INITIALS

Krebs 1928

vii

ESCUELA
DE NAVEGA

TRAJAN INITIALS

Designed by Warren Chappell. The **B**, **E**, **F** and **P** are narrow, the **M** has no top serifs. The **U** has the lower-case design. In the lower-case descenders are short and serifs slightly inclined. The **g** has a small tail compared with the bowl; **t** has a serif at the end of the bar. Numerals are short ranging.

TRAJANUS

Stempel 1940;

Linotype (Frankfurt)

i

ABCDEFGHIJKLM

A Series of Sixteen Promenade Concerts in the Open

Stangjärnshammåre

TRAJANUS

Kortvågssändare

i

TRAJANUS BOLD

TRAVELLER
Monotype 1964

ii

Designed by John Peters and made originally for the British Railways Board.

ABDEGHJKMNQRSTUVWXYZ
abcdefghijklmnopqrstuvwxyz
1234567890

TRAVELLER

**TRENHOLM
INITIALS**
Barnhart Bros. & Spindler

ix

Designed by G.F. Trenholm. A swash calligraphic titling.

TRENHOLM INITIALS

**TRENHOLM
OLD STYLE**
Barnhart Bros. & Spindler 1927

ii

Designed by G.F. Trenholm. The **C** and **G** are wide letters and the **H** rather narrow. The **M** is slightly splayed. In the lower case serifs are inclined on the ascenders as well as on **m**, **n**, etc. The **g** has a sharp-angled link and a straight ear. The italic has a slight inclination. The capitals are swash letters. In the lower case serifs have been eliminated. Numerals are short ranging. There is also a bold.

A B C D E F G H I J K L M N O P Q R S T U
V W X Y Z &

a b c d e f g h i j k l m n o p q r s t u v w x y z
1 2 3 4 5 6 7 8 9 0

A B C D E F G H I J K L M N O P Q R
S T U V W X Y Z &

ii

a b c d e f g h i j k l m n o p q r s t u v w x y z fi fl

1 2 3 4 5 6 7 8 9 0

TRENHOLM OLD STYLE

Designed by Friedrich Bauer. A display roman with thin bracketed serifs and short ascenders and descenders. There are slab serifs on the **A** and **M**. On the lower case the serifs are horizontal. The distinguishing feature is the squared-up shoulders of the **h, m** and **n**. The **g** has the ear on the top and the tail not completed. The italic is a sloped roman. There are also some swash capitals and there are three weights.

Im achtzehnten Jahrhundert wurde die Freiheit

ix

TRENNERT

Neuestes Krematorium in Frankfurt

ix

TRENNERT ITALIC WITH SWASH CAPITALS

den meisten Fällen den Irrweg gegangen, die

ix

TRENNERT SEMI-BOLD

Nordlandreise mit dem modernen Flugzeug

ix

Seit etwa 70 Jahren stellt man die Frage

TRENNERT BOLD

Akademie für Sozial= und Handelswissenschaft in Berlin

ix

HAMBURGS STELLUNG IM HANDEL

TRENNERT BOLD CONDENSED

Designed by Graily Hewitt in accordance with principles laid down in his tract *The Pen and Type Design.* It has therefore the qualities of a script. Serifs are very small, there is little differentiation of colour and the capitals are toned down. **A** has a high bar and the apex extends to the left. **G** has a long terminal, **M** is slightly splayed and **U** has the lower-case design. In the lower case ascenders are shorter than descenders. **v** and **w** are given cursive forms and **y** a vertical stroke. The italic is slightly inclined—seven degrees we are told—and differs from the roman in the one-storeyed **a** and the feet of **m, n**, etc. The matrices were cut by The Monotype Corporation.

ABCDEFGHIJKLMNOPQRSTUVWXYZ

ix

abcdefghijklmnopqrstuvwxyyz

fi fl ff ffi ffl ft & 1234567890

ABCDEFGHIJKLMNOPQRSTUVWXYZ

abcdefghijklmnopqrstuvwxyyz

fiflffffifflft gg & 1234567890

TREYFORD

Designed by Oldrich Menhart. A calligraphic text type of good readability even in the small sizes. It is a bold face of italic inclination and angular character. The lower case **k** is unusual as the swash centre does not link up with the main stroke. The **J** descends below the line but depart in form from conventional characters, ending in a slightly inclined node below the line.

A B C D E F G H I J K L M N O P Q R S T U V W X Y Z

ix

1 2 3 4 5 6 7 8 9 0

a b c d e f g h i j k l m n o p q r s t u v w x y z

TRIGA

225

TROY TYPE

Kelmscott Press 1892

Morris's second type was based on early German fifteenth century founts, though not a direct copy of any one of them. It is a round Gothic with leanings toward roman, the design the Germans have called GOTICO ANTIQUA, antiqua being German for roman. Many of the letters are those of a bold roman. In the lower case there are no foot serifs to **m, n, p,** etc. The **g** has an open tail; **v** and **w** have curved forms. The TROY TYPE also was copied by the American Typefounders. They called it SATANICK. Morris's third type, the CHAUCER, 1893, was a smaller size of the Troy, pica instead of great primer. TROY and CHAUCER are now in the possession of the Cambridge University Press.

ix

ABCDEFGHIJKLMNOPQRSTUV
WXYZ &

abcdefghijklmnopqrstuvwxyz

æ œ fi ff fl ffi ffl   1 2 3 4 5 6 7 8 9 0

TROY TYPE

TRUMP MEDIAEVAL

Weber 1954;

Linotype (Frankfurt)

ii

Designed by Georg Trump. The **E** has a short upper arm, and the **M** is splayed. In the lower case ascenders and descenders are short; the **w** has no serifs. The italic is the sloped roman except for the one-storeyed **a**, the **e** and **f**. There are special capitals and alternative lower case. TRUMP GRAVUR is a three-dimensional companion type.

ABCDEFGHIJKLMNOPQRSTUVW
XYZ
abcdefghijklmnopqrstuvwxyz
1234567890 1234567890

ABCDEFGHIJKLMNOPQRSTUVW
XYZ
abcdefghijklmnopqrstuvwxyz
1234567890 1234567890
ABCDEGFMNPRTVW aekmntvwz

TRUMP MEDIAEVAL

ii

ABCDEFGHIJKLMNOPQRSTUVW
XYZ
abcdefghijklmnopqrstuvwxyz
1234567890 1234567890

TRUMP MEDIAEVAL BOLD

ABCDEFGHIJKLMNOPQRST UVWXYZ
abcdefghijklmnopqrstuvwxy
1234567890 1234567890

TRUMP MEDIAEVAL EXTRA BOLD

ABCDEFGHIJKLMNOPQRSTUVWXYZ
abcdefghijklmnopqrstuvwxyz
1234567890 1234567890

*ABCDEFGHIJKLMNOPQRSTU
VWXYZ*
abcdefghijklmnopqrstuvwxyz
1234567890 1234567890

TRUMP MEDIAEVAL BOLD CONDENSED

ABCDEFGHIJKLMNOPQRS
TUVWXYZ 1234567890

TRUMP GRAVUR

Designed by Helmut Tschörtner. Serifs are small. The U follows the lower-case design, and the w has no middle serif. The italic is slightly inclined and has the serifs of the roman. Numerals are ranging and non-ranging.

ABCDEFGHIJKLMNOPQRSTUV
WXYZ&
abcdefghijklmnopqrstuvwxyz?
1234567890
*ABCDEFGHIJKLMNOPQRSTUVW
XYZ&*
abcdefghijklmnopqrstuvwxyz?
1234567890

TSCHÖRTNER

TYFA

Grafotechna 1959

Designed by Josef Tyfa. Serifs are flat and unbracketed. The **t** is unbracketed and the **w** has no middle serif. Numerals are non-ranging.

iv

ABCDEFGHIJKLMNOPQRSTU
VWXYZ
abcdefghijklmnopqrstuvwxyz
1234567890
*ABCDEFGHIJKLMNOPQRSTU
VWXYZ
abcdefghijklmnopqrstuvwxyz
1234567890*

TYFA

TYPO ROMAN

American Typefounders c. 1920

Capitals and ascenders are tall, descenders long. The **M** is splayed and the middle strokes stop short of the line. The **W** has no serif in the short middle stroke. The **g** is a script form with a large tail. There is also a shaded version.

iv

The Susquehanna Literary and Musical Society
Recital of Shakespearean Songs

TYPO ROMAN

ULTRA BODONI

American Typefounders 1928; Monotype

A fat face in which the thick strokes do not curve into the thin but meet them at an angle. Thus the counters in **B, D, O, P, Q** and **R** are bounded by straight lines.

iv

ABCDEFGHIJKLMNOPQ
RSTUVWXYZ
abcdefghijklmnopqrs

MONOTYPE ULTRA BODONI

ABCDEFGHIJKLMNOPQR STUVWXYZ abcdefghijklmnopqrstuvw xyz

MONOTYPE ULTRA BODONI

Designed by Oldrich Menhart. A pen-drawn uncial with an unusual **A**, and the **G** following the style of ordinary romans.

ABCDEFGHIJKLMNOPQRST UVWXYZ 1234567890

UNCIALA

The oldest of the English decorated types, which belonged about 1700 to the Grover Foundry and has descended to the present owners *via* Fry's and the Fann Street Foundry. It is an italic with swash capitals and open letters which are decorated with pearls or unions.

ABCDEFGHIJKLMNOPQRSTUVWXYZ abcdefghijklmnopqrstuvwxyz

UNION PEARL

Designed by Charles Ricketts and named after his house. The type has heavy serifs and the blackness of GOLDEN TYPE. Capitals are wide. The **G** has a long spur. The **g** has the bowl larger than the tail and an ear pointing north-east. The **t** is very short.
AVON, designed by Ricketts for a Shakespeare edition is a small pica of the same design.

Trimalchio autem miti ad nos vultu respexit; et, Vinum, inquit, si non placet, mutabo: vos illud, oportet, bonum faciatis. Deorum beneficio non emo, sed nunc, quidquid ad salivam facit, in suburbano nascitur meo, quod ego adhuc non novi. Dicitur confine esse Tarracinensibus et Tarentinis. Nunc conjungere

VALE

VAN DIJCK ROMAN
Monotype 1935

Designed with the assistance of Jan van Krimpen and based on the roman of Christoffel van Dijck, the leading founder in Amsterdam in the middle of the seventeenth century. It closely resembles CASLON, which is not surprising since Caslon took Van Dijck as his model, especially in his italic. One size of the original Van Dijck italic still survives in the Enschedé foundry. A few small points by which the type can be distinguished from Caslon are: the ear of the **g** is straighter in Van Dijck. In the italic the bar in the **J** is higher up in Caslon and there is no foot serif on the right limb of the **N**. The type bears some resemblance to the larger FELL ROMAN.

ii

ABCDEFGHIJKLMNOPQRSTUVWXYZ
abcdefghijklmnopqrstuvwxyz
1234567890
ABCDEFGHIJKLMNOPQRSTUVWXYZ
abcdefghijklmnopqrstuvwxyz
1234567890

VAN DIJCK

ii

ABCDEFGHIJKLMNOPQRSTUVWXYZÆ
abcdefghijklmnopqrsſtuvvwwxyzijæœ&
as ch ct ff ffi ffl fi fl fr is ll q̃ ſt ſch ſh ſi ſl ſp ſſ ß ſſi ſſl ſt ſz us

ENSCHEDÉ VAN DIJCK ITALIC

VENDÔME
Olive 1952; Bauer 1962

Designed by François Ganeau and related to 17th century French types. The width of the letters varies greatly, but they are of even weight. The foot serifs of lower case letters are generally shorter on the right, and the thin vertical strokes of the capitals are tapered either toward the top or the bottom of the letter. The curve of the **e** is accentuated toward the left, and the **b** has no horizontal foot serif, but instead a tapered vertical touching the base of the, line.

ii

ABCDEFGHIJKLMNOPQRSTUVX
abcdefghijklmnopqrstuvwxyzabcdeg
1234567890
ABCDEFGHIJKLMNOPQRSTUVWZ
abcdefghijklmnopqrstuvwxyzabcdefgho
1234567890

VENDÔME

ABCDEFGHIJKLMNOPQRSTUI
abcdefghijklmnopqrstuvwxyzab
1234567890

ABCDEFGHIJKLMNOPQRSTUVWXYZ
abcdefghijklmnopqrstuvwxyzabcdefgh
1234567890

VENDÔME BOLD

ABCDEFGHIJKLMNOPQRSTUVWXYZABCDEFGHIJKLMNOPQRM
abcdefghijklmnopqrstuvwxyzabcdefghijklmnopqrstuvwxyz
1234567890

VENDÔME CONDENSED

ABCDEFGHIJKLMNOPQRX
abcdefghijklmnopqrstuvxyz
1234567890

VENDÔME EXTRA BOLD

Originally cut by E.P. Prince for George W. Jones at the Sign of the Dolphin. An italic was designed by F.W. Goudy in 1925. The original type had slab serifs on the **M**. The hyphen is oblique and the full-stop diamond shaped. The italic has angular beginning strokes.

ABCDEFGHIJKLMNOPQRSTUVWXYZ
abcdefghijklmnopqrstuvwxyz
ABCDEFGHIJKLMNOPQRSTUVWXYZ
abcdefghijklmnopqrstuvwxyz

VENEZIA

VENEZIANA
Grafotechna 1920

A calligraphic roman with tall ascenders.

ii

ABCDEFGHIJKLMNOPQRSTUV
WXYZ
abcdefghijklmnopqrstuvwxyz
1234567890
ABCDEFGHIJKLMNOPQRSTUV
WXYZ
abcdefghijklmnopqrstuvwxyz
1234567890

VENEZIANA

ii

ABCDEFGHIJKLMNOPQRST
UVWXYZ
abcdefghijklmnopqrstuvwxyz
1234567890

VENEZIANA BOLD

VERDI
Bauer c. 1851

Designed by J.C. Bauer, although the present type, re-issued in 1957, is modified. The shading in letters like the **A, E, H, P**, etc. completely fills the letters.

v

ABCDEFGHIJKLMNOP
QRSTUVWXYZ
1234567890

VERDI

Descenders are short, and the ear of the **g** is quite unorthodox. The italic is moderately inclined and has the serif formation of the roman, except the **A** where the serif is projected to the left, and the curved **V** and **W**. The **p** and **q** are without foot serifs.

American Typefounders' VERONA is quite different.

VERONA IS LACLEDE OLD STYLE and was bought in 1920 by Barnhart Brothers & Spindler from the Laclede Typefoundry of St Louis; it was rechristened MUNDER and supplied with a bold and an italic cut by Robert Wiebking.

ABCDEFGHIJKLMNOPQRSTUVWXYZ
abcdefghijklmnopqrstuvwxyz
1234567890

i

ABCDEFGHIJKLMNOPQRST UVWXYZ
abcdefghijklmnopqrstuvwxyz
1234567890

VERONA

ABCDEFGHIJKLMNOPQRSTUVWXYZ
abcdefghijklmnopqrstuvwxyz

i

ABCDEFGHIJKLMNOPQRSTUVWXYZ
abcdefghijklmnopqrstuvwxyz

VERONA BOLD

ABCDEFGHIJKLMNOPQRSTUVWXYZ
abcdefghijklmnopqrstuvwxyz

i

VERONA BOLD CONDENSED

ABCDEFGHIJKLMNOPQRSTUVWXYZ
abcdefghijklmnopqrstuvwxyz

i

VERONA EXTRA BOLD

A heavy face with short ascenders and descenders. The thick slab serifs and monotone colour of this type give it almost the appearance of an Egyptian. **R** tapers to a point. Note the short tail of the **y**; the ampersand also has a short tail. The italic has the serifs of the roman.

ABCDEFGHIJKLMNOPQRSTUVWXYZ&
abcdefghijklmnopqrstuvwxyz

v

VERONESE

233

VERTICAL

Haas 1955

A condensed and elongated fat face, a re-cutting of a nineteenth-century design. Capitals only. *Cf.* SLIMBLACK

A somewhat heavier face similiar to this one in ROMAN EXTRA BOLD CONDENSED of the former A.D. Farmer & Son Typefoundry

iv

ABCDEFGHIJKLMNOPQRSTUVWXYZ
THE QUICK BROWN FOX

VERTICAL

VESTA

Berthold 1926

Designed by Albert Augspurg. A shaded titling. Black strokes have a serrated edge on the right side.

iv

GEWERBE-MUSEUM IN BREMEN
29 DEUTSCHE KUNST 56

VESTA

VICTORIA

Adler Traldi 1966

iv

A modern line composition type designed for improved photographic reproducibility.

ABCDEFGHIJKLMNOPQRST
abcdefghijklmnopqrstuvwxyz
1234567890

ABCDEFGHIJKLMNOPQRST
abcdefghijklmnopqrstuvwxyz
1234567890

VICTORIA

iv

ABCDEFGHIJKLMNOPQRST
abcdefghijklmnopqrstuvwxyz
1234567890

ABCDEFGHIJKLMNOPQRST
abcdefghijklmnopqrstuvwxyz
1234567890

VICTORIA BOLD

VICTORIA ITALIC

Ludlow 1927

vii

A titling with fine serifs.

ABCDEFGHIJKLMNOPQRSTUVWXYZ

1234567890

VICTORIA ITALIC

234

A titling in the SCOTCH style.

ABCDEFGHIJKLMNOPQRSTUVWXYZ
1234567890
VICTORIA TITLING

ABCDEFGHIJKLMNOPQRSTUVWXYZ
1234567890
VICTORIA TITLING CONDENSED

ABCDEGHIJKMNOPQRSTUVWXYZ
1234567890
VICTORIA TITLING BOLD

ABCDEFGHIJKLMNOPQRSTUVWXYZ
1234567890
VICTORIA TITLING BOLD CONDENSED

VICTORIA
TITLING
Monotype 1924

iv

iv

iv

iv

Designed by Oldrich Menhart. An angular text type.

VICTORY
Intertype 1947

ix

Á B C D E F G H I J K L
M N O P Q R Š Ů T W V Y
Z X & Æ Œ
a b c ď e f g h i j k l
m n o p q ř s ť ů v w x
ý z ff fi fl ß § æ œ
1 2 3 4 5 6 7 8 9 0
Á B C D E F G H I J K L M N O P Q
R Š T Ů V W Y Z X & Æ Œ
a b c d e f g h i j k l m n o p q r š ť
ů v w ý z x œ œ
1 2 3 4 5 6 7 8 9 0
VICTORY

WALBAUM

Berthold; Monotype 1934;

Linotype (Frankfort) 1960

J.E. Walbaum (1768–1839) was a founder at Goslar and at Weimar. His modern face was cut in the early years of the nineteenth century. The original matrices are still extant in Germany in the Berthold foundry, which acquired them in 1919. The type was introduced into England by the Curwen Press in 1925. Walbaum followed Didot rather than Bodoni. His capitals are noticeably wider than Bodoni's; the **J** is short ranging. The **b** has no foot serif and the **t** is unbracketed. There are two sets of figures, old face and modern. In the italic there are the flat roman serifs of all continental modern faces. There are no foot serifs to **p** and **q**; **v** and **w** are of normal design and have not the eighteenth-century curves of BODONI. The Berthold and Linoytpe versions shown here are not cast from Walbaum's original matrices.

iv

ABCDEFGHIJKLMNOPQRSTUVWXYZ
abcdefghijklmnopqrstuvwxyz
1234567890
ABCDEFGHIJKLMNOPQRSTUVWXY
abcdefghijklmnopqrstuvwxyz

BERTHOLD WALBAUM

iv

ABCDEFGHIJKLMNOPQRSTUVWXYZ
abcdefghijklmnopqrstuvwxy

BERTHOLD WALBAUM MEDIUM

WALLAU

Klingspor 1925–30

Designed by Rudolf Koch. The capitals are roman and appear to be quill-drawn. They are without serifs except for a slab serif on the **A**. The lower case is black letter in design.

ix

ABCDEFGHIJKLMNOPQRSTUVWXYZ
abcdefghijklmnopqrstuvwxyz
1234567890

WALLAU

ix

ABCDEFGHIJKLMNOPQRSTU
abcdefghijklmnopqrstuvwxyz

WALLAU BOLD

WAVERLEY

Intertype (New York) 1941

The type has the vertical stress and flat serifs of a modern face, but the gradation of colour is not abrupt and the serifs are strong. **M** is a wide letter and **R** has a curled tail. The **g** has an ear like CASLON and the bar of the **t** is unbracketed. The italic has the serifs of the roman; **p** and **q** are without foot serifs. The figures are short-ranging. It is very similar to WALBAUM.

iv

ABCDEFGHIJKLMNOPQRSTUVWXYZ
ABCDEFGHIJKLMNOPQRSTUVWXYZ
abcdefghijklmnopqrstuvwxyz
1234567890

WAVERLEY

Designed by Emil Rudolf Weiss. The **B** is narrow and **H** wide. **M** has no top serifs. **U** has the lower-case design. In the lower case **a** has the upper story wide open, **f** is unkerned and **w** has no middle serif. Decenders are rather short. The italic (1931) is of the BLADO school, of very slight inclination and with angular beginning strokes. Most of the capitals are swash varieties. The **g** has an open tail drawn from right to left; **p** and **q** have no foot serifs and the uprights ascend well above the bowls. This roman shares the contemporary affection for very small serifs.

WEISS
ROMAN

Bauer 1926;

Intertype (New York);

Intertype (Berlin)

ii

ABCDEFGHIJKLMNOPQQuRSTUV
WXYZ
abcdefghijklmnopqrstuvwxyz
1234567890

ABCDEFGHIJKLMNOPQRSTUVWXYZ
abcdefghijklmnopqrstuvwxyz e m n t
1234567890
AABCDEFGHIJJKLMNOPQuQRST
UVVWWXYYZ

WEISS ROMAN

ABCDEFGHIJKLMNOPQQuRSTUV
WXYZ
abcdefghijklmnopqrstuvwxyz
1234567890

WEISS ROMAN BOLD

ii

ABCDEFGHIJKLMNOPQQuRSTU
VWXYZ
abcdefghijklmnopqrstuvwxyz
1234567890

WEISS ROMAN EXTRA BOLD

ii

ABCDEFGHIJKLMNOPQRST
UVWXYZ   1234567890

WEISS INITIALS SERIES I

ii

WEISS ROMAN
ii

AABCDEFGGHIJKLMNOPQ
RSTUVWXYZ 1234567890

ii

AABCDEEFGGHIJKLMNOP
QRSTUVWXYZ 123456789

ii

ABCDEFGHIJKLMNOPQRS
TUVWXYZ 1234567890

ii

ABCDEFGHIJKLMNOPQRSTUVWXYZ
abcdefghijklmnopqrstuvwxyz
1234567890
ABCDEFGHIJ KLMNOPQRSTUVWXYZ
ABCDEFGHIJKLMNOPQRSTUVWXYZ
abcdefghijklmnopqrstuvwxyz
1234567890

WEISS
RUNDGOTISCH
Bauer 1936

Designed by E.R. Weiss. A calligraphic type following the German style of the period and leaning on black letter, but also on Italian and Spanish manuscript writing. Descenders are very short.

ix

ABCDEF6HIJKLMNOPQRST
UDWXYZ

abcdefghijklmnopqrſstuvwxyz

1234567890

Designed by Hans Wagner. The **G** has a wide horizontal serif. The **M** is splayed. The **t** is flat across the top and has a curved terminal. Nebiolo's inline version LANDI ECHO is a titling with short-ranging figures and the outline version LANDI LINEAR has black horizontal feet and tops of letters. The type is also known as LUXOR. Nebiolo call it LANDI, Fonderie Française RAMSES and Amsterdam Typefoundry ATLAS.

WELT
Ludwig & Mayer 1931;
Nebiolo; Française;
Amsterdam;
Linotype (Frankfurt)

ABCDEFGHIJKLMNOPQRSTUVWXYZ
abcdefghijklmnopqrstuvwxyz
1234567890

ABCDEFGHIJKLMNOPQRSTUVWXYZÇ
abcdefghijklmnopqrstuvwxyzçœœ

WELT LIGHT

ABCDEFGHIJKLMNOPQRSTUVWXYZ
abcdefghijklmnopqrstuvwxyzçæœ
ABCDEFGHIJKLMNOPQRSTUVWXYZ
abcdefghijklmnopqrstuvwxyzçœœ

WELT MEDIUM

ABCDEFGHIJKLMNOPQRSTUVWXYZ
abcdefghijklmnopqrstuvwxyz

WELT BOLD

THE PRIMARY FUNCTION
of type is that it shall be

WELT EXTRA BOLD

ABCDEFGHIJKLMNOPQRSTUVWXYZÇÆŒ&
abcdefghijklmnopqrstuvwxyzçæœ
1234567890

WELT CONDENSED

239

WERBEDRUCK

J. Wagner

A display roman (originally cut by Norddeutsche Schriftgiesserei in 1930), as one may infer from its weight and shortness of ascenders and descenders.

The design is close to NEW CASLON, but the figures are short ranging.

ii

ABCDEFGHIJKLMNOPQ RSTUVWXYZ
abcdefghijklmnopqrstuvwxyz
1234567890

WERBEDRUCK

ii

ABCDEFGHIJKLMNOPQR
abcdefghijklmnopqrstuvwxyz

WERBEDRUCK BOLD

WESTMINSTER OLD STYLE or DELLA ROBBIA

American Typefounders 1903;

Stephenson Blake 1907;

Deberny & Peignot 1911

Lanston Monotype;

Amsterdam

Designed by T.M. Cleland. It is a roman of light colour and monotone. The serifs are small and inclined on the lower case. The bowls of **B**, **P** and **R** are not closed. **H** is wide and has a high bar. **M** is splayed and the middle strokes descend half-way. **W** is very wide. The **e** is Venetian; **g** has a large bowl and the tail not closed. Descenders are short and the figures modern.

The Monotype Corporation's CANTERBURY (1915) based on M.F. Benton's Della Robbia Light (1903) is a closely similar design. It may be distinguished by the straight tail of the **R**. Amsterdam call the type FIRENZE.

ABCDEFGHIJKLMNOPQRSTUVWXYZ
abcdefghijklmnopqrstuvwxyz
1234567890

vii

WESTMINSTER OLD STYLE

WHITEFRIARS BOLD

Chiswick Press

Formerly a roman of the Whitefriars Foundry.

ix

ABCDEFGHIJKLMNOPQR
abcdefghijklmnopqrstuvwxy!
1234567890£

WHITEFRIARS BOLD

240

Designed by Morris F. Benton, and originally called BENTON. Serifs are not quite horizontal and the stress not quite vertical. The **G** is like CASLON.

RINGLET Photographs

WHITEHALL

Designed by Morris F. Benton and originally called BOLD ANTIQUE. A bold type with slab serifs.

ABCDEFGHIJKLMNOPQRS TUVWXYZ
abcdefghijklmnopqrstuvwxyz
1234567890

WHITIN BLACK

ABCDEFGHIJKLMNOPQRSTUVW XYZ
abcdefghijklmnopqrstuvwxyz
1234567890

WHITIN BLACK CONDENSED

Designed under the direction of Edwin W. Shaar. A newspaper type. Stephenson Blake's WINDSOR is quite different.

ABCDEFGHIJKLMNOPQRSTUVWXYZ
abcdefghijklmnopqrstuvwxyz
1234567890

WINDSOR

ABCDEFGHIJKLMNOPQRSTUVWXYZ
abcdefghijklmnopqrstuvwxyz
1234567890

WINDSOR BOLD

WINDSOR

Stephenson Blake c. 1905

A display type of a rich colour, even in the light face. There are many odd forms in both cases. Some of the capitals, E, F, G, T and S, have beak-like serifs. M has small slab serifs. P and R have large bowls. U has a horse-shoe shape. The lower case has oblique serifs and very short descenders. a has a large bowl, e an oblique stroke to the eye, the squat g has the ear at the top, the last limbs of m and n are splayed, and s has serifs like the upper case. The italic (in the medium weight) is regular and has the serifs of the roman. There are three weights of the roman, also a condensed, elongated and outline. Intertype WINDSOR is a newspaper type.

ix

ABCDEFGHIJKLMNOPQ
RST
abcdefghijklmnopqrstuvwxyz
123
WINDSOR

ix

ABCDEFGHIJKLMNOPQRST
abcdefghijklmnopqrstuvwxyz&
WINDSOR CONDENSED

ix

ABCDEFGHIJKLMNOPQRSTUVWX
YZ
abcdefghijklmnopqrstuvwxyz
1234567890
WINDSOR BOLD

ix

ABCDEFGHIJKLMNOPQRSTUVWXYZ
abcdefghijklmnopqrstuvwxyz
WINDSOR ELONGATED

ix

ABCDEFGHIJKLMNOPQRSTUVWXYZ
abcdefghijklmnopqrstuvwxyz
WINDSOR OUTLINE

WOLFRAM

Ludwig & Mayer 1930

Designed by Hans Wagner. A heavy, upright italic. All the serifs are rounded. Some capitals are of the swash variety. There is considerable variation of colour.

ix

Mauxion Schokol
WOLFRAM

Designed by Lucian Zabel. A roman with slight variation of stress and small, horizontal and stubby serifs. The E, F, L and T are narrow letters. E and F have the centre arms above the middle. M has no top serifs. In the lower case descenders are short. The e has a large eye and the g an open tail. Some vertical strokes are thickened towards the top; this feature is more evident in the bold face. There is no italic.

ZABEL
ROMAN
Woellmer 1928–30

SCHRIFTGIESSEREI
ZABEL ROMAN

Die Bilderschrift ist ein Element, und zwar das wichtigste, aus dem sich die Schrift entwickelt hat. Es gibt aber noch andere Anfänge der Schrift DIESE ANFÄNGE DER SCHRIFT FINDET MAN BEI ALLEN VÖLKERN

ZABEL ROMAN BOLD

Designed by Giovanni Mardersteig. Based on the early Italian romans. The punches were cut by Charles Malin.

ZENO
Officina Bodoni 1937

ABCDEFGHIJKLMNOPQURRSTUVWXYZ

ABCDEFGHIJKLMNOPQURRSTUVWXYZ

abccdefghijklmmnopqrrstuvwxyz

1234567890

ZENO

Designed by Michael Harvey. An accentuated outline titling, giving a somewhat three-dimensional effect.

ZEPHYR
Ludlow 1964

ABCDEFGHIJKLMNOPQRST
UVWXYZ&
1234567890

ZEPHYR

Designed by S.H. Roos. A roman based on JENSON. The E, G and L have the large serifs found in several De Roos types. The U has the lower-case design. The g has a large bowl and narrow tail. The t has a serif at the end of the bar.

The matrices were cut by Wagner & Schmidt and the type was cast by Amsterdam Type-foundry.

ZILVER TYPE
Zilverdistel Pers 1915

YZATEN DIEN EERSTEN AVOND NA,
dat wij aan land waren gekomen tot laat in den
tuin van mijn broeder, ik heb nog nimmer zulk
een schoonen maanlichten avond weêr gezien,

ZILVER

LINEALES

THE EARLIEST "SANS SERIFS" appear in the specimen books of Vincent Figgins, of 1830 and Thorowgood, of 1832. The earliest is the type shown by W. Caslon IV in 1816 and called Egyptian, although it is a lineale. Blake and Stephenson in 1833 called their version Sans Surryphs. Thorowgood called the type Grotesque and the American name Gothic was often used. Figgin's name Sans Serif describes the important characteristic. The type was monotone and the capitals were of equal width. The early designs were heavy and it was some years before lighter faces were cut and even longer before a lower case was cut. The Caslon Doric appears in a number of weights in their specimen book of 1854 and there was already an Outline Doric. With some slight exceptions, no great change took place in the design until the German founders in this century reformed the type by varying the width of the letters and by replacing some of the square ends by tapering strokes. The specimen books of many founders show Dorics, Gothics and Grotesques. "Lineales" is the description applied by Maximilien Vox to types without serifs. In some cases, the distinction between a calligraphic roman and a modified lineale approaching a roman of calligraphic style is hard to draw.

Designed by A.M. Cassandre. A titling in which the letters are partly black and partly white.

ACIER NOIR
Deberny & Peignot 1936

iv

SOUVERAINES

CONCERNANT TOUT LE MONDE MÉDICAL

ACIER NOIR

iv

Designed by Freeman Craw. This type was designed by cutting the letter images out and thus has some wood-cut character. Numerous alternative characters are provided, and in the lower case some characters have slight inclination. Several lower-case characters may be turned upside down without losing alignment, to obtain additional alternative character images.

ADLIB
American 1961

iv

ABCDEEFGHIJKLMNNOOPQRRSSTTUV

WXYZ

aabccdeeffgghijkllmmnoopqrrssttuvwxyz

12345678900

ADLIB

ADONIS EXTENDED
Stephenson Blake 1962

vi

Designed by André Bretton on the basis of the same founder's SPARTAN, but entirely without serifs. An expanded type of medium weight with a sloped version. The **M** is square. The **g** has an open tail. There are ranging figures.

ABCDEFGHIJKLMNOP
QRSTUVWXYZ
abcdefghijklmnopqrstu
vwxyzæœ
1234567890

ABCDEFGHIJKLMNOPQ
RSTUVWXYZ
abcaefghijklmnopqrstuvw
xyzæœ
1234567890

ADONIS EXTENDED

ADSANS
Linotype (London) 1959

vi

A newspaper type for classified advertising in $4\frac{3}{4}$ pt only and first used in the London *Evening News*.

CLERK Reqd for cost office, preferably with some experience, age 21 to 26 years.—Apply Employment Department, FIRTH-VICKERS STAINLESS STEELS LTD., Weedon st., Tinsley. COPY TYPIST Reqd by small tool manufacturers, aged 25-30 years; experience in office routine an advantage.—Apply in own writing to Cintride Ltd., Grange Lane Works, Sheffield, 5.

ADELPHI. Tem 7611 7.30 Wed & Sat. 2.30. Van Johnson, Maureen Hartley. THE MUSIC MAN. London's happiest musical with the show-stopping 76 Trombones. ALDWYCH. Tem 6404. (7.30 Mat W & S 2.30). Royal Shakespeare Co. in THE CHERRY ORCHARD (until Jan 6 then Jan 15/17). Peggy Ashcroft, John Gielgud. Also THE HOLLOW CROWN (Feb 1-3). As You Like It joins rep Jan 10.

ABCDEFGHIJKLMNOPQRSTUVWXYZÆŒ   abcdefghijklmnopqrstuvwxyzæœ   fifflffffffl   1234567890
ABCDEFGHIJKLMNOPQRSTUVWXYZÆŒ   **abcdefghijklmnopqrstuvwxyzæœ**   **fifflffffffl**   **1234567890**
ADSANS and ADSANS BOLD

ADVERTISEMENT GROTESQUE
Haas 1945–46

vi

A bold and rather condensed type. In the lower case ascenders and descenders are abbreviated. In the **G** there is a spur as in nineteenth century designs. COMMERCIAL GROTESQUE is the same design in a lighter weight with less abbreviated ascenders and descenders. NARROW GROTESQUE is the condensed face dating back to c.1865.

ABCDEFGHIJKLMNOPQRSTUVWXYZ
abcdefghijklmnopqrstuvwxyz

ADVERTISEMENT GROTESQUE

AGENCY GOTHIC
American 1933

vi

Designed by Morris F. Benton. Lineale capitals and figures in which the normally round strokes are made straight, *e.g.* **C** and **O** are rectangular. There are two **M**'s one with an unusual middle stroke, the **A** has also two versions.

A A B C D E F G H I J K L M M N O P Q R S
T U V W X Y Z & 1 2 3 4 5 6 7 8 9 0

AGENCY GOTHIC

Designed by Carlos Winkow. An inline three-dimensional titling. **A**, **M** and **N** have rounded tops.

ABCDEFGHIJKLMNOPQRSTUVWXYZ

ALCÁZAR

ALCAZAR

Nacional 1944

vi

Designed by M.F. Benton. A narrow bold type following nineteenth-century style.

ABCDEFGHIJKLMNOPQRSTUVWXYZ

abcdefghijklmnopqrstuvwxyz

1234567890

ALTERNATE GOTHIC

ALTERNATE GOTHIC

*American 1903:
Intertype 1958*

vi

An inclined lineale titling which is not monotone. The round letters have considerable variation of colour and look like pen-drawn letters. These initials are also intended for use with the lower case of BURGUND.

THERMOS

AMBASSADOR

AMBASSADOR

Schriftguss 1937

ix

Originally issued by Wagner & Schmidt in 1914, when it was called GROTESK V and later KRUPP HALLO. This is one of the most widely distributed type faces, and appears in the catalogues (either following or copying the original design) of many Dutch, Spanish, German, French and Italian type-founders. Amsterdam call the type ANNONCE. John called their version KOLOSS, Wagner EDÉL GROTESQUE EXTRA BOLD WIDE, Weber PROGRESS and Weisert FAVORIT. ANTIQUES DOUBLES LARGES of Deberny & Peignot is identical. Nebiolo called the type CAIROLI. Ludwig & Mayer now call the type HALLO and added an italic in 1959.

ABCDEFGHIJKLMNO
PQRSTUVWXYZÆŒ
abcdefghijklmnopqr
stuvwxyz
1234567890£&æœ

ANNONCE GROTESQUE

ANNONCE GROTESQUE or HALLO

Many founders

vi

ABCDEFGHIJKLMNOPQRSTUVW
XYZ
abcdefghijklmnopqrstuvwxyz
1234567890

HALLO ITALIC

vi

A condensed lineale of nineteenth-century design. The **Q** has a curiously wedge-shaped tail. Ascenders are short.

ABCDEFGHIJKLMNOPQRSTUVWXYZÆŒ
abcdefghijklmnopqrstuvwxyzæœ
1234567890

ANTIQUE BOLD CONDENSED

Designed by Roger Excoffon. Ascenders and descenders are short. The extra bold and ultra bold are known as COMPACT and NORD respectively.

ABCDEFGHIJKLMNOPQRSTUVWX
abcdefghijklmnopqrstuvwxyz
1234567890

ABCDEFGHIJKLMNOPQRSTUVWXY
abcdefghijklmnopqrstuvwxyz
1234567890

ANTIQUE OLIVE

ABCDEFGHJKLMNOPQRSTUWXY
abcdefghijklmnopqrstuvwxyz
1234567890

ANTIQUE OLIVE MEDIUM

ABCDEFGHIJKLMNOPQRSTUVWXYZ
abcdefghijklmnopqrstuvwxyz
1234567890

ANTIQUE OLIVE CONDENSED

ABCDEFGHIKLMNOPQRS
abcdefghiklmnopqrstv
1234567890

vi

ANTIQUE OLIVE WIDE

ABCDEFGHIJKLMNOPQRSTUVWXYZ
abcdefghijklmnopqrstuvwxyz
1234567890

vi

ANTIQUE OLIVE CONDENSED BOLD

ABCDEFGHJKLMNOPQRSTUVW
abcdefghijklmnopqrstuvwx
1234567890

vi

ANTIQUE OLIVE BOLD

ABCDEFGHKLMNOPQRSTU
abcdefghjlmnopqrstuvz
1234567890

vi

ANTIQUE OLIVE COMPACT

ABCDEFGHIKMNORX
abcdefghijklmnost
1234567890

vi

ABCDEFGHILMNOPRST
abcdefghijklmnoprstz
1234567890

NORD

ASTUR
Nacional

A three-dimensional type with an informal effect. The letters are somewhat shaded and angular.. Most strokes overlap. In some of the rounded letters the curves are broken.

ix

ABCDEFGHIJKL
MNOPQRSTU
VWXY&Z
abcdefghijklmnopq
rstuvwxyz
1234567890

ASTUR

ATLANTIS
Weber

A lineale following German style. The position of the bar in A and the one-storeyed **a** are characteristic features.

vi

ABCDEFGHIJKLMNOPQRSTUVWXYZ
abcdefghijklmnopqrstuvwxyz

ATLANTIS GROTESQUE

vi

ABCDEFGHIJKLMNOPQRSTUVWXYZ
abcdefghijklmnopqrstuvwxyz

ATLANTIS GROTESQUE MEDIUM

vi

ABCDEFGHIJKLMNOPQRSTUVWXYZ
abcdefghijklmnopqrstuvwxyz

ATLANTIS GROTESQUE BOLD

Designed by K.H. Schaefer. A shaded lineale with five parallel shading lines. Schriftguss called the type FATIMA and were the original founders.

ATLAS
Française 1933

vi

ATLAS

Designed by M.R. Kaufmann. Freely drawn characters and figures are slightly inclined. Counters and bowls are not completely closed. The bars of **A** and **H** and the arms of **E** and **F** protrude to the left. *Cf.* CARTOON.

BALLOON or LASSO
*American 1939;
Amsterdam*

ix

ABCDEFGHIJKLMNOPQRSTUVWXYZ
1234567890

BALLOON

ABCDEFGHIJKLMNOPQRSTUV
WXYZ

ix

BALLOON EXTRA BOLD

Designed by Roger Excoffon. A lineale titling with figures, which is not monotone. Letters are slightly inclined. Some vertical strokes extend above the general level. There are no lower case letters and the strokes are often cut at uneven angles at the ends. The **C** has a short down stroke at the top right. Most letters consist basically of individual heavy strokes arranged next to each other.

BANCO
Olive 1951

ABCDEFGHIJKLMNOPQRSTUVXYZ
1234567890

ix

BANCO

A titling which in the main alphabet is very wide, but for about half the letters a second version is shown which is very narrow. Some letters resemble VOGUE (Stephenson Blake).

BANJO
Deberny & Peignot 1930

vi

AA B CC DD EE FF G H HH I J K LL M
NN O PP Q RR SS TT UU V W X Y Z
Æ Œ &
1234567890

BANJO

BANK GOTHIC

American

vi

Probably designed by M.F. Benton. Capitals in which the normally round letters are squared, *e.g.* the **C, G, O, P, Q, R** and **U**. COMMERCE GOTHIC is a Ludlow version.

ABCDEFGHIJKLMNOPQRSTUVWXYZ&

1234567890

BANK GOTHIC LIGHT

vi

ABCDEFGHIJKLMNOPQRSTUVWXYZ&

1234567890

BANK GOTHIC MEDIUM

vi

ABCDEFGHIJKLMNOPQRSTUVWXYZ&

1234567890

BANK GOTHIC BOLD

vi

ABCDEFGHIJKLMNOPQRSTUVWXYZ&

1234567890

BANK GOTHIC CONDENSED MEDIUM

vi

ABCDEFGHIJKLMNOPQRSTUVWXYZ&

1234567890

BANK GOTHIC CONDENSED LIGHT

BASALT

Genzsch & Heyse 1927

ix

Designed by W. Ege. Bold capitals which have some relatively thin strokes, *e.g.* the arm of the **E**. The type was redesigned in 1934.

ENMITGLIED

BASALT

BASUTO

Stephenson Blake 1927

ix

An extra bold titling distinguished by the shape of the counters. In the **O** the counter is an inclined oval; in the **P** and **R** they have the shape of a D.

ABCDEFGHIJKLMNOPQRSTU VWXYZ1234?

BASUTO

BELL GOTHIC

Mergenthaler Linotype c. 1938; Intertype 1958; Linotype; Monotype

vi

A type designed initially by the Bell Telephone Company's typographer and Mergenthaler Linotype for use in directories and due to its slender design very space saving. The weight of the line is moderate and uniform.

ABCDEFGHIJKLMNOPQRSTUVWXYZ
abcdefghijklmnopqrstuvwxyz
Æ fi ff fl ffi ffl Œ
1234567890

ABCDEFGHIJKLMNOPQRSTUVWXYZ
abcdefghijklmnopqrstuvwxyz
Æ fi ff fl ffi ffl Œ
1234567890

BELL GOTHIC and GOTHIC BOLD

BERNHARD FASHION

American 1929; Intertype

vi

Designed by Lucian Bernhard. An extra light type. The bars of **A** and **H** and the arms of **E** and **F** protrude to the left. Ascenders are tall and the **a** is one-storeyed.

AABCDEEEFGHIJKLMNOP

QRSSTUVWXYZ&

abcdefghijklm nopqrstuvwxyz

1234567890

BERNHARD FASHION

Designed by Lucian Bernhard. The arms of **E** and **F** and the bar of **H** are low. **M** is splayed and pointed (but not in the light face). The tail of the **Q** is external to the bowl. **a** is two-storeyed and **g** has an open tail. There are four weights, with italics to the two lightest.

ABCDEFGHIJKLMNOPQRSTUVW
XYZ abcdefghijklmnopqrstuvwxyz
1234567890

BERNHARD GOTHIC LIGHT

ABCDEFGHIJKLMNOPQRSTUVW
XYZ abcdefghijklmnopqrstuvwxyz
1234567890

ABCDEFGHIJKLMNOPQRSTUV
WXYZ abcdefghijklmnopqrstuvwxyz
1234567890

BERNHARD GOTHIC MEDIUM

ABCDEFGHIJKLMNOPQRSTUVWXYZ
abcdefghijklmnopqrstuvwxyz
1234567890

BERNHARD GOTHIC MEDIUM CONDENSED

ABCDEFGHIJKLMNOPQRSTUVW
XYZ abcdefghijklmnopqrstuvwxyz
1234567890

BERNHARD GOTHIC HEAVY

ABCDEEFGHIJKKLMNOPQRST
UVWXYZ
abcdefghijklmnopqrstuvwxyz
1234567890

BERNHARD GOTHIC EXTRA HEAVY

A true lineale of the usual continental design. There are five weights, two of them with italics. The ascender of the **t** is pointed, and the bottom curve of the **G** is broken. PLASTICA is a shaded titling fount based on this type. NOBEL is very similar.

vi

ABCDEFGHIJKLMNOPQRSTUVWXYZ
abcdefghijklmnopqrstuvwxyz

ABCDEFGHIJKLMNOPQRSTUVWXYZ
abcdefghijklmnopqrstuvwxyz

BERTHOLD GROTESQUE LIGHT

vi

ABCDEFGHIJKLMNOPQRSTUVWXYZ
abcdefghijklmnopqrstuvwxyz1234567890

ABCDEFGHIJKLMNOPQRSTUVWXYZ
abcdefghijklmnopqrstuvwxyz

BERTHOLD GROTESQUE

vi

ABCDEFGHIJKLMNOPQRSTUVWXYZ
abcdefghijklmnopqrstuvwxyz

BERTHOLD GROTESQUE CONDENSED

vi

ABCDEFGHIJKLMNOPQRSTUVWXYZ
abcdefghijklmnopqrstuvwxyz

BERTHOLD GROTESQUE BOLD CONDENSED

vi

ABCDEFGHIJKLMNOPQRSTUVWXYZ
abcdefghijklmnopqrstuvwxyz

BERTHOLD GROTESQUE MEDIUM

vi

ABCDEFGHIJKLMNOPQRSTUVWXY
abcdefghijklmnopqrstuvwxyz

BERTHOLD GROTESQUE BOLD

BIFUR
Deberny & Peignot 1929

Designed by A.M. Cassandre. A lineale in which about half of each letter is omitted. The **A** has no bar, **E** has arms only, **G** is represented by the lower half only and **N** has the middle stroke only. A shaded background helps the eye to the recognition of the whole letter. This daring innovation was applied to an upper case only. It has been called a stencil letter.

vi

DANGER

BIFUR

Designed by J. Binder. A condensed and elongated type face with very short ascenders and descenders. *Cf.* PLACARD.

ABCDEFGHIJKLMNOPQRSTUVWXYZ

abcdefghijklmnopqrstuvwxyz

1234567890

BINDER STYLE

ABCDEFGHIJKLMNOPQRSTUVWXYZ

abcdefghijklmnopqrstuvwxyz

1234567890

BINDER STYLE BOLD

Designed by J. Trochut Blanchard as a lineale with vertical stress and rounded letters.

Alegría de Viena - CONDESTABLE

BISONTE

Alegría de Viena - CONDESTABLE

BISONTE ITALIC

Alegría de Viena-CONDESTABLE

BISONTE BOLD

Designed by H. Hoffmann and setting a style-trend which was soon followed by others. Woellmer called their version HERMES. A bold sans of the usual German pattern. Ascenders and descenders are much abbreviated. There is also a condensed face.

ABCDEFGHIJKLMNOPQRSTUVW
abcdefghijklmnopqrstuvwxyz
1234567890

BLOCK

ABCDEFGHIJKLMNOPQRSTUVWXYZ
abcdefghijklmnopqrstuvwxyz

BLOCK CONDENSED

trische Personen- und Transportw
KIELER ELEKTROMOBIL-WERKE

HERMES GROTESQUE SEMI-BOLD

DRESDEN Genf

HERMES GROTESQUE SHADED

BOUL MICH

American c. 1928

vi

An inline titling version of this founder's BROADWAY and different from BROADWAY ENGRAVED.

SEASON

BOUL MICH

BOWERY

Bruce c. 1890

vi

A rounded three-dimensional and bold type, also known as ROUND SHADED.

ABCDEFGHIJKLMNOPQRSTUVWXYZ

BOWERY

BRAGGA DOCIO

Monotype 1930

vi

Designed by W.A. Woolley. A heavy type face with a resemblance to FUTURA BLACK by the omission of thin strokes. But the letters are wider and the main strokes thicker; ascenders and descenders are shorter. The G has a spur; the J tapers to a point on the line. In the lower case c and s with their blobs approach more closely to the usual fat face design.

ABCDEFGHIJKLMNOPQRSTUVW
XYZ
abcdefghijklmnopqrstuvwxyz
1234567890

BRAGGADOCIO

BRITANNIC

Stephenson Blake

vi

A type like ROTHBURY, combining the qualities of a fat face. The thins have a considerable weight. The G has a spur and the Q a curled tail. The lower case follows the usual English design, as in the a, e, g and t. Ascenders are short. The thins are thicker than in ROTHBURY.

ABCDEFGHIJKLM NOPQRSTUV
WXYZ!?
abcdefghijklmno pqrstuvwxyz
1234

BRITANNIC

BROADWAY

American 1929;
Lanston Monotype 1928–29

vi

The American Typefounders type, designed by M.F. Benton, has a condensed version. A type combining characteristics of fat face and lineale. In most of the letters only the main stroke is fat, the thins taking over the rest of the letter. Thins and thicks meet at an angle and not in a curve.

A B C D E F G HIJKLMN O P Q R ſ S ſſ
T U V W X Y Z & ! ?
a b c d e f g h i j k l m n o p q r ſ t u v w
x y z
1 2 3 4 5 6 7 8 9 0

BROADWAY

ABCDEFGHIJKLMNOPQ

RƧƧSƧƧTUVWXYZ&!?

1234567890

BROADWAY INLINE

Designed by Rudolf Koch. In some points it resembles the designer's LOCARNO, *e.g.* in the varying width of the capitals. **G** has no terminal bar. **J** is short and has a wide loop. **M** is slightly splayed. The arms of **E**, **F** and **L** and the top of the **T** are sheared off obliquely. **U** has the lower-case design. The **a**, **e** and **g** have the same design in the normalised version as in LOCARNO. **t** has a curved terminal. The Klingspor versions, which are the original, are no longer cast.

There are four weights (the heaviest being modified considerably) italics or sloped romans, condensed faces and an inline, which is also called ZEPPELIN.

ABCDEFGHIJKLMNOPQRSTUV

abcdefghijklmnopqrstuvwxyz

ABCDEFGHIJKLMNOPQRSTUVWX

CABLE LIGHT

ABCDEFGHIJKLMNOPQRSTUV

abcdefghijklmnopqrstuvwxyz

CABLE MEDIUM

ABCDEFGHIJKLMNOPQRSTU

abcdefghijklmnopqrstuvwxyz

ABCDEFGHIJKLMNOPQRSTUV

abcdefghijklmnopqrstuvwxyz

CABLE BOLD

ABCDEFGHIJKLMNOPQRSTU

abcdefghijklmnopqrstuvwxy

CABLE HEAVY

CABLE or KABEL

vi

ABCDEFGHIJKLMNOPQRSTU

abcdefghijklmnopqrstuvwxyz

CABLE CONDENSED

vi

ABCDEFGHIJKLMNOPQRSTUVWXYZ

abcdefghijklmnopqrstuvwxyz

CABLE BOLD CONDENSED

ix

LOPQRS

CABLE INITIALS

vi

Romeo and Juliet

LORD BYRON

ZEPPELIN

CALYPSO

Olive 1958

Designed by Roger Excoffon. Decorated and three-dimensional capitals. The letters are formed from shaped material.

ix

ABCDEFGHIJLMNOPQRSTU
VWXYZABCDEFGHIJKLMNO

CALYPSO

CANTORIA

Grafotechna 1969

Designed by Bronislav Maly. A text lineale in which vertical stokes expand at the feet.

vi

AÁBCČDĎEÉĚFGHIÍJKLMNÑOÓPQRŘSŠTŤU
ÚŮVWXYÝZŽÆŒ

aábcčdďeéěfghiíjklmnňoópqrřsštťuúvw
xyýzžæœ

1234567890

CANTORIA

CAPITOL

Schriftguss 1931

Designed by K.H. Schaefer. The shading of this lineale consists simply of an additional stroke on the outside of the main strokes.

vi

BELVEDERE

CAPITOL

Designed by H.A. Trafton. A series of freely-drawn capitals and figures. There is little variation in colour and serifs are almost entirely lacking. The bars of the **A** and **H**, and the centre arm of the **E** protrude. The bowls of **B** and **R** are not closed. The capitals of STUDIO are similar. There are two weights. In Germany the type is called FRESKO.

ABCDEFGHIJKLMNOPQRST
UVWXYZ 1234567890

ix

CARTOON

ABCDEFGHIJKLMNOPQRST
UVWXYZ 1234567890

ix

CARTOON BOLD

Designed by Roger Excoffon as a lineale with stressed down strokes.

ABCDEFGHIJKLMNOPQRSTUVWXYZ
abcdefghijklmnopqrstuvwxyz
1234567890

vi

CHAMBORD MEDIUM

ABCDEFGHIJKLMNOPQRSTUVWYZ
abcdefghijklmnopqrstuvwxyz
1234567890
ABCDEFGHJKLMNOPQRSTUVWXYZ
abcdefghijklmnopqrstuvwxyz
1234567890

vi

CHAMBORD SEMI-BOLD

ABCDEFGHIKLMNOPQRSTUW
abcdefghijklmnopqrstuvwxyz
1234567890

vi

CHAMBORD BOLD

ABCDEFGHIJKLMNOPQRSTUVWXYZ
abcdefghijklmnopqrstuvwxyz 1234567890

vi

CHAMBORD CONDENSED

CHAMFER GOTHIC
Ludlow

vi

An angular type without a lower case.

ABCDEFGHIJKLMNOPQRSTUVWXYZ&
1234567890

CHAMFER GOTHIC

COLONIA
Ludwig & Mayer 1938

vi

Designed by W.F. Kemper. A type in which the strokes vary in weight. The U is like the lower case; the ends of many letters are cut at a single angle. VIDEO ROMA has some similarity.

ABCDEFGHIJKLMNOPQRSTUV
WXYZ
abcdefghijklmnopqrstuvwxyz
1234567890
ABCDEFGHIJKLMNOPQRSTUV
WXYZ
abcdefghijklmnopqrstuvwxyz
1234567890

COLONIA

vi

ABCDEFGHIJKLMNOPQRST
UVWXYZ
abcdefghijklmnopqrstuvwxyz
1234567890

COLONIA BOLD

COMMERCE GOTHIC
Ludlow 1939

vi

Capitals in which the normally round letters are squared. BANK GOTHIC is similar.

ABCDEFGHIJKLMNOPQRSTUVWXYZ&
1234567890

COMMERCE GOTHIC LIGHT

vi

ABCDEFGHIJKLMNOPQRSTUVWXYZ&   1234567890

COMMERCE GOTHIC LIGHT CONDENSED

vi

ABCDEFGHIJKLMNOPQRSTUVWXYZ&
1234567890

COMMERCE GOTHIC MEDIUM

vi

ABCDEFGHIJKLMNOPQRSTUVWXYZ&   1234567890

COMMERCE GOTHIC MEDIUM CONDENSED

260

A bold rather condensed lineale. COMMERCIALE COMPACTE is a companion type for larger sizes.

ABCDEFGHIJKLMNOPQRSTUVWXYZ
abcdefghijklmnopqrstuvwxyz
1234567890

COMMERCIAL GROTESQUE

ABCDEFGHIJKLMNOPQRSTUVWXYZ
abcdefghijklmnopqrstuvwxyz

COMMERCIAL GROTESQUE BOLD

A condensed extra bold variation of the same founder's COMMERCIAL GROTESQUE BOLD.

Modelle der diesjährigen Winter-Damenmode
Einladung zur Ausstellung der schönsten

COMMERCIALE COMPACTE

A rimmed fat lineale. Bauer call their version ASTORIA.

ABCDEFGHIJKLMNOPQR
STUVWXYZ&
abcdefghijklmnopqrstuvw
xyz
1234567890

COMSTOCK

A condensed inclined type. Ascenders and descenders are very short. The lower case is not entirely without serifs, the **m**, **n** and **u** having foot serifs.

ABCDEFGHIJKLMNOPQRSTUVWXYZ&
abcdefghijklmnopqrstuvwxyz

CONDENSA

Designed by R. Hunter Middleton. An outline lineale following the nineteenth-century model.

ABCDEFGHIJKLMNOPQRSTUVWXYZ&
abcdefghijklmnopqrstuvwxyz
1234567890

CONDENSED GOTHIC OUTLINE

CONTACT

Ludwig & Mayer 1968

ix

Designed by Imre Reiner.   A bold slightly inclined brush script.   There are a few slight serifs and some vertical strokes are curved. In the lower case ascenders and descenders are very short. The **a** and **y** have italic forms. There are two weights.

ABCDEFGHIJKLM
NOPQRSTUVWXYZ
abcdefghijklmnopqr
stuvwxyzæœ ff fi ffi fl ffl
1234567890

CONTACT

CYCLONE

Fanfare Press

vi

Designed by W. Ingram. An inclined and condensed titling. The tail of the **Q** is short and entirely outside the bowl. The **G** has a pointed spur, and the vertical strokes in straight letters are inclined at the foot and top.

ABCDEFGHIJKLMNOPQRSTUVWXYZ
1234567890

CYCLONE

DELIA

Simoncini 1962

vi

Designed by Francesco Simoncini. A newspaper type for classified advertisements almost linear in style but with expanding feet. The characters avoid parallel lines, there is variation of stress, normally straight lines are slightly curved, and especially in the lower case there are gaps between the strokes. All this is designed to prevent any filling in on newsprint.

ABCDEFGHIJKLMNOPQRSTUVWXYZ abcdefghijklmnopqrstuvwxyz 1234567890
ABCDEFGHIJKLMNOPQRSTUVWXYZ abcdefghijklmnopqrstuvwxyz 1234567890

DELIA

**DIGI
GROTESK**

Hell 1968

vi

A lineale specially designed for cathode ray tube phototypesetting and based on German lineals. VIDEO TECHNICA is similar.

ABCDEFGHIJKLMNOPQRSTUVWXYZ
abcdefghijklmnopqrstuvwxyz
1234567890

DIGI GROTESK

ABCDEFGHIJKLMNOPQRSTUVW
XYZ
1234567890

DIGI GROTESK BOLD

A stencil type following the DIN German industrial standard lettering style used by engineers and drawing offices.

DIN
Stempel 1923; Berthold 1929

vi

ABCDEFGHIJKLMNOPQRSTUVW
abcdefghijklmnopqrstuvwxyz
1234567890

DIN

Designed by Max Salzmann. A heavy type with considerable variation in colour. The bars of **A** and **H** are triangular pieces. The lower-case letters are very wide and descenders very short. The **j**, **p** and **q** are cut off obliquely at the feet. There is also a decorated face, called ZIERDOLMEN.

DOLMEN
Schelter & Giesecke 1922

Aus römischen Sagen   MAINZER JAHRBUCH

ix

DOLMEN

GUNTHER

ix

ZIERDOLMEN

Designed by Pete Dom. A lineale which is almost monotone and has letters freely or casually drawn. Vertical strokes are irregular ending at different heights, and some are slightly shaped. There is some variation of stress in the rounded letters. Lanston Monotype's FLASH is similar and was designed by Edwin W. Sharr in 1939.
Amsterdam call the type POLKA.

DOM
American 1951–53;
Amsterdam

DOM CASUAL   abcdefghijklmnopqrstuvw

ix

DOM CASUAL

ABCDEFGHIJKLMNOPQRSTUVWXYZTT
abcdefghijklmnopqrstuvwxyz 12345678

ix

DOM DIAGONAL

ALL KNIGHTS OF THE MIDDLE AG
After an apprenticeship as page and

ix

DOM BOLD

DORIC 1 ITALIC
Stephenson Blake

vi

One of the late nineteenth-century designs from Germany cut by John in Hambury in 1892. Amsterdam call the type OLD GOTHIC BOLD and Fonderie Typographique Française call it WASHINGTON.

ABCDEFGHIJKLMNOPQRSTU

VWXYZÆŒ

abcdefghijklmnopqrstuvwxyz

1234567890

DORIC No. 1 ITALIC

DORIC 12
Stephenson Blake

vi

One of the early sans serif designs from Caslon. It has the two English characteristics of a uniform width of capitals and a nearer approach to contemporary romans in the lower case. Note the wide **E** and **R**, and the design of the **a** and **g**. Intertype DORIC (1962) is a quite different type design and is duplexed with ROYAL under which heading it is shown.

MANCHESTER HO
Distinguished Master

DORIC 12

DRESCHER INITIALS
Schriftguss 1927

vi

Designed by A. Drescher. An open lineale titling with letters of equal width. The **M** is square.

UNIVERSUM

DRESCHER INITIALS

DUPLEX
Typoart 1930

vi

Designed by Arno Drescher. A titling type with fine incline and heavy centre strokes.

ABCDEFGHIJKLMNOPQRSTUVWXYZAMW
DIE SCHRIFT WURDE DIE TRÄGERIN DES

DUPLEX

Designed by K. Sommer. Vertical strokes are thickened slightly where normally serifs would be found. Some of the capitals are unequal across the top. MOTOR is a partially shaded version of this type.

DYNAMO
Ludwig & Mayer 1930

ix

ABCDEFGHIJKLMNO
PORSTUVWXYZ
1234567890

DYNAMO

ABCDEFGHIJKLMNO
PORSTUVWXYZ
1234567890

MOTOR

A type face designed to meet the needs of magnetic character recognition in automatic cheque and document reading equipment. MOORE COMPUTER complements the numerals.

E 13 B
Monotype and others

ix

1234567890

E 13 B

Designed by Peter Bell. A three-dimensional lineale with open letters.

ECHO
Stephenson Blake 1956

vi

ABCDEFGHIJKLMN
OPQRSTUVWXYZ
abcdefghijklmnop
qrstuvwxyz
1234567890

ECHO

EDEL GROTESQUE
J. Wagner

Originally issued by Wagner & Schmidt around 1914 as WOTAN, and taken on by many German typefounders. Wagner have combined their LESSING, WOTAN and REICHSGROTESK under this name. The extra bold wide is ANNONCE GROTESQUE. Several versions were added to the original type faces.

vi

ABCDEFGHIJKLMNOPQ
RSTUVWXZ
1234567890
abcdefghijklmnopqrstuvwz

EDEL GROTESQUE LIGHT EXTENDED or GROTESQUE LIGHT

vi

ABCDEFGHIJKLMNOPQRSTUVW
abcdefghijklmnopqrstuvwxyz

EDEL GROTESQUE LIGHT or WOTAN LIGHT

vi

ABCDEFGHIJKLMNOPQRSTUVW
abcdefghijklmnopqrstuvwxyz
1234567890

EDEL GROTESQUE MEDIUM or WOTAN MEDIUM

vi

ABCDEFGHIJKLMNOPQRSTU
abcdefghijklmnopqrstuvwxyz

WOTAN BOLD

vi

ABCDEFGHIJKLMNOP
QRSTUVWXYZ
abcdefghijklmnopqrstuvz

EDEL GROTESQUE BOLD EXTENDED or LESSING GROTESQUE BOLD

vi

ABCDEFGHIJKLMNOPQRSTUVWXYZ
abcdefghijklmnopqrstuvwxyz

EDEL GROTESQUE BOLD CONDENSED or WOTAN BOLD CONDENSED

266

Designed by Carlos Winkow. A sans serif following Continental models. In the **A** and **E** the bars protude to the left, and the **M** is splayed. The **a** is one storeyed. There is a semi-bold and a bold, and in these the bar of the **A** becomes a triangle. There are condensed faces for two weights and also an inline version.

Demostraciones científicas sobre gases metaloides
PROPIAS TRIBULACIONES

vi

ELECTRA FINA

El doctor Merino en la Cátedra de Alta Cultura
CAMINO INADECUADO

vi

ELECTRA SEMINEGRA

Deliciosa e inconfundiblemente encantadora
CONOCIMIENTO GENERAL

vi

ELECTRA NEGRA

Dieron la vuelta al mundo montados en bicicleta
MARAVILLOSO PANORAMA

vi

ELECTRA CURSIVA

Conferencia del doctor Rodrigáñez sobre los valores nutritivos de la miel
ARQUITECTURA ARABE EN LA PENINSULA

vi

ELECTRA ESTRECHA FINA

Recepción en honor de los Miembros del Congreso Internacional
GRAN CONCIERTO DE MUSICA CLASICA

vi

ELECTRA ESTRECHA NEGRA

ABCDEFGHIJKLMNOPQRSTUVWXYZ

vi

ELECTRA CLARA

267

Designed by Hans Möhring. The **G** is wide, the **M** square with the middle strokes stopping short of the line. **E** and especially **T** are narrow. The lower case follows the usual continental model. There are many pointed terminations of vertical strokes. There are three weights and an inline. Stephenson Blake's GUILDFORD SANS is identical.

vi

NeueRundschau

ELEGANT GROTESQUE LIGHT

vi

ABCDEFGHIJKLMNOPQRSTU VWXYZ
abcdefghijklmnopqrstuvwxyz
1234567890

ELEGANT GROTESQUE

vi

Ein kurzer Rückblick mag über die Verwendung der Elektrizität in der Medizin

ELEGANT GROTESQUE   MEDIUM BOLD

vi

ABCDEFGHIJKLMN OPQRSTUVWXYZ&

ELEGANT GROTESQUE INLINE

vi

SPORTKLUB

ELEGANT GROTESQUE BOLD

A condensed titling. The top of the **A** is rounded, and the horizontal strokes of **A, E, H** and **R** are central.

vi

ABCDEFGHIJKLMNOPQRSTUVWXYZ
1234567890

IRIS

Letters have very slight inclination, originally designed as a photolettering style by Studio Hollenstein of Paris. The type supplements the large display sizes of the photolettering design.

vi

ABCDEFGHIJKLMNOPQRSTUVWXYZ ÄÖÜ ÆOE
abcdefghijklmnopqrstuvwxyz
§& 1234567890 ß

ERAS

Designed by J. Erbar. One of the first and most popular of the new sans. **A** has a low bar. **E, F, L** and especially **T** are narrow. The tail of the **Q** is a short horizontal stroke. The **a** is one-storeyed, **g** has an open tail, and **t** has the top cut off at any angle.

There are four weights, with italic and condensed faces. The bold face has also an inline called PHOSPHOR. A set of capitals, white on black, is called LUCINA and an open version LUMINA. There are four weights of ERBAR CONDENSED on Mergenthaler Linotype and two weights on Linotype (London).

ERBAR

Ludwig & Mayer 1922–30 & 1960;

Linotype (Frankfurt);

Mergenthaler Linotype 1933–37;

Linotype (London);

Typograph

ABCDEFGHIJKLMNOPQRSTUVWXYZ

abcdefghijklmnopqrstuvwxyz

1234567890

ERBAR BOOK (LUDWIG & MAYER)

ABCDEFGHIJKLMNOPQRSTUVWXYZ

12345   abcdefghijklmnopqrstuvwxyz   67890

When it is considered that it was the intention to make the book one of practical instruction, and that it was written with the hope that it might be placed in the hands of each printer's boy on entering the business, I trust this sin of inelegance may [from Savage's Dictionary

LINOTYPE ERBAR BOLD

vi

ABCDEFGHIJKLMNOPQRSTUVWXYZ

12345   abcdefghijklmnopqrstuvwxyz   67890

MERGENTHALER LINOTYPE ERBAR MEDIUM CONDENSED

vi

ABCDEFGHIJKLMNOPQRSTUVWXYZ

12345   abcdefghijklmnopqrstuvwxyz   67890

ABCDEFGHIJKLMNOPQRSTUVWXYZ

When it is considered that it was the intention to make the book one of practical instruction, and that it was written with the hope that it might be placed in the hands of each printer's boy on entering the business, I trust this sin of inelegance may be pardoned. No one but [from Savage's Dictionary

LINOTYPE ERBAR LIGHT CONDENSED

vi

ABCDEFGHIJKLMNOPQRSTUVWXYZ

12345   abcdefghijklmnopqrstuvwxyz   67890

ABCDEFGHIJKLMNOPQRSTUVWXYZ

When it is considered that it was the intention to make the book one of practical instruction, and that it was written with the hope that it might be placed in the hands of each printer's boy on entering the business, I trust this sin of inelegance may be pardoned. No one but [from Savage's Dictionary

LINOTYPE ERBAR BOLD CONDENSED

vi

THE · PRIMARY FUNCTION of type is

ERBAR LIGHT

vi

THE PRIMARY FUNCTION of type is that it shall be read, and the first considera-

vi

THE PRIMARY FUNCTION of type is that it

ERBAR

THE PRIMARY FUNCTION of type is

ERBAR MEDIUM.

THE PRIMARY FUNCTION of type is that it shall be read, and the first

THE PRIMARY FUNCTION of type

ERBAR BOLD

THE PRIMARY FUNCTION of type is that it shall be read,

ERBAR CONDENSED

THE PRIMARY FUNCTION of type is that it shall

ERBAR MEDIUM CONDENSED

JAHRESBERICHT

LUCINA

FERD

LUMINA

ABCDEFGHIJKLMNOPQRST
UVWXYZ
1234567890

LUX

ABCDEFGHIJKLMNOPQRS
TUVWXYZ
1234567890

PHOSPHOR

Designed by A. Novarese. A new series to complement the same founder's MICROGRAMMA titling types by offering a lower case. Letters are square-shaped, and have some pen-drawn characteristics. There are several weights in preparation.

ABCDEFGHIJKLMNOPQRSTUVXY
ZW
abcdefghijklmnopqrstuvxyzw
1234567890

EUROSTILE

vi

ABCDEFGHIJKLMNOPQRSTUVXYZW
abcdefghijklmnopqrstuvxyzw
1234567890

EUROSTILE CONDENSED

vi

ABCDEFGHIJKLMNOPQ
RSTUVXYZW
abcdefghijklmnopqrstuvx
yzw
1234567890

EUROSTILE EXTENDED

vi

ABCDEFGHIJKLMNO
PQRSTUVXYZW
abcdefghijklmnopqrstu
vxyzw
1234567890

EUROSTILE BOLD EXTENDED

vi

ABCDEFGHIJKLMNOPQRSTUVXYZW

abcdefghijklmnopqrstuvxyzw

1234567890

EUROSTILE BOLD CONDENSED

vi

ABCDEFGHIJKLMNOPQRSTUVXYZW

abcdefghijklmnopqrstuvxyzw

1234567890

EUROSTILE COMPACT

vi

ABCDEFGHIJKLMNOPQRSTUV
XYZW

abcdefghijklmnopqrstuvxyzw

1234567890

EUROSTILE BOLD

Designed by Louis Oppenheim. An extra bold lineale of unusual angular design.

Lehrbuch für Gartenbau

FANFARE

FANFARE
Berthold 1927
ix

FEDER GROTESK
Ludwig & Mayer 1910
vi

Designed by J. Erbar. A bold sans serif italic, which is not monotone. The arms of **E** and **F**, etc., are comparatively light. The tops of the short ascenders are cut off obliquely.

ABCCDEFGHIJKLM
NOPQRSTUVWXYZ
1234567890
abcdefghijklmnopqr
ſßstuvwxyz

Frühjahrsmod

FEDER ITALIC

ix

Designed by Phillip Boydell and his associates of the London Press Exchange for Festival advertising and to commemorate the Festival of Britain. Based upon condensed sans italic capitals it has a three-dimensional form making it suitable for use in exhibition display typography. Capitals and numerals only.

FESTIVAL

Monotype 1951

ix

ABCDEFGHIJKLMNOPQRST
UVWXYZ
1234567890

FESTIVAL

Designed by Marcel Jacno. Sans serif capitals and figures. The face of the letters is in white and they are three-dimensional. They are placed on a criblé ground.

FILM

Deberny & Peignot 1934

vi

ABCDEFGHIJKLM
NOPQRSTUVXYZ

FILM

Designed by Hans Möhring. Light sans serif capitals, which are not monotone. Upstrokes, arms, etc., are half the weight of the downstrokes. In the **M** the middle strokes stop short of the line.

FLORIDA

Weber 1931

vi

vi

ABCDEFGHIJKLMNOPQRSTUVW
1234567890

FLORIDA

Designed by Imre Reiner. A three-dimensional angular titling in which the faces of letters are horizontally shaded.

FLORIDE

Deberny & Peignot 1939

vi

ABCDEFGHIJKLMNOPQRS
TUVWXYZ
1234567890

FLORIDE

Designed by Konrad F. Bauer and Walter Baum. Fonderie Typographique Francaise call this type CARAVELLE. A sans serif following nineteenth century models, e.g., the **G** and **M**. There are 17 versions of the basic design.

vi

ABCDEFGHIJKLMNOPQRSTUVO
abcdefghijklmnopqrstuvwxyzabcdel
1234567890

ABCDEFGHIJKLMNOPQRSTUVX
abcdefghijklmnopqrstuvwxyzabcdz
1234567890

FOLIO LIGHT

vi

ABCDEFGHIJKLMNOPQRSTUYZ
abcdefghijklmnopqrstuvwxyzabcde
1234567890

FOLIO MEDIUM

vi

ABCDEFGHIJKLMNOPQRSW
abcdefghijklmnopqrstuvxyz
1234567890

ABCDEFGHIJKLMNOPQRSZ
abcdefghijklmnopqrstuwyr
1234567890

FOLIO MEDIUM EXTENDED

vi

ABCDEFGHIJKLMNOPQRSTW
abcdefghijklmnopqrstuvwj
1234567890

FOLIO EXTRA BOLD

vi

ABCDEFGHIJKLMNOPQRSTUVWXYZABCDEFGH
abcdefghijklmnopqrstuvwxyzabcdefghijklmj
1234567890

FOLIO BOLD CONDENSED

Designed under the direction of Aldo Novarese, by a team of designers including Franco Grignani, Giancarlo Iliprandi, Bruno Munari, Ilio Negri, Till Neuburg, Luigi Oriani and Pino Tovaglia. A "waisted" type with strokes of characters slightly thickened towards their ends to provide for improved readability in continuous texts and better reproducibility.

ABCDEFGHIJKLMNOPQRSTUVX
abcdefghijklmnopqrstuvxyzw
1234567890

vi

ABCDEFGHIJKLMNOPQRSTUVX
abcdefghijklmnopqrstuvxyzw
1234567890

FORMA

ABCDEFGHIJKLMNOPQRSTUVX
abcdefghijklmnopqrstuvxyzw
1234567890

vi

FORMA BOLD

ABCDEFGHIJKLMNOPQRSTUV
abcdefghijklmnopqrstuvwxyz
XYZ1234567890

vi

FORMA CONTORNATA

Designed by Morris F. Benton. A heavy sans serif after the English models. Note the **G**, upper and lower case, and the square **M**. Ludlow's version is somewhat taller.

ABCDEFGHIJKLMNOPQRSTUVWXYZ
abcdefghijklmnopqrstuvwxyz
1234567890

vi

FRANKLIN GOTHIC EXTRA CONDENSED

ABCDEFGHIJKLMNOPQRSTUVWXYZ
abcdefghijklmnopqrstuvwxyz
1234567890

vi

FRANKLIN GOTHIC CONDENSED

ABCDEFGHIJKLMNOPQRSTU
VWXYZ
abcdefghijklmnopqrstuvwxyz
1234567890

ABCDEFGHIJKLMNOPQRSTU
VWXYZ
abcdefghijklmnopqrstuvwxyz
1234567890

FRANKLIN GOTHIC

vi

ABCDEFGHIJKLMNOPQR
STUVWXYZ
abcdefghijklmnopqrstuv
wxyz 1234567890

FRANKLIN GOTHIC WIDE

vi

ABCDEFGHIJKLMNOPQRSTUVW
XYZ 1234567890
abcdefghijklmnopqrstuvwxyz

FRANKLIN GOTHIC CONDENSED ITALIC

FUNDAMENTAL

L. Wagner 1938

Designed by Arno Drescher. A sans serif with short descenders, in four weights and two condensed versions. The **b** has a spur at the foot; dots on letters like **i** and the German *Umlaut*-vowels are square. In the bold versions the curved strokes are narrow where they meet vertical strokes. The type is like SUPER GROTESQUE, but the **M** in the latter is splayed.

vi

Elektrische Geräte im Kraftfahrzeug

FUNDAMENTAL LIGHT ITALIC

vi

des Magnetismus und der Elektrizität

FUNDAMENTAL LIGHT CONDENSED

vi

Kapazität einer Sammlerbatterie

FUNDAMENTAL MEDIUM

Laden der Sammler mit der Lichtmaschine

Unterbrecher und Kondensator

Primär- und Sekundär-Stromkreise

Designed by Paul Renner. One of the popular German sans. The **M** is splayed, the **Q** has a straight tail starting inside the bowl, the **T** is narrow but less so than in Erbar. The **a** is one-storeyed, **g** has the usual open tail, **t** is square across the top, and **u** has the design of the upper case. There are six weights, a condensed in three weights, and an inline. Deberny & Peignot also issue this type and call it EUROPE. SPARTAN (American Typefounders and Mergenthaler Linotype) is rather similar to this German design, although also similar to ERBAR. FUTURA BOOK—not shown here—is also on German Linotype (Frankfurt).

FUTURA BLACK differs considerably from the main series. By the omission of the thin strokes many of the letters are formed of three and others of two detached parts. The lower-case **r** for example consists of a thick vertical stroke and a detached blob. It resembles a stencil type.

Intertype and Intertype (Fotosetter) FUTURA EXTRA BOLD were designed (roman) by Edwin W. Shaar in 1952 and (italic) by Edwin W. Shaar and Tommy Thompson in 1955.

ABCDEFGHIJKLMNOPQRSTUVWXYZ
abcdefghijklmnopqrstuvwxyz
1234567890

vi

ABCDEFGHIJKLMNOPQRSTUVWXYZ
abcdefghijklmnopqrstuvwxyz
1234567890

vi

ABCDEFGHIJKLMNOPQRSTUVWXYZ
abcdefghijklmnopqrstuvwxyz
1234567890

vi

ABCDEFGHIJKLMNOPQRSTUVWXYZ
abcdefghijklmnopqrstuvwxyz
1234567890

INTERTYPE FUTURA EXTRA BOLD CONDENSED OBLIQUE

vi

ABCDEFGHIJKLMNOPQRSTUVWXYZ
abcdefghijklmnopqrstuvwxyz
1234567890

ABCDEFGHIJKLMNOPQRSTUVWXYZ
abcdefghijklmnopqrstuvwxyz
1234567890

INTERTYPE FUTURA EXTRA BOLD WITH OBLIQUE

vi

ABCDEFGHIJKLMNOPQRSTUVWXYZ
abcdefghijklmnopqrstuvwxyz
123456789

FUTURA DISPLAY

vi

ABCDEFGHIJKLMNOPQRSTU
VWXYZ
abcdefghijklmnopqrstuvwxyz
1234567890

FUTURA BLACK

vi

ABCDEFGHIJKLMNOPQRSTUVW
XYZ
1234567890

FUTURA INLINE

ABCDEFGHIJKLMNOPQRSTUVWXYZ
abcdefghijklmnopqrstuvwxyz
1234567890

ABCDEFGHIJKLMNOPQRSTUVWXYZ
abcdefghijklmnopqrstuvwxyz
1234567890

FUTURA BOOK

ABCDEFGHIJKLMNOPQRSTUVWXYZ
abcdefghijklmnopqrstuvwxyz
1234567890

ABCDEFGHIJKLMNOPQRSTUVWXYZ
abcdefghijklmnopqrstuvwxyz
1234567890

FUTURA BOOK WITH OBLIQUE

ABCDEFGHIJKLMNOPQRSTUVWXYZ
abcdefghijklmnopqrstuvwxyz
1234567890

FUTURA BOOK BOLD

ABCDEFGHIJKLMNOPQRSTUVWXYZ
abcdefghijklmnopqrstuvwxyz
1234567890

ABCDEFGHIJKLMNOPQRSTUVWXYZ
abcdefghijklmnopqrstuvwxyz
1234567890

FUTURA MEDIUM

ABCDEFGHIJKLMNOPQRSTUVWXYZ
abcdefghijklmnopqrstuvwxyz
1234567890

FUTURA MEDIUM CONDENSED

ABCDEFGHIJKLMNOPQRSTUVW
XYZ
abcdefghijklmnopqrstuvwxyz

FUTURA SEMI-BOLD

ABCDEFGHIJKLMNOPQRSTUV
WXYZ
abcdefghijklmnopqrstuvwxyz
1234567890

ABCDEFGHIJKLMNOPQRSTUV
WXYZ
abcdefghijklmnopqrstuvwxyz
1234567890

FUTURA BOLD AND FUTURA BOLD OBLIQUE

ABCDEFGHIJKLMNOPQRSTUVWXYZ
abcdefghijklmnopqrstuvwxyz
1234567890

FUTURA BOLD CONDENSED

ABCDEFGHIJKLMNOPQRSTUVWXYZ
abcdefghijklmnopqrstuvwxyz
1234567890

INTERTYPE FUTURA EXTRA BOLD CONDENSED

A newspaper type of large x-height.

ABCDEFGHIJKLMNOPQRSTUVWXYZ

abcdefghijklmnopqrstuvwxyz

1234567890

ABCDEFGHIJKLMNOPQRSTUVWXYZ

abcdefghijklmnopqrstuvwxyz

1234567890

GALAXY

vi

ABCDEFGHIJKLMNOPQRSTUVWXYZ

abcdefghijklmnopqrstuvwxyz

1234567890

GALAXY BOLD

Designed by Eric Gill. It owes something to the letters designed by Edward Johnston for the Underground Railways in 1918. In some ways it is closer in design to the original sans serifs than the modern German versions. There is a more uniform width of the capitals and the only points are at the feet of **V** and **W**. The final stroke in the **G** is shorter than in the German versions. The **M** is square and the middle strokes descend half-way. In the lower case the **a**, **g** and **t** follow the normal roman designs, but there are alternative sorts.

There are four weights, italic (with a one-storeyed **a**), a condensed and a GILL SHADOW, a three-dimensional letter. GILL CAMEO and KAYO are shown separately.

ABCDEFGHIJKLMNOPQRSTUVWXYZ

abcdefghijklmnopqrstuvwxyz

1234567890

vi

ABCDEFGHIJKLMNOPQRSTUVWXYZ

abcdefghijklmnopqrstuvwxyz

1234567890

GILL SANS LIGHT

ABCDEFGHIJKLMNOPQRSTUVWXYZ

abcdefghijklmnopqrstuvwxyz

1234567890

vi

ABCDEFGHIJKLMNOPQRSTUVWXYZ

abcdefghijklmnopqrstuvwxyz

1234567890

GILL SANS

ABCDEFGHIJKLMNOPQRSTUVWXYZ

1234567890

vi

GILL SANS MEDIUM

GILL SANS

ABCDEFGHIJKLMNOPQRSTUVWXYZ

abcdefghijklmnopqrstuvwxyz

1234567890

GILL SANS MEDIUM CONDENSED

vi

ABCDEFGHIJKLMNOPQRSTUVWXYZ

abcdefghijklmnopqrstuvwxyz

1234567890

ABCDEFGHIJKLMNOPQRSTUVWXYZ

abcdefghijklmnopqrstuvwxyz

1234567890

GILL SANS BOLD

vi

ABCDEFGHIJKLMNOPQRSTUVWXYZ

abcdefghijklmnopqrstuvwxyz

1234567890

GILL BOLD CONDENSED

vi

ABCDEFGHIJKLMNOPQRSTUVWXYZ

abcdefghijklmnopqrstuvwxyz

1234567890

GILL BOLD EXTRA CONDENSED

vi

ABCDEFGHIJKLMNOPQRSTUVWXYZ

abcdefghijklmnopqrstuvwxyz

1234567890

GILL EXTRA BOLD

vi

ABCDEFGHIJKLMNOPQRSTUVWXYZ

abcdefghijklmnopqrstuvwxyz

1234567890

GILL KAYO or SANS ULTRABOLD

282

THE MANY TYPES 12

GILL CAMEO

THE MANY TYPES 123

GILL CAMEO RULED

VISIT CORNWALL

GILL SHADOW TITLING

VISIT CORNWALL

GILL SHADOW No. 1

ABCDEFGHIJKLMNOPQRSTU VWXYZ

abcdefghijklmnopqrstuvwxyz

1234567890

GILL SANS SHADOW LINE

First cut around 1906. There are condensed and extra condensed versions. The **E**, **F** and **H** have high cross-bars, and **V** and **W** in capitals and lower case have an angular finish to the stems of the caps.

ABCDEFGHIJKLMNOPQRS
TUVWXYZ&
abcdefghijklmnopqrstuv
wxyz
1234567890

GLOBE GOTHIC

ABCDEFGHIJKLMNOPQRSTUVWXYZ

abcdefghijklmnopqrstuvwxyz

1234567890

GLOBE GOTHIC CONDENSED

A traditional American condensed gothic or lineale.

ABCDEFGHIJKLMNOPQRSTUVWXYZ&
abcdefghijklmnopqrstuvwxyz
1234567890

GOTHIC NO. 13

A sans serif after the English models, as in the spur of the **G** and the regularity in the width of the capitals.

ABCDEFGHIJKLMNOPQRSTUVWXYZ
abcdefghijklmnopqrstuvwxyz
1234567890

GOTHIC CONDENSED No. 25

A set of outline sans serif capitals of nineteenth-century design. Note the **G** and **R**. The type was originally introduced by another American foundry around 1890.

BRAZIL AND OTHER COUNTRIES
WERE SENDING TO PORTUGAL

GOTHIC OUTLINE NO. 61

Designed by F.W. Goudy in 1925, with the bold originally called GOUDY GOTHIC and first shown in 1922. Some capitals are scriptorial.

AABCDEFGHIJKLMNOPQRRSSTTUVWXYZ
aabcdeεfghijklmnopqrstuvwxyz fiflffffiffl&
$1234567890

GOUDY SANSERIF

AABCDEFGHIJKLMNNOPQRRSSTTUVWXYZ
aabcdeεfghijklmnopqrstuvwxyz fiflffffiffl&
$1234567890

GOUDY SANSERIF BOLD

The **M** is like GILL and the tail of the **Q** like FUTURA. The lower case follows the German model, except the **t** with a curved foot. The dot is diamond-shaped. There are four weights, with italic, a condensed face, an inline, white on black called CAMEO, and a GRANBY SHADOW, a three-dimensional letter.

ABCDEFGHIJKLMNOPQRSTUV
WXYZÆ
abcdefghijklmnopqrstuvwxyz
123456780

ABCDEFGHIJKLMNOPQRSTUVWXYZ
abcdefghijklmnopqrstuvwxyz
12345

GRANBY

vi

ABCDEFGHIJKLMNOPQRSTUVWXYZ
abcdefghijklmnopqrstuvwxyz

ABCDEFGHIJKLMNOPQRSTUVWXYZ
abcdefghijklmnopqrstuvwxyz

GRANBY LIGHT

vi

ABCDEFGHIJKLMNOPQRSTUVWXYZÆŒ
abcdefghijklmnopqrstuvwxyzæœ
1234567890

GRANBY LIGHT CONDENSED

vi

ABCDEFGHIJKLMNOPQRSTUVWXYZÆŒ
abcdefghijklmnopqrstuvwxyzæœ
123456

GRANBY CONDENSED

vi

ABCDEFGHIJKLMNOPQRSTUVWXYZ
abcdefghijklmnopqrstuvwxyz
123456

GRANBY BOLD CONDENSED

vi

ABCDEFGHIJKLMNOPQRSTUVWX
YZ&
abcdefghijklmnopqrstuvwxyz
£1234567890

GRANBY BOLD

vi

ABCDEFGHIJKLMNOPQRSTUVWX
YZÆŒ
abcdefghijklmnopqrstuvwxyzæœ
1234567890

GRANBY EXTRA BOLD

vi

ABCDEFGHIJKLMNOPQRSTU
VWXYZÆŒ
abcdefghijklmnopqrstuvwxyz
1234567890

GRANBY ELEPHANT

vi

ABCDEFGHIJKLMNOPQRST
UVWXYZ
£1234567890

GRANBY SHADOW

vi

ABCDEFGHIJKLMNOPQRSTUVWXYZ
abcdefghijklmnopqrstuvwxyzæœ
1234567890

GRANBY INLINE

vi

ABCDEFGHIJK&

GRANBY CAMEO

Cut after original designs by Hermann Eidenbenz. A set of open, three-dimensional and condensed sans serif capitals and figures. The design is derived from a nineteenth-century model.

ABCDEFGHIJKLMNOPQRSTUVWXYZ
1234567890

GRAPHIQUE

A sans serif with thick and thin strokes. The thicks and thins meet at an angle and not in a curve. There is an additional oddity of a partial inline. Capitals and figures only.

ABDEGHIJKMNPQRSTUVWXYZ
1234567890

GROCK

A modified light sans serif not unlike VOGUE and with tall ascenders. The Z has a bar at x-height level.

ABCDEFGHIJKLMNOPQRSTUVWXYZ

bdfhkllßt   Switzerland

GROTESKPFEILER

One of the early sans serifs, that of Thorowgood, 1832, was called GROTESQUE, and the name is still in use for sans serif types based on nineteenth-century models. The capitals are of equal width, the **G** has a spur and the **M** is square. The lower case follows the usual design of contemporary English romans, as in the **a, e, g** and **t**. The Monotype Corporation's HEADLINE BOLD closely follows Stephenson Blake's GROTESQUE NO. 9.

ABCDEFGHIJKLMNOPQRSTUVWXYZ
abcdefghijklmnopqrstuvwxyz

MONOTYPE GROTESQUE No. 1 BOLD

ABCDEFGHIJKLMNOPQRSTUV
WXYZ

GROTESQUE No. 3

ABCDEFGHIJKLMNOPQRSTUVWXYZ

abcdefghijklmnopqrstuvwxyz

MONOTYPE GROTESQUE CONDENSED No. 4

vi

ABCDEFGHIJKLMNOPQRSTUV WXYZÆŒ& abcdefghijklmnopqrstuvwxyzæ œ£1234567890

GROTESQUE No. 8

vi

ABCDEFGHIJKLMNOPQRSTUVWXYZ abcdefghijklmnopqrstuvwxyz 1234567890

ABCDEFGHIJKLMNOPQRSTUVWXYZ abcdefghijklmnopqrstuvwxyz 1234567890

GROTESQUE NO. 9 (MONOTYPE HEADLINE BOLD)

vi

ABCDEFGHIJKLMNOPQRST UVWXYZ abcdefghijklmnoqrstuvwxyz 1234567890

GROTESQUE No. 10

vi

ABCDEFGHIJKLMNOPQRSTUV WXYZ 1234567890

GROTESQUE No. 12

vi

ABCDEFGHIJKLMNOPQRSTUVWXYZÆ Œ abcdefghijklmnopqrstuvwxyz æœ& £1234567890

GROTESQUE No. 18

ABCDEFGHIJKLMNOPQRSTUVWXYZ
abcdefghijklmnopqrstuvwxyz
1234567890

GROTESQUE CONDENSED No. 33

ABCDEFGHIJKLMNO
PQRSTUVWXYZ
abcdefghijklmnopq
rstuvwxyzæœ
£&1234567890

GROTESQUE No. 66

ABCDEFGHIJKLMNOPQRSTUVWXYZÆŒ
abcdefghijklmnopqrstuvwxyzæœ&
£1234567890

GROTESQUE No. 77 ´

ABCDEFGHIJKLMNOPQRSTUVWXYZ
abcdefghijklmnopqrstuvwxyz
1234567890
ABCDEFGHIJKLMNOPQRSTUVWXYZ
abcdefghijklmnopqrstuvwxyz
1234567890

GROTESQUE LIGHT No. 126

ABCDEFGHIJKLMNOPQRSTUVWXYZ
abcdefghijklmnopqrstuvwxyz
1234567890

GROTESQUE BOLD EXTENDED No. 150

ABCDEFGHIJKLMNOPQRSTUVWXYZ
abcdefghijklmnopqrstuvwxyz
1234567890

vi

GROTESQUE BOLD EXTENDED No. 150

vi

ABCDEFGHIJKLMNOPQRSTUVWXYZ
abcdefghijklmnopqrstuvwxyz
1234567890

ABCDEFGHIJKLMNOPQRSTUVWXYZ
abcdefghijklmnopqrstuvwxyz
1234567890

GROTESQUE No. 215

vi

ABCDEFGHIJKLMNOPQRSTUVWXYZ
abcdefghijklmnopqrstuvwxyz
1234567890

GROTESQUE BOLD No. 216

vi

ABCDEFGHIJKLMNOPQRSTUVWXYZ
abcdefghijklmnopqrstuvwxyz
1234567890

GROTESQUE CONDENSED No. 318

vi

ABCDEFGHIJKLMNOPQRSTUVWXYZ
abcdefghijklmnopqrstuvwxyz
1234567890

vi

ABCDEFGHIJKLMNOPQRSTUVWXYZ
abcdefghijklmnopqrstuvwxyz
1234567890

ABCDEFGHIJKLMNOPQRSTUVWXYZ
abcdefghijklmnopqrstuvwxyz
1234567890

GROTESQUE BOLD CONDENSED

ABCDEFGHIJKLMNOPQRSTUVWXYZ
1234567890

GROTESQUE BOLD CONDENSED TITLING

A condensed considerably elongated titling.

ABCDEFGHIJKLMNOP
QRSTUVWXYZ12345

GROTESQUE CONDENSED TITLING

A condensed lineale with short descenders.

ABCDEFGHIJKLMNOPQRSTUVWXYZ
abcdefghijklmnopqrstuvwxyz
1234567890

HANSEATIC

ABCDEFGHIJKLMNOPQRSTUVWXYZ
abcdefghijklmnopqrstuvwxyz
1234567890

HANSEATIC BOLD

A condensed and elongated sans serif, with short ascenders and descenders. The bars of **A**, **E**, **F** and **H**, and some of the up-strokes are thin. There is also a bold.

ABCDEFGHIJKLMNOPQRSTUVXYWZ
abcdefghijklmnopqrstuvyxwz
1234567890

HASTILE

ABCDEFGHIJKLMNOPQRSTUVXYWZ
abcdefghijklmnopqrstuvxywz
1234567890

HASTILE BOLD

HELION

Schriftguss 1935; Française 1935

Designed by Arno Drescher. Three-dimensional sans serif capitals, similar to FILM but on a white ground. The shading does not give a true three-dimensional effect and is very wide. In France the type is called HELIOS.

vi

ABCDEFGHIJKLMNOPQRSTUVWXYZ

HELION

HELVETICA

Haas 1957; Stempel; Linotype (Frankfurt, London & New York); Typograph

Designed by M. Miedinger. A traditional following the nineteenth-century style. The **a** has a curved spur and the tail of the **Q** is oblique. The type was formerly called NEUE HAAS GROTESK.

vi

ABCDEFGHIJKLMNOPQRSTUVWXYZ
abcdefghijklmnopqrstuvwxyz
£1234567890

ABCDEFGHIJKLMNOPQRSTUVWXYZ
abcdefghijklmnopqrstuvwxyz
£1234567890

HELVETICA LIGHT

vi

ABCDEFGHIJKLMNOPQRSTUVWXYZ&
abcdefghijklmnopqrstuvwxyz
1234567890

ABCDEFGHIJKLMNOPQRSTUVWXYZ&
abcdefghijklmnopqrstuvwxyz
1234567890

MERGENTHALER LINOTYPE HELVETICA LIGHT

vi

ABCDEFGHIJKLMNOPQRSTUVWXYZ
abcdefghijklmnopqrstuvwxyz
1234567890

ABCDEFGHIJKLMNOPQRSTUVWXYZ
abcdefghijklmnopqrstuvwxyz
1234567890

HELVETICA

292

ABCDEFGHIJKLMNOPQRSTUVWXYZ
abcdefghijklmnopqrstuvwxyz
£1234567890

HELVETICA CONDENSED

ABCDEFGHIJKLMNOPQRSTUVWXYZ&
abcdefghijklmnopqrstuvwxyz
1234567890

ABCDEFGHIJKLMNOPQRSTUVWXYZ&
abcdefghijklmnopqrstuvwxyz
1234567890

MERGENTHALER LINOTYPE HELVETICA

ABCDEFGHIJKLMNOPQRSTUV
abcdefghijklmnopqrstuvwxyz
£ 1234567890

HELVETICA EXTENDED

ABCDEFGHIJKLMNOPQRSTUVWXYZ
abcdefghijklmnopqrstuvwxyz
1234567890

ABCDEFGHIJKLMNOPQRSTUVWXYZ
abcdefghijklmnopqrstuvwxyz
1234567890

HELVETICA MEDIUM

ABCDEFGHIJKLMNOPQRSTUVWXYZ&
abcdefghijklmnopqrstuvwxyz
1234567890

ABCDEFGHIJKLMNOPQRSTUVWXYZ&
abcdefghijklmnopqrstuvwxyz
1234567890

MERGENTHALER LINOTYPE HELVETICA BOLD

ABCDEFGHIJKLMNOPQRSTUVWXYZ

abcdefghijklmnopqrstuvwxyz

1234567890

HELVETICA BOLD

vi

ABCDEFGHIJKLMNOPQRSTUVWXYZ

abcdefghijklmnopqrstuvwxyz

1234567890

ABCDEFGHIJKLMNOPQRSTUVWXYZ

abcdefghijklmnopqrstuvwxyz

1234567890

HELVETICA EXTRA BOLD

vi

ABCDEFGHIJKLMNOPQRSTUVWXYZ

abcdefghijklmnopqrstuvwxyz

1234567890

HELVETICA BOLD CONDENSED

vi

ABCDEFGHIJKLMNOPQRSTUVWXYZ

abcdefghijklmnopqrstuvwxyz

1234567890

HELVETICA COMPACT

vi

ABCDEFGHIJKLMNOPQRSTUVWXYZ

abcdefghijklmnopqrstuvwxyz

1234567890

MERGENTHALER LINOTYPE HELVETICA EXTRA COMPRESSED

vi

ABCDEFGHIJKLMNOPQRSTUVWXYZ

abcdefghijklmnopqrstuvwxyz

1234567890

MERGENTHALER LINOTYPE HELVETICA ULTRA COMPRESSED

Designed by Werner Rebhuhn in 1955 for Genzsch & Heyse. A heavy type with letters drawn casually. There is some variation of stress in the rounded, somewhat angular letters.

Die Wahl der richtigen Schrift

ABCDEFGHIJKLMNOPQRSTUVWXYZ

abcdefghijklmnopqrstuvwxyz

1234567890

HOBBY

Designed by Morris F. Benton. Vertical strokes and bars are curved, and there is some variation of stress. Descenders have been eliminated.

ABCDEFGHIJKLMNOPQRSTUV WXYZ

abcdefghijklmnopqrstuvwxyz

1234567890

HOBO

Designed by Max Miedinger. A heavy titling with almost square letters.

ABCDEFGHIJKLMN OPQRSTUVWXYZ 1234567890

HORIZONTAL

Designed and cut in wood by A. van der Vossen. A heavy almost monotone lineale with very short ascenders and descenders. The chief characteristic is the squaring off of the curves in the lower case which is almost uncial.

ABCDEFGHIJKLMNOPQRSTUVWXYZ
abcdefghijklmnopqrstuvwxyz

HOUTSNEELETTER

Designed by Walter Huxley. The bars of the **A**, **B**, **E**, **F**, etc., are low and project to the left. **A**, **M** and **N** have each two sorts, one with a rounded top. There is also a second, rounded **W**.

HUXLEY VERTICAL

Designed by E. Crous-Vidal. A lineale type but by no means monotone. In the bold face there is much variation of colour. In the semi-bold there are two capital **O**'s, one with vertical and one oblique stress. The **M** is splayed.

ABCDEFGHIJKLMNOPQRSTUVWXY

abcdefghijklmnopqrstuvwxyz

1234567890

ILE DE FRANCE

vi

ABCDEFGHIJKLMNOPQRSTUVW

abcdefghijklmnopqrstuvwxyz

1234567890

ILE DE FRANCE BOLD

vi

ABCDEFGHIJKLMNOPQRSTU
VWXYZ

abcdefghijklmnopqrstuvwxyz

1234567890

ILE DE FRANCE EXTRA BOLD

Designed by E. Crous-Vidal. A condensed slightly inclined lineale in the Continental style. The **A** has a rounded top, the **E** a low bar, and the lower case **t** an unusually low cross bar.

La vanidad, el orgullo, la soberbia y otras pasiones ciegan la inteligencia humana

LA EDUCACION DE LA VOLUNTAD

ILERDA

Designed by Geoffrey Lee. An extra bold type.

ABCDEFGHIJKLMNPOQRSTUVWX YZ J
abcdefghijklmnopqrstuvwxyz r
1234567890&£$

IMPACT

Designed by G. Collette and J. Dufour. An extra bold stylized lineale.

Steam Traction NEIGHBOURS

INDEPENDANT

A rounded titling type with a horizontal straight white line running at half height through all characters. The type can also be used in two-colours using upper and lower halves to print in different colours.

ABCDEFGHIJKLMNOPQRSTUVW

INTERPOL

Designed by Rea Irvin and made by Lanston Monotype for the American magazine. Some letters of POST ROMAN are similar, but this type was designed for straight setting and no letter-spacing or fitting is being done in the columns of the *New Yorker*, thus retaining the informal character.

ABCDEFGHIJKLMNOPQRSTUVWXYZ

1234567890 &

IRVIN

Designed by Marcel Jacno. A lineale which is not monotone. The capitals **A**, **M**, **N** and **U** have the lower-case design; the **A** is one-storeyed.

a B C Ç D E F G

JACNO

A condensed titling with alternative rounded characters.

ABCDEFGHIJKLMNOPQRSTUVWXYZ KRSWM
1234567890

JEFFERSON GOTHIC

JIM CROW
American Typefounders c. 1890

vi

One of the quaint types of the period, a shaded three-dimensional and angular titling. Originally cast by the Dickinson Type Foundry, of Boston.

ABCDEFGHIJKLMNOPQR
STUVWXYZ
1234567890

JIM CROW

JOCUNDA
Monotype 1933

vi

Designed by Stanley Baxter. A type in which the bars of **A** and **H**, the centre arms of **E** and **F** protrude to the left, and these strokes are shaped. The tails of **K** and **R** and the top of **T** also are shaped.

ABCDEFGHIJKLMNOPQRSTUV
WXYZ

JOCUNDA

JOHNSTON'S RAILWAY TYPE
or
UNDERGROUND
London Transport (1918)

iv

Designed by Edward Johnston for the London Underground Railways. It is the first of the twentieth-century sans serifs. The proportions of the letters are based on old face and not on the designs of the nineteenth century. Eric Gill based some of his GILL SANS on this type, it is said.

ABCDEFGHIJKLMNOP
QRSTUVWXYZ
abcdefghijklmnopqrst
uvwxyz
1234567890&£

JOHNSTON'S RAILWAY TYPE

KAMENE
Grafotechna 1956

vi

Designed by Stanislav Marso.

ABCDEFGHIJKLMNOPQRSTUVWXYZ
abcdefghijklmnopqrstuvwxyz
1234567890

KAMENE

vi

ABCDEFGHIJKLMNOPQRSTUVWXYZ
abcdefghijklmnopqrstuvwxyz
1234567890

KAMENE BOLD

Designed by M. Dovey. A modified lineale type. The bars of the **A** and **H** are triangular pieces. The distinguishing feature is that in both upper and lower case the round letters are flat across the top.

KINO
Monotype 1930

ix

ABCDEFGHIJKLMNOPQRSTUVWXYZ

abcdefghijklmnopqrstuvwxyz

1234567890

KINO

Designed by J. Erbar. An extra bold type face which is not monotone and thus suggests a fat face. It needs only the addition of thin serifs to become a type like NUBIAN.

KOLOSS
Ludwig & Mayer 1923

vi

The best publicity

COMES FROM THE

KOLOSS

Sans serif bold capitals with horizontal shading. The **A**, **M** and **N** have rounded tops. Nebiolo's FREGIA MECANO is similar.

KOMBINETTE
Ludwig & Mayer 1932

vi

ABCDEF

KOMBINETTE

The **G** has a spur. The lower case follows the usual German model, with a one-storeyed **a**. The **t** has the top cut obliquely and a curved tail. There are four weights, with oblique faces, several extended faces, a condensed and an inline. Only caps in small sizes are now cast by Typoart.

KORALLE
Schelter & Giesecke 1913

vi

ABCDEFGHIJKLMNOPQRSTUVWXYZ
ABCDEFGHIJKLMNOPQRSTUVWXYZ

KORALLE LIGHT

vi

ABCDEFGHIJKLMNOPQRSTUVWXYZ
ABCDEFGHIJKLMNOPQRSTUVWXYZ

KORALLE LIGHT EXTENDED

vi

ABCDEFGHIJKLMNOPQRSTUVWXYZ
ABCDEFGHIJKLMNOPQRSTUVWXYZ

KORALLE EXTENDED

KORALLE BOLD INLINE

vi

KRISTALL GROTESQUE
J. Wagner 1937

The tail of the J descends below the line, the M is splayed and the Q has a short tail outside the bowl. Alternative A, M, N, V and W have flattened vertical strokes. The lower case follows the usual German model. The ascenders are rather taller than in most sans. There are three weights and a bold condensed. Originally cut by Wagner & Schmidt, and called POLAR by John in 1930 and also sold by Weber (RUND GROTESK), Berling (SAXO) and Iranzo (PREDILECTA), and under other names.

vi

ABCDEFGHIJKLMNOPQRSTUVWXYZ

abcdefghijklmnopqrstuvwxyz

KRISTALL GROTESQUE

vi

ABCDEFGHIJKLMNOPQRSTUVWXYZABCDEFGHIJKLMNOPQRSTUVWX

abcdefghijklmnopqrstuvwxyzabcdefghijklmnopqrstuvwxyzabcdefghijklmnopqrstuvwxyz

KRISTALL BOOK

vi

ABCDEFGHIJKLMNOPQRSTUVWXYZ

abcdefghijklmnopqrstuvwxyz

1234567890

ABCDEFGHIJKLMNOPQRSTUVWXYZ

abcdefghijklmnopqrstuvwxyz

KRISTALL GROTESQUE BOLD

vi

ABCDEFGHIJKLMNOPQRSTUVWXYZ

abcdefghijklmnoprqstuvwxyz

KRISTALL GROTESQUE BOLD CONDENSED

vi

ABCDEFGHIJKLMNOPQRSTUV

abcdefghijklmnopqrstuvwxyz

KRISTALL GROTESQUE EXTRA BOLD

vi

ABCDEFGHIJKLMNOPQRSTUVWXYZ

abcdefghijklmnopqrstuvwxyz

KRISTALL GROTESQUE EXTRA BOLD CONDENSED

vi

ABCDEFGHIJKLMNOPQRSTUVZ

KRISTALL BOOK INLINE

A three-dimensional lineale titling. The shadow is deeper and the letters are narrower than in HELION.

LEUCHT GROTESK
Schriftguss 1932

vi

LEUCHT GROTESK

A light lineale following American style.

ABCDEFGHIJKLMNOPQRSTUVWXYZ&
abcdefghijklmnopqrstuvwxyz
1234567890

LIGHTLINE GOTHIC
American Typefounders

vi

LIGHTLINE GOTHIC

Designed by Umberto Fenocchio.

ABCDEFGHIJKLMNOPQRSTUVY
XWZ&GR
abcdefghijklmnopqrstuvwxyza
1234567890

LINEA
Cooperativa 1966–69

iv

LINEA

ABCDEFGHIJKLMNOPQRSTUV
WXYZ&GR
abcdefghijklmnopqrstuvwxyza
1234567890

iv

LINEA BOLD

ABCDEFGHIJKLMNOPQRSTUVWXYZ&GR
abcdefghijklmnopqrstuvwxyza
1234567890

vi

LINEA BOLD CONDENSED

ABCDEFGHIJKLMNOPQRSTUVWXYZ&
abcdefghijklmnopqrstuvwxyza
1234567890

LINEA EXTRA BOLD CONDENSED

A grotesque following the English model.

vi

ABCDEFGHIJKLMNOPQRSTUVWXYZ&ÆŒ
abcdefghijklmnopqrstuvwxyzæœ
1234567890
LINING GOTHIC TEXT

vi

ABCDEFGHIJKLMNOPQRSTUVWXYZ&
1234567890
LINING GOTHIC COMPRESSED CAPITALS

vi

A B C D E F G H I J K L M N O P Q R S T U V W X Y
Z & Æ Œ
a b c d e f g h i j k l m n o p q r s t u v w x y z æ œ
fi fl ff ffi ffl
1 2 3 4 5 6 7 8 9 0 £
LINING GOTHIC

vi

A B C D E F G H I J K L M N O P Q R S T U V W
X Y Z & Æ Œ
a b c d e f g h i j k l m n o p q r s t u v w x y z æ œ
fi fl ff ffi ffl
1 2 3 4 5 6 7 8 9 0 £
LINING GOTHIC BOLD

vi

A B C D E F G H I J K L M N O P Q R S T U V
W X Y Z & Æ Œ
a b c d e f g h i j k l m n o p q r s t u v w x y z æ œ
fi fl ff ffi ffl
1 2 3 4 5 6 7 8 9 0 £
LINING GOTHIC CONDENSED BOLD

vi

A B C D E F G H I J K L M N O P Q R S T U V W X Y Z
a b c d e f g h i j k l m n o p q r s t u v w x y z
1 2 3 4 5 6 7 8 9 0 &
LINING GOTHIC CONDENSED EXTRA BOLD

vi

ABCDEFGHIJKLMNOPQRSTUVWXYZ&ÆŒ
abcdefghijklmnopqrstuvwxyzæœ fiflffffiffl
1234567890
LINING GOTHIC BOLD EXPANDED

An English lineale with an expanding tail to the **Q**. For body sizes there is also a titling. "Lining" means that the face is cast on standard line.

ABCDEFGHIJKLMNOPQRSTUV WXYZÆŒ
abcdefghijklmnopqrstuvwxyz
1234567890£&œæ

LINING SANS SERIF 25

A heavy type of even colour. The ends of all strokes are rounded. The dot on the **i** is an oval. There is also an inline version.

Hilario WATER

MAMMOTH BLACK   MAMMOTH INLINE

Designed by Stanislav Marso.

ABCDEFGHIJKLMNOPQRS TUVWXYZ
abcdefghijklmnopqrstuvwxyz
1234567890

MARSO GROTESQUE

ABCDEFGHIJKLMNOPQRS TUVWXYZ
abcdefghijklmnopqrstuvwxyz
1234567890

MARSO GROTESQUE BOLD

ABCDEFGHIJKLMNOPQRS TUVWXYZ
abcdefghijklmnopqrstuvwxyz
1234567890

MARSO GROTESQUE EXTRA BOLD

Designed by Dick Dooijes. The **R** has a straight tail, and the tail of the **Q** is oblique and is outside the bowl only.

vi

ABCDEFGHIJKLMNOPQRSTUV
WXYZÆŒ
abcdefghijklmnopqrstuvwxyz
1234567890£&æœ

MERCATOR LIGHT

vi

ABCDEFGHIJKLMNOPQRSTUV
WXYZ
abcdefghijklmnopqrstuvwxyz
1234567890£&æœ

*ABCDEFGHIJKLMNOPQRSTU
VWXYZÆŒ
abcdefghijklmnopqrstuvwxyz
1234567890£&æœ*

MERCATOR

vi

ABCDEFGHIJKLMNOPQRSTUVWXYZ
abcdefghijklmnopqrstuvwxyz
1234567890

MERCATOR CONDENSED LIGHT

vi

**ABCDEFGHIJKLMNOPQRSTU
VWXYZÆŒ
abcdefghijklmnopqrstuvwxyz
1234567890£&æœ**

MERCATOR BOLD

ABCDEFGHIJKLMNOPQRS TUVWXYZÆŒ
abcdefghijklmnopqrstuvwxyz
1234567890£&æœ

MERCATOR BOLD ITALIC

ABCDEFGHIJKLMNOPQRSTUVWXYZ
abcdefghijklmnopqrstuvwxyz
1234567890

MERCATOR BOLD CONDENSED ITALIC

Designed by Imre Reiner. A bold type which is not monotone and thus suggests a fat face. It is like KOLOSS, but is less bold and the thins are tapered.

ABCDEFGHIJKLMNOPQRST
abcdefghijklmnopqrstuvwxyz
123456789

MERIDIAN

Designed by Albert Auspurg. This sans has several peculiarities. The bars of the **A** and **H**, the centre arms of **E** and **F** are diamond-shaped. The tails of the **K** and **R** descend below the line. The **e** has an oblique stroke to the eye. There are three weights, the bold being capitals only, and an inline.

Euler & Hotz   LONDON

MESSE GROTESK

PAPIERFABRIK

MESSE GROTESK INLINE

METRO

Mergenthaler Linotype 1929–30;
Linotype (London)

Designed by W.A. Dwiggins. In the No. 1 series the **M** is straight-sided and **N, W, V** are un-pointed; in the No. 2 series the letters are splayed and pointed. The alternative characters convert No. 2 into No. 1. The **Q** has the tail attached to the left corner of the bowl. The lower case follows the Continental design. The **t** has a curved foot. The three weights are called METROLITE, METROMEDIUM and METROBLACK, and there is also a very light METROTHIN of the Mergenthaler Linotype.

vi

ABCDEFGHIJKLMNOPQRSTUVWXYZ AGJMNVWW

abcdefghijklmnopqrstuvwxyz agvwe

1234567890

METROTHIN No. 2

vi

ABCDEFGHIJKLMNOPQRSTUVWXYZ AGJMNVWW

abcdefghijklmnopqrstuvwxyz agvwe

1234567890

ABCDEFGHIJKLMNOPQRSTUVWXYZ AGJMNVWW

abcdefghijklmnopqrstuvwxyz agvwe

1234567890

METROMEDIUM No. 2

vi

ABCDEFGHIJKLMNOPQRSTUVWXYZ AGJMNVWW

abcdefghijklmnopqrstuvwxyz agvwe

123456789

ABCDEFGHIJKLMNOPQRSTUVWXYZ

abcdefghijklmnopqrstuvwxyz

234567890

METROLITE No. 2

vi

ABCDEFGHIJKLMNOPQRSTUVWXYZ

abcdefghijklmnopqrstuvwx

12345

METROBLACK

vi

ABCDEFGHIJKLMNOPQRSTUVWXYZ AGJMNVW

abcdefghijklmnopqrstuvwxyz agvwe

123456789

ABCDEFGHIJKLMNOPQRSTUVWXYZ AGJMNVW

abcdefghijklmnopqrstuvwxyz agvwe

234567890

METROBLACK No. 2

METROPOL

Nebiolo 1967

Designed by Aldo Novarese. A condensed extra bold type.

vi

ABCDEFGHIJKLMNOPQRSTUVXYZW

abcdefghijklmnopqrstuvxyzw

1234567890

METROPOL

Designed by A. Butti and A. Novarese. An angular titling face with no lower case. Basically these letters consist of squares with rounded corners. **M** and **N** have wide flattened strokes at the top and bottom. EUROSTYLE is similar and has a lower case.

ABCDEFGHIJKLMNOPQRSTUVXY WZÆŒ& 1234567890

MICROGRAMMA CONDENSED

ABCDEFGHIJKLMNOPQ RSTUVXYWZÇÆŒ& 1234567890

MICROGRAMMA

ABCDEFGHIJKLM NOPQRSTUVXYZ 1234567890

MICROGRAMMA EXTENDED

ABCDEFGHIJKLMNOP QRSTUVWXYZÇÆŒ& 1234567890

MICROGRAMMA BOLD

ABCDEFGHIJKL MNOPQRSTUV XYWZÇÆŒ& 1234567890

MICROGRAMMA BOLD EXTENDED

vi

vi

vi

vi

vi

307

MODERNIQUE
American Typefounders 1928

Designed by M.F. Benton. A type very like MERIDIEN, that is a mixture of lineale and fat face; the thick strokes are heavier than in Meridien. In place of the dot on **i** and **j** there is a solid segment.

vi

ABCDEFGHIJKLMNOP
QRSTUVWXYZ&
abcdefghijklmn
opqrstuvwxyz
1234567890

MODERNIQUE

MONTAN
Stempel 1954

Designed by A.M. Schildbach. A bold, condensed titling. In the **M** the centre arms stop short of the line.

vi

ABCDEFGHIJKLMNOPQRSTUVW
1234567890

MONTAN

MONUMENT
Genzsch & Heyse 1924

Designed by Heinrich Schmidt, and now incorporated in the REFORM or INFORMATION family of types. A lineale type of nineteenth-century design. The capitals are of equal width and the **M** square. In the lower case the **a** is two-storeyed and the **t** is rounded at the base. There are three weights and also extended faces.

vi

Constantin ROSENHEIM

MONUMENT LIGHT

vi

Liedertafel

MONUMENT LIGHT EXTENDED

vi

Hansestädte

MONUMENT SEMI-BOLD

vi

Reisebild BREM

MONUMENT MEDIUM BOLD EXTENDED

vi

Holland MARN

MONUMENT BOLD EXTENDED

Designed by Martin Kausche. A set of bold sans serif capitals and figures of irregular design. The **C**, **D** and **Q** are like lower-case letters. The **M** is wide and splayed. The **W** equally wide. In some ways the design is like that of uncials.

ABCDEFGHIJKLMNOPQRSTUVWXYZ
1234567890

MOSAIK

A nineteenth-century design of tall, condensed letters with two-storeyed **a** and square dots on **i** and **j**. The **G** has a spur. ANTIQUES BOLD CONDENSED of Fonderie Typographique Française is identical. The type is also known as ADVERTISEMENT GROTESQUE CONDENSED.

ABCDEFGHIJKLMNOPQRSTUVWXYZ
abcdefghijklmnopqrstvwxyz
1234567890

NARROW GROTESQUE

Designed by G. de Milano. A modified lineale titling. The **A** has a rounded apex. **E**, **M**, **N** and **U** have lower-case design. NEON OMBRATA is a three-dimensional version.

ABCDEFGHIJKLMNOPQRSTUVWXYZ
1234567890

NEON BOLD

ABCDEFGHIJKLMNOPQRSTUVWXYZ
1234567890

NEON

ABCDEFGHIJKLMNOPQRSTUU
WXYZÇÆŒ&
1234567890

NEON OMBRATA

NEON
Weber 1936

Designed by W. Schaefer. A three-dimensional lineale titling. The face of the letters is thin and the shadow is deep. The bar of the **A** is low and in the **M** the middle stroke stops short of the line.

ABCDEFGHIJKLMNOPQRSTUV
WXYZ
1234567890

NEON

NEULAND
Klingspor 1923

Designed by Rudolf Koch. Bold sans serif capitals, with some modifications. There is some angularity about the round letters, especially the **C** and **G**. Many strokes are cut off obliquely, as the centre arm of the **E**, the **S**, top of the **T** and the **U**. The **M** is splayed. Some vertical strokes are slightly concave. Monotype OTHELLO is an imitation of this design. This type is said to have been designed as cut, the shapes of individual letters therefore vary considerably from one size to another.

ix

ABCDEFGHIJKLMN
OPQRSTUVWXYZ
1234567890

NEULAND

NEW AURORA GROTESQUE
Weber 1966

A type face identical with NORMAL GROTESQUE but with ("new") bold condensed and extra bold condensed added later.

vi

ABCDEFGHIJKLMNOPQRSTUVWXYZ
abcdefghijklmnopqrstuvwxyz
1234567890

NEW AURORA GROTESQUE BOLD CONDENSED

vi

ABCDEFGHIJKLMNOPQRSTUVWXYZ
abcdefghijklmnopqrstuvwxyz
1234567890

NEW AURORA GROTESQUE EXTRA BOLD CONDENSED

The light faces were designed by Morris F. Benton for American Typefounders, but the new companion bold faces for Intertype were designed under the direction of H.R. Freund and are generally narrower than the original. New additional weights were added 1958–66, including designs by Frank Bartuska for American Typefounders.

ABCDEFGHIJKLMNOPQRSTUVWXYZ
abcdefghijklmnopqrstuvwxyz
1234567890

NEWS GOTHIC

vi

ABCDEFGHIJKLMNOPQRSTUVWXYZ
abcdefghijklmnopqrstuvwxyz
1234567890

NEWS GOTHIC CONDENSED

vi

ABCDEFGHIJKLMNOPQRSTUVWXYZ
abcdefghijklmnopqrstuvwxyz
1234567890

NEWS GOTHIC EXTRA CONDENSED

vi

ABCDEFGHIJKLMNOPQRSTUVWX
YZ abcdefghijklmnopqrstuvwxyz
1234567890

NEWS GOTHIC BOLD

vi

ABCDEFGHIJKLMNOPQRSTUVWXYZ
abcdefghijklmnopqrstuvwxyz
1234567890

INTERTYPE NEWS GOTHIC CONDENSED

vi

ABCDEFGHIJKLMNOPQRSTUVWXYZ
abcdefghijklmnopqrstuvwxyz
1234567890

INTERTYPE NEWS GOTHIC BOLD CONDENSED

vi

ABCDEFGHIJKLMNOPQRSTUVWXYZ
abcdefghijklmnopqrstuvwxyz
1234567890

INTERTYPE NEWS GOTHIC

vi

ABCDEFGHIJKLMNOPQRSTUVWXYZ
abcdefghijklmnopqrstuvwxyz
1234567890

INTERTYPE NEWS GOTHIC BOLD

vi

ABCDEFGHIJKLMNOPQRSTUVWXYZ
abcdefghijklmnopqrstuvwxyz
1234567890

INTERTYPE NEWS GOTHIC EXTENDED

vi

ABCDEFGHIJKLMNOPQRSTUVWXYZ
abcdefghijklmnopqrstuvwxyz
1234567890

INTERTYPE NEWS GOTHIC BOLD EXTENDED

NOBEL
GROTESQUE
Amsterdam 1929–31; Intertype

A lineale after the Continental model, with some vertical strokes pointed. There are two **M**'s, one square with the middle strokes ending half-way, and the other splayed. The **T** is narrowed. The **a** is one-storeyed and **g** has an open tail. The **t** has a curved terminal. There are three weights, with italics, a condensed medium and an inline.

vi

ABCDEFGHIJKLMNOPQRSTUVWXYZ
abcdefghijklmnopqrstuvwxyz
1234567890

ABCDEFGHIJKLMNOPQRSTUVWXY
abcdefghijklmnopqrstuvwxyz

NOBEL

ABCDEFGHIJKLMNOPQRSTUVWXYZ

abcdefghijklmnopqrstuvwxyz

ABCDEFGHIJKLMNOPQRSTUVWXYZ

abcdefghijklmnopqrstuvwxyz

NOBEL LIGHT

ABCDEFGHIJKLMNOPQRSTUVWXY

abcdefghijklmnopqrstuvwxyz

NOBEL BOLD

ABCDEFGHIJKLMNOPQRSTUVWXYZ

abcdefghijklmnopqrstuvwxyz

NOBEL NARROW

ABCDEFGHIJKLMNOPQRSTUVWXYZ

abcdefghijklmnopqrstuvwxyz

NOBEL NARROW BOLD

ABCDEFGHIJKLMMN

OPQRSTUVWXYZ&

1234567890

NOBEL INLINE CAPITALS

NORMAL GROTESQUE

Haas;
Linotype (Frankfurt) 1955

Based on AKZIDENZ GROTESK or STANDARD and modified by Edmund Thiele. The Berthold type of this name is different. In design this lineale is like English nineteenth-century models, *e.g.* the capitals are square and the **G** has a spur. But the lower-case **g** is of the German variety.

NORMAL GROTESQUE REGULAR was added in 1943. In the Linotype version the design of some of the letters has been modified.

vi

ABCDEFGHIJKLMNOPQRSTUVW
abcdefghijklmnopqrstuvwxyz

NORMAL GROTESQUE

vi

ABCDEFGHIJKLMNOPQRSTUV
abcdefghijklmnopqrstuvwxyz
1234567890

NORMAL GROTESQUE MEDIUM

vi

ABCDEFGHIJKLMNOPQRS
abcdefghijklmnopqrstuvwxy

NORMAL GROTESQUE BOLD

vi

ABCDEFGHIJKLMNOPQ
abcdefghijklmnopqrstuvw

NORMAL GROTESQUE LIGHT EXTENDED

vi

ABCDEFGHIJKLMNOP
abcdefghijklmnopqrstuv

NORMAL GROTESQUE MEDIUM EXTENDED

vi

ABCDEFGHIJKLMNO
abcdefghijklmnopqr

NORMAL GROTESQUE BOLD EXTENDED

vi

ABCDEFGHIJKLMNOPQRSTUVWXYZ
abcdefghijklmnopqrstuvwxyz
1234567890

NORMAL GROTESQUE REGULAR LIGHT

Designed by Morris F. Benton. A fat lineale face somewhat similar to KOLOSS but the arms of **E** and **F** are triangular pieces. Many of the vertical strokes are cut off obliquely.

A B C D E F G H I J K L M N O P

Q R S T U V W X Y Z &

NOVEL GOTHIC

A lineale designed to meet optical character recognition criteria as defined by the US Bureau of Standards for business machine input and output printing.

ABCDEFGHIJKLM NOPQRSTUVWXYZ

0123456789

OCR–A

Designed by Adrian Frutiger. In 1961 a technical committee was established by the European Computer Manufacturers Association (ECMA) to recommend standards for character recognition systems. The committee recommended two fount designs: the one to satisfy immediate requirements and the other (OCR—B) to "permit and encourage the widest possible use of optical character recognition by the use of character shapes which are as distinguishable as possible without undue sacrifice of their acceptability by the public as a general-purpose type fount".

The ECMA standard defines three sizes of letters (and envisages a fourth), but only sizes 1 and 2 are for normal printing purposes. If combined in a matrix-case arrangement for composition with some other fount, the OCR—B characters must be 10 to the inch.

ABCDEFGHIJKLMNOPQRSTUVWXYZ

1234567890

OCR—B

Designed by Rudolf Koch. A set of capitals without serifs but not monotone. They have the appearance of having been drawn with a quill pen. The ends of arms and verticals are cut off obliquely. The capitals are intended for use with a gothic lower case. However, STEEL provides a roman lower case.

ABCDEFGHIKLMNOPQRSTUVWXYZ

aabcdefghijklmnopqrſstuvwxyzzchckßtz&

+1234567890

OFFENBACH

Designed by F.W. Kleukens. A fat face in which the serifs have almost disappeared; there is just a slight thickening at the ends of strokes. The thins have a considerable weight. The dot over the **i** is oblong.

Süddeutschland
REFORMATION

OMEGA

ONDINA
Schriftguss 1935

Designed by K. Kranke. Shaded and inclined roman capitals.

vi

DIPLOMA

ONDINA

OPTIMA
Stempel 1958; Linotype (Frankfurt) 1960

Designed by Hermann Zapf. A stressed sans serif with strokes thickened towards the end. The **M** is slightly splayed and the **g** has the Venetian form. This is a modified sans serif, intended as a text type. Like KLANG, which it does not, however, resemble, it can be described as either a calligraphic roman or a modified sans serif.

vi

ABCDEFGHIJKLMNOPQRSTUVW
abcdefghijklmnopqrstuvwxyz
1234567890
ABCDEFGHIJKLMNOPQRSTUVWXY
abcdefghijklmnopqrstuvwxyz
1234567890

OPTIMA

vi

ABCDEFGHIJKLMNOPQRSTUVW
abcdefghijklmnopqrstuvwxyz
1234567890

OPTIMA BOLD

vi

ABCDEFGHIJKLMNOPQRSTUVWXYZ&
abcdefghijklmnopqrstuvwxyz
1234567890

ABCDEFGHIJKLMNOPQRSTUVWXYZ&
abcdefghijklmnopqrstuvwxyz
1234567890

LINOTYPE (FRANKFURT) OPTIMA

vi

ABCDEFGHIJKLMNOPQRSTUVWXYZ&
abcdefghijklmnopqrstuvwxyz
1234567890

MERGENTHALER LINOTYPE OPTIMA MEDIUM

vi

ABCDEFGHIJKLMNOPQRSTUVWXYZ&
abcdefghijklmnopqrstuvwxyz
1234567890

LINOTYPE (FRANKFURT) OPTIMA BOLD

vi

ABCDEFGHIJKLMNOPQRSTUVWXYZ&
abcdefghijklmnopqrstuvwxyz
1234567890

MERGENTHALER LINOTYPE OPTIMA BLACK

An angular type in which curves are almost eliminated. **C, G, O,** etc., have straight sides. **A** has a flat top, **M, N** and **W** are like the lower-case letters. The **g** has an open tail.

The Monotype Corporation's OTHELLO, an imitation of NEULAND, is a set of capitals differing from the normal in some angular letters, *e.g.* the **G.** The **M** is slightly splayed. There is also OTHELLO SHADOW.

OTHELLO

American Typefounders 1896;
Monotype

ix

A B C D E F G H I J K L M N O P Q R S T U V W
X Y Z &
a b c d e f g h i j k l m n o p q r s t u v
1 2 3 4 5 6 7 8 9 0

AMERICAN TYPEFOUNDERS OTHELLO

ABCDEFGHIJKLMNOPQRSTUVWXYZ
1234567890

MONOTYPE OTHELLO

ix

ABCDEFGHIJKLMN

MONOTYPE OTHELLO SHADOW

ix

Designed by W. Brudi. A three-dimensional open lineale titling, with somewhat condensed letters.

ORBIS

Stempel 1953

vi

ABCDEFGHIJKLMNOPQRSTUVWXYZ
1234567890

ORBIS

Designed by Hans Bohn. A three-dimensional lineale titling. **A** and **M** have flat tops. **K** and **R** have vertical tails. There are additional rounded-top **A** and **M**, and a round-based **W.**

ORPLID

Klingspor 1929

vi

ABCDEFGHIJKLMNOP QRSTUVWXYZ
1234567890

ORPLID

Designed by E. Crous-Vidal. A modified inclined lineale titling with a shaded version called FLASH (quite different from the Monotype Corporation's type of the same name). Letters have a calligraphic quality, and upward and horizontal strokes extend towards the ends. The **G** has a slight spur, and the cross-bar of the **T** gives the impression of being slightly curved. The tail of the **Q** is a wedge cutting through the foot of the bowl.

PARIS

Française 1953

ABCDEFGHIJKLMNOPQRSTUV
WXYZÆŒ1234567890

ix

PARIS LIGHT

ABCDEFGHIJKLMNOPQRSTU VWXYZÆŒ 1234567890

PARIS

ABCDEFGHIJKLMN OOPQRSTUVWXYZ ÆŒ1234567890

PARIS BOLD

ABCDEFGHIJKLM NOOPQRSTUVWX 1234567890

FLASH

Designed by M.F. Benton. The type is not monotone, but has abrupt variation of colour. The thins occupy much of the letter. There are two **E**'s and two **M**'s, one with short middle strokes. In the lower case the ascenders are tall. The lower-case **r** has a bowl. The **t** is a cross with an oblique top. Intertype's version is considerably modified.

IMPORTED GOWNS
Enthusiastic Buyer Rewarded

PARISIAN

Designed by José Mendoza y Almeida. A type face with some variation in colour and of considerable weight. The **M** is somewhat splayed; the **g** has an open tail. Ascenders and descenders are short and the figures ranging. ILE DE FRANCE of Fonderie Typographique Française is similar; and also has a bold.

ABCDEFGHIJKLMNOPQRSTUV WXYZÆŒ

abcdefghijklmnopqrstuvwxyz 1234567890£&æœ

PASCAL

Designed by A.M. Cassandre. A lineale in which the lower-case letters with the exception of
b, d and **f**, are small capitals. It is an attempt to revive the original form of the roman alphabet.
In the **h** the left-hand vertical is taller than the right. There are three weights and a titling.
Central Typefoundry had a type not unlike this one, which was called QUAINT GOTHIC.

vi

ABCDEFGHIJKLMNOPQRSTUVWXYZ
abcdefghijklmnopqrstuvwxyz
1234567890 1234567890

PEIGNOT LIGHT

ABCDEFGHIJKLMNOPQRSTUVWXYZ
abcdefghijklmnopqrstuvwxyz
1234567890

PEIGNOT

vi

ABCDEFGHIJKLMNOPQRSTUV
WXYZ
abcdefghijklmnopqrstuvwxyz
1234567890   1234567890

PEIGNOT BOLD

vi

A B C D E F G H I J K L M N O P Q R S T U V
W X Y Z Œ &
1 2 3 4 5 6 7 8 9 0

INITIALS PEIGNOT ETROIT

Designed by Robert Foster. An angular titling with an unusual **E**. The tail of the **R** extends
and is bent at a right angle.

vi

A B C D E Ɛ F G H I J K L M N O P Q
W X Y Z & Ʀ R S T U V
1 2 3 4 5 6 7 8 9 0

PERICLES

PERMANENT
Ludwig & Mayer 1962;
Simoncini

vi

Designed by Karlgeorg Hoefer.

ABCDEFGHIJKLMNOPQRSTUVWXYZ

abcdefghijklmnopqrstuvwxyz

1234567890

ABCDEFGHIJKLMNOPQRSTUVWXYZ
abcdefghijklmnopqrstuvwxyz
1234567890

ABCDEFGHIJKLMNOPQRSTUVWXYZ
abcdefghijklmnopqrstuvwxyz
1234567890
PERMANENT

vi

ABCDEFGHIJKLMNOPQRSTUVW
XYZ
abcdefghijklmnopqrstuvwxyz
1234567890

ABCDEFGHIJKLMNOPQRSTUVWXYZ
abcdefghijklmnopqrstuvwxyz
1234567890
PERMANENT MEDIUM

vi

ABCDEFGHIJKLMNOPQRSTUVWXYZ
abcdefghijklmnopqrstuvwxyz
1234567890
PERMANENT CONDENSED

vi

ABCDEFGHIJKLMNOPQRSTUVWXYZ
abcdefghijklmnopqrstuvwxyz
1234567890
PERMANENT BOLD CONDENSED

vi

ABCDEFGHIJKLMNOPQRSTUVW
XYZ
abcdefghijklmnopqrstuvwxyz
1234567890

PERMANENT BOLD

ABCDEFGHIJKLMNOPQRSTUVWX YZ
abcdefghijklmnopqrstuvwxyz
1234567890

PERMANENT ULTRA BOLD COMPRESSED

Designed by M.F. Benton. A condensed type with rounded tops to **A** and **M**, and rounded base to the **W**. The bar of the **A** and arms of the **E** and **F** overlap to the left. The **g** has an open tail and **t** is a plain cross.
SHADOW is an open, three-dimensional set of capitals based on this design.

ABCDEFGHIJKLM NOPQRSTUVWXYZ&
abcdefghijklmnopqrstuvwxyz
1234567890

PHENIX

A condensed lineale with very short ascenders and descenders. The **M** is slightly splayed. The **g** has an open tail and the **t** is a cross.

ABCDEFGHIJKLMNOPQRSTUVWXYZ
abcdefghijklmnopqrstuvwxyz
1234567890

PLACARD BOLD CONDENSED

ABCDEFGHIJKLMNOPQRSTUVWXYZ
abcdefghijklmnopqrstuvwxyz
1234567890

PLACARD LIGHT EXTRA CONDENSED

ABCDEFGHIJKLMNOPQRSTUVWXYZ
abcdefghijklmnopqrstuvwxyz
1234567890

PLACARD CONDENSED

PLASTICA
Berthold

A three-dimensional version of BERTHOLD GROTESQUE without lower case. The plastic effect of this face is enhanced by the shading, which is done in perspective. UMBRA (Ludlow) is very similar and was designed by R. H. Middleton in 1935.

vi

FINE OLD TABLE WIN

PLASTICA

vi

ABCDEFGHIJKLMNOPQRSTUV
1234567890

UMBRA

POST MARCATO
Berthold 1963

Designed by Herbert Post. A bold display type having wood-cut qualities, with short ascenders and descenders.

vi

ABCDEFGHIJKLMNOPQRSTUVWXYZ
abcdefghijklmnopqrstuvwxyz

PRAZKE KAMENE
Grafotechna 1958

vi

Designed by Stanislav Marso. A condensed and elongated sans serif of medium weight.

ABCDEFGHIJKLMNOPQRSTUVWXYZ
abcdefghijklmnopqrstuvwxyz
1234567890

PRAZKE KAMENE

PRISMA
Klingspor 1931

An inline version of Rudolf Koch's CABLE. The shading is made by three parallel white lines. Capitals and ranging figures only.

vi

ABCDEFGHIJKLMNO
PQRSTUVWXYZ
1234567890

PRISMA

PSSITT
Française 1953

Designed by René Ponot. A lineale with some variation of colour. Note the lower-case **g** with a straight ear pointing north-east.

ix

ABCDEFGHIJKLMNOPQRSTUVWXYZÆŒ
abcdefghijklmnopqrstuvwxyzæœ

PSSITT

Designed by R.H. Middleton. The type is not monotone, and is somewhat condensed. The **G** has no spur and the **M** is square. The lower-case **g** has an open tail. The heavy version is like BRITANNIC or ROTHBURY.

Advertising Increases

ABCDEFGHIJKLMNOPQRSTUVWXYZ&
abcdefghijklmnopqrstuvwxyz
1234567890$

RADIANT MEDIUM

vi

More Composition

RADIANT BOLD

vi

Installed the Ludlow System

ABCDEFGHIJKLMNOPQRSTUVWXYZ&
abcdefghijklmnopqrstuvwxyz
1234567890$

RADIANT BOLD CONDENSED

vi

Greater Appeal with Strong Dignity

RADIANT BOLD EXTRA CONDENSED

vi

Big Machinery Ad

RADIANT HEAVY

vi

Designed by G. da Milano. A condensed lineale titling which is negative on a square mesh background.

FREGIO RAZIONALE

FREGIO RAZIONALE

vi

ABCDEFGHIJKLMNOPQRSTUVXYZW
1234567890

vi

RAZIONALE

Designed by R.H. Middleton (except the earliest versions). A lineale type following the English design with several weights and with extended and condensed versions of both roman and italic. RECORD GOTHIC OFFSET is a mirror type.

vi

ABCDEFGHIJKLMNOPQRSTUVWXYZ&
abcdefghijklmnopqrstuvwxyz
1234567890$

RECORD GOTHIC

vi

ABCDEFGHIJKLMNOPQRSTUVWXYZ&
abcdefghijklmnopqrstuvwxyz
1234567890$

RECORD GOTHIC CONDENSED

vi

ABCDEFGHIJKLMNOPQRSTUVWXYZ&
abcdefghijklmnopqrstuvwxyz
1234567890$

ABCDEFGHIJKLMNOPQRSTUVWXYZ&
abcdefghijklmnopqrstuvwxyz
1234567890$

RECORD GOTHIC EXTRA CONDENSED

vi

ABCDEFGHIJKLMNOPQRSTUVWXYZ&
abcdefghijklmnopqrstuvwxyz
1234567890$

RECORD GOTHIC THINLINE CONDENSED

vi

ABCDEFGHIJKLMNOPQRSTUVWXYZ
abcdefgghijklmnopqrstuvwxyz
11234567890$

RECORD GOTHIC LIGHT MEDIUM EXTENDED

ABCDEFGHIJKLMNOPQRSTUVW
XYZ&
abcdefghijklmnopqrstuvwxyz
1234567890$

ABCDEFGHIJKLMNOPQRSTUV
WXYZ&
abcdefghijklmnopqrstuv
wxyz
1234567890$

RECORD GOTHIC EXTENDED

ABCDEFGHIJKLMNOPQRSTUV
WXYZ&
abcdefghijklmnopqrstuvwxyz
1234567890$

vi

RECORD GOTHIC MEDIUM EXTENDED

ABCDEFGHIJKLMNOPQRSTUVWXYZ&
abcdefghijklmnopqrstuvwxyz
1234567890$

vi

ABCDEFGHIJKLMNOPQRSTUVWXYZ&
abcdefghijklmnopqrstuvwxyz
1234567890$

RECORD GOTHIC BOLD

ABCDEFGHIJKLMNOPQRSTU
VWXYZ&
abcdefghijklmnopqrstuvwxyz
1234567890$

vi

RECORD GOTHIC BOLD MEDIUM EXTENDED

*ABCDEFGHIJKLMNOPQRST
UVWXYZ&
abcdefghijklmnopqrstuvw
xyz
1234567890$*

vi

RECORD GOTHIC BOLD EXTENDED

vi

ABCDEFGHIJKLMNOPQRSTUVW
XYZ&
abcdefghijklmnopqrstuvwxyz
1234567890$

RECORD GOTHIC BOLD MEDIUM EXTENDED

vi

ABCDEFGHIJKLMNOPQRSTUVWXYZ
abcdefghijklmnopqrstuvwxyz
1234567890

RECORD GOTHIC BOLD CONDENSED

vi

ABCDEFGHIJKLMNOPQRSTUVWXY
abcdefghijklmnopqrstuvwxyz
Z1234567890

RECORD GOTHIC HEAVY CONDENSED

RECTA
Nebiolo 1958–61

Designed by Aldo Novarese. The **a** has a roman design and the **g** an open tail. There are ranging figures.

vi

ABCDEFGHIJKLMNOPQRSTUVXYZW
abcdefghijklmnopqrstuvxyzw
1234567890

RECTA LIGHT

vi

ABCDEFGHIJKLMNOPQRSTUVXYZW
abcdefghijklmnopqrstuvxyzw
1234567890

RECTA LIGHT CONDENSED

ABCDEFGHIJKLMNOPQRSTUVXYZW

abcdefghijklmnopqrstuvxyzw

1234567890

ABCDEFGHIJKLMNOPQRSTUVXYZW

abcdefghijklmnopqrstuvxyzw

1234567890

RECTA

A B C D E F G H I J K L M N O P Q R S T U
V W X Y Z

a b c d e f g h i j k l m n o p q r s t u v w x y z
1 2 3 4 5 6 7 8 9 0

RECTA MEDIUM CONDENSED

ABCDEFGHIJKLMNOPQRSTUVXYZW

abcdefghijklmnopqrstuvxyzw

1234567890

RECTA EXTRA CONDENSED

**ABCDEFGHIJKLMNOPQRSTU
V W X Y Z**

**abcdefghijklmnopqrstuvwxyz
1234567890**

***ABCDEFGHIJKLMNOPQRSTU
VWXYZ***

***abcdefghijklmnopqrstuvwxyz
1234567890***

RECTA BOLD

ABCDEFGHIJKLMNOPQRSTU
VWXYZ
abcdefghijklmnopqrstuvwxyz
1234567890

ABCDEFGHIJKLMNOPQRSTU
VWXYZ
abcdefghijklmnopqrstuvwxyz
1234567890

RECTA CONDENSED BOLD

vi

ABCDEFGHIJKLMNOPQRSTUVX
YZW
1234567890
ABCDEFGHIJKLMNOPQRSTUVX
YZW
1234567890

RECTA CONDENSED BOLD

The **A** has a low bar, **E** and **F** are wide, **M** is square and **R** has a wide and short bowl. There is a slight variation of colour in the lower case—but not in the light face. The design was modernised in the 1930s. Klingspor called the type INFORMATION.

INFORMATION EXTRA BOLD WIDE was designed by F.K. Sallway in 1958 for Klingspor and taken over by Stempel, and in Germany called BREITE FETTE INFORMATION. Some of the MONUMENT types now also appear under this name.

vi

ABCDEFGHIJKLMNOPQRS
abcdefghijklmnopqrstuvz1234

REFORM GROTESQUE

vi

ABCDEFGHIJKLMNOPQRST
abcdefghijklmnopqrstuvwxyz

INFORMATION MEDIUM

ABCDEFGHIJKLMNOPQRSTUVW

abcdefghijklmnopqrstuvwxyz

INFORMATION MEDIUM

ABCDEFGHIJKLMN

abcdefghijklmnopqrst

INFORMATION LIGHT EXTENDED

ABCDEFGHIJKLM

abcdefghijklmnopqr

INFORMATION BOLD EXTENDED

ABCDEFGHIJKLMNOPQR

abcdefghijklmnopqrstuvw

ABCDEFGHIJKLMNOPQRSTUVW

abcdefghijklmnopqrstuvwxyz

INFORMATION BOLD

ABCDEFGHIJKLMNOPQRSTUVWXYZ

abcdefghijklmnopqrstuvwxyz

INFORMATION MEDIUM CONDENSED

ABCDEFGHIJKLMNOPQRSTUWXYZ

abcdefghijklmnopqrstuvwxyz

INFORMATION BOLD CONDENSED

ABCDEFGHIJKLMNOPQRSTUVWXYZ

abcdefghijklmnopqrstuvwxyz

INFORMATION EXTRA BOLD CONDENSED

329

DEFGHIJKLMNOPQRSTUVWXY
abcdefghijklmnopqrstuvw
1234567
ABCDEFGHIJKLMNOPQRSTUVW

REFORM GROTESQUE LIGHT

vi

ABCDEFGHIJKLMNOPQRS
abcdefghijklmnopqr
1234567
ABCDEFGHIJKLMNOPQRS
defghijklmnopqrst
1234567

REFORM GROTESQUE BOLD

vi

ABCDEFGHIJKLMNOPQR
bcdefghijklmno
12345678

REFORM GROTESQUE EXTRA BOLD

vi

ABCDEFGHIJKLMNOPQRSTUVWXYZ
abcdefghijklmnopqrstuvwxyz

REFORM GROTESQUE EXTRA BOLD CONDENSED

vi

ABCDEFGHIJKLM
abcdefghijklmnop
1234567890

INFORMATION EXTRA BOLD WIDE

Designed by Zoltan Nagy as a display titling of calligraphic character. The **g** is curious.

REKLAM
Magyar

ix

ABCDEFGHIJKLM
NOPQRSTUVWXYZ
fghijklmnopqrstuvwxyz

REKLAM

Designed by H. Brünnel. A mixture of fat face and lineale type. The letters where there would be normally hair lines there are complete breaks in the strokes. The **M** is splayed. Ascenders and descenders are very small, the **g** having an abbreviated tail. *Cf.* BASALT.

RESOLUT
Nebiolo 1937

ix

ABCDEFGHIJKLMNOPQRSTUVXYZ
abcdefghijklmnopqrstuvxywz

RESOLUT

A German lineale. The bar of the **A** is low. The **G** has no spur. The **M** is pointed and the middle strokes stop short of the line. The **T** is narrow. The lower-case **a** is two-storeyed, the **g** has an open tail and the **t** is a plain cross. There are three weights.

RHYTHMUS
Schelter & Giesecke 1931

vi

Der Architekt und die moderne Baukunst   **Erzeugnisse der optischen Industrie**

RYTHMUS   RHYTHMUS MEDIUM

Synthetic Fibres and Plastics   vi·

RYTHMUS BOLD

Designed by A. Novarese. The bars and some upstrokes are thinner than the main strokes.

RITMO
Nebiolo 1955

ix

ABCDEFGHIJKLMNOPQRSTUVXYZ
abcdefghijklmnopqrstuvxywz

RITMO

Originally designed by Matthews of the Inland Typefoundry around 1906 and cast by Caslon. A bold lineale which is not monotone, resembling KOLOSS and BRITANNIC.

ROTHBURY
Stephenson Blake

vi

MONMOUTH JOURNAL

Newport Parish Magazine

Christmas Reading

182nd Special Number

ROTHBURY

ROYAL GOTHIC

Stevens Shanks

vi

An extra bold type face with some variation of colour. The **g** has an open tail and the ascender of the **t** is not shorter than that of other letters with ascenders. The **G** has a spur on the foot of the line.

ABCDEFGHIJKLMNOPQRSTUVWXYZÆŒ
abcdefghijklmnopqrstuvwxyzæœ&$
1234657890

ABCDEFGHIJKLMNOPQRSTUVWXYZ
abcdefghijklmnoqrpstuvwxzæ
1234567890

ROYAL GOTHIC

SAMSON

Ludlow 1940

ix

Designed by R.H. Middleton. A heavy type face in which there is some gradation of colour.

ABCDEFGHIJKLMNOPQRST
UVWXYZ&
abcdefghijklmnopqrs
tuvwxyz

SAMSON

NARROW SANS ITALIC

Stephenson Blake

vi

This condensed and inclined sans serif follows the usual English nineteenth century model. *Cf.* NARROW GROTESQUE.

ABCDEFGHIJKLMNOPQRSTUVWXYZ
abcdefghijklmnopqrstuvwxyz
1234567890

SANS ITALIC NARROW

SANS SERIF CONDENSED

Stephenson Blake

vi

These designs are lighter versions of the same founders' GROTESQUE types.

ABCDEFGHIJKLMNOPQRSTUVWXYZ
abcdefghijklmnopqrstuvwxyz
1234567890

CONDENSED SANS SERIF No. 5

vi

ABCDEFGHIJKLMNOPQRSTUVWXYZ
abcdefghijklmnopqrstuvwxyz

CONDENSED SANS SERIF No. 7

A sans serif based on the GILL SANS family and practically identical, but with a straight tail to the **R**.

ABCDEFGHIJKLMNOPQRSTUVWXYZ
abcdefghijklmnopqrstuvwxyz
1234567890 &£

SANS SERIF No. 2

ABCDEFGHIJKLMNOPQRSTUVWXYZ
abcdefghijklmnopqrstuvwxyz
1234567890 &£

SANS SERIF No. 2 BOLD

A three-dimensional lineale titling. This is the type first shown by Thorowgood in 1839 as SANS SURRYPHS SHADED and forerunner of the English "sans serifs". Several founders had this type around the middle of the nineteenth century. The letters are of equal width, the **G** has a spur and the **M** is square.

ABCDEFGHIJKLMN
OPQRSTUVWXYZ
ÆŒ&£
1234567890

SANS SERIF SHADED

Designed by K.H. Schaefer. A heavy modified lineale titling on shaded ground. There are a few small serifs as on the **E** and **R**.

SCHAEFER VERSALIEN

Designed by Walter Diethelm. A three-dimensional condensed grotesque, with fine white inline.

ABCDEFGHIJKLMNOPQRS
TUVWXYZ
1234567890

SCULPTURA

333

SEMPLICITA
Nebiolo 1931

A lineale following the Continental model. It may be distinguished by the vertical strokes in the **a** and **d**, which do not descend below the bowls. The **t** is a vertical with a bar on the right only.

vi

ABCDEFGHIJKLMNOPQRSTUVWXYZ
abcdefghijklmnopqrstuvwxyz
1234567890

ABCDEFGHIJKLMNOPQRSTUVWXYZ
abcdefghijklmnopqrstuvwxyz
1234567890

SEMPLICITÀ LIGHT

vi

ABCDEFGHIJKLMNOPQRSTUVWXYZ
abcdefghijklmnopqrstuvwxyz
1234567890

ABCDEFGHIJKLMNOPQRSTUVWXYZ
abcdefghijklmnopqrstuvwxyz
1234567890

SEMPLICITÀ

vi

ABCDEFGHIJKLMNOPQRSTUVWXYZ
abcdefghijklmnopqrstuvwxyz
1234567890

SEMPLICITÀ BOLD

vi

ABCDEFGHIJKLMNOPQRSTUVWXYZ
abcdefghijklmnopqrstuvwxyz
1234567890

SEMPLICITÀ CONDENSED

vi

ABCDEFGHIJKLMNOPQRS
TUVWXYZ
1234567890

SEMPLICITÀ OMBRA

334

Designed by George Trump. A highly condensed type. The **Q** has the tail separate from the bowl. The **T** is particularly narrow. In the lower case ascenders and descenders are short. There are two **g**'s.

ABCDEFGHIJKLMNOPQRSTUVWXYZ

abcdefghijklmnopqrstuvwxyz

1234567890

SIGNUM

Designed by S.H. de Roos and based on the same founder's LIBRA as a lineale which incorporates a number of uncial forms, for example, the **a**, **d** and **e**. Some of the letters have the upper-case design. Ascenders are short.

art must not be a superficial talent

but must begin farther back in man

SIMPLEX

die kraft reichtümer zu schaffen, ist

wichtiger, als der reichtum selbst

SIMPLEX SEMI-BOLD

Designed by H. Sinkwitz. A lineale titling of calligraphic appearance.

ABCDEFGHIJKLMN

OPQRSTUVWXYZ

1234567890 &

SINKWITZ-VERSALIEN

The most widely used lineale in the USA and copied from FUTURA. The **t** is designed like a cross. **A** and **V** are flattened at top or bottom respectively; the **g** has an open tail. Two versions of the **a** are supplied. There are several weights. The Lanston Monotype version is called TWENTIETH CENTURY and was designed by Sol Hess.

ABCDEFGHIJKLMNOPQRSTUVWXYZ

abcdefghijklmnopqrstuvwxyz

1234567890

MERGENTHALER LINOTYPE SPARTAN LIGHT

ABCDEFGHIJKLMNOPQRSTUVWXYZ

abcdefghijklmnopqrstuvwxyz

1234567890

ABCDEFGHIJKLMNOPQRSTUVWXYZ

abcdefghijklmnopqrstuvwxyz

1234567890

ABCDEFGHIJKLMNOPQRSTUVWXYZ

MERGENTHALER LINOTYPE SPARTAN BOOK

ABCDEFGHIJKLMNOPQRSTUVWXYZ
abcdefghijklmnopqrstuvwxyz
1234567890

MERGENTHALER LINOTYPE SPARTAN BOOK CONDENSED

vi

ABCDEFGHIJKLMNOPQRSTUVWXYZ
abcdefghijklmnopqrstuvwxyz
1234567890
ABCDEFGHIJKLMNOPQRSTUVWXYZ
abcdefghijklmnopqrstuvwxyz
1234567890

MERGENTHALER LINOTYPE SPARTAN MEDIUM

vi

ABCDEFGHIJKLMNOPQRSTUVWXYZ
abcdefghijklmnopqrstuvwxyz
1234567890

MERGENTHALER LINOTYPE SPARTAN MEDIUM CONDENSED

vi

ABCDEFGHIJKLMNOPQRSTUVWXYZ
abcdefghijklmnopqrstuvwxyz
1234567
ABCDEFGHIJKLMNOPQRSTUVWXYZ
abcdefghijklmnopqrstuvwxyz
4567890

MERGENTHALER LINOTYPE SPARTAN BOLD

vi

ABCDEFGHIJKLMNOPQRSTUVWXYZ
abcdefghijklmnopqrstuvwxyz
1234567890
ABCDEFGHIJKLMNOPQRSTUVWXYZ
abcdefghijklmnopqrstuvwxyz
1234567890

MERGENTHALER LINOTYPE SPARTAN BOLD CONDENSED

vi

ABCDEFGHIJKLMNOPQRSTUVWXYZ
abcdefghijklmnopqrstuvwxyz
1234567890
ABCDEFGHIJKLMNOPQRSTUVWXYZ
abcdefghijklmnopqrstuvwxyz
1234567890

MERGENTHALER LINOTYPE SPARTAN HEAVY

ABCDEFGHIJKLMNOPQRSTUVWXYZ
abcdefghijklmnopqrstuvw
1234567
ABCDEFGHIJKLMNOPQRSTUVWXYZ
defghijklmnopqrstuvwxyz
4567890

MERGENTHALER LINOTYPE SPARTAN BLACK

vi

ABCDEFGHIJKLMNOPQRSTUVWXYZ
abcdefghijklmnopqrstuvwxyz
1234567890

MERGENTHALER LINOTYPE SPARTAN HEAVY CONDENSED

vi

ABCDEFGHIJKLMNOPQRSTUVWXYZ
abcdefghijklmnopqrstuvwxyz
1234567890
ABCDEFGHIJKLMNOPQRSTUVWXYZ
abcdefghijklmnopqrstuvwxyz
1234567890

MERGENTHALER LINOTYPE SPARTAN BLACK CONDENSED

vi

ABCDEFGHIJKLMNOPQRSTUVWXYZ
abcdefghijklmnopqrstuv
12345
ABCDEFGHIJKLMNOPQRSTUVWXYZ
fghijklmnopqrstuvwxyz
67890

MERGENTHALER LINOTYPE SPARTAN EXTRA BLACK

vi

ABCDEFGHIJKLMNOPQRSTUVWXYZ
abcdefghijklmnopqrstuvwxyz
1234567890

MERGENTHALER LINOTYPE SPARTAN EXTRA BLACK CONDENSED

vi

ABCDEFGHIJKLMNOPQR
STUVWYXZ
abcdefghijklmnopqrstuv
wxyz 1234567890&$

LANSTON MONOTYPE 20th CENTURY ULTRABOLD EXTENDED

vi

ABCDEFGHIJKLMNOPQRSTUV
WXYZ

SPARTAN OUTLINE

vi

337

Designed by R.H. Middleton. A square lineale following the nineteenth-century model.

ABCDEFGHIJKLMNOPQRST UVWXYZ& abcdefghijklmnopqrstuvwxyz 1234567890$

SQUARE GOTHIC

A Continental lineale in four weights. The **G** has a spur, the **A** is flattened at the top. The **a,** in some weights, has a curved flat serif at the bottom, and the **g** has an open tail, the **y** a flattened tail. Also called AKZIDENZ GROTESK, this is one of the types so frequently used in Swiss typography of the 1950's and followed in the U.S.A. and Germany.

STANDARD MEDIUM CONDENSED was first shown in Berthold's 1896 specimen. The extra bold extended and condensed were added in 1956 and 1957. Book weights were added in 1970. Intertype ALTERNATE GOTHIC is very much like the medium condensed of this type. STANDARD GOTHIC is a newspaper type for classified advertisements.

vi

ABCDEFGHIJKLMNOPQRSTUVWXYZ
abcdefghijklmnopqrstuvwxyz

STANDARD LIGHT

vi

ABCDEFGHIJKLMNOPQRSTUVWXYZ
abcdefghijklmnopqrstuvwxyz

STANDARD LIGHT CONDENSED

vi

ABCDEFGHIJKLMNOPQRSTUV
abcdefghijklmnopqrstuvwxyz

STANDARD EXTRA LIGHT EXTENDED

vi

ABCDEFGHIJKLMNOPQRSTU
abcdefghijklmnopqrstuvwxyz

STANDARD LIGHT EXTENDED

vi

ABCDEFGHIJKLMNOPQRSTUVWXYZ
abcdefghijklmnopqrstuvwxyz
1234567890

STANDARD

vi

ABCDEFGHIJKLMNOPQRS
abcdefghijklmnopqrstuvwxyz

STANDARD EXTENDED

338

ABCDEFGHIJKLMNOPQRSTUVWXYZ
abcdefghijklmnopqrstuvwxyz

STANDARD CONDENSED

ABCDEFGHIJKLMNOPQRSTUVW
abcdefghijklmnopqrstuvwxyz
1234

ABCDEFGHIJKLMNOPRSTUWXZ
abcdefghijklmnopqrstuvwxyz
5890

STANDARD BOOK

ABCDEFGHIJKLMNOPQRSTUVWXYZ
abcdefghijklmnopqrstuvwxyz

STANDARD MEDIUM

ABCDEFGHIJKLMNOPQRSTUVWXYZ
abcdefghijklmnopqrstuvwxyz
1234567890

STANDARD MEDIUM CONDENSED

ABCDEFGHIJKLMNOPQRSTUVW
XYZ
abcdefghijklmnopqrstuvwxyz
1234567890

ABCDEFGHIJKLMNOPQRSTUVWXYZ
abcdefghijklmnopqrstuvwxyz
1234567890

STANDARD BOOK MEDIUM

ABCDEFGHIJKLMNOPQRSTUVWX
abcdefghijklmnopqrstuvwxyz

STANDARD BOLD

STANDARD

vi

ABCDEFGHIJKLMNOPQRSTUVWXYZ
abcdefghijklmnopqrstuvwxyz

STANDARD BOLD CONDENSED

vi

ABCDEFGHIJKLMNOPQRSTUVWXYZ
abcdefghijklmnopqrstuvwxyz
1234567890

STANDARD EXTRA BOLD CONDENSED

vi

ABCDEFGHIJKLMNOPQRSTUVWXYZ
abcdefghijklmnopqrstuvwxyz
1234567

STANDARD COMPACT

vi

ABCDEFGHIJKLMNOPQRSTUV
WXYZ
abcdefghijklmnopqrstuvwxyz
1234567890

STANDARD GOTHIC EXTRA BOLD EXTENDED

STEINSCHRIFT
Haas c. 1860

A revival of an early lineale. A condensed design, following nineteenth-century models. The **G** has a long spur, the **M** is square, **R** has a curved tail. The narrow **T** is unlike the usual letter of that period.

vi

ABCDEFGHIJKLMNOPQRSTUVWXYZ
abcdefghijklmnopqrstuvwxyz
1234567890

STEINSCHRIFT

STELLAR
Ludlow 1929

Designed by R.H. Middleton. The type is not quite monotone. The main strokes are thickened towards the ends. The bars of the **A** and **H**, and the arms of **E** and **F** are comparatively thin. The feet of the **A**, **M** and **R** are cut off obliquely.

vi

RENDERS THE LUDLOW
system particularly worthy of the

STELLAR

vi

FEW PARTICULAR POIN
ints of utility and adaptability

STELLAR BOLD

Designed by C.W. Pischiner. The **M** and round capitals are wide. **E**, **F** and **T** are narrow, **J** is short-ranging. The **a** is one-storeyed; **g** has the usual continental open tail. There are four weights. NEUZEIT BOOK was added in 1959.

ABCDEFGHIJKLMNOPQRSTUVWXY
abcdefghijklmnopqrstuvwxyz

ABCDEFGHIJKLMNOPQRSTUVWXYZ
abcdefghijklmnopqrstuvwxyz

STEMPEL SANS LIGHT

ABCDEFGHIJKLMNOPQRSTUVW
abcdefghijklmnopqrstuvwxyz
1234567890

STEMPEL SANS MEDIUM

vi

ABCDEFGHIJKLMNOPQRSTUVW
$XYZ£
abcdefghijklmnopqrstuvwxyz
1234567890

STEMPEL SANS BOLD

vi

ABCDEFGHIJKLMNOPQRSTUVWXYZ
abcdefghijklmnopqrstuvwxyz

STEMPEL SANS MEDIUM CONDENSED

vi

ABCDEFGHIJKLMNOPQRSTUVWXYZ
abcdefghijklmnopqrstuvwxyz

STEMPEL SANS SEMI-BOLD CONDENSED

vi

ABCDEFGHIJKLMNOPQRSTUVWXYZ
abcdefghijklmnopqrstuvwxyz
$1234567890£

NEUZEIT BOOK

vi

341

ABCDEFGHIJKLMNOPQRSTUVW
abcdefghijklmnopqrstuvwxyz
1234567890

NEUZEIT BOOK-S

vi

ABCDEFGHIJKLMNOPQRSTUVWXYZ
abcdefghijklmnopqrstuvwxyz

$1234567890£

NEUZEIT BOOK BOLD

STEREO

Ludwig & Mayer 1968

vi

A three-dimensional lineale of stencil design.

ABCDEFGHIJKLM
NOPQRSTUVWXYZ
1234567890

STEREO

STOP

Nebiolo 1970

vi

Designed by Aldo Novarese. A bold lineale based on computer printout and neon-lighting lettering somewhat in the again fashionable style of the 1930s. Several letters have unusual shape, such as the A which follows the Greek A, the Q and 9 are almost identical.

ABCDEFGHIJKLMNOPQ
RSTUVWXYZ
1234567890%

STOP

STRIDON

Warnery 1952

vi

An inclined upper case and short-ranging figures. Three-dimensional.

ABCDEFGHIJK
LMNOPQR

STRIDON

Designed by A. Overbeek. One of those almost monotone types with freely drawn letters which seem to be based on "print script" writing as taught in schools. *Cf.* CARTOON. Ascenders and descenders are short and serifs are almost non-existent. The **a** is one-storeyed, the eye of the **e** has an oblique stroke and the **g** an open tail. The bold is also called FLAMBARD.

STUDIO
Amsterdam 1946

ix

ABCDEFGHIJKLMNOPQRSTUVW XYZ abcdefghijklmnopqrstuvwxyz 1234567890

STUDIO

ABCDEFGHIJKLMNOPQRSTUVW abcdefghijklmnopqrstuvwxyz

STUDIO BOLD

A heavy lineale which is not monotone and thus has the effect of a fat face. It has some resemblance to the same founders' ULTRA MODERN, but the counters are much smaller. Ascenders and the feet of **p** and **q** are cut off obliquely. There is an italic, which has swash capitals.

STYGIAN BLACK
Ludlow 1929

ix

Unique and Popular Designs

Attention Compelling Designs

STYGIAN BLACK

Designed by Arno Drescher. The **M** is square and the middle strokes stop short of the line. The **a** is one-storeyed, **g** has an open tail and the **t** is curved at the foot.

There are four weights and a book face, as well as similar types called SUPREMO, shaded capitals called SUPER REFLEX, others shaded obliquely called SUPER ELEKTRIK.

SUPER
Schriftguss 1930

vi

ABCDEFGHIJKLMNOPQRSTUVWXYZ& abcdefghijklmnopqrstuvwxyz? 1234567890

ABCDEFGHIJKLMNOPQRSTUV WXYZ abcdefghijklmnopqrstuvwxyz& 1234567890

SUPER LIGHT

ABCDEFGHIJKLMNOPQRSTUVWXYZ&
abcdefghijklmnopqrstuvwxyz?
1234567890

ABCDEFGHIJKLMNOPQRSTU
VWXYZ
abcdefghijklmnopqrstuvwxyz&
1234567890

SUPER

ABCDEFGHIJKLMNOPQRSTUVWXYZ&
abcdefghijklmnopqrstuvwxyz?
1234567890

SUPER CONDENSED

ABCDEFGHIJKLMNOPQRSTUV
WXYZ&
abcdefghijklmnopqrstuvwxyz?
1234567890

SUPER GROTESQUE BOLD

ABCDEFGHIJKLMNOPQRSTUVWXYZ&
abcdefghijklmnopqrstuvwxyz?
1234567890

SUPER BOLD CONDENSED

ABCDEFGHIJKLMNOPQRSTU
VWXYZ&
abcdefghijklmnopqrstuvwxyz?
1234567890

SUPER GROTESQUE EXTRA BOLD

ABCDEFGHIJKLMNOPQRS
TUVWXYZ
abcdefghijklmnopqrstuvw vi
xyz&
1234567890

SUPER EXTRA BOLD ITALIC

ABCDEFGHIJKLMNOPQRSTUVWXYZ& vi
abcdefghijklmnopqrstuvwxyz?
1234567890

SUPER GROTESQUE EXTRA BOLD CONDENSED

ABCDEFGHIJKLMNOPQRSTUVWXYZ vi
abcdefghijklmnopqrstuvwxyz
1234567890

SUPER GROTESQUE BOOK LIGHT

ABCDEFGHIJKLMNOPQRSTUVWXYZ vi
abcdefghijklmnopqrstuvwxyz
1234567890

SUPER GROTESQUE BOOK BOLD

ABCDEFGHIJKLMNOPQRSTUVWXYZ vi
abcdefghijklmnopqrstuvwxyz
1234567890

SUPER GROTESQUE BOOK LIGHT ITALIC

KEDİ PENCESİ vi
SUPER ELEKTRIK

ESCURSIONE vi
SUPER REFLEX

345

Designed by Hand Eduard Meyer, and leaning on Renaissance minuscule writing, while capitals follow the roman "lapidar" style. All terminal strokes are cut off at right angle.

vi

ABCDEFGHIJKLMMNOPQRSTUVWXYZ
abcdefghijklmnopqrstuvwxyz
1234567890
SYNTAX

vi

ABCDEFGHIJKLMMNOPQRSTUVWXY
abcdefghijklmnopqrstuvwxyz
1234567890
SYNTAX BOLD

Designed by R.H. Middleton. A sans serif after the continental model. The **B, E, F, P, R** and **T** are narrow letters. The **M** is splayed. The lower-case **g** has an open tail and the **t** is a vertical stroke with a bar. The italic acquires some foot serifs on the **a, d, h, m,** etc. There are five weights, condensed faces, and also a heavy inline. Additional weights were added in 1961.

vi

ABCDEFGHIJKLMNOPQRSTUVWXYZ&
abcdefghijklmnopqrstuvwxyz
1234567890

ABCDEFGHIJKLMNOPQRSTUVWXYZ&
abcdefghijklmnopqrstuvwxyz
1234567890
TEMPO LIGHT

vi

ABCDEFGHIJKLMNOPQRSTUVWXYZ&
abcdefghijklmnopqrstuvwxyz
1234567890

ABCDEFGHIJKLMNOPQRSTUVWXYZ&
abcdefghijklmnopqrstuvwxyz
1234567890
TEMPO MEDIUM

ABCDEFGHIJKLMNOPQRSTUVWXY
Z&
abcdefghijklmnopqrstuvwxyz
1234567890

ABCDEFGHIJKLMNOPQRSTUVWXYZ
abcdefghijklmnopqrstuvwxyz
1234567890

TEMPO BOLD

ABCDEFGHIJKLMNOPQRSTUVWXYZ&
abcdefghijklmnopqrstuvwxyz
1234567890

TEMPO BOLD CONDENSED

ABCDEFGHIJKLMNOPQRSTUVW
XYZ&
abcdefghijklmnopqrstuvwxyz
1234567890

TEMPO HEAVY

ABCDEFGHIJKLMNOPQRSTUVWXYZ&
abcdefghijklmnopqrstuvwxyz
1234567890

TEMPO HEAVY CONDENSED

ABCDEFGHIJKLMNOPQRSTUV
WXYZ&
abcdefghijklmnopqrstuvwxyz
12345678

TEMPO EXTRA HEAVY

ABCDEFGHIJKLMNOPQ RSTUVWXYZ& abcdefghijklmnopqrstuv wxyz 1234567890

TEMPO BOLD EXTENDED

ABCDEFGHIJKLMNOP QRSTUVWXYZ& abcdefghijklmnopqrst uvwxyz 1234567890

TEMPO BLACK EXTENDED ITALIC

ABCDEFGHIJK LMNOPQRSTU VWXYZ 1234567890

TEMPO INLINE

TIMES GOTHIC

Intertype (New York) 1960

vi

A type face specially designed for classified advertising, and first used by the *New York Times*. The type face is cut in one size only, and joins the ranks of such specialised types as ADSANS, etc.

ABCDEFGHIJKLMNOPQRSTUVWXYZ
abcdefghijklmnopqrstuvwxyz
1234567890

TIMES GOTHIC

ABCDEFGHIJKLMNOPQRSTUVWXYZ
abcdefghijklmnopqrstuvwxyz
1234567890

TIMES GOTHIC BOLD

Designed by Paul Renner and based on his FUTURA. It is a condensed type in which the normally round letters acquire straight sides. The capitals **A**, **E**, **M** and **W** appear in two forms, the second designs being rounded.

AABCDEEFGHIJKKLMMNNOPQRSTUVWWXYZ
abcdefghijklmnopqrstuvwxyz
1234567890

ABCDEFGHIJKLMNOPQRSTUVWXYZ
abcdefghijklmnopqrstuvwxyz
1234567890

TOPIC MEDIUM

AABCDEEFGHIJKKLMMNNOPQRSTUVW
WXYZ
abcdefghijklmnopqrstuvwxyz
1234

ABCDEFGHIJKLMNOPQRSTUVWXYZ
abcdefghijklmnopqrstuvwxyz
1234567890

TOPIC BOLD

Designed by A.M. Cassandre, in collaboration with Charles Peignot, following the style of the PEIGNOT face of the same founders, but eight of the lower-case letters have been modified to give them the more traditional appearance of the standard lower-case alphabets.

HER Bord ÉDITEUR

TOURAINE

Touraine MIN

TOURAINE BOLD

TOURIST GOTHIC
Lanston Monotype 1909

vi

Designed by Sol Hess, with an italic added in 1938. A bold type of even weight.

AABCCDEEEFFGGHIJJKLMMNN OPQRRSSTUV
WWXXYYZ&ÆŒ£$
abcdefghijklmnopqrstuvwxyzæœ
1234567890

ABCDEFGHIJKLMNOPQRSTUVWXYZ&
abcdefghijklmnopqrstuvwxyz
1234567890

TOURIST GOTHIC

TRADE GOTHIC
Mergenthaler Linotype 1948-60; Linotype (London)

vi

Designed by Jackson Burke. A lineale type with short ascenders and descenders. The design is nineteenth century, except for the **g**. There are also bold, condensed, and extra condensed faces. Linotype (London) issue the condensed forms.

ABCDEFGHIJKLMNOPQRSTUVWXYZ
abcdefghijklmnopqrstuvwxyz
1234567890

TRADE GOTHIC

ABCDEFGHIJKLMNOPQRSTUVWXYZ&
abcdefghijklmnopqrstuvwxyz
1234567890

ABCDEFGHIJKLMNOPQRSTUVWXYZ&
abcdefghijklmnopqrstuvwxyz
1234567890

TRADE GOTHIC LIGHT

vi

ABCDEFGHIJKLMNOPQRSTUVWXYZ
abcdefghijklmnopqrstuvwxyz
1234567890

TRADE GOTHIC CONDENSED (No. 18)

vi

ABCDEFGHIJKLMNOPQRSTUVWXYZ
abcdefghijklmnopqrstuvwxyz
1234567890

TRADE GOTHIC EXTRA CONDENSED (No. 17)

vi

ABCDEFGHIJKLMNOPQRSTUVWXYZ
abcdefghijklmnopqrstuvwxyz
1234567890

TRADE GOTHIC BOLD EXTRA CONDENSED (No. 19)

vi

ABCDEFGHIJKLMNOPQRSTUVWXYZ
abcdefghijklmnopqrstuvwxyz
1234567890

TRADE GOTHIC EXTENDED

ABCDEFGHIJKLMNOPQRSTUVWXYZ
abcdefghijklmnopqrstuvwxyz
1234567890

TRADE GOTHIC ITALIC BOLD

ABCDEFGHIJKLMNOPQRSTUVWXYZ
abcdefghijklmnopqrstuvwxyz
1234567890

TRADE GOTHIC BOLD NO. 2

vi

ABCDEFGHIJKLMNOPQRSTUVWXYZ
abcdefghijklmnopqrstuvwxyz
1234567890

ABCDEFGHIJKLMNOPQRSTUVWXYZ
abcdefghijklmnopqrstuvwxyz
1234567890

TRADE GOTHIC BOLD

vi

ABCDEFGHIJKLMNOPQRSTUVWXYZ
abcdefghijklmnopqrstuvwxyz
1234567890

TRADE GOTHIC BOLD CONDENSED (No. 20)

vi

ABCDEFGHIJKLMNOPQRSTUVWXYZ
abcdefghijklmnopqrstuvwxyz
1234567890

TRADE GOTHIC EXTENDED BOLD

vi

Designed by J. Tschichold. A heavy stencil type. Most of the letters are in two and some in three parts. The arms of the **E** and **F** are separate triangular pieces. The **r** consists of a fat vertical stroke and a separate circle. The **t** is a vertical rounded at the foot with the remains of a bar on the right.

TRANSITO
Amsterdam 1931

The Local Government Examiner
DISTINGUISHED ELOCUTIONIST 3

vi

TRANSITO

Designed by H.R. Möller. The thin strokes, hair lines, occupy one half of most of the letters in the same manner as in BROADWAY. The **M** is pointed and splayed. Capitals and figures only. TRIO B is a shaded version and TRIO C an inline version, with three white lines.

TRIO
Schriftguss 1937

ABCDEFGHIJKLMNOPQRSTUVWXYZ

vi

TRIO A

ABCDEFGHIJKLM

TRIO B

NOPQRSTUVWXYZ

TRIO C

Designed by Douglas C. McMurtrie. Vertical strokes are slightly concave. The arms of **E** and **F** are shaped. The **R** has a curled tail. The counters of some of the round letters have straight edges, *e.g.* in the **G**, **O** and **Q**, and the lower-case **a**, **e**, **o**, etc.

INQUIRIES conducted

ULTRA MODERN

A type based on German Standard DIN 1451 engineering lettering. There is also a light and a condensed version.

UTSRQPONMLKJIHGFEDCBA
ZYXWV
ɒ zʎxwvutsrqponmlʞɾiʜgʇɘdɔʙɒ
0987654321

UMKEHRSCHRIFT

Designed by Adrian Frutiger. A new lineale of individual style incorporating characteristics of weights, but unfortunately several of the versions now available are slightly varied so that they are not always truly compatible. This is different from SABON, the other purpose-designed UNIVERSAL foundry, machine composition and phototypesetting type of the 1960s.

Univers   *Univers*

UNIVERS 45   UNIVERS 46

ABCDEFGHIJKLMNOPQRSTUVWXYZ
abcdefghijklmnopqrstuvwxyz
1234567890

UNIVERS 47

ABCDEFGHIJKLMNOPQRSTUVWXYZ
abcdefghijklmnopqrstuvwxyz
1234567890

UNIVERS 48

ABCDEFGHIJKLMNOPQRSTUVWXYZ
abcdefghijklmnopqrstuvwxyz
1234567890

UNIVERS LIGHT EXTRA CONDENSED

Univers

UNIVERS 53

ABCDEFGHIJKLMNOPQRSTUVW
XYZ
abcdefghijklmnopqrstuvwxyz
1234567890

UNIVERS 55

ABCDEFGHIJKLMNOPQRSTUV
12345 WXYZ 67890
abcdefghijklmnopqrstuvwxyz

UNIVERS 56

ABCDEFGHIJKLMNOPQRSTUVWXYZ
abcdefghijklmnopqrstuvwxyz
1234567890

UNIVERS 57

ABCDEFGHIJKLMNOPQRSTUVWXYZ
abcdefghijklmnopqrstuvwxyz
1234567890

UNIVERS 58

Univers

UNIVERS 59

Univers

UNIVERS 63

**ABCDEFGHIJKLMNOPQRSTU
VWXYZ
abcdefghijklmnopqrstuvwxyz
1234567890**

UNIVERS 65

*ABCDEFGHIJKLMNOPQRSTU
VWXYZ
abcdefghijklmnopqrstuvwxyz
1234567890*

UNIVERS 66

vi

ABCDEFGHIJKLMNOPQRSTUVWXYZ
abcdefghijklmnopqrstuvwxyz
1234567890

UNIVERS 67

vi

*ABCDEFGHIJKLMNOPQRSTUVWXYZ
abcdefghijklmnopqrstuvwxyz
1234567890*

UNIVERS 68

vi

ABCDEFGHIJKLMNOPQRSTUVWXYZ
abcdefghijklmnopqrstuvwxyz
1234567890

UNIVERS MEDIUM EXTRA CONDENSED

Univers

UNIVERS 73

vi

ABCDEFGHIJKLMNOPQRST
UVWXYZ
abcdefghijklmnopqrstuvwxyz
1234567890

UNIVERS 75

vi

*ABCDEFGHIJKLMNOPQRST
UVWXYZ
abcdefghijklmnopqrstuvwxyz
1234567890*

UNIVERS 76

Univers

UNIVERS 83

A lineale following German design of the period.

ABCDEFGHIJKLMNOPQRS
TUVWXYZ
abcdefghijklmnopqrstuvwxyz
1234567890

ABCDEFGHIJKLMNOPQRS
TUVWXYZ
abcdefghijklmnopqrstuvwxyz
1234567890

UNIVERSAL

vi

ABCDEFGHIJKLMNOPQRS
TUVWXYZ
abcdefghijklmnopqrstuvwxyz
1234567890

UNIVERSAL BOLD

vi

ABCDEFGHIJKLMNOPQRS
TUVWXYZ
abcdefghijklmnopqrstuvwxyz
1234567890

UNIVERSAL EXTRA BOLD

vi

ABCDEFGHIJKLMNOPQRS
TUVWXYZ
abcdefghijklmnopqrstuvwxyz
1234567890

UNIVERSAL EXTRA BOLD ITALIC

ABCDEFGHIJKLMNOPQRSTUVWXYZ
abcdefghijklmnopqrstuvwxyz
1234567890

UNIVERSAL EXTRA BOLD CONDENSED

VALIANT
Lanston Monotype 1941
vi

Designed by Edwin W. Shaar as an angular bold display type.

ABCDEFGHIJKLMNOPQRSTUVWXYZ&
aabcdefgghijkklmnopqrstuvwxyz
1234567890

VALIANT

VEGA
Grafotechna 1965
vi

An angular lineale with variation in stress between down and up strokes.

ABCDEFGHIJKLMNOPQRS
TUVWXYZ
abcdefghijklmnopqrstuvwxyz
1234567890

VEGA

vi

ABCDEFGHIJKLMNOPQRS
TUVWXYZ
abcdefghijklmnopqrstuvwxyz
1234567890

VEGA BOLD

VENUS
Bauer 1907–27

Originally a Wagner & Schmidt design, and some weights sold to several founders. A lineale which looks, in the upper case, like a revival of a nineteenth-century type. Capitals are of equal width. The **M** is square. The **a** is two-storeyed, the **g** has an open tail and the **t** a curved terminal.

vi

ABCDEFGHIJKLMNOPQRSTUVW
XYZ
abcdefghijklmnopqrstuvwxyz
1234567890

VENUS LIGHT

356

ABCDEFGHIJKLMNOPQRSTUVWXYZ
abcdefghijklmnop qrstuvwxyz
1234567890

VENUS LIGHT

ABCDEFGHIJKLMNOPQRSTUVWXYZ
abcdefghijklmnopqrstuvwxyz
1234567890

VENUS LIGHT CONDENSED

ABCDEFGHIJKLMNOPQRSTUVW
XYZ
abcdefghijklmnopqrstuvwxyz
1234567890

ABCDEFGHIJKLMNOPQRSTUVWXYZ
abcdefghijklmnopqrstuvwxyz
1234567890

VENUS MEDIUM

ABCDEFGHIJKLMNOPQRSTUV
abcdefghijklmnopqrstuvwxyz
1234567890

ABCDEFGHIJKLMNOPQRST
abcdefghijklmnopqrstuvwxyz
1234567890

VENUS BOLD

ABCDEFGHIJKLMNOPV
abcdefghijklmnopqrstuv
1234567890

VENUS BOLD EXTENDED

vi

ABCDEFGHIJKLMNOPQR STUVWXYZ abcdefghijklmnopqrstuvwx yz 1234567890

VENUS MEDIUM EXTENDED

vi

ABCDEFGHIJKLMNOPQR STUVWXYZ abcdefghijklmnopqrstuvwxyz 1234567890

VENUS LIGHT EXTENDED

vi

ABCDEFGHIJKLMNOPQRSTUVWXYZ abcdefghijkl mnopqrstuvwxyz 1234567890

VENUS MEDIUM CONDENSED

vi

ABCDEFGHIJKLMNOPQRSTUVWXYZ abcdefghijklmnopqrstuvwxyz 1234567890

VENUS BOLD CONDENSED

vi

ABCDEFGHIJKLMNTI abcdefghijklmnopqri 1234567890

VENUS EXTRA BOLD EXTENDED

A type designed for optical character recognition machines.

ABCDEFGHIJKLMNOPQRSTU VWXYZ 1234567890

VIAFONT

A type similar to FOLIO.

ABCDEFGHIJKLMNOPQRSTUVWXYZ& abcdefghijklmnopqrstuvwxyz$1234567890
VIDEO SPECTRA

ABCDEFGHIJKLMNOPQRSTUVWXYZ& abcdefghijklmnopqrstuvwxyz$1234567890
VIDEO SPECTRA BOLD

A light titling. The bars of **A** and **H** overhang to the left. In the **M** the middle strokes stop short of the line. **E**, **N**, **S** and **T** are narrow and the round letters wide.

Quite different from INTERTYPE VOGUE, which follows lineale style, but has a very unusual **g** in the light and bold versions, and has the CABLE **a**, **e** and **g**, but also FUTURA characters.

ABCDEFGHIJKLMNOPQRSTUVWXYZ 12345678

VOGUE

ABCDEFGHIJKLMNOPQRSTUVWXYZ

abcdefghijklmnopqrstuvwxyz

1234567890 &£

INTERTYPE VOGUE LIGHT

ABCDEFGHIJKLMNOPQRSTUVWXYZ

abcdefghijklmnopqrstuvwxyz

1234567890 &£

INTERTYPE VOGUE BOLD

ABCDEFGHIJKLMNOPQRSTUVWXYZ

abcdefghijklmnopqrstuvwxyz

1234567890 &£

ABCDEFGHIJKLMNOPQRSTUVWXYZ

abcdefghijklmnopqrstuvwxyz

1234567890 &£

INTERTYPE VOGUE EXTRA BOLD WITH OBLIQUE

Designed by Whedon Davis. This type matches others in the normal GOTHIC types of this foundry.

ABCDEFGHIJKLMNOPQRSTUVWX YZ
abcdefghijklmnopqrstuvwxyz
£1234567890 &

WHEDONS GOTHIC OUTLINE

SCRIPT TYPES

A SCRIPT is a type based on cursive or current handwriting. In the sixteenth century there was a script known as Secretary, which was based on an Elizabethan gothic hand. It has not survived and has not been revived, although a French type, Civilité, of similar style has been. The earliest Latin scripts are the Scriptorials of the Grover foundry which have survived. They appear in Stanley Morison's *Ichabod Dawks*. Towards the end of the eighteenth century scripts were cut based on the engraved copperplate writing. In the end the letters were made to fit so closely as to give the impression of being actually engraved lettering.

A heavy display italic. It is monotone and the letters are not close-setting. Very like ATTRAKTION; the two may be distinguished by the **e**'s; in ACHTUNG the **e** is italic, in Attraktion it is an inclined roman **e**.

ACHTUNG

Ludwig & Mayer 1932

viii

ABCDEFGHIJKLMNOPQRSTUV
ABCDEFGHIJKLM
abcdefghijklmnopqrstuvwxyz

ACHTUNG

Designed by Karl Klauss for Geuzsch & Heyse in 1953.

ADAGIO

Bauer

viii

ABCDEFGHIJKLMNOP
QRSTUVWXYZ
abcdefghijklmnopqrstuvwxyz 1234567890

ADAGIO

Designed by R. Hunter Middleton. A pen script with swash caps.

ADMIRAL SCRIPT

Ludlow 1953

viii

ABCDEFGHIJKLMNOPQ
RSTUVWXYZ&
abcdefghijklmnopqrstuvwxyz 1234567890$

ADMIRAL SCRIPT

AGITATOR
Typoart 1960

viii

Designed by Wolfgang Eickhoff. Freely drawn capitals of a semi bold script. There is little variation of stress. It is almost an inclined sans serif.

ABCDEFGHIJKLMNOPQR STUVWXYZ&? 1234567890

AGITATOR

AKTUELL
or PENFLOW
Schriftguss 1935

viii

Designed by Walter Schnippering. An informal script of medium weight and with the letters closely set. The alignment is irregular. PENTAPE or ORIGINELL is a heavier face of the same design but an inline conveying the idea of a flowing ribbon.

International European Fairs

Modische Neuheiten für den Herbstanfang

ACTUELLE or PENFLOW

AMANDA
Stephenson Blake 1939

viii

A script of medium weight with flourished capitals and a somewhat stiff lower case. The ascenders are looped. The **m** and **n** have serifs and give an appearance of formality.

ABCDEFGHIJKLMNOPQRSTUV WXYZ

abcdefghijklmnopqrstuvwxyz 1234567890

AMANDA

AMAZONE
Amsterdam 1959

viii

Designed by Leonard H.D. Smit. A formal script of medium weight. The capitals are flourished. The lower case letters adjoin. Ascenders are looped and tall, as are the descenders.

ABCDEFGHIJKLMNOPQRST UVWXYZÆŒ

abcdefgijklmnopqrstuvwxyz1234567890£&œæ

AMAZONE

ANDROMAQUE
Anvil Press 1960

viii

Designed by Victor Hammer and cast by *Deberny & Peignot* as a cursive uncial for private press use and originally intended for a printing of Racine's *Andromaque* by the Stamparia del Santuccio.

one light, one ray and it will be the angels' spring:
one flash, one glance upon the shiny pond, and then
asperges me! sweet wilderness, and lo! we are redeemed!

ANDROMAQUE

362

Designed by A. Drescher. A script with flourishing capitals and a formal lower case. Two sets of capitals, one even more flourished, are provided. The ascenders in the lower case are tall. The **f** and **r** are unusual forms, a number of ligatures are supplied. A heavier face is called ARABELLA FAVORIT.

ABCDEFGHIJKLMNOPQu
RSTUVWXYZ 1234567890
abcdefghijklmnopqrstuvwxyzchck ff fi fl ft ll st ß ttt z

ABCDEFGHIJ
KLMNOPQuRS

ARABELLA

ABCDEFGHIJKLMNOPQu
RSTUVWXYZ
abcdefghijklmnopqrstuvwxyz ff fi fl ft ll st ß tt

ABCDEFGHIJ
KLMNOPQuRST

ARABELLA FAVORIT

Designed by G. Zapf–v. Hesse. A set of initials of flowing design with considerable variation of stress. *Cf.* GAVOTTE.

ABCDEFGHIJKLMNOP

ARIADNE

Designed by M. Wilke. A script originally cut in three weights (matrices of the bold were destroyed in the war), with abrupt variation in colour. The capitals are flourished. In the lower case the thin, hair-line upstrokes take off from the feet of the down strokes. Ascenders are of moderate height, and descenders rather short.

ABCDEFGHIJKLMNOPQRSTU
abcdefghijklmnopqrstuvwxyz

ARISTON LIGHT

ABCDEFGHIJKLMNOPQRST
abcdefghijklmnopqrstuvwxyz
1234567890

ARISTON MEDIUM

ARKONA
Genzsch & Heyse 1935

viii

Designed by Karl Klauss. A formal script with considerable variation of stress and slight inclination. Ascenders have no serifs but are thickened towards the top. Descenders are short. It makes an impression of rigidity.

ABCDEFGHIJKLMNOPQRST
UVWXYZ 1234567890
abcdefghijklmnopqrstuvwxyz

ARKONA

viii

ABCDEFGHIJKLMNOPQRS
TUVWXYZ 1234567890
abcdefghijklmnopqrstuvwxyz

ARKONA MEDIUM

ARTISTA
Schelter & Giesecke 1936

viii

Designed by Rudolf Sternberg. A light script with cursive capitals and a lower case which might almost be an italic. There are second varieties of **r** and **s** which are more script-like.

Dresden, the City of Art and Flowers

ARTISTA

ARTSCRIPT
Lanston Monotype 1940

viii

Designed by Sol Hess and based on the writing of Servidori of Madrid, 1798. Servidori was an admirer of the calligraphers of the sixteenth century, and this script is a good revival of an Italian or Spanish Cancellaresca formata of that period. The serifs on the **m**, **n** and **r** are somewhat unusual.

ABCDEFGHIJKLMNOPQRSTUVW
XYZ&
abcdefghijklmnopqrstuvwxyz   fiflff ffiffl   1234567890

ARTSCRIPT

ASHLEY SCRIPT
Monotype 1955

viii

Designed by Ashley Havinden. A heavy monotone brush script with informal sans serif capitals.

ABCDEFGHIJKLMNOPQRST
UVWXYZ 12345
abcdefghijklmnopqrstuvwxyz

viii

ASHLEY SCRIPT

364

A three-dimensional script.

ABCDEFGHIJKLMNOP
QRSTUVWXYZ

ATLANTIDA

A heavy display italic, monotone in colour. The capitals are of the swash variety. A somewhat condensed version is called BEROLINA.

Noch schneller   Berolina

ATTRAKTION   BEROLINA

A strong brush script, designed by Johannes Boehland. The type, which is especially suited for uncoated stock, has a certain similarity to Chinese brush lettering. The lower case **d** and **g** extend over the body. The capital **W** is supplied in two versions, one of these with a strong cross-bar closing the top.

ABCDEFGHIJKLMNOPQRSTUVWX
abcdefghijklmnopqrstuvwxyz
1234567890

BALZAC

A light script of slight inclination of the visiting-card class. The capitals are flowing and the lower-case letters round, with tall ascenders and short descenders. The lower case has thin oblique serifs.

Reise-Erlebnisse aus dem sonnigen Italien

BARBERINA

Designed by Imre Reiner. A bold, informal brush script with irregularly inclined letters and uneven ascender and descender lengths. BRAVO has some similarity to this type.

ABCDEFGHIJKLMNOPQRSTU
VWXYZ abcdefghijklmnopqrstuvwxyz

BAZAAR

BERNHARD BRUSH SCRIPT

Bauer

viii

Designed by Lucian Bernhard. A heavy informal script, which has the appearance of having been drawn with a brush. The variation of stress is considerable. Ascenders are looped.

The York Times

BERNHARD BRUSH SCRIPT

BERNHARD CURSIVE or MADONNA

Bauer 1925
Stephenson Blake

viii

Designed by Lucian Bernhard before the roman and italic, which it now accompanies. The lower case has very tall ascenders and short descenders. **b**, **d** and **l** have no top serifs, but **h** has a finishing stroke. The vertical strokes of **p** and **q** project high above the bowls. The capitals are flowing pen-forms. There is also a bold face. Stephenson Blake call the type MADONNA RONDE, but their MADONNA BOLD is a different design.

ABCDEFGHIJKLMNOPQ
RSTUVWXYZ

abcdefghijklmnopqrstuvwxyz 1234567890

BERNHARD CURSIVE

viii

ABCDEFGHIJKLMNOPQ
RSTUVWXYZ

abcdefghijklmnopqrst uvwxyz 1234567890

BERNARD CURSIVE BOLD

BERNHARD TANGO

American 1934

viii

Designed by Lucian Bernhard. A stylised script with contrasting bold and hair-line strokes. The **e** is angular, and there are swash capitals.

ABCDEFGHIJKLMNOPQRSTUVWXYZ

abcdefghijklmnopqrstuvwxyz 1234567890

BERNHARD TANGO

BISON

Weber 1935

viii

Designed by Julius Kirn. A heavy brush script of slight inclination. Ascenders and descenders, as well as capitals, are rather short. The **t** is a slightly inclined cross, cut diagonally at top and foot. The **r** is very narrow; and the **W** follows the lower-case design.
BLIZZARD cut by Trennert is identical.

ABCDEFGHIJKLMNOPQRSTUVWXYZ

abcdefghijklmnopqrstuvwxyz

1234567890

BISON

BOULEVARD

Berthold 1955

viii

Designed by G.G. Lange. A formal script with much variation of stress. The capitals are flourished and the lower case approaches the English copperplate, but ascenders are short.

ABCDEFGHIJKLMNOPQ

abcdefghijklmnopqrstuvwxyz 1234567890

BOULEVARD

Designed by E.A. Neukomm. A heavy informal script with tall ascenders. The inclination of the letters is irregular, many of them being upright. There are no looped letters and the descenders taper to points. The differentiation of colour is slight. The letters are not close-setting.

ABCDEFGHIJKLMNOPQRST
abcdefghijklmnopqrstuvwxyz 1234567890

viii

BRAVO

Designed by Harold Brodersen. An informal brush script of heavy weight. The lower case letters are close-setting, ascenders and descenders short.

ABCDEFGHIJKLMNOPQRSTUVWXYZ
abcdefghijklmnopqrstuvwxyz 1234567890

viii

BRODY

Designed by Robert E. Smith. An informal brush script of heavy weight. The lower-case letters are close-setting and have the appearance of being brush drawn. The set is deliberately irregular. *Cf.* BERNHARD BRUSH and SIGNAL.

ABCDEFGHIJKLM
NOPQRSTUVWXYZ
abcdefghijklmn1234567890

viii

BRUSH

Designed by M. Wilke. A formal script of slight inclination. The lower-case letters are round and the curves have the qualities of pen strokes. Descenders are short and the **g** has an open tail. AMBASSADOR is a second set of plain capitals to accompany BURGUND.

Metropol-Cinema
Schönheit und Kosmetik

viii

BURGUND

Designed by Willy Schumann. A script with flowing capitals and round, broad letters in the lower case. There is only moderate variation in stress. There is also a bold and special initials.

Modehaus Brühl & Co., Dresden

viii

BUTTERFLY LIGHT

Porzellanmanufaktur

viii

BUTTERFLY BOLD

CALLIGRAPH-IQUES
Deberny & Peignot

viii

A copperplate script in the English nineteenth-century fashion, and available from many founders. *Cf.* GRAPHIC SCRIPT, PALACE SCRIPT or COMMERCIAL SCRIPT.

ABCDEFGHIJKLMM
NOPQRSTUVWXYZŒ

abbcdeeffgghijkkllmnopp
qgrrssttuvwxyyzz çœœon
12345 & 67890

CALLIGRAPHIQUES

CANTATE
Bauer 1958

viii

Designed by J.J. Siercke. A formal script with abrupt variation of colour. Hair lines are frequent. The lower case letters adjoin and ascenders are looped.

ABCDEFGHIJKLMNOPQX
abcdefghijklmnopqrstuvwxyzabcdefghk
1234567890

CANTATE

CAPRICE
Berthold 1939

viii

Designed by M. Wilke. A script of medium weight with freely drawn capitals and a more formal lower case. The pen-drawn characteristic is so pronounced in the larger sizes that the type seems to be almost three-dimensional.

ABCDEFGHIJKLMNOPQR
abcdefghijklmnopqrstuvwxyz 1234567890

CAPRICE

CASCADE SCRIPT
Linofilm 1966

viii

Designed by Matthew Carter.

ABCDEFGHIJKLMNOPQRSTUVWXYZ
abcdefghijklmnopqrstuvwxyz
1234567890

CASCADE SCRIPT

CATALINA
Intertype (F) 1955

viii

Designed by Emil Klumpp. An informal script with close-setting lower case and little variation of stress. There are two sets of capitals for this face designed specially for the Fotosetter.

AABCDEEFGGHIJKLMNOPQRSTTUVWXYYZ
ABCDEFGHIJKLMNOP
QRSTUVWXYZ
abbcdeffghijklmnopqrstuvwxyz 1234567890$

CATALINA

368

Designed by G.G. Lange. A script of very informal design and medium weight. There is some variation of colour. The lower case letters are not close-fitting.

ABCDEFGHIJKLMNOPQRSTUVWXYZ

abcdefghijklmnopqrstuvwxyz

1234567890

CHAMPION

CHAMPION
Berthold 1957

viii

Designed by Paul Hayden-Duensing for his private press. The characters have a very low x-height. Many alternative characters are to be added.

ABCDEFGHI JKLMNOPQRSTUVWXYZ

abcdefghijklmnopqrstuvwxyz

CHANCERY ITALIC

CHANCERY ITALIC
Hayden-Duensing 1966

viii

Designed by Helmut Matheis. An informal script of medium weight and some variation of colour. The capitals are flowing and the lower case letters are close fitting. There is a set of ranging figures. The bold introduced in 1959, is called SLOGAN but quite different from Nebiolo's SLOGAN.

ABCDEFGHIJKLMNOPQR STUVWXYZ

abcdefghijklmnopqrstuvwxyz

1234567890

CHARME

CHARME
Ludwig & Mayer 1958

viii

Designed by Roger Excoffon. A heavy and uniform script. *Cf.* REINER BLACK, but the lettering is even rougher than in that design. In fact it is the most informal of all scripts, although its characters are not as close-setting as those in MISTRAL.

ABCDEFGHIJKLMNOPQRSTUVWXY

abcdefghijklmnopqrstuvwxyz

1234567890

CHOC

CHOC
Olive 1955; Amsterdam 1964

viii

Designed by A. Novarese. A formal script heavier in weight than the same founder's CIGOGNA. The capitals are freely drawn and the ascenders in the lower case are without loops.

ABCDEFGHIJKLMNOPQRST UVWXYZÇÆŒ&

abcdefghijklmnopqrstuvwxyzçæœ

1234567890

CIGNO

CIGNO
Nebiolo 1954

viii

CIGOGNA
Nebiolo

Designed by A. Butti. This is a script type resembling quill pen lettering. The heavy strokes are finely tapered in some letters. The bowls of the lower-case **a** and **o** are not closed, and the **s** descends below the line. The capital **Q** resembles a hand-written figure 2.

viii

ABCDEFGHIJKLM NOPQQuRSTUVWXYZÇ

abcdefghijklmnopqrstuvwxyzçœœ   1234567890

CIGOGNA LIGHT

viii

ABCDEFGHIJKLM NOPQQuRST UVWXYZÇŒŒIVX

abcdefghijklmnopqrstuvwxyzçœœ

1234567890

CIGOGNA BOLD

CIVILITÉ
American 1922

Designed by Louis Ferrand. A script with flourished capitals and a formal lower case. There are no serifs.

viii

ABCDEFGHIJKLMNOPQRS TUVWXYZ&

abcdefghijklmnopq. rstuvwxyz
1234567890

CIVILITÉ
Enschedé

Probably cut by Robert Granjon at Lyons in 1557, although some records seem to indicate that this particular type stems from Plantin's Leyden office, around 1584. It now ranks as a private press type, as it is no longer available from the foundry. The type is heavy, with swash letters, and close setting. M. F. Benton designed a type after this style for American Typefounder's in 1922. *Cf.* LA CIVILITÉ.

viii

ABEDEFGHIJKLMNOHRESTWWXYZ

abcdefghijklmnopqrstuswxyz

As Frederic Warde aptly put it, 'as long as we work with the arbitrary signs of the alphabet, we shall be dependent on the past and-like the Greek vase

CIVILITÉ

CLIPPER
Française 1951

Designed by M.F. Benton. Based on the French cursive first cut by Robert Granjon at Lyons in 1557. It corresponds to the English SECRETARY. Compared with the original the modern version has been considerably Latinised, especially in the upper case. The **A, D, R, S, V** and **W** are Latin forms. The letters are upright and the gothic form of the **d**, with the top stroke inclined to the left, and the **h** with the tail sweeping round below the line, have been preserved. The **m, n**, and initial, are other sixteenth-century forms.

viii

ABCDEFGHIJKLMNOPQRSTUV WXYZ

abcdefghijklmnopqrstuvwxyzœœ 1234567890

CLIPPER

Designed by Helmut Matheis.. An angular vertical script.

ABCDEFGHJJKLMNOPQRSTUVW
XYZ
abcdefghijklmnopqrstuvwxyz
1234567890
COMPLIMENT

Designed by Joachim Romann. A light Latin script, similar to GAVOTTE.

ABCDEFGHIJKLMN
OPQRSTUVWXYZ
abcdefghijklmnopqrstuvwxyz
1234567890
CONSTANCE

A bold slightly inclined brush script.

ABCDEFGHIJKLMNOPQRSTUVWXYZ
abcdefghijklmnopqrstuvwxyz
1234567890
CONTACT

A bold face of the English copperplate script, similar in style, but not in weight, to MARINA. This is a bolder version of YOUTHLINE.

ABCDEFGHIJKLMNO
PQRSTUVWXYZ
abcdefghijklmnopqrstuvwxyz
1234567890
COPPERPLATE BOLD

CORONET
Ludlow 1937

Designed by R.H. Middleton. A script very like TRAFTON with freely drawn capitals and a more formal lower case. The descenders are not quite so long as in Trafton; the **d** is not looped, whereas the **l** is, the reverse being the case in Trafton. There is also a bold.

viii

ABCDEFGHIJKLMNOPQRSTUVWXYZ

abcdefghijklmnopqrstuvwxyz

1234567890

CORONET

viii

ABCDEFGHIJKLMNOPQRSTUVW XYZ

abcdefghijklmnopqrstuvwxyz

1234567890

CORONET BOLD

DERBY
Berthold 1953

Designed by G.G. Lange. A formal script of considerable weight and with pen-drawn characteristics. The lower case has oblique serifs and short ascenders. The lower case resembles TEMPLE SCRIPT, but the capitals are more freely drawn.

viii

ABCDEFGHIJKLMNOPQRSTU

abcdefghijklmnopqrstuvwxyz 1234567890

DERBY

DIANE
Olive 1956

Designed by Roger Excoffon. A modern version of eighteenth-century copperplate scripts with flourished capitals and an angular lower case with joining letters.

viii

A B C D E F G H I J

K L M N O P Q R S T

U V W X Y Z

abcdefghijklmnopqrstuvw

xyz

1 2 3 4 5 6 7 8 9 0

DIANE

Designed by M. Wilke. A formal script with moderate variation of stress and slight inclination. The capitals are freely drawn. The lower case has no serifs and short descenders. The **f** and **l** are looped.

ABCDEFGHIJKLMNO

abcdefghijklmnopqrstuvwxyz

1234567890

DISCUS

ABCDEFGHIJKLMNO

abcdefghijklmnopqrstuvwxyz

DISCUS BOLD

A visiting-card script. A nearly upright type with curly capitals. The lower case has looped ascenders and long descenders.

The Monotype Corporation's GROSVENOR is a similar design but of larger height and with very short descenders.

ABCDEFGHIJKLMN

OPQRSTUVWXYZ&

abcdefghijklmnopqrstuvwxyz

DORCHESTER SCRIPT

An adaptation of flourished book initials after the Victorian model.

DUTCH INITIALS

DYNAMIC
Berthold 1952

viii

Designed by Herbert Post. A heavy, forceful script with several unusual letters. The down strokes of **B** and **P** are crossed by the bottom line of the bowls. The **G** has an open, descending tail, and the **g** an open tail. All down strokes are very pronounced. The bowls of **R** and **e** are open, the upstroke of the **A** descends below the line.

ABCDEFGHIJKLMNOPQRSTUVWZ
abcdefghijklmnopqrstuvwxyz
1234567890

DYNAMIC

ELAN
Stempel 1937

viii

Designed by Hans Möhring. A heavy, informal script resembling SIGNAL. The letters are monotone and close-setting, but the alignment is not so irregular as in Signal.

Besuchen Sie das Seebad

ELAN

ELEGANCE
Ludwig & Mayer 1968

viii

Designed by Karlgeorg Hoefer. A spidery wide script.

ABCDEFGHIJKLMNOPQ
RSTUVWXYZ
abcdefghijklmnopqrstuvwxyz
1234567890

ELEGANCE

EL GRECO
Berthold 1964

viii

Designed by G.G. Lange. An angular pen script.

ABCDEFGHIJKLMNOPQRSTUV
abcdefghijklmnopqrstuvwxyz th
1234567890

EL GRECO

ELITE
Nebiolo 1968

viii

Designed by Aldo Novarese as a linear script.

ABCDEFGHIJKLMN
OPQRSTUVWXYZ&
abcdefghijklmnopqrstuvwxyz
1234567890%

ELITE

Designed by S.H. de Roos. A serifed spidery script, almost an inclined roman but without variation in stress.

ELLA
Amsterdam 1915

viii

Birmingham Industrial Residences

ELLA

Designed by Arno Drescher. A heavy script of monotone colour, with close-fitting letters. It resembles SIGNAL. The alignment is not quite so irregular as in SIGNAL. ENERGOS is a bold version of APPELL.

ENERGOS
Schriftguss 1932

The Royal Bank of Canada

viii

Sonderschau der Deutschen Graphik

viii

ENERGOS

Designed by Walter Höhnisch. A tall, bold script with even inclination.

EXPRESS
Ludwig & Mayer 1957

viii

ABCDEFGHIJKLMNOPQR STUVWXYZ

abcdefghijklmnopqrstuvwxyz

1234567890

EXPRESS

A fairly heavy, informal script resembling PENFLOW. The lower-case letters are close-setting. There is some variation of stress but there are no hair lines.
A rather heavier face which is partially shaded, like PENTAPE, is called FLAMME.

FANAL
Schelter & Giesecke 1933

ABCDEFGHIJKLMNOPQRSTU VWXYZ

viii

abcdefghijklmnopqrstuvwxyz

1234567890

FANAL

Designed by R. Hunter Middleton.

*A B C D E F G H I J K
L M N O P Q R S T
U V W X Y 3
1 2 3 4 5 6 7 8 9 0*

FLAIR

A heavy script, which is slightly shaded. The lower-case letters are close setting. *Cf.* FANAL.

*ABCDEFGHIJKLMNOPQR
STUVWXYZ
abcdefghijklmnopqrstuvwxyz&
£1234567890*

FLAMME

Designed by George Salter. A ribbon type, or partially shaded script, resembling PENTAPE. The capitals are swash forms and the lower case almost an italic.

Amicable Resolutions Introduced

FLEX

Designed by R.H. Middleton. A narrow pen script with tall ascenders and swash capitals.

*ABCDEFGHIJKLMNOPQRSTUVW
XYZ&
abcdefghijklmnopqrstuvwxyz 1234567890*

FLORENTINE CURSIVE

Designed by A. Butti. A script in which the thin strokes are hair lines starting from the foot of the main strokes.

FLUIDUM

Nebiolo 1951

ABCDEFGHIJKLMNOPQRSTUVWXYZÇÆŒ
abcdefghijklmnopqrstuvwxyzçœœ
1234567890

FLUIDUM

viii

ABCDEFGHIJKLMNOPQRSTU
VWXYZÇ 1234567890
abcdefghijklmnopqrstuvwxyz

FLUIDUM BOLD

viii

Designed by Erich Mollowitz. A script of medium weight and colour with flourished capitals and tall ascenders in the lower case. There are no serifs. Descenders are short. There are also bold face and swash capitals. MERCURY (Stephenson Blake) was copied from the original design. Originally a type designed for Trennert in 1936.

FORELLE or
RHINEGOLD
and MERCURY

Weber 1936

ABCDEFGHIJKL MNOPQRSTUV
WXYZ
abcdefghijklmnopqrstuvwxyz 1234567890

FORELLE

viii

ABCDEFGHIJKL MNOPQRSTUV
WXYZ
abcdefghijklmnopqrstuvwxyz 1234567890

FORELLE

viii

Designed by R. Hunter Middleton.

ABCDEFGHIJKLMNOPQRSTUV
WXYZ&
abcdefghijklmnopqrstuvwxyz
1234567890

FORMAL SCRIPT

FORMAL
SCRIPT

Ludlow 1956

viii

FORTE
Monotype 1962

viii

A bold script designed by Carl Reissberger. The type has neither kerns nor connecting strokes.

*ABCDEFGHIJKLMNOPQRSTUV
WXYZ   1234567890
abcdefghijklmnopqrstuvwxyz*

FORTE

FOX
Berthold

viii

Designed by W. Rebhuhn for Genzsch & Heyse in 1955. A heavy brush script of angular design.

*ABCDEFGHIJKLMNOPQRSTUVW
XYZ   1234567890
abcdefghijklmnopqrstuvwxyz*

FOX

FRANCESCA RONDE
Stephenson Blake c. 1948

viii

An informal script of medium weight and little variation in colour. The type has a slight but irregular inclination, some letters being upright. Ascenders and descenders are of medium size. The letters are not close-setting.

*ABCDEFGHIJKLMNOPQRSTU
VWXYZ   1234567890
abcdefghijklmnopqrstuvwyxz*

FRANCESCA RONDE

FUTURA DEMIBOLD SCRIPT
Intertype (F) 1954

viii

Designed by Edwin W. Shaar. A formal script of heavy weight and almost monotone. Ascenders and descenders are short. The design is intended to complement the FUTURA range.

*ABCDEFGHIJKLMNOPQRSTUVWXYZ
abcdefghijklmnopqrstuvwxyz   1234567890$*

FUTURA DEMIBOLD SCRIPT

GABRIELE
Weber 1947

viii

Designed by Hans Möhring. A formal script of medium weight. The capitals are swash letters. The letters of the lower case are rather wide and ascenders are tall. The serifs are sharp and oblique. There are no looped ascenders.

*ABCDEFGHIJKLMNOPQR
STUVWXYZ
abcdefghijklmnopqrstuvwxyz
1234567890*

GABRIELE

Designed by Hans-Jürg Hunziker and Matthew Carter as a formal script for phototypesetting.

GANDO
RONDE
Mergenthaler Linofilm 1970

viii

ABCDEFGHIJ

KLMNOPQRSTUVWXYZ

abcdefghijklmnopqrstuvwxyz

$1234567890

GANDO RONDE

Designed by Rudo· Spemann. A light script in which several capitals descend below the line. The ascenders are long. There are also swash capitals.

GAVOTTE
Klingspor 1940

viii

ABCDEFGHIJKLMNOPQR

abcdefghijklmnopqrstuvwxyz

GAVOTTE

Designed by William S. Gillies. A script monotone in colour with flowing capitals and a more rigid lower case. Some of the lower-case letters resemble the italic letters in a sans serif, *e.g.*, the **m**, **n** and **t**; perhaps that trait coupled with the uniform colour accounts for the name Gothic. It is also called FLOTT. There is also a bold version.

GILLIES
GOTHIC or
FLOTT
Bauer 1935

viii

ABCDEFGHIJKLMNOPQRSTUVWXYZ

abcdefghijklmnopqrstuvwxyz   Th

1234567890

GILLIES GOTHIC LIGHT

viii

ABCDEFGHIJKLMNOPQRSTUVWXYZ

abcdefghijklmnopqrstuvwxyz   Th

1234567890

GILLIES GOTHIC

Designed by Hans Möhring, originally a Schriftguss type. An informal and heavy brush script.

GLADIATOR
Typoart

viii

As the New Year Opens

GLADIATOR

GLADIOLA
Stempel 1936

viii

Designed by Martin Wilke. An upright and monotone script. The capitals are freely drawn. In the lower case ascenders and descenders are short and the letters are round.

Der Zauber

GLADIOLA

GLENMOY
Stephenson Blake 1931

viii

The Sheffield version of the heavy pen scripts. The letters set closely in a deceptive way. The alignment is more regular than in some of these heavy scripts.

Enterprising Printers

GLENMOY

GLORIA
Gans c. 1930

viii

A formal and rather heavy script, with considerable variation of stress. The capitals are italic swash forms. In the lower case the ascenders have small loops. The **i**, **p** and **q** have large foot serifs, but otherwise there are no serifs. The dots over **i** and **j** are diamond-shaped. The type is also called FULGOR.

ABCDEFGHIJKLMNOPQRSTUV
abcdefghijklmnopqrstuvwxyz fi ff fl

GLORIA

GONG
J. Wagner 1953

viii

A chalk script of a design similar to the same founder's REPORTER, with mottled shading.

ABCDEFGHIJKLMNOPQRST
UVWXYZ
abcddeemaffffiffghchijkcklllmnopqrsst
tßžŭwwxyzg
1234567890

GONG

GRAFICO
Cooperativa 1965

viii

Designed by Umberto Fenocchio as a pen script of large x-height.

ABCDEFGHIJKLMNOPQR
STUVWXYZ&ÆŒ
abcdefghijklmnopqrstuvwxyzœœ
1234567890

GRAFICO

380

A nineteenth-century copperplate script. *Cf.* CALLIGRAPHIQUES, PALACE SCRIPT, etc. There are two varieties of many letters, the lower-case ascending letters being without loops.

A B C D E F G G H I J K L
M M N O P Q Q R S T U V W
X Y Z abcdefghijklmnopqrstuvwxyz e h l r s t z
1234567890

GRAPHIC SCRIPT

viii

A A B C D E F F G H H I
J K K L M M N N O P Q Q R
S S T U V W X Y Z 1234567890
abcdefghijklmnopqrstuvwxyz e h l r s t z

GRAPHIC SCRIPT BOLD

Designed by F.H.E. Schneidler (originally cast by Otto Weissert in Stuttgart). A bold, slightly inclined script following the style of other German bold display scripts.

ABCDEFGHIJKLMNOPQRSTUVWXYZ
abcdefghijklmnopqrstuvwxyz 1234567890

GRAPHIK

Designed by F.H. Riley. A script of medium weight with considerable variation of stress. In the lower case the thickest parts of the stroke seem to come in an unnatural place. This is also in part true of the upper case.

ABCDEFGHIJKLMNO
abcdefghijklmnopqrstuvwxyz 12345

GRAYDA

A light script of the visiting card class. It has a slight inclination, swash capitals, looped ascenders, except the **d**, and short descenders. The lower-case letters are regular and round, and the variation of stress is slight.

For those interested in the Art of fine Printing, there is nothing

GROSVENOR SCRIPT

HAUSER SCRIPT
Ludlow 1937

viii

Designed by George Hauser. A heavy brush script like RADAR. The alignment is irregular, but the letters are not close-setting.

ABCDEFGHIJKLMNOPQRSTUVWXYZ&

abcdefghijklmnopqrstuvwxyz 1234567890

HAUSER SCRIPT

HERITAGE
American 1952

viii

Designed by Walter H. McKay. A calligraphic type of slight inclination. The pen-drawn quality is most evident in the serifs. The **a** is unusual in type.

A B C D E F G H I J K L M N O P Q R S T U V W X Y Z Qu &

a a b c d e f g h i j k l m n o p q r s t u v w x y z   ff fi fl ft ffi ffl t. tt

1 2 3 4 5 6 7 8 9 0

HERITAGE

HOLLA
Klingspor 1932

viii

viii

Designed by Rudolf Koch. A quill pen-drawn script of medium weight. The capitals are freely drawn. **O** and **Q** have an unusual finish at the top of the bowls.

In the lower case ascenders and descenders are short and the letters are somewhat condensed and almost upright. The new version shown here with modified weight was issued in 1951.

ABCDEFGHIJKLMNOPQRSTUV

abcdefghijklmnopqrstuvwxyz

1234567890

HOLLA

BCDEFGIKOUVWY

HOLLA INITIALS

HOYER SCHÖN- SCHRIFT
Stempel

viii

Designed by Hans T. Hoyer. A formal, light script, with flourished capitals and a lower case in which most of the letters are based on the formal Italian hand of the sixteenth century. The inclination is slight. Ascenders are tall and the terminals hooked. The **p** (with an extended upright), the **r**, **v** and **w** vary from the general design.

ABCDEFG

abcdefghijklmnopqrstuvwxyz

1234567890

HOYER SCHÖNSCHRIFT

A ribbon script with slight inclination. Fine white hair lines interrupt the black of the strokes where they change from down to up stroke, a suggestion of three-dimensional treatment. Some of the capitals, like the **E**, look as if they fall backwards.

El Escorial situado al pié

IMPERIO

Designed by L. Zimmermann. A heavy script with normal lower case and short thickened ascenders.

ABCDEFGHIJKLMNOPQR
STUVWXYZ ADELMORZ
abcdefghijklmnopqrstuvwxyzhchchchckffllsstß
ttzzenrt 1234567890

IMPULS

A set of calligraphic capitals of the sixteenth century, founder unknown. In 1582 Jan van Hout of Leyden acquired a fount. Enschedé bought them from Ploos van Amstel in 1799.

INITIALS 13

An English copperplate script in the traditional style using the caps of MARINA SCRIPT and the lower case of YOUTHLINE.

ABCDEFGHIJKLMNOPQ
RSTUVWXYZ

abcdefghijklmnopqrstuvwxyz   1234567890

INVITATION SCRIPT

Designed by Jacoby-Boy. A formal script which is nearly upright and has considerable variation of stress. There are two versions of many of the capitals, italic letters and swash varieties.

Echte Spitzen

JACOBEA

JAGUAR
Weber 1967

viii

Designed by Georg Trump. A calligraphic script with very short descenders.

ABCDEFGHIJKLMNOPQRSTUVW
XYZ
abcdefghijklmnopqrstuvwxyz
1234567890

JAGUAR

JOWA SCRIPT
Wagner 1967

viii

Designed by J. Wagner and following the style of GONG as a light informal pen script.

ABCDEFGHIJKLMNOPQRST
UVWXYZ ÄÖÜ
abcdefghijklmnopqrstuvwxyz äöü chckffffiflßtz
uenerdellstsgæœ ÆÖ
1234567890 &

JOWA SCRIPT

JULIET
Nebiolo 1955

viii

Designed by A. Novarese. A light formal script. The capitals are flourished and the lower case has tall ascenders with small loops.

ABCDEFGHIJKLMNOPQRSTUVWXYZÆŒW

abcdefghijklmnopqrsftuvxyzæœw

1 2 3 4 5 6 7 8 9 0

JULIET

JUNIOR
Schelter & Giesecke 1936

viii

Designed by Hans Heimbeck. A light script with a very slight inclination. Pen-drawn qualities are evident in both the freely drawn capitals and the more formal lower case. There are no looped ascenders and descenders are short.

ABCDEFGHIJKLMN
OPQRSTUVWXYZ
abcdefghijklmnopqrstuvwxyz
1234567890

JUNIOR

Designed by Trochut Blanchard. An unusual script which is nearly upright. Ascenders and descenders are long and the ascenders looped. The lower-case **o** is not closed at the top, and the **r** and **s** are very unusual.

The rotation is continuous and the bottom part touches the color

JUVENTUD

JUVENTUD
or MURIEL
Gans 1950; Française

viii

Designed by M.R. Kaufmann. A monotone script of medium weight. The capitals are freely drawn. In the lower case the letters are close-fitting. The **d** is looped. There is also a light face.

A B C D E F G H I J K L M N O P Q R S T U V W X Y Z &

a b c d e f g h i j k l m n o p q r s s t u v w x y z

1 2 3 4 5 6 7 8 9 0

KAUFMANN

KAUFMANN
American 1936

viii

A B C D E F G H I J K L M N O P Q R S T U V W X Y Z &

a b c d e f g h i j k l m n o p q r s s t u v w x y z

1 2 3 4 5 6 7 8 9 0

KAUFMANN BOLD

viii

Designed by W.T. Sniffin. A bold, non-joining, slightly inclined script without serifs. The **Q** almost resembles a figure 2, and **G, J, S** and **Y** descend below the line. The bowls of many round letters, as for instance, **A, B, D, O, Q, R**, and some of their lower-case counterparts, are open. The tail of the **y** is vertical and that of the **g** is open.

A B C D E F G H I J K L M N O P Q R S T U V W X Y Z &

a b c d e f g h i j k l m n o p q r s t u v w x y z   er es is or os Th th tt

1 2 3 4 5 6 7 8 9 0

KEYNOTE

KEYNOTE
American 1933

viii

Designed by Karl Klauss. A fat face pen-script following German handwriting style, notably in the **s** and **f**. The **d** is open and has no spur, and capitals are swash letters.

Reisen in das Mittelmeer

KLAUSS CURSIVE

KLAUSS
CURSIVE
Genzsch & Heyse 1956

viii

Designed by Rudolf Koch for children's books and primers to instruct in the German cursive handwriting style then taught in schools.

Winterolympiade in Innsbruck

KOCH KURRENT

KOCH
KURRENT
Klingspor c. 1930

viii

KONZEPT
Stempel 1968

viii

Designed by Martin Wilke as an informal script departing from pen or brush script style by using a fibre pen in drawing the original characters.

ABCDEFGHIJKLMNOPQRSTU

abcdefghijklmnopqrstuvwxyz

1234567890

KONZEPT

KÜNSTLER-SCHREIB-SCHRIFT
Stempel 1957

viii

Designed by Hans Bohn. There are three weights of this type and the bold shown here is more rounded and compact than the normal and medium. The script has the design of a copperplate in a bold weight.

ABCDEFGHIJKLM

NOPQRSTUVWXYZ

abcdefghijklmnopqrstuvwxyz

KÜNSTLERSCHREIBSCHRIFT

KURIER
Typoart

viii

Designed by Herbert Thannhaeuser, originally a Schelter & Giesecke face. An informal and heavy brush script, similar to the same founder's GLADIATOR and LOTTO.

ABCDEFGHIJKLM

NOPQRSTUVWXYZ

abcdefghijklmnopqrzsstuvwxyz

1234567890

KURIER

LA CIVILITÉ
Deberny & Peignot

viii

A script based on French sixteenth-century cursive. There are several alternative swash letters The design is very similar to Enschedè's original CIVILITÉ, which is, however, somewhat bolder American Typefounders' CIVILITÉ is less correct in design.

Observez bien la modestie en vous couchant

LA CIVILITÉ

LAPIS
Nebiolo

viii

A pen-script based on Italian writing styles around the turn of the century. Similar types are cast by other Italian founders.

ABCDEFGHIJKLM

NOPQRSEUVXYZWG

abcdefghijklmnopqrstuvxyzw

1234567890

LAPIS

Designed by F.H.E. Schneidler. A script of some distinction. The capitals are flowing. The lower case has long ascenders and descenders and is upright. Some letters, *e.g.*, the **d**, **g** and **h**, together with some second varieties in the capitals, are derived from gothic scripts. The figures are non-ranging.

LEGEND
Bauer 1937

viii

AABCDDEF FG HIJKLMN
OPQRRSSTUVWXYZ Th
abcdefghijklmnopqrstuvwxyz th
1234567890
LEGEND

Designed by W.T. Sniffin. A light, formal script resembling BERNHARD CURSIVE. The capitals are flourished and the variation of stress is considerable. The ascenders are very tall and hooked at the top. The letters are round and the thin strokes take off from the feet of the thick strokes.

LIBERTY
American 1927

viii

ABCDEFGHIJKLMNOPQRSTUVWX
YZ&
abcdefghijklmnopqrstuvwxyz
1 2 3 4 5 6 7 8 9 0
LIBERTY

Designed by Imre Reiner. Not a true script and somewhat reminiscent of TIME SCRIPT.

LONDON SCRIPT
Stephenson Blake 1957

viii

ABCDEFGHIJKLMNOPQRSTUVW
XYZabcdefghijklmnopqrstuvwxyz&£$!?
aschfffethtt§h 1234567890
LONDON SCRIPT

Designed by Herbert Thannhaeuser. An informal and heavy brush script, similar to the same founders' GLADIATOR.

LOTTO
Typoart 1955

viii

Newspapers and Periodicals
LOTTO

Designed by R.H. Middleton. A medium heavy, informal script. The variation of stress is slight and the lower-case letters are close-setting. The ascenders are short and without loops. *Cf.* ELAN.

MANDATE
Ludlow 1934

viii

ABCDEFGHIJKLMNOPQRSTU
VWXYZ&
abcdefghijklmnopqrstuvwxyz
1234567890
MANDATE

MARGGRAFF LIGHT ITALIC
Schriftguss 1929

viii

Designed by G. Marggraff. Although called a cursive, the type is really a script. There is considerable variation of colour. In some letters, *e.g.*, **g**, **m**, **n** and **r**, the thin upstroke is quite separate from the downstroke, giving the appearance of an inline type. Ascenders terminate in a hook to the left. There is also a bold.

Morgenfeier im Eldorado
MARGGRAFF LIGHT ITALIC*

MARINA
Stephenson Blake 1936
viii

A copperplate script of rather heavier weight than PALACE SCRIPT.

ABCDEFGHIJKLMNOP2RST U V
WXYZ
abcdefghijklmnopqrstuvwxyz
1234567890
MARINA

MAXIM
Bauer 1955

viii

Designed by Peter Schneidler. A heavy informal script of the brush variety. The inclination is extreme, some letters appearing to be toppling over. The irregularity adds to the informal character of the design.

ABCDEFGHIJ
KLMNOPQRSTU
VWXYZ1234567890
abcdefghijklmnnop
qrstuvwxyz
MAXIM

MISTRAL
Olive 1953; Amsterdam 1955
viii

Designed by Roger Excoffon. An informal, true script. The letters of the lower case are joining and the descenders fairly long.

ABCDEFGHIJKLMNOPQRSTUVWXYZ
abcdefghijklmnopqrstuvwxyz
1234567
MISTRAL

388

Designed by R.H. Middleton. A script of medium weight and sharp variation of stress. The capitals are flourished. In the lower case ascenders are tall and vertical strokes of uniform thickness. The letters are round. *Cf.* BERNHARD CURSIVE BOLD and MERCURY.

ABCDEFGHIJKLMNOPQRSTU
VWXYZ&
1234567890
abcdefghijklmnopqrstuvwxyz

viii

MAYFAIR CURSIVE

Designed by Imre Reiner and drawn with a pen made from bamboo.

ABCDEFGHIJKLM
NOPQRSTUVWYZ
abcdefghijklmnopqrs
tuvwxyz

MERCURIUS

An informal, monotone script of medium weight. The lower case letters are close setting. There are more looped ascenders than in SWING BOLD.

ABCDEFGHIJKLMNOPQRSTUVWXYZ
abcdefghijklmnopqrstuvwxyz 12345
MONOLINE

Designed by E.J. Klumpp. A light script with swash capitals and an informal, condensed lower case. The letters are almost upright.

ABCDEFGHIJKLMNOPQRSTUV
WXYZ& abcdefghijklmnopqrstuvwxyz 1234567890
MURRAY HILL

ABCDEFGHIJKLMNOPQRST
UVWX abcdefghijklmnopqrstuvwxyz
1234567890
MURRAY HILL BOLD

MUSTANG
Stempel 1956

viii

viii

Designed by Imre Reiner. A heavy brush script, less irregular than some similar types.

ABCDEGHIJKLMNOPQRSTUVWXYZ

abcdefghijklmnopqrstuvwxyz

MUSTANG

NOVA SCRIPT
Intertype (New York) 1937

viii

Designed by George F. Trenholm. A script with freely drawn capitals and rather more formal lower case. Ascenders are tall and have slight serifs. The figures are ranging.

ABCDEFGHIJKLMNOPQRSTUVWXYZ

abcdefghijklmnopqrstuvwxyz

1234567890

NOVA SCRIPT

ONDINE
Deberny & Peignot 1954

viii

Designed by A. Frutiger. A formal upright script of heavy weight. There are four additional capitals, including extra wide **M** and **N**.

ABCDEFGHIJKLMNOPQRSTUVW
XYZ QVEMNQu
abcdefghijklmnopqrstuvwxyz
1234567890

ONDINE

ORIENTE
American

viii

A Victorian flourished script.

ABCDEFGHIJKLMNOPQRS
TUVWXYZ
1234567890

ORIENTE

OSCAR
Nebiolo 1966

viii

viii

Designed by Aldo Novarese. A pen script with open bowls to letters and tapered strokes.

ABCDEFGHIJKLMNOPQRSTUVW
XYZ
abcdefghijklmnopqrstuvxyzw
1234567890

OSCAR

An English copperplate script. It is steeply inclined and has abrupt variation in colour. The ascenders are not looped, except the **f**, but there are second looped versions of the **h** and **l**. In combination the letters appear to be engraved and not the impression from type.

EMBASSY SCRIPT (Caslon, 1924) is a similar type. Stephenson Blake have other closely similar copperplates, called MARINA and IMPERIAL. SOCIETY SCRIPT is another, but rather lighter in colour.

ABCDEFGHIJKLMNOP
QRSTUVWXYZ

abcdefghijklmnopqrstuvwxyz

STEPHENSON BLAKE PALACE SCRIPT

ABCDEFGHIJKLMNOPQRST
UVWXYZ abcdefghijklmnopqrstuvwxyz12345

MONOTYPE PALACE SCRIPT

Designed by Martin Wilke. A strong brush script giving an even black in print. The long descenders are characteristic of some capital letters, as for instance **A, G, M, N, P, T** and **B** have very long upper serifs. The ascender of the **d** is curved backwards.

PALETTE
Berthold 1951

viii

ABCDEFGHIJKLMNOPQRSTUVWX

abcdefghijklmnopqrstuvwxyz

1234567890

PALETTE

Designed by Georg Trump. A script of heavy weight with flourished capitals and an upright lower case. Ascenders are tall and the letters have a pen-drawn quality with little variation of colour.

PALOMBA
Weber 1955

viii

ABCDEFGHIJKLMNO
PQRSTUVWXYZ

abcdefghijklmnopqrstuvwxyz
1234567890

PALOMBA

Designed by Richard Weber. A heavy brush script, without serifs. The counters are circular and the figures non-ranging.

PAPAGENO
Bauer 1958

viii

ABCDEFGHIJKLMNOPQRSTUVW
abcdefghijklmnopqrstuvwxyzabi
1234567890

PAPAGENO

PARISIAN RONDE
Stephenson Blake

A faithful reproduction of the common French script of the nineteenth century. It is an upright script with flourished capitals and considerable variation of colour. The lower-case letters are close-fitting, the ascenders looped and fairly tall. Descenders are equally long. The original design was called FRENCH SCRIPT by the Inland Type Foundry and American Typefounders called it TYPO UPRIGHT.

viii

ABCDEFGHIJKLMNOPQRSTUVWXYZ

abcdefghijklmnopqrstuvwxyz

1234567890

PARISIAN RONDE

PARK AVENUE
American 1933

Designed by R.E. Smith. A light script with freely drawn capitals. The pen-drawn quality is very evident in the lower case. Ascenders and descenders are long; the ascenders are bent over at the top. The figures are non-ranging and the capitals are similar to TRAFTON.

viii

A B C D E F G H I J K L M N O P Q R S T U V

W X Y Z &

a b c d e f g h i j k l m n o p q r s t u v w x y z er es rs

1 2 3 4 5 6 7 8 9 0

PARK AVENUE

PARKWAY SCRIPT
Ludlow 1964

Designed by Emil Hirt as a calligraphic script following European contemporary models.

viii

ABCDEFGHIJKLMNOPQRS

TUVWXYZ&

abcdefghijklmnopqrstuvwxyz

1234567890

PARKWAY SCRIPT

PENTAPE
Schriftguss 1935

Designed by Walter Schnippering. An inline script, conveying the idea of a flowing ribbon. The type is also known as ORIGINELL.

viii

ABCEGJKLMOUZ

PENTAPE

PEPITA
Monotype 1959

Designed by Imre Reiner. An informal script of medium weight. The lower-case letters are irregularly aligned and are not close-fitting. There is moderate variation on stress. The figures are non-ranging.

viii

ABCDEFGHIJKLMNOPQRSTUVWXYZ

abcdefghijklmnopqrstuvwxyz

1234567890

PEPITA

Designed by Heinrich Pauser. A script of heavy face. The capitals are of a flowing design. The lower case has tall ascenders and descenders and is almost an italic, with serifs on some letters, *e.g.* **m**, **n** and **u**.

ABCDEFGHIJKLMNO

abcdefghijklmnopqrstuvwxyz

1234567890

PETRA

Designed by F. Riedinger. A heavy, informal script, but regular in alignment.

Großer Ausverkauf in

PHÄNOMEN

Designed by H. Wieynck. A script with flourished capitals and a lower case which is practically an italic. It has oblique serifs. The **a** is two-storeyed. The **v**, **w** and **y** are script forms.

Volkskonzert in der Philharmon

PHYLLIS

Designed by Carl Pohl. A brush script, which is almost upright. The variation in colour is slight, and serifs are all but eliminated.

ABCDEFGHIJKLMNOPQRSTUV
WXYZ&

abcdefghijklmnopqrstuvwxyz?

1234567890

POLO

Designed by E. Lautenbach. A heavy German script, regular in alignment and close setting. Also called SAMSON SCRIPT. *Cf.* SCRIPT BOLD

*ABCDEFGHIJKLMNOPQRSTU
VWXYZ
abcdefghijklmnopqrstuvwxyz
1234567890*

PRÄGEFEST

PRIVAT
Bauer 1966

viii

Designed by J.J. Siercke as an informal pen script.

A ABCD ƏE EFGHIƷKLMMNOPQRS TƐUVWXYZ

abcdefghijklmnopqrstuvwxyz
1234567890

PRIVAT

PRIMA
Stempel 1957

viii

Designed by Martin Hermersdorf as a pen-drawn type used by the Moritz Diesterweg educational publishing house in reading primers.

ABCDEFGHIJKLMNOPQRSTU
abcdefghijklmnopqrstuvwxyz
1234567890

PRIMA

PRIMADONNA
Ludwig & Mayer

viii

Designed by Helmut Matheis. A light and formal script with considerable variation of stress. The **m**, **n** and **p** have roman serifs, which adds to the formality of the design.

ABCDEFGHIJKLMNOPQ
RSTUVWXYZ
abcdefghijklmnopqrstuvwxyz
1234567890

PRIMADONNA

PULIDO
Iranzo

viii

A formal, tall script with pen-drawn qualities and considerable variation of stress.

Competición Internacional de Ajedrez

PULIDO

RADAR
Nacional

viii

A heavy brush script with slight inclination. Descenders are short, and some letters have lower-case handwriting characteristics, as for instance **n**, **o** and **p**. The cross-beam of the **A** ascends from the right foot of the letter on the line and cuts half-way through the up-stroke. The bowl of the **R** is not closed.

Alpinismo en Navas del Rey

RADAR

Decorated pen-drawn initials in elaborately baroque style, designed by Henk Krijger. The face is characterised by an abundance of pen flourishes.

RAFFIA INITIALS

Designed by Imre Reiner. A strong brush script. *Cf.* CHOC and others. The bowl of the e is open at the top and the **r** is curiously shaped.

ABCDEFGHIJKLMNOPQRSTUVW
XYZ& 1234567890

abcdefghijklmnopqrssttthuvwxyz

REINER BLACK

Designed by Imre Reiner. An informal pen script which is almost upright. The variation in colour is slight.

ABCDEFGHIJKLMNOPQRSTUVWXYZ

abcdefghijklmnopqrstuvwxyz

The Quick Brown Fox Jumped Over the Lazy Dog

REINER SCRIPT

Designed by C. Winkow. An informal script of medium weight which is slightly shaded. The capitals are not unlike SIGNAL, and the alignment has a similar irregularity. There are two versions of some letters and a number of tied letters. There is a slight variation of colour. RUSINOL (Fundicion Tipografica National) is identical but has some different alternative letters.

ABCDEFTGHFJKLMNOPQÜRSSchSFTTh
UVWXYZ 1234567890

áãubcdecienerentffffifllft ghhchheitijkckkeit

lllmmunmaoopãürsschsssftßtrthHßũũũ̃zuvwxyz

REPORTER

REPRO SCRIPT
American 1954

viii

Designed by Jerry Mullen. A script of lighter weight than the same founders' BRODY, but equally informal and with close-setting lower-case letters.

A B C D E F G H I J K L M N O P Q R S T U V W

X Y Z &

a b c d e f g h i j k l m n o p q r s t u v w x y z

1 2 3 4 5 6 7 8 9 0

REPRO SCRIPT

RHAPSODY
Ludwig & Mayer

viii

Designed by Ilse Schuele. Mainly intended as a display face, the type was later also issued in the smaller sizes. A modern roman adaptation of Schwabacher. The descenders of **P** and **f** are finely tapered.

ABCDEFGHIJKLMNOPQRSTUVWXYZ

abcdefghijklmnopqrstuvwxyz

1234567890

RHAPSODY

ROMANY
American 1934

viii

Designed by A.R. Bosco. An upright script bearing a general resemblance to GLADIOLA. There are however many differences in detail. For instance, the **d** has a looped ascender and the **e** an uncial form.

A A B C D E F G H I J K L M N O P Q R S T U V W

X Y Z &

a b c d e a f g h i j k l m n o p q r s t u v w x y z

1 2 3 4 5 6 7 8 9 0

ROMANY

RONDINE
Nebiolo 1948

viii

Designed by A. Butti. A formal script of medium weight. The capitals are freely drawn, and in the lower case the ascenders are tall and looped.

ABCDEFGHIJKLMNOPQuRSTUVWXYZÇÆŒ

abcdefghijklmnopqrstuvwxyzçœœ

1234567890

RONDINE

396

Designed by Stefan Schlesinger and Dick Dooijes. The flourished capitals have some resemblance to those of the traditional French Ronde, but not the lower case. The variation of colour is small, ascenders and descenders are short and there are no looped letters. The type has a slight inclination. There are two weights.

ABCDEFGHIJKLMNOP QuRSTUVWXYZ
abcdefghijklmnopqrstuvwxyz 1234567890

RONDO

ABCDEFGHIJKLMNOP QuRSTUVWXYZ
abcdefghijklmnopqrstuvwxyz

RONDO BOLD

Designed by Karlgeorg Hoefer. An informal Latin script of heavy weight and considerable variation of stress. On the lower case serifs are either stubby or non-existent.

ABCDEFGHIJKLMNOP
QRSTUVWXYZ
abcdefghijklmnopqrstuvwxyz

SALTINO

Designed by Karlgeorg Hoefer. A brush script of slight inclination with strong emphasised down strokes. The capitals are higher than the ascenders of lower-case letters. Some lower-case letters, like **a, n, m** and **u,** have foot serifs on the right, the **h** has a descender with a small spur; the dot on the **i** is a flat stroke.

The Annual Dinner of the Club

SALTO

Designed by Marcel Jacno. An informal and almost monotone script of medium weight, with close-fitting letters in the lower case. Not unlike FANAL, but the letters are more upright.

ABCDEFGHIJ
abcçdefghijklmnopqrs

SCRIBE

SCRIPT BOLD

Monotype 1931

A German script based on PRAEGEFEST and also resembling BRUSH SCRIPT or SIGNAL in its informality and blackness. But there is more variation in stress. The small looped tail of **g** and **y** may be noted.

MONOSCRIPT 351 is a rather similar informal and close-setting script, but lighter in weight.

viii

His family has farmed the land for

SCRIPT BOLD

SCRIPTURA

Stempel 1926

Designed by F.W. Kleukens. A light script of slight inclination, with flowing capitals and round letters in the lower case. The ascenders are tall and looped and the descenders short. There is an extra set of open initials.

The type was originally called KLEUKENS SCRIPTURA.

viii

Die Sculptur in Rom

SCRIPTURA

SIGNAL

Berthold 1931

Designed by W. Wege. A heavy script based on an entirely informal hand. It is practically monotone and the letters are deceptively close-fitting. The alignment also is deliberately irregular. The open **o** and irregular **w** may be noted. There are also two lighter weights. Very many German script types resemble this design.

viii

ABCDEFGHIJKLMNOPQRSTUVWXYZ
abcdefghijklmnopqrstuvwxyz

SIGNAL LIGHT

viii

ABCDEFGHIJKLMNOPQRSTUVWXYZ
abcdefghijklmnopqrstuvwxyz 1234567890

SIGNAL MEDIUM

viii

ABCDEFGHIJKLMNOPQRSTUVWXYZ
abcdefghijklmnopqrstuvwxyz

SIGNAL BLACK

SKETCH or SKIZZE

Ludwig & Mayer 1935

viii

Designed by W. Höhnisch. A normal script. The capitals are flourished and the lower case without eccentricity. The **l** is the only looped ascender, the others terminating with hooks.

ABCDEFGHIJKLMNOP
QRSTUVWXYZ
abcdefghijklmnopqrstuvwxyz
1234567890

SKETCH or SKIZZE

Designed by Helmut Matheis. A rather heavy script with considerable variation in colour. The capitals are freely drawn. The lower-case letters are close-fitting and more regular than in other similar scripts. There are ranging figures. Nebiolo's SLOGAN is quite different.

SLOGAN
Ludwig & Mayer 1959

viii

ABCDEFGHIJKLMNOPQR
STUVWXYZ
abcdefghijklmnopqrstuvwxyz
1234567890

SLOGAN

viii

Designed by A. Novarese. A brush script with swash letters and rather narrow lower case.

SLOGAN
Nebiolo 1957

viii

ABCDEFGHIJKLMNOPQRSTUV
abcdefghijklmnopqrstuvwxyzææw
1234567890

SLOGAN

Designed by Matthew Carter. Based on the hand of Charles Snell, English writing master and author of *The Pen-man's Treasury open'd* of 1694, whose standard rules for forming letters lend themselves particularly well to phototypesetting scripts. Lower case letters, and some capitals, have joining strokes on the right that run into the following character to allow more than one sort of link than the usual butt joint of the formal script.

SNELL
ROUNDHAND
Linofilm 1966

viii

ABCDEFGHIJ
KLMNOPQRS
TUVWXYZ
abcdefghijklmnopqrstuvwxyz
1234567890

SNELL ROUNDHAND

Designed by Heinz Schumann. A narrow brush script.

STENTOR
Typoart 1964

viii

ABCDEFGHIJKLMNOPQuRS
TUVWXYZ
abcdefghijklmnopqrstuvwxyz&
1234567890

STENTOR

STOP

Ludwig & Mayer 1939

viii

Designed by Walter Höhnisch. A dry brush script. The shading is irregular and the endings of vertical strokes and arcs are ragged.

ABCDEFGHIJKLMNOPQRS
TUVWXYZ
abcdefghijklmnopqrstuvw
xyz
1234567890

STOP

STRADIVARIUS

Bauer 1945

viii

Designed by Imre Reiner. An unusual script with flourished capitals and a stiff lower case. There is considerable variation of colour. Ascenders are tall and there are no serifs. The rigid appearance is produced by the squaring of the normally round letters. In Germany the type is called SYMPHONIE.

ABCDEFGHIJKLMNOPQ
RSTUVWXYZ
abcdefghijklmnopqrstuvwxyz
1234567890

STRADIVARIUS

STYLO

Française

viii

An informal, monotone script of medium weight. The capitals are flourished and the lower-case is close setting.

ABCDEFGHIJKLMNOPQR
TUVWXYZ
abcdefghijklmnopqrstuvwxyzœæ
1234567890

STYLO

SWING BOLD

Monotype 1955

viii

An informal script of medium weight and monotone in colour. The lower-case letters are joining.

ABCDEFGHIJKLMNOP2RSTUVWXYZ
abcdefghijklmnopqrstuvwxyz 12345

SWING BOLD

A pen script lighter in weight and more formal, in the lower case at least, than the brush scripts like SIGNAL, etc. The lower case has oblique serifs. The o has a quill-drawn form but such as no quill could manage. There are short-ranging figures.

ABCDEFGHIJKLMNOPQRST
UVWXYZ
abcdeßghijklmnopqrstuvwxyz
1234567890

TEMPLE SCRIPT

Designed by Tommy Thompson. A calligraphic script with slight inclination, in which some lower-case letters, as for instance, the **f**, are almost roman. The **g** has an open tail, and the **p** a slab serif on the foot. Most lower-case letters have no serifs. There are various alternative capital letters.

ABCDEFGHIJKLMNOPQRSTUVWXYZ&
AAEFGHIKLMNTVW&fh
abcdefghijklmnopqrstuvwxyz
1234567890

THOMPSON QUILLSCRIPT

Designed by G. Trump. An informal calligraphic type with letters of uneven x-height and several capitals descending below the line. Ascenders have spur serifs, which are also found in the **K, N, V, W** and **X**.

ABCDEFGHIIJKLMNOPQRSTU
UWXYZ
abcddefgghijklmnopqrsstuvwxyz
1234567890

TIME

ABCDEFGHIJKLMNOPQR
STUVWXYZ
abcddefgghijklmnopqrsstuvwx
yz 1234567890

TIME MEDIUM

TIME

ABCDEFGHIJKLMNOPQ
RSTUVWXYZ
abcddefgghijklmnopqrsstuv
wxyz
1234567890

viii

TIME BOLD

TITANTYPO
Wagner 1966

Originally a Wagner & Schmidt type first cast around 1905, and formerly known as STANLEY. A fat script with rounded letters and tall ascenders. Amsterdam called this type HERCULES and Wagner in the 1927 version TITAN.

viii

ABCDEFGHIJKLMNOSQRSTUVW
XYZ
abcdefghijklmnopqrstuvwxyz
1234567890

TITANTYPO

TRAFTON
SCRIPT
Bauer 1933

Designed by H.A. Trafton. A light script with freely drawn capitals. The lower case has long ascenders and descenders and the descenders are looped. There is a considerable gradation of colour, but the vertical strokes are of uniform width. In Germany the type is called QUICK and in France ETOILE.

viii

ABCDEFGHIJKLMNOPQuQRS
TUVWXYZ
abcdefghijklmnopqrstuvwxyz 12345678

TRAFTON SCRIPT

TRIANON
Bauer 1905

Designed by H. Wieynck. A formal cursive script with bold strokes, generally in eighteenth-century design. Some letters are not unlike the italic of TRADITION. Capitals are wide and flourished, and serifs very pronounced. There is also an outline version, TRIANON OPEN.

viii

Haus für Qualitätsdruck

TRIANON

Rheinländer

TRIANON OPEN

Designed by Albert Auspurg. A light script with flourished capitals and a round lower case. The ascenders are tall and nicked at the top. The vertical strokes taper. The **g** has a vertical ear. The **w** is of German design.

Hôtel David Petterson

TROCADERO KURSIV

A ZIRKULAR KARTENSCHRIFT, cut by Wagner & Schmidt in 1926, was cast around 1927 by many foundries. Willy Schumann designed some initials to it for BUTTERFLY of Schriftguss; Georg Belwe another set for L. Wagner (as SCHÖNSCHRIFT MOZART INITIALEN); E. Thiele designed an exclusive series for Haas, TROUBADOUR OPEN, which was also sold by Stempel* and Berthold.* Amsterdam sells this type as GRACIA, Nebiolo as DONATELLO and Berling as HERTHA.

ABCDEFGHIJKLMNOPQRS

abcdefghijklmnopqrstuvwxyz

1234567890

TROUBADOUR

ABCDEFGHIJKLMNOPQR

abcdefghijklmnopqrstuvwxyz

TROUBADOUR BOLD

ABCDEFGHIJKLMNOPQR

abcdefghijklmnopqrstuvwxyz

TROUBADOUR OPEN

Designed by Hildegard Korger. A calligraphic type with some similarity in style to TIME, though narrower and less free in form.

ABCDEFGHIJKLMNOPQRSTUVWXYZ

abcdefghijklm nopqrstu vwxyz

TYPO-SKRIPT

Designed by Joachim Romann. Several letters of this script, with no lower case, resemble the same founder's GAVOTTE. The weight, however, is much heavier, and the contrast between thick and thin strokes much stronger.

ABCDEFGHIJKLM NOPQRSTUVWXY

VARIANTE

VELTRO
Nebiolo 1931

An informal script, very like SIGNAL. It is similar in its irregular alignment, the close setting of the letters, and is also monotone. There are two weights.

viii

ABCDEFFGHIIJKLMNOPQRSSTUV.
abcdefghijklmnopqrsstuvwxyzwçœœ 1234567890

VELTRO

viii

ABCDEFGHIIJKLMNOPQRSS.
TUVWXYZçÇÆŒ&
abcdefghijklmnopqrsstuvwxyzçœœ
1234567890

VELTRO BOLD

VENTURE
Linofilm 1969

Designed by Hermann Zapf.

ABCDEFGHIJKLMNOPQRSTUVWXYZ

viii

abcdefghijklmnopqurstuvwxyz

1234567890

VENTURE

VERONA
Berthold

Designed by Helmuth Matheis for Genzsch & Heyse in 1958. A script of medium weight and nearly upright.
American Typefounders and Stephenson Blake have quite different types of this name.

viii

ABCDEFGHIJKLMNOPQRSTUVW
XYZ
abcdefghijklmnopqrstuvwxyz
123456780

VERONA

VICTORIANA
Nacional

A formal script with fine up-strokes and bold main strokes. The capitals are higher than the ascenders of lower-case letters. The **r** is slightly higher than other lower-case letters.

viii

Luxemburgo Alemania

VICTORIANA

Designed by Hermann Zapf. A fairly condensed formal script with strong hair lines. Descenders and ascenders have been designed to avoid overhanging the kerns whenever possible, thus giving extra strength for printing. There are alternative versions for some letters.

ABCDEFGHIJKLMNOPQu

abcdefghijklmnopqurstuvwxyz

1234567890

VIRTUOSA I

ABCDEFGHIJKLMNOPQuR

VIRTUOSA II

Designed by R. Hunter Middleton.

ABCDEFGHIJKLMNOPQRST UVWXYZ

abcdefghijklmnopqrstuvwxyz 1234567890

WAVE

A non-kerning copperplate script without joins, but very much heavier in weight. Some capitals, as for instance the **Y**, descend below the line. The foot of the **t** is horizontal and has sharp corners. In contrast with other copperplate scripts the letters in this type do not link up. The ascender of the **l** gives the optical illusion of being taller than those of other letters. The type was originally designed for a corsetry brand. Stephenson Blake's COPPERPLATE BOLD (1953) is a bolder version of this type.

ABCDEFGHIJKLMNOPQ RSTUVWXYZ

abcdefghijklmnopqrstuvwxyz 1234567890

YOUTHLINE

Designed by Karl Georg Hoefer. A bold brush script with tinted shading.

ABCDEFGHIJKLMN

abcdefghijklmnopqrst

1234567890

ZEBRA

INDEX TO DESIGNERS

408

INDEX TO TYPE FACES

Bold figures indicate pages where the type faces are shown. Other figures are to textual references. The absence of a comma before numerals means that this is part of the typeface name, i.e., Initials 13